# Advanced Information and Knowledge Processing

*Series Editors*
Professor Lakhmi Jain
Xindong Wu

## *Also in this series*

Manuel Graña, Richard Duro, Alicia d'Anjou and Paul P. Wang (Eds)
*Information Processing with Evolutionary Algorithms*
1-85233-886-0

Colin Fyfe
*Hebbian Learning and Negative Feedback Networks*
1-85233-883-0

Yun-Heh Chen-Burger and Dave Robertson
*Automatic Business Modelling*
1-85233-835-0

Dirk Husmeier, Richard Dybowski and Stephen Roberts (Eds)
*Probabilistic Modeling in Bioinformatics and Medical Informatics*
1-85233-778-8

K.C. Tan, E.F. Khor and T.H. Lee
*Multiobjective Evolutionary Algorithms and Applications*
1-85233-863-9

Ajith Abraham, Lakhmi Jain and
Robert Goldberg (Eds)

# Evolutionary Multiobjective Optimization

## Theoretical Advances and Applications

With 173 Figures

 Springer

Ajith Abraham
Department of Computer Science, Oklahoma State University, USA

Lakhmi Jain
KES Center, University of South Australia, Australia

Robert Goldberg
Department of Computer Science, Queens College, New York, USA  ⌐

*Series Editors*
Xindong Wu
Lakhmi Jain

British Library Cataloguing in Publication Data
Evolutionary multiobjective optimization : theoretical
    Advances and applications. – (Advanced information and knowledge processing)
    1. Mathematical optimization  2. Evolutionary computing
    I. Abraham, Ajith, 1968–  II. Jain, L.C.  III. Goldberg, Robert, 1939–
    519.6


Library of Congress Cataloging-in-Publication Data
Evolutionary multiobjective optimization : theoretical advances and applications /
[edited by] Ajith Abraham, Lakhmi Jain, Robert Goldberg.
    p .cm. -- (Advanced information and knowledge processing)
    Includes bibliographical references and index.

    1. Evolutionary programming (Computer science)  2. Genetic algorithms.  3. Mathematical
    optimization. I. Abraham, Ajith, 1968–  II. Jain, L. C.  III. Goldberg, Robert, 1939–  IV. Series

    T57.E95 2004
    005.1--dc22                                                                 2004052555

AI&KP ISSN 1610-3947

ISBN-13: 978-1-84996-916-1      e-ISBN-13: 978-1-84628-137-2
Springer Science+Business Media
springeronline.com

34/3830-543210  Printed on acid-free paper

# Preface

Multiobjective optimization has been available for about two decades, and its application in real world problems is continuously increasing. An important task in multiobjective optimization is to identify the set of Pareto-optimal solutions. An evolutionary algorithm is characterized by a population of solution candidates and the reproduction operator enables the process to combine existing solutions to generate new solutions. As a result, the computation finds several members of the Pareto-optimal set in a single run instead of performing a series of separate runs, which is the case for some of the conventional stochastic processes. The main challenge in a multiobjective optimization environment is to minimize the distance of the generated solutions to the Pareto set and to maximize the diversity of the developed Pareto set. A good Pareto set may be obtained by appropriate guiding of the search process through careful design of reproduction operators and fitness assignment strategies. To obtain diversification special care has to be taken in the selection process. Special care is also to be taken to prevent non-dominated solutions from being lost.

Addressing the various issues of evolutionary multiobjective optimization problems and the various design challenges using different intelligent approaches is the novelty of this edited volume. This volume comprises 12 chapters' including two introductory chapters giving the fundamental definitions and some important research challenges. Several complex test functions and a practical problem involving the multiobjective optimization of space structures under static and seismic loading conditions used to illustrate the importance of the evolutionary algorithm approach.

First, we would like to thank Lance Chambers (Australia) for initiating this book project in 2001. We are very much grateful to the authors of this volume and to the reviewers for their tremendous service by critically reviewing the chapters. The editors would like to thank Beverly Ford and Catherine Drury of Springer Verlag, London office and Jenny Wolkowicki of Springer Verlag, New York Office for the editorial assistance and excellent cooperative collaboration to produce this important scientific work. We are also indebted to Berend Jan

van der Zwaag (University of Twente, The Netherlands) for the tremendous
help during the preparation of the manuscript. We hope that the reader will
share our excitement to present this volume on 'Evolutionary Multiobjective
Optimization: Theoretical Advances and Applications' and will find it useful.

Oklahoma State University, USA                                    Ajith Abraham
University of South Australia, Australia                          Lakhmi Jain
Queens College, USA                                          Robert Goldberg
                                                                    (Editors)

# Contents

9    **MOGADES: Multiobjective Genetic Algorithm**
**with Distributed Environment Scheme**                                    **210**
*Tomoyuki Hiroyasu, Mitsunori Miki, Jiro Kamiura, Shinya*
*Watanabe, and Hiro Hiroyasu*

# List of Contributors

**Ajith Abraham (Ed.)**
Department of Computer Science, Oklahoma State University, USA
ajith.abraham@ieee.org

**Carlos A. Coello Coello**
Depto. de Ingeniería Eléctrica, Sección de Computación,
Av. Instituto Politécnico Nacional No. 2508,
Col. San Pedro Zacatenco, D.F. 07300, México
ccoello@cs.cinvestav.mx

**Kalyanmoy Deb**
Kanpur Genetic Algorithms Laboratory (KanGAL),
Indian Institute of Technology Kanpur, PIN 208016, India
deb@iitk.ac.in

**D. Dumitrescu**
Department of Computer Science,
Faculty of Mathematics and Computer Science, University Babes-Bolyai,
Cluj-Napoca, 3400 Cluj – Napoca, Romania
ddumitr@cs.ubbcluj.ro

**Robert Goldberg (Ed.)**
Department of Computer Science, 65-30 Kissena Blvd.,
Queens College, Flushing, NY 11367, USA
rrg@solomon.cs.qc.edu

**Crina Grosan**
Department of Computer Science,
Faculty of Mathematics and Computer Science, University Babes-Bolyai,
Cluj-Napoca, 3400 Cluj – Napoca, Romania
cgrosan@cs.ubbcluj.ro

**Natalie Hammerman**
Department of Mathematics and Computer Science,
Molloy College, 1000 Hempstead Avenue, Rockville Centre, NY 11571, USA
nhammerman@molloy.edu

**Hiro Hiroyasu**
Department of Mechanical System Engineering,
Kinki University, Hiroshima, Japan
hiro@hiro.kindai.ac.jp

**Tomoyuki Hiroyasu**
Department of Knowledge Engineering and Computer Sciences,
Doshisha University, Tatara Miyakodani Kyotanabe-shi, Kyoto Japan
tomo@is.doshisha.ac.jp

**Lakhmi Jain (Ed.)**
University of South Australia, Adelaide, Australia
lakhmi.jain@unisa.edu.au

**Jiro Kamiura**
Department of Knowledge Engineering and Computer Sciences,
Doshisha University, Tatara Miyakodani Kyotanabe-shi, Kyoto Japan

**Nikos D. Lagaros**
Institute of Structural Analysis & Seismic Research
National Technical University Athens
Zografou Campus, Athens 157 80, Greece
nlagaros@central.ntua.gr

**Marco Laumanns**
Swiss Federal Institute of Technology (ETH) Zürich,
Computer Engineering and Networks Laboratory (TIK),
CH-8092 Zürich, Switzerland
laumanns@tik.ee.ethz.ch

**Efrén Mezura-Montes**
Computer Science Section, Electrical Engineering Department
CINVESTAV-IPN, Av. Instituto Politécnico Nacional No. 2508
Col. San Pedro Zacatenco, México, D.F. 07300
emezura@computacion.cs.cinvestav.mx

**Mitsunori Miki**
Department of Knowledge Engineering and Computer Sciences,
Doshisha University, Tatara Miyakodani Kyotanabe-shi, Kyoto Japan
mmiki@mail.doshisha.ac.jp

**Sanaz Mostaghim**
Electrical Engineering Department,
University of Paderborn, Paderborn, Germany
mostaghim@date.upb.de

**Christine L. Mumford-Valenzuela**
School of Computer Science, Cardiff University, United Kingdom
christine@cs.cardiff.ac.uk

**Mihai Oltean**
Department of Computer Science,
Faculty of Mathematics and Computer Science, University Babes-Bolyai,
Cluj-Napoca, 3400 Cluj – Napoca, Romania
molteang@cs.ubbcluj.ro

**Manolis Papadrakakis**
Institute of Structural Analysis & Seismic Research
National Technical University Athens
Zografou Campus, Athens 157 80, Greece
mpapadra@central.ntua.gr

**Vagelis Plevris**
Institute of Structural Analysis & Seismic Research
National Technical University Athens
Zografou Campus, Athens 157 80, Greece
vplevrisg@central.ntua.gr

**Tian Hou Seow**
10 Kent Ridge Crescent, Singapore 119260
Department of Electrical & Computer Engineering
National University of Singapore

**Dipti Srinivasan**
10 Kent Ridge Crescent, Singapore 119260
Department of Electrical & Computer Engineering
National University of Singapore

**Jürgen Teich**
Computer Science Department, Friedrich-Alexander-University,
Erlangen, Germany
teich@informatik.uni-erlangen.de

**Lothar Thiele**
Swiss Federal Institute of Technology (ETH) Zürich
Computer Engineering and Networks Laboratory (TIK),
CH-8092 Zürich, Switzerland
thiele@tik.ee.ethz.ch

**Shinya Watanabe**
Department of Knowledge Engineering and Computer Sciences,
Doshisha University, Tatara Miyakodani Kyotanabe-shi, Kyoto Japan

**Eckart Zitzler**
Swiss Federal Institute of Technology (ETH) Zürich
Computer Engineering and Networks Laboratory (TIK),
CH-8092 Zürich, Switzerland
zitzlerg@tik.ee.ethz.ch

# 1

# Evolutionary Multiobjective Optimization

Ajith Abraham and Lakhmi Jain

**Summary.** Very often real-world applications have several multiple conflicting objectives. Recently there has been a growing interest in evolutionary multiobjective optimization algorithms that combine two major disciplines: evolutionary computation and the theoretical frameworks of multicriteria decision making. In this introductory chapter, some fundamental concepts of multiobjective optimization are introduced, emphasizing the motivation and advantages of using evolutionary algorithms. We then lay out the important contributions of the remaining chapters of this volume.

## 1.1 What Is Multiobjective Optimization?

Even though some real-world problems can be reduced to a matter of a single objective very often it is hard to define all the aspects in terms of a single objective. Defining multiple objectives often gives a better idea of the task. Multiobjective optimization has been available for about two decades, and its application in real-world problems is continuously increasing. In contrast to the plethora of techniques available for single-objective optimization, relatively few techniques have been developed for multiobjective optimization.

In single-objective optimization, the search space is often well defined. As soon as there are several possibly contradicting objectives to be optimized simultaneously, there is no longer a single optimal solution but rather a whole set of possible solutions of equivalent quality. When we try to optimize several objectives at the same time the search space also becomes partially ordered. To obtain the optimal solution, there will be a set of optimal trade-offs between the conflicting objectives.

A multiobjective optimization problem could be written in the form minimize $[f_1(x), f_2(x), \ldots, f_k(x)]$ for $k$ objective functions $f_i: \Re^n \to \Re$ subject to several equality and inequality constraints. For $x = [x_1, x_2, \ldots, x_n]^T$, the vector of decision variables, our task is to determine the set $F$ of all vectors which satisfy all the constraints, the particular set of values $[x_1^*, x_2^* \ldots, x_n^*]$ and also yields the optimum values for all the objective functions [1].

As shown in Figure 1.1, a solution could be best, worst and also indifferent to other solutions (neither dominating or dominated) with respect to the objective values. Best solution means a solution not worst in any of the objectives and at least better in one objective than the other. An optimal solution is the solution that is not dominated by any other solution in the search space. Such an optimal solution is called a Pareto-optimal and the entire set of such optimal trade-offs solutions is called a Pareto- optimal set. As evident, in a real world situation a decision making (trade-off) process is required to obtain the optimal solution. Even though there are several ways to approach a multiobjective optimization problem, most work is concentrated on the approximation of the Pareto set.

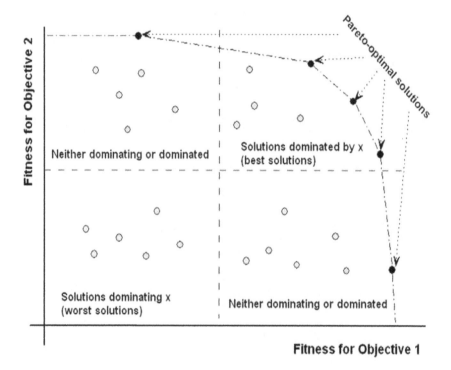

**Figure 1.1.** Concept of Pareto optimality.

## 1.2 Why Use Evolutionary Algorithms for Multiobjective Optimization?

A number of stochastic optimization techniques such as simulated annealing, tabu search, ant colony optimization etc., could be used to generate the

Pareto set. Just because of the working procedure of these algorithms, the solutions obtained very often tend to be stuck at a good approximation and they do not guarantee to identify optimal trade-offs. Evolutionary algorithm is characterized by a population of solution candidates and the reproduction process enables the combination of existing solutions to generate new solutions. This enables finding several members of the Pareto-optimal set in a single run instead of performing a series of separate runs, which is the case for some of the conventional stochastic processes. Finally, natural selection determines which individuals of the current population participate in the new population.

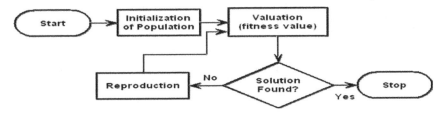

**Figure 1.2.** Flowchart of evolutionary algorithm iteration.

The iterative computation process of an evolutionary algorithm is illustrated in Figure 1.2. Multiobjective evolutionary algorithms can yield a whole set of potential solutions, which are all optimal in some sense. After the first pioneering work on multiobjective evolutionary optimization by Schaffer in the mid-1980s [2], several different algorithms have been proposed and successfully applied to various problems. For comprehensive overviews and discussions, the reader is referred to Coello Coello [1] and Deb [3]. Some of the other advantages of having evolutionary algorithms is that they require very little knowledge about the problem being solved, less susceptible to the shape or continuity of the Pareto front, easy to implement, robust, and could be implemented in a parallel environment.

## 1.3 Evolutionary Multiobjective Optimization: Challenges, Advances and Applications

The main challenge in a multiobjective optimization environment is to minimize the distance of the generated solutions to the Pareto set and to maximize the diversity of the developed Pareto set. A good Pareto set may be obtained by appropriate guiding of the search process through careful design of reproduction operators and fitness assignment strategies. To obtain diversification special care has to be taken in the selection process. Special care is also to be taken to prevent non-dominated solutions from being lost [4, 5]. Elitism addresses the problem of losing good solutions during the optimization process. Addressing the evolutionary multiobjective optimization problem and the various design challenges using different intelligent approaches is the novelty of this edited volume. This volume comprises 12 chapters and the rest of the volume is organized as follows.

In the following Chapter, Coello Coello presents the basic concepts of evolutionary multiobjective algorithms, their potential applications, metrics, test functions and concludes with some of the most promising future research directions.

Laumanns begins Chapter 3 by presenting the convergence behavior of simple evolutionary algorithms with different selection strategies on a continuous multiobjective optimization problem. Special focus is given to the problem of controlling the mutation strength, since an adaptation of the mutation strength is necessary to converge to the optimum with arbitrary precision, and to achieve linear convergence order. Experiment results reveal that the convergence properties achieved by a self-adaptation of the mutation strength on single-objective problems do not carry over to the multiobjective case, if a simple dominance-based selection scheme is used. As a solution, a combined strategy is proposed using dominance-based selection in the archive and scalarizing functions in the working population.

In Chapter 4, Mumford-Valenzuela explains a Pareto-based approach to evolutionary multi-objective optimization, that avoids most of the time-consuming global calculations typical of other multiobjective evolutionary techniques. The new approach uses a simple uniform selection strategy within a steady-state evolutionary algorithm and employs a straightforward elitist mechanism for replacing population members with their offspring. An important advantage of the proposed method is that global calculations for fitness and Pareto dominance are not needed. The performance of the algorithm is demonstrated using some benchmark combinatorial problems and continuous functions.

Mostaghim and Teich in Chapter 5 shows the importance of special data structures for storing and updating archives which would have a great impact on the required computational time, especially when optimizing higher-dimensional problems with large Pareto sets. The authors introduce Quad-trees as an alternative data structure to linear lists for storing Pareto sets. Performance of the quad-trees data structures are evaluated and compared using several multiobjective example problems. The results presented show that typically, linear lists perform better for small population sizes and higher-dimensional Pareto fronts (large archives) whereas Quad-trees perform better for larger population sizes and Pareto sets of small cardinality.

In Chapter 6, Deb et al. suggest three different approaches for systematically designing test problems for evaluating multiobjective evolutionary algorithms. The simplicity of construction, scalability to any number of decision variables and objectives, knowledge of the shape and the location of the resulting Pareto-optimal front, and introduction of controlled difficulties in both converging to the true Pareto-optimal front and maintaining a widely distributed set of solutions are the main features of the suggested test problems. These test problems should be found useful in various research activities on new multiobjective evolutionary algorithms and to enhance the understanding of the working principles of multiobjective evolutionary algorithms.

Srinivasan and Seow in Chapter 7 present a hybrid combination of particle swarm optimization and evolutionary algorithm for multiobjective optimization problems. The main algorithm for swarm intelligence is particle swarm optimization, which is inspired by the paradigm of birds flocking. The core updating mechanism of the particle swarm optimization algorithm relies only on two simple self-updating equations and the process of updating the individuals per iteration is fast as compared to the computationally expensive reproduction mechanism using mutation or crossover operations in a typical evolutionary algorithm. While additional domain-specific heuristics related to the real-world problems cannot be easily incorporated in the particle swarm optimization algorithm; in an evolutionary algorithm, heuristics can be easily incorporated in the population generator and mutation operator to prevent leading the individuals to infeasible solutions. Therefore, a direct particle swarm optimization does not perform well in its search in complex multi-constrained solution spaces, which are the case for many complex real world problems. To overcome the limitations of particle swarm optimization and evolutionary algorithms, a hybridized algorithm is proposed to use a synergistic combination of particle swarm optimization and evolutionary algorithm. Experiment results using some test functions illustrate the feasibility of the hybrid approach as a multiobjective search algorithm.

In Chapter 8, Dumitrescu et al. propose a new evolutionary elitist approach combining a non-standard solution representation and an evolutionary optimization technique which permits the detection of continuous decision regions. Each solution in the final population corresponds to a decision region of the Pareto-optimal set. The proposed method is evaluated using some test functions.

Hiroyasu et al. in Chapter 9 address the parallel implementation of multiobjective evolutionary algorithms to manage the computational costs especially for higher-dimensional problems with large Pareto sets. They propose a parallel evolutionary algorithm for multiobjective optimization problems called Multiobjective Genetic Algorithm with Distributed Environment Scheme (MOGADES). Further, a new mechanism is added to multiobjective genetic algorithms called Distributed Cooperation model of Multiobjective Genetic Algorithm (DCMOGA). In DCMOGA, there are not only individuals for searching Pareto-optimum solutions but also individuals for searching the solution of one object. After illustrating MOGADES and DCMOGA, these two algorithms were combined. This hybrid algorithm is called Distributed Cooperation model of Multiobjective Genetic Algorithm with Environmental Scheme (DCMOGADES). The performance of DCMOGADES is illustrated using some test functions.

6    Abraham and Jain

In Chapter 10, Mezura-Montes and Coello Coello describe the general
multiobjective optimization concepts that can be used to incorporate
constraints of any type (linear, non-linear, equality, and inequality) into the
fitness function of a genetic algorithm used for global optimization. Several
approaches reported in the literature are also described and four of them are
compared using several test functions.

Goldberg and Hammerman in Chapter 11 present a new operator, which
when added to a genetic algorithm (GA), improved the performance of the GA
for locating optimal finite state automata. The new operator (termed MTF)
reorganizes a finite state automaton (FSA) genome during the execution of the
genetic algorithm. MTF systematically renames the states and moves them
to the front of the genome. The operator was tested on the ant trail problem.
Across different criteria (failure rate, processing time to locate a solution,
number of generations needed to locate a solution), the MTF-enhanced GA
realized speedups between 110% and 579% over the non-enhanced version. In
addition, the successful FSAs found by the genetic algorithm augmented with
MTF were 25% to 46% smaller in size than those found by the original GA.

In the last chapter, Lagaros et al. deal with a practical problem of
structural sizing. The aim is to minimize the weight of the structure under
certain restrictions imposed by design codes. Authors present two approaches
(rigorous and simplified) with respect to the loading condition, and their
efficiency is compared to find the optimum design of a structure under
multiple objectives. In the context of the rigorous approach a number of
artificial accelerograms are produced from the design response spectrum of the
region for elastic structural response, which constitutes the multiple loading
conditions under which the structures are optimally designed. This approach
is compared with the approximate one based on simplifications adopted by
the seismic codes. Experiment results reveal that the Pareto sets obtained by
the rigorous approach and the simplified one were different.

# References

1. Coello Coello, CA, Comprehensive Survey of Evolutionary-Based Multiobjective
   Optimization Techniques, International Journal of Knowledge and Information
   Systems, 1999; 1(3):269-308.
2. Schaffer, JD, Multiple Objective Optimization with Vector Evaluated Genetic
   Algorithms, PhD Thesis, Vanderbilt University, Nashville, USA, 1984.
3. Deb, K, Multiobjective Optimization using Evolutionary Algorithms, John Wiley
   & Sons, Chichester, 2001.
4. Laumanns, M, Thiele, L, Deb, K and Zitzler, E, Combining Convergence
   and Diversity in Evolutionary Multi-objective Optimization. Evolutionary
   Computation, MIT Press, 2002; 10(3):263-282.
5. Zitzler, E, Laumanns, M and Bleuler, S, A Tutorial on Evolutionary
   Multiobjective Optimization, Workshop on Multiple Objective Metaheuristics
   (MOMH), Springer-Verlag, Berlin, 2004.

# 2

# Recent Trends in Evolutionary Multiobjective Optimization

Carlos A. Coello Coello

**Summary.** This chapter presents a brief review of some of the most relevant research currently taking place in evolutionary multiobjective optimization. The main topics covered include algorithms, applications, metrics, test functions, and theory. Some of the most promising future paths of research are also addressed.

## 2.1 Introduction

Evolutionary algorithms (EAs) are heuristics that use natural selection as their search engine to solve problems. The use of EAs for search and optimization tasks has become very popular in the last few years with a constant development of new algorithms, theoretical achievements and novel applications [1, 2, 3]. One of the emergent research areas in which EAs have become increasingly popular is multiobjective optimization. In multiobjective optimization problems, we have two or more objective functions to be optimized at the same time, instead of having only one. As a consequence, there is no unique solution to multiobjective optimization problems, but instead, we aim to find all of the good trade-off solutions available (the so-called Pareto optimal set).

The first implementation of a multiobjective evolutionary algorithm (MOEA) dates back to the mid-1980s [4, 5]. Since then, a considerable amount of research has been done in this area, now known as evolutionary multiobjective optimization (EMO for short). The growing importance of this field is reflected by a significant increment (mainly during the last ten years) of technical papers in international conferences and peer-reviewed journals, books, special sessions at international conferences and interest groups on the Internet [6].[1]

---

[1] The author maintains an EMO repository which currently contains over 1450 bibliographical entries at: http://delta.cs.cinvestav.mx/~ccoello/EMOO, with a mirror at http://www.lania.mx/~ccoello/EMOO/

The main motivation for using EAs to solve multiobjective optimization problems is because EAs deal simultaneously with a set of possible solutions (the so-called population) which allows us to find several members of the Pareto-optimal set in a single run of the algorithm, instead of having to perform a series of separate runs as in the case of the traditional mathematical programming techniques [7]. Additionally, EAs are less susceptible to the shape or continuity of the Pareto front (e.g., they can easily deal with discontinuous and concave Pareto fronts), whereas these two issues are a real concern for mathematical programming techniques [6, 8, 9].

## 2.2 Basic Concepts

The emphasis of this chapter is the solution of multiobjective optimization problems (MOPs) of the form:

$$\text{minimize } [f_1(\mathbf{x}), f_2(\mathbf{x}), \ldots, f_k(\mathbf{x})] \tag{2.1}$$

subject to the $m$ inequality constraints:

$$g_i(\mathbf{x}) \leq 0 \quad i = 1, 2, \ldots, m \tag{2.2}$$

and the $p$ equality constraints:

$$h_i(\mathbf{x}) = 0 \quad i = 1, 2, \ldots, p \tag{2.3}$$

where $k$ is the number of objective functions $f_i : \mathbb{R}^n \to \mathbb{R}$. We call $\mathbf{x} = [x_1, x_2, \ldots, x_n]^T$ the vector of decision variables. We wish to determine from among the set $\mathcal{F}$ of all vectors which satisfy Equations 2.2 and 2.3 the particular set of values $x_1^*, x_2^*, \ldots, x_n^*$ which yield the optimum values of all the objective functions.

### 2.2.1 Pareto Optimality

It is rarely the case that there is a single point that simultaneously optimizes all the objective functions of a multiobjective optimization problem. Therefore, we normally look for "trade-offs", rather than single solutions when dealing with multiobjective optimization problems. The notion of "optimality" is therefore different in this case. The most commonly adopted notion of optimality is that originally proposed by Francis Ysidro Edgeworth [10] and later generalized by Vilfredo Pareto [11]. Although some authors call this notion *Edgeworth-Pareto optimality* (see for example [12]), we will use the most commonly accepted term: *Pareto optimality*.

We say that a vector of decision variables $\mathbf{x}^* \in \mathcal{F}$ is *Pareto optimal* if there does not exist another $\mathbf{x} \in \mathcal{F}$ such that $f_i(\mathbf{x}) \leq f_i(\mathbf{x}^*)$ for all $i = 1, \ldots, k$ and $f_j(\mathbf{x}) < f_j(\mathbf{x}^*)$ for at least one $j$.

In words, this definition says that $\mathbf{x}^*$ is Pareto optimal if there exists no feasible vector of decision variables $\mathbf{x} \in \mathcal{F}$ which would decrease some criterion without causing a simultaneous increase in at least one other criterion. Unfortunately, this concept almost always gives not a single solution, but rather a set of solutions called the *Pareto-optimal set*. The vectors $\mathbf{x}^*$ correspoding to the solutions included in the Pareto-optimal set are called *non-dominated*. The image of the Pareto-optimal set under the objective functions is called *Pareto front*.

## 2.3 Algorithms

The potential of evolutionary algorithms for solving multiobjective optimization problems was hinted at in the late 1960s by Rosenberg in his PhD thesis [13]. Rosenberg's study contained a suggestion that would have led to multiobjective optimization if he had carried it out as presented. His suggestion was to use multiple *properties* (nearness to some specified chemical composition) in his simulation of the genetics and chemistry of a population of single-celled organisms. Since his actual implementation contained only one single property, the multiobjective approach could not be shown in his work.

The first actual implementation of what is now called a multiobjective evolutionary algorithm (or MOEA, for short) was Schaffer's *Vector Evaluation Genetic Algorithm* (VEGA), which was introduced in the mid-1980s, mainly aimed at solving problems in machine learning [4, 5, 14]. Since then, a wide variety of algorithms have been proposed in the literature [6, 8, 15].

We can roughly divide MOEAs into the following types:

- Aggregating functions
- Population-based approaches
- Pareto-based approaches

We will briefly discuss each of them in the following subsections.

### 2.3.1 Aggregating Functions

Perhaps the most straightforward approach to handling multiple objectives with any technique is to combine all the objectives into a single one using either an addition, multiplication or any other combination of arithmetical operations. These techniques are normally known as "aggregating functions" because they combine (or "aggregate") all the objectives of the problem into a single one. In fact, aggregating approaches are the oldest mathematical programming methods for multiobjective optimization, since they can be derived from the Kuhn-Tucker conditions for non-dominated solutions [16].

An example of this approach is a linear sum of weights of the form:

$$\min \sum_{i=1}^{k} w_i f_i(\mathbf{x}) \tag{2.4}$$

where $w_i \geq 0$ are the weighting coefficients representing the relative importance of the $k$ objective functions of our problem. It is usually assumed that

$$\sum_{i=1}^{k} w_i = 1 . \tag{2.5}$$

Aggregating functions may be linear (as in the previous example) or nonlinear (e.g., the aggregating functions adopted by game theory [17, 18], goal programming [19, 20], goal attainment [21, 22] and the min-max algorithm [23, 24]). Both types of aggregating functions have been used with evolutionary algorithms in a number of occasions, with relative success.

Aggregating functions have been largely underestimated by EMO researchers mainly because of the well-known limitation of linear aggregating functions (i.e., they cannot generate non-convex portions of the Pareto front regardless of the weight combination used [25]). Note, however, that non-linear aggregating functions do not necessarily present such limitation [6]. In fact, even linear aggregating functions can be cleverly defined such that concave Pareto fronts can be generated [26]. However, the EMO community tends to show little interest in new algorithms based on aggregating functions, hence their relatively low popularity among EMO researchers.

### 2.3.2 Population-based Approaches

In these techniques, the population of an EA is used to diversify the search, but the concept of Pareto dominance is not directly incorporated into the selection process. The classical example of this sort of approach is the Vector Evaluated Genetic Algorithm (VEGA), proposed by Schaffer [5]. VEGA basically consists of a simple genetic algorithm with a modified selection mechanism. At each generation, a number of sub-populations are generated by performing proportional selection according to each objective function in turn. Thus, for a problem with $k$ objectives, $k$ sub-populations of size $M/k$ each are generated (assuming a total population size of $M$). These sub-populations are then shuffled together to obtain a new population of size $M$, on which the genetic algorithm (GA) applies the crossover and mutation operators.

VEGA has several problems, from which the most serious is that its selection scheme is opposed to the concept of Pareto dominance. If, for example, there is an individual that encodes a good compromise solution for all the objectives, but it is not the best in any of them, it will be discarded. Note however, that such individual should really be preserved because it encodes a Pareto-optimal solution. Schaffer suggested some heuristics to deal with this problem. For example, to use a heuristic selection preference approach for non-dominated individuals in each generation, to protect individuals that encode

Pareto-optimal solutions but are not the best in any single objective function. Also, crossbreeding among the "species" could be encouraged by adding some mate selection heuristics instead of using the random mate selection of the traditional GA. Nevertheless, the fact that Pareto dominance is not directly incorporated into the selection process of the algorithm remains its main disadvantage.

One interesting aspect of VEGA is that despite its drawbacks it remains in current use by some researchers mainly because it is appropriate for problems in which we want the selection process to be biased and in which we have to deal with a large number of objectives (e.g., when handling constraints as objectives in single-objective optimization [27]).

Other researchers have proposed variations of VEGA or other similar population-based approaches (e.g., [28, 29, 30, 31]). Despite the limitations of these approaches, their simplicity has attracted several researchers and we should expect to see more work on population-based approaches in the next few years.

### 2.3.3 Pareto-based Approaches

Taking as a basis the main drawbacks of VEGA, Goldberg discussed on pages 199 to 201 of his famous book on genetic algorithms [1] a way of tackling multiobjective problems. His procedure consists of a selection scheme based on the concept of Pareto optimality. Goldberg not only suggested what would become the standard MOEA for several years, but also indicated that stochastic noise would make such algorithms useless unless some special mechanism was adopted to block convergence. Niching or fitness sharing [32] was suggested by Goldberg as a way to maintain diversity and avoid convergence of the GA to a single solution.

Pareto-based approaches can be historically studied as covering two generations. The first generation is characterized by the use of fitness sharing and niching combined with Pareto ranking (as defined by Goldberg or adopting a slight variation). The most representative algorithms from the first generation are the following:

1. **Non-dominated Sorting Genetic Algorithm** (NSGA): This algorithm was proposed by Srinivas and Deb [33]. The approach is based on several layers of classifications of the individuals as suggested by Goldberg [1]. Before selection is performed, the population is ranked on the basis of non-domination: all non-dominated individuals are classified into one category (with a dummy fitness value, which is proportional to the population size, to provide an equal reproductive potential for these individuals). To maintain the diversity of the population, these classified individuals are shared with their dummy fitness values. Then this group of classified individuals is ignored and another layer of non-dominated individuals is considered. The process continues until all individuals in the

population are classified. Stochastic remainder proportionate selection is adopted for this technique. Since individuals in the first front have the maximum fitness value, they always get more copies than the rest of the population. This allows to search for non-dominated regions, and results in convergence of the population toward such regions. Sharing, its part, helps to distribute the population over this region (i.e., the Pareto front of the problem).

2. **Niched-Pareto Genetic Algorithm** (NPGA): Proposed by Horn et al. [34]. The NPGA uses a tournament selection scheme based on Pareto dominance. The basic idea of the algorithm is the following: Two individuals are randomly chosen and compared against a subset from the entire population (typically, around 10% of the population). If one of them is dominated (by the individuals randomly chosen from the population) and the other is not, then the non-dominated individual wins. When both competitors are either dominated or non-dominated (i.e., there is a tie), the result of the tournament is decided through fitness sharing [35].

3. **Multiobjective Genetic Algorithm** (MOGA): Proposed by Fonseca and Fleming [36]. In MOGA, the rank of a certain individual corresponds to the number of chromosomes in the current population by which it is dominated. Consider, for example, an individual $x_i$ at generation $t$, which is dominated by $p_i^{(t)}$ individuals in the current generation. The rank of an individual is given by [36]:

$$\text{rank}(x_i, t) = 1 + p_i^{(t)} . \tag{2.6}$$

All non-dominated individuals are assigned rank 1, while dominated ones are penalized according to the population density of the corresponding region of the trade-off surface.

Fitness assignment is performed in the following way [36]:

a) Sort population according to rank.
b) Assign fitness to individuals by interpolating from the best (rank 1) to the worst (rank $n \leq M$) in the way proposed by Goldberg (1989), according to some function, usually linear, but not necessarily.
c) Average the fitnesses of individuals with the same rank, so that all of them are sampled at the same rate. This procedure keeps the global population fitness constant while maintaining appropriate selective pressure, as defined by the function used.

The second generation of MOEAs was born with the introduction of the notion of elitism. In the context of multiobjective optimization, elitism usually (althought not necessarily) refers to the use of an external population (also called secondary population) to retain the non-dominated individuals. However, the use of this external file raises several questions:

- How does the external file interact with the main population?
- What do we do when the external file is full?
- Do we impose additional criteria to enter the file instead of just using Pareto dominance?

Note that elitism can also be introduced through the use of a $(\mu + \lambda)$-selection in which parents compete with their children, and those which are non-dominated (and possibly comply with some additional criterion such as providing a better distribution of solutions) are selected for the following generation.

The most representative second generation MOEAs are the following:

1. **Strength Pareto Evolutionary Algorithm** (SPEA): This algorithm was introduced by Zitzler and Thiele [37]. This approach was conceived as a way of integrating different MOEAs. SPEA uses an archive containing non-dominated solutions previously found (the so-called external non-dominated set). At each generation, non-dominated individuals are copied to the external non-dominated set. For each individual in this external set, a *strength* value is computed. This strength is similar to the ranking value of MOGA, since it is proportional to the number of solutions to which a certain individual dominates.

   In SPEA, the fitness of each member of the current population is computed according to the strengths of all external non-dominated solutions that dominate it. Additionally, a clustering technique called "average linkage method" [38] is used to keep diversity.

2. **Strength Pareto Evolutionary Algorithm 2** (SPEA2): This approach has three main differences with respect to its predecessor [39]: (1) it incorporates a fine-grained fitness assignment strategy which takes into account for each individual the number of individuals that dominate it and the number of individuals by which it is dominated; (2) it uses a nearest neighbor density estimation technique which guides the search more efficiently, and (3) it has an enhanced archive truncation method that guarantees the preservation of boundary solutions.

3. **Pareto Archived Evolution Strategy** (PAES): This algorithm was introduced by Knowles and Corne [40]. PAES consists of a (1+1) evolution strategy (i.e., a single parent that generates a single offspring) in combination with a historical archive that records some of the non-dominated solutions previously found. This archive is used as a reference set against which each mutated individual is being compared. An interesting aspect of this algorithm is its procedure used to maintain diversity which consists of a crowding procedure that divides objective space in a recursive manner. Each solution is placed in a certain grid location based on the values of its objectives (which are used as its "coordinates" or "geographical location"). A map of this grid is

maintained, indicating the number of solutions that reside in each grid location. Since the procedure is adaptive, no extra parameters are required (except for the number of divisions of the objective space).

4. **Non-dominated Sorting Genetic Algorithm II** (NSGA-II): Deb et al. [41, 42, 43] proposed a revised version of the NSGA [33], called NSGA-II, which is more efficient (computationally speaking), uses elitism and a crowded comparison operator that keeps diversity without specifying any additional parameters. The NSGA-II does not use an external memory as in the previous algorithms. Instead, its elitist mechanism consists of combining the best parents with the best offspring obtained (i.e., a $(\mu+\lambda)$-selection).

5. **Niched Pareto Genetic Algorithm 2** (NPGA 2): Erickson et al. [44] proposed a revised version of the NPGA [34] called the NPGA 2. This algorithm uses Pareto ranking but keeps tournament selection (solving ties through fitness sharing as in the original NPGA). In this case, no external memory is used and the elitist mechanism is similar to the one adopted by the NSGA-II. Niche counts in the NPGA 2 are calculated using individuals in the partially filled next generation, rather than using the current generation. This is called continuously updated fitness sharing, and was proposed by Oei et al. [45].

6. **Pareto Envelope-based Selection Algorithm** (PESA): This algorithm was proposed by Corne et al. [46]. This approach uses a small internal population and a larger external (or secondary) population. PESA uses the same hyper-grid division of phenotype (i.e., objective function) space adopted by PAES to maintain diversity. However, its selection mechanism is based on the crowding measure used by the hyper-grid previously mentioned. This same crowding measure is used to decide what solutions to introduce into the external population (i.e., the archive of non-dominated vectors found along the evolutionary process). Therefore, in PESA, the external memory plays a crucial role in the algorithm since it determines not only the diversity scheme, but also the selection performed by the method. There is also a revised version of this algorithm, called PESA-II [47]. This algorithm is identical to PESA, except for the fact that region-based selection is used in this case. In region-based selection, the unit of selection is a hyperbox rather than an individual. The procedure consists of selecting (using any of the traditional selection techniques [48]) a hyperbox and then randomly selecting an individual within that hyperbox. The main motivation of this approach is to reduce the computational costs associated with traditional MOEAs (i.e., those based on Pareto ranking).

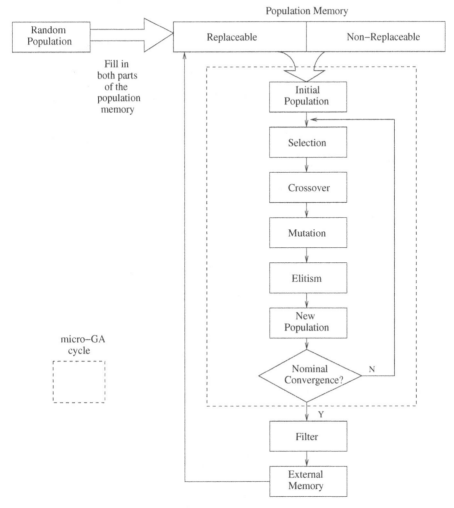

**Figure 2.1.** Diagram that illustrates the way in which the micro-GA for multiobjective optimization works [50].

7. **Micro-Genetic Algorithm**: This approach was introduced by Coello Coello and Toscano Pulido [49, 50]. A micro-genetic algorithm is a GA with a small population and a reinitialization process. The way in which the micro-GA works is illustrated in Figure 2.1. First, a random population is generated. This random population feeds the population memory, which is divided in two parts: a replaceable and a non-replaceable portion. The non-replaceable portion of the population memory never changes during the entire run and is meant to provide the required diversity for the algorithm. In contrast, the replaceable portion experiences changes after each cycle of the micro-GA.

The population of the micro-GA at the beginning of each of its cycles is taken (with a certain probability) from both portions of the population memory so that there is a mixture of randomly generated individuals (non-replaceable portion) and evolved individuals (replaceable portion). During each cycle, the micro-GA undergoes conventional genetic operators. After the micro-GA finishes one cycle, two non-dominated vectors are chosen[2] from the final population and they are compared with the contents of the external memory (this memory is initially empty). If either of them (or both) remains as non-dominated after comparing it against the vectors in this external memory, then they are included there (i.e., in the external memory). This is the historical archive of non-dominated vectors. All dominated vectors contained in the external memory are eliminated.

The micro-GA then uses three forms of elitism: (1) it retains non-dominated solutions found within the internal cycle of the micro-GA, (2) it uses a replaceable memory whose contents is partially "refreshed" at certain intervals, and (3) it replaces the population of the micro-GA by the nominal solutions produced (i.e., the best solutions found after a full internal cycle of the micro-GA).

EMO researchers are still wondering about the sort of algorithms that will give rise to the third generation, but the emphasis seems to be on algorithmic efficiency [51, 52] and on spatial data structures that improve the efficiency of the storage in the external population [53, 54, 55, 56]. We should also expect to see more work on the true role of elitism in evolutionary multiobjective optimization [57, 58].

## 2.4 Applications

An analysis of the evolution of the EMO literature reveals some interesting facts. From the first EMO approach published in 1985 [5] up to the first survey of the area published in 1995 [59], the number of published papers related to EMO is relatively low. However, from 1995 to date, the increase of EMO-related papers is exponential. The EMO repository registers over 1450 papers, from which a vast majority are applications. The vast number of EMO papers currently available makes it impossible to attempt to produce a detailed review of them in this section. Instead, we will discuss the most popular application fields, indicating some of the specific areas within them in which researchers have focused their main efforts.

Current EMO applications can be roughly classified in three large groups: engineering, industrial, and scientific. Some specific areas within each of these groups are indicated next.

---

[2]This is assuming that there are two or more non-dominated vectors. If there is only one, then this vector is the only one selected.

We will start with the engineering applications, which are, by far, the most popular in the literature. This should not be too surprising, since engineering disciplines normally have problems with better understood mathematical models which facilitates the use of evolutionary algorithms. A representative sample of engineering applications is the following (aeronautical engineering seems to be the most popular subdiscipline within this group):

- Electrical engineering [60, 61, 62]
- Hydraulic engineering [63, 44, 64]
- Structural engineering [65, 66, 67]
- Aeronautical engineering [68, 69, 70]
- Robotics [71, 72, 73]
- Control [74, 75, 76]
- Telecommunications [77, 78, 79]
- Civil engineering [80, 81, 82]
- Transport engineering [83, 84, 85]

Industrial applications occupy the second place in popularity in the EMO literature. Within this group, scheduling is the most popular subdiscipline. A representative sample of industrial applications is the following:

- Design and manufacture [86, 87, 88]
- Scheduling [89, 90, 91]
- Management [92, 93, 94]

Finally, we have a variety of scientific applications, from which the most popular are (for obvious reasons) those related to computer science:

- Chemistry [95, 96, 97]
- Physics [98, 18, 99]
- Medicine [100, 101, 102]
- Computer science [103, 104, 105, 106]

The above distribution of applications indicates a strong interest for developing real-world applications of EMO algorithms (something not surprising considering that most real-world problems are of a multiobjective nature). Furthermore, the previous sample of EMO applications should give a general idea of the application areas that have not been explored yet, some of which are mentioned in the following section.

## 2.5 Test Functions

One of the fundamental issues when proposing an algorithm is to have a standard methodology to validate it. As part of this methodology, certain test functions (i.e., a benchmark) are required. In the early days of EMO research, very simple unconstrained bi-objective test functions were adopted

[23, 33, 34]. However, in the last few years several researchers have produced an important number of test functions that have become standard in the EMO community [107, 108, 6, 109]. Such test functions present certain difficulties for traditional EAs and mathematical programming techniques used for multiobjective optimization (e.g., multifrontality, disconnected or concave Pareto fronts). Note, however, that no serious theoretical study has been performed regarding the characteristics that make a multiobjective problem difficult for an MOEA and some apparently "difficult" test functions have been found to be relatively easy for most MOEAs [6].

The transition from two to three objective functions is taking place in the literature, and high-dimensional problems are the current focus of study among EMO researchers [110]. We should expect that more complex test functions appear in the literature in the next few years, emphasizing aspects such as the presence of noise, uncertainty, dynamic objective functions, and epistasis, among other issues [111, 6, 112, 113].

## 2.6 Metrics

The definition of appropriate metrics is very important to be able to validate an algorithm. However, when dealing with multiobjective optimization problems, there are several reasons why the qualitative assessment of results becomes difficult. The initial problem is that we will be generating several solutions, instead of only one (we aim to generate as many elements as possible of the Pareto-optimal set). The second problem is that the stochastic nature of evolutionary algorithms makes it necessary to perform several runs to assess their performance. Thus, our results have to be validated using statistical analysis tools. Finally, we may be interested in measuring different things. For example, we may be interested in having a robust algorithm that approximates the global Pareto front of a problem consistently, rather than an algorithm that converges to the global Pareto front but only occasionally. Also, we may be interested in analyzing the behavior of an evolutionary algorithm during the evolutionary process, trying to establish its capabilities to keep diversity and to progressively converge to a set of solutions close to the global Pareto front of a problem.

There are normally the issues to take into consideration to design a good metric in this domain [114]:

1. Minimize the distance of the Pareto front produced by our algorithm with respect to the global Pareto front (assuming we know its location).
2. Maximize the spread of solutions found, so that we can have a distribution of vectors as smooth and uniform as possible.
3. Maximize the number of elements of the Pareto-optimal set found.

The research produced in the last few years has included a wide variety of metrics that assess the performance of an MOEA in one of the three aspects previously indicated [6]. Some examples are the following:

1. **Error Ratio** (ER): This metric was proposed by Van Veldhuizen [115] to indicate the percentage of solutions (from the non-dominated vectors found so far) that are not members of the true Pareto-optimal set:

$$ER = \frac{\sum_{i=1}^{n} e_i}{n},$$

(2.7)

where $n$ is the number of vectors in the current set of non-dominated vectors available; $e_i = 0$ if vector $i$ is a member of the Pareto-optimal set, and $e_i = 1$ otherwise. It should then be clear that $ER = 0$ indicates an ideal behavior, since it would mean that all the vectors generated by our MOEA belong to the Pareto-optimal set of the problem. This metric addresses the third issue from the list previously provided.

2. **Generational Distance** (GD): The concept of generational distance was introduced by Van Veldhuizen and Lamont [116] as a way of estimating how far the elements in the set of non-dominated vectors are found from those in the Pareto-optimal set and is defined as:

$$GD = \frac{\sqrt{\sum_{i=1}^{n} d_i^2}}{n}$$

(2.8)

where $n$ is the number of vectors in the set of non-dominated solutions found so far and $d_i$ is the Euclidean distance (measured in objective space) between each of these and the nearest member of the Pareto-optimal set. It should be clear that a value of $GD = 0$ indicates that all the elements generated are in the Pareto-optimal set. Therefore, any other value will indicate how "far" we are from the global Pareto front of our problem. This metric addresses the first issue from the list previously provided.

3. **Spacing** (SP): Here, one desires to measure the spread (distribution) of vectors throughout the non-dominated vectors found so far. Since the "beginning" and "end" of the current Pareto front found are known, a suitably defined metric judges how well the solutions in this front are distributed. Schott [117] proposed such a metric measuring the range (distance) variance of neighboring vectors in the non-dominated vectors found so far. This metric is defined as:

$$S \triangleq \sqrt{\frac{1}{n-1} \sum_{i=1}^{n} (\overline{d} - d_i)^2},$$

(2.9)

where $d_i = \min_j(| f_1^i(\mathbf{x}) - f_1^j(\mathbf{x}) | + | f_2^i(\mathbf{x}) - f_2^j(\mathbf{x}) |)$, $i, j = 1, \ldots, n$, $\overline{d}$ is the mean of all $d_i$, and $n$ is the number of non-dominated vectors found so far. A value of zero for this metric indicates all members of the Pareto front currently available are equidistantly spaced. This metric addresses the second issue from the list previously provided.

Many other metrics exist (see for example [118, 108, 6, 9]), but some recent theoretical results seem to indicate that they may not be as reliable as we think and further research in this direction is necessary [119, 120, 121].

## 2.7 Theory

The weakest aspect of the current EMO research lies on the theoretical foundations of the area. Most of the current research concentrates on proving convergence of MOEAs [122, 123, 124, 125, 126, 127].

However, several research topics are still open. For example:

- Study the structure of fitness landscapes in multiobjective optimization problems [128, 129].
- There are no current attempts to answer a fundamental question: what makes difficult a multiobjective optimization problem for an MOEA?
- Develop a formal framework to analyze and prove convergence of parallel MOEAs.
- We know that if too many objective functions are used, the concept of Pareto dominance will eventually lead us to a situation in which all the individuals in the population will be non-dominated. The question is then, what is the theoretical limit for Pareto ranking assuming finite size populations?
- Perform run-time analysis of an MOEA [130].
- It is necessary to provide definitions of robustness, convergence, and diversity (among others) in the context of evolutionary multiobjective optimization that are acceptable by the EMO community at large [131].

## 2.8 Promising Paths for Future Research

After providing a general overview of the research currently done in evolutionary multiobjective optimization, it is important to indicate now what are some of the areas and problems that represent the most promising research challenges for the next few years. Some of these promising paths for future research are the following:

- **Incorporation of preferences in MOEAs**: Despite the efforts of some researchers to incorporate users preferences into MOEAs so as to narrow the search, most of the multicriteria decision-making techniques developed in Operations Research have not been applied in evolutionary multiobjective optimization [132, 133]. Such incorporation of preferences is very important in real-world applications since the user will only need one Pareto-optimal solution and not the whole set as normally assumed by EMO researchers.

- **Dynamic Test Functions**: After tackling static problems with two and three objective functions, the next logical step is to develop MOEAs that can deal with dynamic test functions [134] (i.e., test functions in which the Pareto front moves over time due to the existence of random variables).

- **Highly Constrained Search Spaces**: There is little work in the current literature regarding the solution of multiobjective problems with highly constrained search spaces. However, it is rather common to have such problems in real-world applications and it is then necessary to develop novel constraint-handling techniques that can deal with highly constrained search spaces efficiently.

- **Parallelism**: We should expect more work on parallel MOEAs in the next few years. Currently, there is a noticeable lack of research in this area [6, 135] and it is therefore open to new ideas. It is necessary to have more algorithms, formal models to prove convergence, and more real-world applications that use parallelism.

- **Theoretical Foundations**: It is quite important to develop the theoretical foundations of MOEAs. Although a few steps have been taken regarding proving convergence using Markov Chains (e.g., [122, 123]), much more work remains to be done as indicated in Section 2.7 (see [6]).

## 2.9 Conclusions

This chapter has discussed some of the most relevant research currently taking place in evolutionary multiobjective optimization. The main topics discussed include algorithms, metrics, test functions and theoretical foundations of EMO. The overview provided intends to give the reader a general picture of the current state of the field so that newcomers can analyze the current progress in their areas of interest.

Additionally, we have provided some possible paths of future research that seem promising in the short and medium term. The areas indicated should provide research material for those interested in making contributions in evolutionary multiobjective optimization. The areas described present challenges that are likely to determine the future research directions in this area.

## Acknowledgments

This chapter is representative of the research performed by the Evolutionary Computation Group at CINVESTAV-IPN (EVOCINV). The author acknowledges support from the mexican Consejo Nacional de Ciencia y Tecnología (CONACyT) through project number 34201-A.

## References

1. Goldberg, DE, *Genetic Algorithms in Search, Optimization and Machine Learning*. Addison-Wesley Publishing Company, Reading, MA, 1989.
2. Bäck, T, Fogel, DB, and Michalewicz, Z (eds.), *Handbook of Evolutionary Computation*. Institute of Physics Publishing and Oxford University Press, 1997.
3. Mitchell, M, *An Introduction to Genetic Algorithms*. MIT Press, Cambridge, MA, 1996.
4. Schaffer, JD, *Multiple Objective Optimization with Vector Evaluated Genetic Algorithms*. PhD thesis, Vanderbilt University, Nashville, TN, 1984.
5. Schaffer, JD, Multiple objective optimization with vector evaluated genetic algorithms. In *Genetic Algorithms and their Applications: Proceedings of the First International Conference on Genetic Algorithms*, pp. 93–100, Hillsdale, NJ, 1985. Lawrence Erlbaum.
6. Coello Coello, CA, Van Veldhuizen, DA, and Lamont, GB, *Evolutionary Algorithms for Solving Multi-Objective Problems*. Kluwer Academic Publishers, New York, May 2002. ISBN 0-3064-6762-3.
7. Miettinen, KM, *Nonlinear Multiobjective Optimization*. Kluwer Academic Publishers, Boston, Massachusetts, 1998.
8. Coello Coello, CA, A Comprehensive Survey of Evolutionary-Based Multiobjective Optimization Techniques. *Knowledge and Information Systems. An International Journal*, 1(3):269–308, August 1999.
9. Deb, K, *Multi-Objective Optimization using Evolutionary Algorithms*. John Wiley & Sons, Chichester, UK, 2001. ISBN 0-471-87339-X.
10. Edgeworth, FY, *Mathematical Physics*. P. Keagan, London, England, 1881.
11. Pareto, V, *Cours D'Economie Politique*, volume I and II. F. Rouge, Lausanne, 1896.
12. Stadler, W, Fundamentals of multicriteria optimization. In Stadler, W (ed), *Multicriteria Optimization in Engineering and the Sciences*, pp. 1–25. Plenum Press, New York, NY, 1988.
13. Rosenberg, RS, *Simulation of genetic populations with biochemical properties*. PhD thesis, University of Michigan, Ann Arbor, MI, 1967.
14. Schaffer, JD and Grefenstette, JJ, Multiobjective learning via genetic algorithms. In *Proceedings of the 9th International Joint Conference on Artificial Intelligence (IJCAI-85)*, pp. 593–595, Los Angeles, CA, 1985. AAAI.
15. Coello Coello, CA and Mariano Romero, CE, Evolutionary Algorithms and Multiple Objective Optimization. In Ehrgott, M and Gandibleux, X (eds.), *Multiple Criteria Optimization: State of the Art Annotated Bibliographic Surveys*, pp. 277–331. Kluwer Academic Publishers, Boston, 2002.

16. Kuhn, HW and Tucker, AW, Nonlinear programming. In Neyman, J (ed), *Proceedings of the Second Berkeley Symposium on Mathematical Statistics and Probability*, pp. 481–492, Berkeley, CA, 1951. University of California Press.
17. Rao, SS, Game theory approach for multiobjective structural optimization. *Computers and Structures*, 25(1):119–127, 1987.
18. Périaux, J, Sefrioui, M, and Mantel, B, GA multiple objective optimization strategies for electromagnetic backscattering. In Quagliarella, D, Périaux, J, Poloni, C, and Winter, G (eds.), *Genetic Algorithms and Evolution Strategies in Engineering and Computer Science. Recent Advances and Industrial Applications*, chapter 11, pp. 225–243. John Wiley and Sons, West Sussex, England, 1997.
19. Deb, K, Solving goal programming problems using multi-objective genetic algorithms. In *1999 Congress on Evolutionary Computation*, pp. 77–84, Piscataway, NJ, July 1999. IEEE Service Center.
20. Wienke, PB, Lucasius, C, and Kateman, G, Multicriteria target optimization of analytical procedures using a genetic algorithm. *Analytical Chimica Acta*, 265(2):211–225, 1992.
21. Wilson, PB and Macleod, MD, Low implementation cost IIR digital filter design using genetic algorithms. In *IEE/IEEE Workshop on Natural Algorithms in Signal Processing*, pp. 4/1–4/8, Chelmsford, U.K., 1993.
22. Zebulum, RS, Pacheco, MA, and Vellasco, M, A multi-objective optimisation methodology applied to the synthesis of low-power operational amplifiers. In Cheuri, IJ and dos Reis Filho, CA (eds.), *Proceedings of the XIII International Conference in Microelectronics and Packaging*, volume 1, pp. 264–271, Curitiba, Brazil, August 1998.
23. Hajela, P and Lin, CY, Genetic search strategies in multicriterion optimal design. *Structural Optimization*, 4:99–107, 1992.
24. Coello Coello, CA and Christiansen, AD, Two new GA-based methods for multiobjective optimization. *Civil Engineering Systems*, 15(3):207–243, 1998.
25. Das, I and Dennis, J, A closer look at drawbacks of minimizing weighted sums of objectives for pareto set generation in multicriteria optimization problems. *Structural Optimization*, 14(1):63–69, 1997.
26. Jin, Y, Okabe, T, and Sendhoff, B, Dynamic Weighted Aggregation for Evolutionary Multi-Objective Optimization: Why Does It Work and How? In Spector, L, Goodman, ED, Wu, A, Langdon, WB, Voigt, HM, Gen, M, Sen, S, Dorigo, M, Pezeshk, S, Garzon, MH, and Burke, E (eds.), *Proceedings of the Genetic and Evolutionary Computation Conference (GECCO'2001)*, pp. 1042–1049, San Francisco, California, 2001. Morgan Kaufmann Publishers.
27. Coello Coello, CA, Treating Constraints as Objectives for Single-Objective Evolutionary Optimization. *Engineering Optimization*, 32(3):275–308, 2000.
28. Norris, SR and Crossley, WA, Pareto-optimal controller gains generated by a genetic algorithm. In *AIAA 36th Aerospace Sciences Meeting and Exhibit*, Reno, Nevada, January 1998. AIAA Paper 98-0010.
29. Rogers, JL, A parallel approach to optimum actuator selection with a genetic algorithm. In *AIAA Paper No. 2000-4484, AIAA Guidance, Navigation, and Control Conference*, Denver, CO, August 14–17 2000.
30. Sridhar, J and Rajendran, C, Scheduling in Flowshop and Cellular Manufacturing Systems with Multiple Objectives – A Genetic Algorithmic Approach. *Production Planning & Control*, 7(4):374–382, 1996.

31. Venugopal, V and Narendran, TT, A genetic algorithm approach to the machine-component grouping problem with multiple objectives. *Computers and Industrial Engineering*, 22(4):469–480, 1992.
32. Deb, K and Goldberg, DE, An investigation of niche and species formation in genetic function optimization. In Schaffer, JD (ed), *Proceedings of the Third International Conference on Genetic Algorithms*, pp. 42–50, San Mateo, CA, June 1989. Morgan Kaufmann Publishers.
33. Srinivas, N and Deb, K, Multiobjective optimization using nondominated sorting in genetic algorithms. *Evolutionary Computation*, 2(3):221–248, Fall 1994.
34. Horn, J, Nafpliotis, N, and Goldberg, DE, A niched pareto genetic algorithm for multiobjective optimization. In *Proceedings of the First IEEE Conference on Evolutionary Computation, IEEE World Congress on Computational Intelligence*, volume 1, pp. 82–87, Piscataway, NJ, June 1994. IEEE Service Center.
35. Goldberg, DE and Richardson, J, Genetic algorithm with sharing for multimodal function optimization. In Grefenstette, JJ (ed), *Genetic Algorithms and Their Applications: Proceedings of the Second International Conference on Genetic Algorithms*, pp. 41–49, Hillsdale, NJ, 1987. Lawrence Erlbaum.
36. Fonseca, CM and Fleming, PJ, Genetic algorithms for multiobjective optimization: Formulation, discussion and generalization. In Forrest, S (ed), *Proceedings of the Fifth International Conference on Genetic Algorithms*, pp. 416–423, San Mateo, CA, 1993. Morgan Kaufmann Publishers.
37. Zitzler, E and Thiele, L, Multiobjective evolutionary algorithms: A comparative case study and the strength pareto approach. *IEEE Transactions on Evolutionary Computation*, 3(4):257–271, November 1999.
38. Morse, JN, Reducing the size of the nondominated set: Pruning by clustering. *Computers and Operations Research*, 7(1–2):55–66, 1980.
39. Zitzler, E, Laumanns, M, and Thiele, L, SPEA2: Improving the Strength Pareto Evolutionary Algorithm. Technical Report 103, Computer Engineering and Networks Laboratory (TIK), Swiss Federal Institute of Technology (ETH) Zurich, Gloriastrasse 35, CH-8092 Zurich, Switzerland, May 2001.
40. Knowles, JD and Corne, DW, Approximating the nondominated front using the pareto archived evolution strategy. *Evolutionary Computation*, 8(2):149–172, 2000.
41. Deb, K, Agrawal, S, Pratab, A, and Meyarivan, T, A fast elitist non-dominated sorting genetic algorithm for multi-objective optimization: NSGA-II. KanGAL report 200001, Indian Institute of Technology, Kanpur, India, 2000.
42. Deb, K, Agrawal, S, Pratab, A, and Meyarivan, T, A fast elitist non-dominated sorting genetic algorithm for multi-objective optimization: NSGA-II. In Schoenauer, M, Deb, K, Rudolph, G, Yao, X, Lutton, E, Merelo, JJ, and Schwefel, H-P (eds.), *Proceedings of the Parallel Problem Solving from Nature VI Conference*, pp. 849–858, Paris, France, 2000. Springer. Lecture Notes in Computer Science No. 1917.
43. Deb, K, Pratap, A, Agarwal, S, and Meyarivan, T, A Fast and Elitist Multiobjective Genetic Algorithm: NSGA-II. *IEEE Transactions on Evolutionary Computation*, 6(2):182–197, April 2002.
44. Erickson, M, Mayer, A, and Horn, J, The Niched Pareto Genetic Algorithm 2 Applied to the Design of Groundwater Remediation Systems. In Zitzler, E,

Deb, K, Thiele, L, Coello Coello, CA, and Corne, D (eds.), *First International Conference on Evolutionary Multi-Criterion Optimization*, pp. 681–695. Springer-Verlag. Lecture Notes in Computer Science No. 1993, 2001.

45. Oei, CK, Goldberg, DE, and Chang, S-J, Tournament Selection, Niching, and the Preservation of Diversity. Technical Report 91011, Illinois Genetic Algorithms Laboratory, University of Illinois at Urbana-Champaign, Urbana, Illinois, December 1991.

46. Corne, DW, Knowles, JD, and Oates, MJ, The Pareto Envelope-based Selection Algorithm for Multiobjective Optimization. In Schoenauer, M, Deb, K, Rudolph, G, Yao, X, Lutton, E, Merelo, JJ, and Schwefel, H-P (eds.), *Proceedings of the Parallel Problem Solving from Nature VI Conference*, pp. 839–848, Paris, France, 2000. Springer. Lecture Notes in Computer Science No. 1917.

47. Corne, DW, Jerram, NR, Knowles, JD, and Oates, MJ, PESA-II: Region-based Selection in Evolutionary Multiobjective Optimization. In Spector, L, Goodman, ED, Wu, A, Langdon, WB, Voigt, H-M, Gen, M, Sen, S, Dorigo, M, Pezeshk, S, Garzon, MH, and Burke, E (eds.), *Proceedings of the Genetic and Evolutionary Computation Conference (GECCO'2001)*, pp. 283–290, San Francisco, California, 2001. Morgan Kaufmann Publishers.

48. Goldberg, DE and Deb, K, A comparison of selection schemes used in genetic algorithms. In Rawlins, GJE (ed), *Foundations of Genetic Algorithms*, pp. 69–93. Morgan Kaufmann, San Mateo, CA, 1991.

49. Coello Coello, CA and Toscano Pulido, G, A Micro-Genetic Algorithm for Multiobjective Optimization. In Zitzler, E, Deb, K, Thiele, L, Coello Coello, CA, and Corne, D (eds.), *First International Conference on Evolutionary Multi-Criterion Optimization*, pp. 126–140. Springer-Verlag. Lecture Notes in Computer Science No. 1993, 2001.

50. Coello Coello, CA and Toscano Pulido, G, Multiobjective Optimization using a Micro-Genetic Algorithm. In Spector, L, Goodman, ED, Wu, A, Langdon, WB, Voigt, H-M, Gen, M, Sen, S, Dorigo, M, Pezeshk, S, Garzon, MH, and Burke, E (eds.), *Proceedings of the Genetic and Evolutionary Computation Conference (GECCO'2001)*, pp. 274–282, San Francisco, California, 2001. Morgan Kaufmann Publishers.

51. Coello Coello, CA and Salazar Lechuga, M, MOPSO: A Proposal for Multiple Objective Particle Swarm Optimization. In *Congress on Evolutionary Computation (CEC'2002)*, volume 2, pp. 1051–1056, Piscataway, New Jersey, May 2002. IEEE Service Center.

52. Jensen, MT, Reducing the run-time complexity of multiobjective eas: The nsga-ii and other algorithms. *IEEE Transactions on Evolutionary Computation*, 7(5):503–515, October 2003.

53. Everson, RM, Fieldsend, JE, and Singh, S, Full Elite Sets for Multi-Objective Optimisation. In Parmee, IC (ed), *Proceedings of the Fifth International Conference on Adaptive Computing Design and Manufacture (ACDM 2002)*, volume 5, pp. 343–354, University of Exeter, Devon, UK, April 2002. Springer-Verlag.

54. Fieldsend, JE, Everson, RM, and Singh, S, Using Unconstrained Elite Archives for Multiobjective Optimization. *IEEE Transactions on Evolutionary Computation*, 7(3):305–323, June 2003.

55. Habenicht, W, Quad trees: A data structure for discrete vector optimization problems. In *Lecture Notes in Economics and Mathematical Systems*, volume 209, pp. 136–145, 1982.

56. Mostaghim, S, Teich, J, and Tyagi, A, Comparison of Data Structures for Storing Pareto-sets in MOEAs. In *Congress on Evolutionary Computation (CEC'2002)*, volume 1, pp. 843–848, Piscataway, New Jersey, May 2002. IEEE Service Center.

57. Purshouse, RC and Fleming, PJ, Why use Elitism and Sharing in a Multi-Objective Genetic Algorithm? In Langdon, WB, Cantú-Paz, E, Mathias, K, Roy, R, Davis, D, Poli, R, Balakrishnan, K, Honavar, V, Rudolph, G, Wegener, J, Bull, L, Potter, MA, Schultz, AC, Miller, JF, Burke, E, and Jonoska, N (eds.), *Proceedings of the Genetic and Evolutionary Computation Conference (GECCO'2002)*, pp. 520–527, San Francisco, California, July 2002. Morgan Kaufmann Publishers.

58. Laumanns, M, Zitzler, E, and Thiele, L, On the Effects of Archiving, Elitism, and Density Based Selection in Evolutionary Multi-objective Optimization. In Zitzler, E, Deb, K, Thiele, L, Coello Coello, CA, and Corne, D (eds.), *First International Conference on Evolutionary Multi-Criterion Optimization*, pp. 181–196. Springer-Verlag. Lecture Notes in Computer Science No. 1993, 2001.

59. Fonseca, CM and Fleming, PJ, An overview of evolutionary algorithms in multiobjective optimization. *Evolutionary Computation*, 3(1):1–16, Spring 1995.

60. Thomson, R and Arslan, T, The Evolutionary Design and Synthesis of Non-Linear Digital VLSI Systems. In Lohn, J, Zebulum, R, Steincamp, J, Keymeulen, D, Stoica, A, and Ferguson, MI (eds.), *Proceedings of the 2003 NASA/DoD Conference on Evolvable Hardware*, pp. 125–134, Los Alamitos, California, July 2003. IEEE Computer Society Press.

61. Abdel-Magid, YL and Abido, MA, Optimal Multiobjective Design of Robust Power System Stabilizers Using Genetic Algorithms. *IEEE Transactions on Power Systems*, 18(3):1125–1132, August 2003.

62. Ramírez Rosado, IJ and Bernal Agustín, JL, Reliability and cost optimization for distribution networks expansion using an evolutionary algorithm. *IEEE Transactions on Power Systems*, 16(1):111–118, February 2001.

63. Reed, PM, Minsker, BS, and Goldberg, DE, A multiobjective approach to cost effective long-term groundwater monitoring using an elitist nondominated sorted genetic algorithm with historical data. *Journal of Hydroinformatics*, 3(2):71–89, April 2001.

64. Formiga, KTM, Chaufhry, FH, Cheung, PB, and Reis, LFR, Optimal Design of Water Distribution System by Multiobjective Evolutionary Methods. In Fonseca, CM, Fleming, PJ, Zitzler, E, Deb, K, and Thiele, L (eds.), *Evolutionary Multi-Criterion Optimization. Second International Conference, EMO 2003*, pp. 677–691, Faro, Portugal, April 2003. Springer. Lecture Notes in Computer Science. Volume 2632.

65. Kurapati, A and Azarm, S, Immune Network Simulation with Multiobjective Genetic Algorithms for Multidisciplinary Design Optimization. *Engineering Optimization*, 33:245–260, 2000.

66. Coello Coello, CA and Christiansen, AD, Multiobjective optimization of trusses using genetic algorithms. *Computers and Structures*, 75(6):647–660, May 2000.

67. Aguilar Madeira, JF, Rodrigues, H, and Pina, H, Genetic Methods in Multi-objective Optimization of Structures with an Equality Constraint on Volume. In Fonseca, CM, Fleming, PJ, Zitzler, E, Deb, K, and Thiele, L (eds.), *Evolutionary Multi-Criterion Optimization. Second International Conference, EMO 2003*, pp. 767–781, Faro, Portugal, April 2003. Springer. Lecture Notes in Computer Science. Volume 2632.

68. Pulliam, TH, Nemec, M, Hoslt, T, and Zingg, DW, Comparison of Evolutionary (Genetic) Algorithm and Adjoint Methods for Multi-Objective Viscous Airfoil Optimizations. In *41st Aerospace Sciences Meeting. Paper AIAA 2003-0298*, Reno, Nevada, January 2003.

69. Obayashi, S, Tsukahara, T, and Nakamura, T, Multiobjective evolutionary computation for supersonic wing-shape optimization. *IEEE Transactions on Evolutionary Computation*, 4(2):182–187, July 2000.

70. Lavagna, MR and Ercoli Finzi, A, Concurrent Processes within Preliminary Spacecraft Design: An Autonomous Decisional Support Based on Genetic Algorithms and Analytic Hierarchical Process. In *Proceedings of the 17th International Symposium on Space Flight Dynamics*, Moscow, Russia, June 2003.

71. Osyczka, A, Krenich, S, and Karaś, K, Optimum design of robot grippers using genetic algorithms. In *Proceedings of the Third World Congress of Structural and Multidisciplinary Optimization (WCSMO)*, Buffalo, New York, May 1999.

72. Teo, J and Abbass, HA, Is a Self-Adaptive Pareto Approach Beneficial for Controlling Embodied Virtual Robots. In Cantú-Paz, E et al. (eds), *Genetic and Evolutionary Computation—GECCO 2003. Proceedings, Part II*, pp. 1612–1613. Springer. Lecture Notes in Computer Science Vol. 2724, July 2003.

73. Ortmann, M and Weber, W, Multi-criterion optimization of robot trajectories with evolutionary strategies. In *Proceedings of the 2001 Genetic and Evolutionary Computation Conference. Late-Breaking Papers*, pp. 310–316, San Francisco, CA, July 2001.

74. Blumel, AL, Hughes, EJ, and White, BA, Multi-objective Evolutionary Design of Fuzzy Autopilot Controller. In Zitzler, E, Deb, K, Thiele, L, Coello Coello, CA, and Corne, D (eds.), *First International Conference on Evolutionary Multi-Criterion Optimization*, pp. 668–680. Springer-Verlag. Lecture Notes in Computer Science No. 1993, 2001.

75. Tan, KC, Lee, TH, Khor, EF, and Ou, K, Control system design unification and automation using an incremented multi-objective evolutionary algorithm. In Hamza, MH (ed), *Proceedings of the 19th IASTED International Conference on Modeling, Identification and Control*. IASTED, Innsbruck, Austria, 2000.

76. Kundu, S and Kawata, S, Evolutionary Multicriteria Optimization for Improved Design of Optimal Control Systems. In Parmee, IC (ed), *Proceedings of the Fifth International Conference on Adaptive Computing Design and Manufacture (ACDM 2002)*, volume 5, pp. 207–218, University of Exeter, Devon, UK, April 2002. Springer-Verlag.

77. Caswell, DJ and Lamont, GB, Wire-Antenna Geometry Design with Multiobjective Genetic Algorithms. In *Congress on Evolutionary Computation (CEC'2002)*, volume 1, pp. 103–108, Piscataway, New Jersey, May 2002. IEEE Service Center.

78. Kumar, R, and Banerjee, N, Multicriteria Network Design Using Evolutionary Algorithm. In Cantú-Paz, E et al. (eds), *Genetic and Evolutionary*

*Computation—GECCO 2003. Proceedings, Part II*, pp. 2179–2190. Springer. Lecture Notes in Computer Science Vol. 2724, July 2003.

79. Pullan, W, Optimising Multiple Aspects of Network Survivability. In *Congress on Evolutionary Computation (CEC'2002)*, volume 1, pp. 115–120, Piscataway, New Jersey, May 2002. IEEE Service Center.

80. Feng, CW, Liu, L, and Burns, SA, Using genetic algorithms to solve construction time-cost trade-off problems. *Journal of Computing in Civil Engineering*, 10(3):184–189, 1999.

81. Balling, R, The Maximin Fitness Function; Multiobjective City and Regional Planning. In Fonseca, CM, Fleming, PJ, Zitzler, E, Deb, K, and Thiele, L (eds.), *Evolutionary Multi-Criterion Optimization. Second International Conference, EMO 2003*, pp. 1–15, Faro, Portugal, April 2003. Springer. Lecture Notes in Computer Science. Volume 2632.

82. Khajehpour, S, *Optimal Conceptual Design of High-Rise Office Buldings*. PhD thesis, Civil Engineering Department, University of Waterloo, Ontario, Canada, 2001.

83. Cheng, R, Gen, M, and Oren, SS, An Adaptive Hyperplane Approach for Multiple Objective Optimization Problems with Complex Constraints. In Whitley, D, Goldberg, D, Cantú-Paz, E, Spector, L, Parmee, I, and Beyer, H-G (eds.), *Proceedings of the Genetic and Evolutionary Computation Conference (GECCO'2000)*, pp. 299–306, San Francisco, California, 2000. Morgan Kaufmann.

84. Gen, M and Li, Y-Z, Solving multi-objective transportation problems by spanning tree-based genetic algorithm. In Parmee, I (ed), *The Integration of Evolutionary and Adaptive Computing Technologies with Product/System Design and Realisation*, pp. 95–108, Plymouth, United Kingdom, April 1998. Plymouth Engineering Design Centre, Springer-Verlag.

85. Laumanns, N, Laumanns, M, and Neunzig, D, Multi-objective design space exploration of road trains with evolutionary algorithms. In Zitzler, E, Deb, K, Thiele, L, Coello Coello, CA, and Corne, D (eds.), *First International Conference on Evolutionary Multi-Criterion Optimization*, pp. 612–623. Springer-Verlag. Lecture Notes in Computer Science No. 1993, Berlin, Germany, 2001.

86. Andersson, J, Applications of a Multi-objective Genetic Algorithm to Engineering Design Problems. In Fonseca, CM, Fleming, PJ, Zitzler, E, Deb, K, and Thiele, L (eds.), *Evolutionary Multi-Criterion Optimization. Second International Conference, EMO 2003*, pp. 737–751, Faro, Portugal, April 2003. Springer. Lecture Notes in Computer Science. Volume 2632.

87. Ramos, RM, Saldanha, RR, Takahashi, RHC, and Moreira, FJS, The Real-Biased Multiobjective Genetic Algorithm and Its Application to the Design of Wire Antennas. *IEEE Transactions on Magnetics*, 39(3):1329–1332, May 2003.

88. Sbalzarini, IF, Müller, S, and Koumoutsakos, P, Microchannel Optimization Using Multiobjective Evolution Strategies. In Zitzler, E, Deb, K, Thiele, L, Coello Coello, CA, and Corne, D (eds.), *First International Conference on Evolutionary Multi-Criterion Optimization*, pp. 516–530. Springer-Verlag. Lecture Notes in Computer Science No. 1993, 2001.

89. Ishibuchi, H, Yoshida, T, and Murata, T, Balance Between Genetic Search and Local Search in Memetic Algorithms for Multiobjective Permutation Flowshop Scheduling. *IEEE Transactions on Evolutionary Computation*, 7(2):204–223, April 2003.

90. Talbi, E-G, Rahoual, M, Mabed, MH, and Dhaenens, C, A Hybrid Evolutionary Approach for Multicriteria Optimization Problems: Application to the Flow Shop. In Zitzler, E, Deb, K, Thiele, L, Coello Coello, CA, and Corne, D (eds.), *First International Conference on Evolutionary Multi-Criterion Optimization*, pp. 416–428. Springer-Verlag. Lecture Notes in Computer Science No. 1993, 2001.

91. Brizuela, C, Sannomiya, N, and Zhao, Y, Multi-Objective Flow-Shop: Preliminary Results. In Zitzler, E, Deb, K, Thiele, L, Coello Coello, CA, and Corne, D (eds.), *First International Conference on Evolutionary Multi-Criterion Optimization*, pp. 443–457. Springer-Verlag. Lecture Notes in Computer Science No. 1993, 2001.

92. Jaszkiewicz, A, Hapke, M, and Kominek, P, Performance of Multiple Objective Evolutionary Algorithms on a Distribution System Design Problem—Computational Experiment. In Zitzler, E, Deb, K, Thiele, L, Coello Coello, CA, and Corne, D (eds.), *First International Conference on Evolutionary Multi-Criterion Optimization*, pp. 241–255. Springer-Verlag. Lecture Notes in Computer Science No. 1993, 2001.

93. Krause, M and Nissen, V, On using penalty functions and multicriteria optimisation techniques in facility layout. In Biethahn, J and Nissen, V (eds.), *Evolutionary Algorithms in Management Applications*. Springer-Verlag, Berlin, Germany, 1995.

94. Ducheyne, EI, De Wulf, RR, and De Baets, B, Bi-objective genetic algorithm for forest management: a comparative study. In *Proceedings of the 2001 Genetic and Evolutionary Computation Conference. Late-Breaking Papers*, pp. 63–66, San Francisco, CA, July 2001.

95. Jones, G, Brown, RD, Clark, DE, Willett, P, and Glen, RC, Searching databases of two-dimensional and three-dimensional chemical structures using genetic algorithms. In Forrest, S (ed), *Proceedings of the Fifth International Conference on Genetic Algorithms*, pp. 597–602, San Mateo, California, 1993. Morgan Kaufmann.

96. Hinchliffe, M, Willis, M, and Tham, M, Chemical process systems modelling using multi-objective genetic programming. In Koza, JR, Banzhaf, W, Chellapilla, K, Deb, K, Dorigo, M, Fogel, DB, Garzon, MH, Goldberg, DE, Iba, H, and Riolo, RL (eds.), *Proceedings of the Third Annual Conference on Genetic Programming*, pp. 134–139, San Mateo, CA, July 1998. Morgan Kaufmann Publishers.

97. Kunha, A, Oliveira, P, and Covas, JA, Genetic algorithms in multiobjective optimization problems: An application to polymer extrusion. In Wu, AS (ed), *Proceedings of the 1999 Genetic and Evolutionary Computation Conference. Workshop Program*, pp. 129–130, Orlando, FL, July 1999.

98. Parks, GT, Multiobjective pressurized water reactor reload core design by nondominated genetic algorithm search. *Nuclear Science and Engineering*, 124(1):178–187, 1996.

99. Golovkin, I, Mancini, R, Louis, S, Ochi, Y, Fujita, K, Nishimura, H, Shirga, H, Miyanaga, N, Azechi, H, Butzbach, R, Uschmann, I, Förster, E, Delettrez, J, Koch, J, Lee, RW, and Klein, L, Spectroscopic Determination of Dynamic Plasma Gradients in Implosion Cores. *Physical Review Letters*, 88(4), January 2002.

100. de Toro, F, Ros, E, Mota, S, and Ortega, J, Non-invasive Atrial Disease Diagnosis Using Decision Rules: A Multi-objective Optimization Approach.

In Fonseca, CM, Fleming, PJ, Zitzler, E, Deb, K, and Thiele, L (eds.), *Evolutionary Multi-Criterion Optimization. Second International Conference, EMO 2003*, pp. 638–647, Faro, Portugal, April 2003. Springer. Lecture Notes in Computer Science. Volume 2632.

101. Aguilar, J and Miranda, P, Approaches Based on Genetic Algorithms for Multiobjective Optimization Problems. In Banzhaf, W, Daida, J, Eiben, AE, Garzon, MH, Honavar, V, Jakiela, M, and Smith, RE (eds.), *Proceedings of the Genetic and Evolutionary Computation Conference (GECCO'99)*, volume 1, pp. 3–10, Orlando, Florida, USA, 1999. Morgan Kaufmann Publishers.

102. Lahanas, M, Schreibmann, E, Milickovic, N, and Baltas, D, Intensity Modulated Beam Radiation Therapy Dose Optimization with Multiobjective Evolutionary Algorithms. In Fonseca, CM, Fleming, PJ, Zitzler, E, Deb, K, and Thiele, L (eds.), *Evolutionary Multi-Criterion Optimization. Second International Conference, EMO 2003*, pp. 648–661, Faro, Portugal, April 2003. Springer. Lecture Notes in Computer Science. Volume 2632.

103. Dasgupta, D and González, FA, Evolving Complex Fuzzy Classifier Rules Using a Linear Tree Genetic Representation. In Spector, L, Goodman, ED, Wu, A, Langdon, WB, Voigt, H-M, Gen, M, Sen, S, Dorigo, M, Pezeshk, S, Garzon, MH, and Burke, E (eds.), *Proceedings of the Genetic and Evolutionary Computation Conference (GECCO'2001)*, pp. 299–305, San Francisco, California, 2001. Morgan Kaufmann Publishers.

104. Fornaciari, W, Micheli, P, Salice, F, and Zampella, L, A First Step Towards Hw/Sw Partitioning of UML Specifications. In *IEEE/ACM Design Automation and Test in Europe (DATE'03)*, pp. 668–673, Munich, Germany, March 2003. IEEE.

105. Ekárt, A and Németh, SZ, Selection Based on the Pareto Nondomination Criterion for Controlling Code Growth in Genetic Programming. *Genetic Programming and Evolvable Machines*, 2(1):61–73, March 2001.

106. Llorà, X and Goldberg, DE, Bounding the Effect of Noise in Multiobjective Learning Classifier Systems. *Evolutionary Computation*, 11(3):279–298, Fall 2003.

107. Deb, K, Multi-Objective Genetic Algorithms: Problem Difficulties and Construction of Test Problems. *Evolutionary Computation*, 7(3):205–230, Fall 1999.

108. Van Veldhuizen, DA and Lamont, GB, Multiobjective optimization with messy genetic algorithms. In *Proceedings of the 2000 ACM Symposium on Applied Computing*, pp. 470–476, Villa Olmo, Como, Italy, 2000. ACM.

109. Deb, K, Pratap, A, and Meyarivan, T, Constrained test problems for multi-objective evolutionary optimization. In Zitzler, E, Deb, K, Thiele, L, Coello Coello, CA, and Corne, D (eds.), *First International Conference on Evolutionary Multi-Criterion Optimization*, pp. 284–298. Springer-Verlag. Lecture Notes in Computer Science No. 1993, Berlin, Germany, 2001.

110. Deb, K, Thiele, L, Laumanns, M, and Zitzler, E, Scalable Multi-Objective Optimization Test Problems. In *Congress on Evolutionary Computation (CEC'2002)*, volume 1, pp. 825–830, Piscataway, New Jersey, May 2002. IEEE Service Center.

111. Parmee, IC, Poor-Definition, Uncertainty, and Human Factors—Satisfying Multiple Objectives in Real-World Decision-Making Environments. In Zitzler, E, Deb, K, Thiele, L, Coello Coello, CA, and Corne, D (eds.), *First*

*International Conference on Evolutionary Multi-Criterion Optimization*, pp. 67–81. Springer-Verlag. Lecture Notes in Computer Science No. 1993, 2001.

112. Tiwari, A, Roy, R, Jared, G, and Munaux, O, Interaction and Multi-Objective Optimisation. In Spector, L, Goodman, ED, Wu, A, Langdon, WB, Voigt, H-M, Gen, M, Sen, S, Dorigo, M, Pezeshk, S, Garzon, MH, and Burke, E (eds.), *Proceedings of the Genetic and Evolutionary Computation Conference (GECCO'2001)*, pp. 671–678, San Francisco, California, 2001. Morgan Kaufmann Publishers.

113. Hughes, EJ, Constraint Handling With Uncertain and Noisy Multi-Objective Evolution. In *Proceedings of the Congress on Evolutionary Computation 2001 (CEC'2001)*, volume 2, pp. 963–970, Piscataway, New Jersey, May 2001. IEEE Service Center.

114. Zitzler, E, Deb, K, and Thiele, L, Comparison of Multiobjective Evolutionary Algorithms: Empirical Results. *Evolutionary Computation*, 8(2):173–195, Summer 2000.

115. Van Veldhuizen, DA, *Multiobjective Evolutionary Algorithms: Classifications, Analyses, and New Innovations*. PhD thesis, Department of Electrical and Computer Engineering. Graduate School of Engineering. Air Force Institute of Technology, Wright-Patterson AFB, OH, May 1999.

116. Van Veldhuizen, DA and Lamont, GB, Multiobjective evolutionary algorithm research: A history and analysis. Technical Report TR-98-03, Department of Electrical and Computer Engineering, Graduate School of Engineering, Air Force Institute of Technology, Wright-Patterson AFB, OH, 1998.

117. Schott, JR, Fault tolerant design using single and multicriteria genetic algorithm optimization. Master's thesis, Department of Aeronautics and Astronautics, Massachusetts Institute of Technology, Cambridge, MA, May 1995.

118. Van Veldhuizen, DA and Lamont, GB, Multiobjective evolutionary algorithm test suites. In Carroll, J, Haddad, H, Oppenheim, D, Bryant, B, and Lamont, GB (eds.), *Proceedings of the 1999 ACM Symposium on Applied Computing*, pp. 351–357, San Antonio, TX, 1999. ACM.

119. Zitzler, E, Laumanns, M, Thiele, L, Fonseca, CM, and Grunert da Fonseca, V, Why Quality Assessment of Multiobjective Optimizers Is Difficult. In Langdon, WB, Cantú-Paz, E, Mathias, K, Roy, R, Davis, D, Poli, R, Balakrishnan, K, Honavar, V, Rudolph, G, Wegener, J, Bull, L, Potter, MA, Schultz, AC, Miller, JF, Burke, E, and Jonoska, N (eds.), *Proceedings of the Genetic and Evolutionary Computation Conference (GECCO'2002)*, pp. 666–673, San Francisco, California, July 2002. Morgan Kaufmann Publishers.

120. Knowles, J and Corne, D, On Metrics for Comparing Nondominated Sets. In *Congress on Evolutionary Computation (CEC'2002)*, volume 1, pp. 711–716, Piscataway, New Jersey, May 2002. IEEE Service Center.

121. Zitzler, E, Thiele, L, Laumanns, M, Fonseca, CM, and Grunert da Fonseca, V, Performance Assessment of Multiobjective Optimizers: An Analysis and Review. *IEEE Transactions on Evolutionary Computation*, 7(2):117–132, April 2003.

122. Rudolph, G, On a Multi-Objective Evolutionary Algorithm and Its Convergence to the Pareto Set. In *Proceedings of the 5th IEEE Conference on Evolutionary Computation*, pp. 511–516, Piscataway, NJ, 1998. IEEE Press.

123. Rudolph, G and Agapie, A, Convergence Properties of Some Multi-Objective Evolutionary Algorithms. In *Proceedings of the 2000 Conference on*

*Evolutionary Computation*, volume 2, pp. 1010–1016, Piscataway, NJ, July 2000. IEEE Press.

124. Hanne, T, On the convergence of multiobjective evolutionary algorithms. *European Journal of Operational Research*, 117(3):553–564, September 2000.

125. Hanne, T, Global multiobjective optimization using evolutionary algorithms. *Journal of Heuristics*, 6(3):347–360, August 2000.

126. Van Veldhuizen, DA and Lamont, GB, Evolutionary computation and convergence to a pareto front. In Koza, JR (ed), *Late Breaking Papers at the Genetic Programming 1998 Conference*, pp. 221–228, Stanford, CA, July 1998. Stanford University Bookstore.

127. Laumanns, M, Thiele, L, Zitzler, E, and Deb, K, Archiving with Guaranteed Convergence and Diversity in Multi-Objective Optimization. In Langdon, WB, Cantú-Paz, E, Mathias, K, Roy, R, Davis, D, Poli, R, Balakrishnan, K, Honavar, V, Rudolph, G, Wegener, J, Bull, L, Potter, MA, Schultz, AC, Miller, JF, Burke, E, and Jonoska, N (eds.), *Proceedings of the Genetic and Evolutionary Computation Conference (GECCO'2002)*, pp. 439–447, San Francisco, California, July 2002. Morgan Kaufmann Publishers.

128. Wright, S, The roles of mutation, inbreeding, crossbreeding and selection in evolution. In Jones, DF (ed), *Proceedings of the Sixth International Conference on Genetics*, volume 1, pp. 356–366, 1932.

129. Altenberg, L, NK fitness landscapes. In Bäck, T, Fogel, DB, and Michalewicz, Z (eds.), *Handbook of Evolutionary Computation*, chapter B2.7.2, pp. B2.7:5–B2.7:10. Oxford University Press, New York, NY, 1997.

130. Laumanns, M, Thiele, L, Zitzler, E, Welzl, E, and Deb, K, Running Time Analysis of Multi-objective Evolutionary Algorithms on a Simple Discrete Optimization Problem. In Merelo Guervós, JJ, Adamidis, P, Beyer, H-G, Fernández-Villacañas, JL, and Schwefel, H-P (eds.), *Parallel Problem Solving from Nature—PPSN VII*, pp. 44–53, Granada, Spain, September 2002. Springer. Lecture Notes in Computer Science No. 2439.

131. Laumanns, M, Thiele, L, Deb, K, and Zitzler, E, Combining Convergence and Diversity in Evolutionary Multi-objective Optimization. *Evolutionary Computation*, 10(3):263–282, Fall 2002.

132. Coello Coello, CA, Handling Preferences in Evolutionary Multiobjective Optimization: A Survey. In *2000 Congress on Evolutionary Computation*, volume 1, pp. 30–37, Piscataway, New Jersey, July 2000. IEEE Service Center.

133. Cvetković, D and Parmee, IC, Preferences and their Application in Evolutionary Multiobjective Optimisation. *IEEE Transactions on Evolutionary Computation*, 6(1):42–57, February 2002.

134. Farina, M, Deb, K, and Amato, P Dynamic Multiobjective Optimization Problems: Test Cases, Approximation, and Applications. In Fonseca, CM, Fleming, PJ, Zitzler, E, Deb, K, and Thiele, L (eds.), *Evolutionary Multi-Criterion Optimization. Second International Conference, EMO 2003*, pp. 311–326, Faro, Portugal, April 2003. Springer. Lecture Notes in Computer Science. Volume 2632.

135. Van Veldhuizen, DA, Zydallis, JB, and Lamont, GB, Considerations in Engineering Parallel Multiobjective Evolutionary Algorithms. *IEEE Transactions on Evolutionary Computation*, 7(2):144–173, April 2003.

# 3

# Self-adaptation and Convergence of Multiobjective Evolutionary Algorithms in Continuous Search Spaces

Marco Laumanns

**Summary.** This chapter investigates the convergence behavior of simple evolutionary algorithms with different selection strategies on a continuous multiobjective model problem. Special focus is given to the problem of controlling the mutation strength, since an adaptation of the mutation strength is necessary to converge to the optimum with arbitrary precision, and to achieve linear convergence order. Adaptive parameter control represents a major research topic in the field of evolutionary computation, and several methods have been proposed and applied successfully for single-objective optimization problems. We demonstrate that the convergence properties achieved by a self-adaptation of the mutation strength on single-objective problems do not carry over to the multiobjective case, if a simple dominance-based selection scheme is used. As a solution, a combined strategy is proposed using dominance-based selection in the archive and scalarizing functions in the working population.

## 3.1 Introduction

An important task in multiobjective optimization is to identify or to approximate the set of Pareto-optimal solutions. When evolutionary algorithms (EAs) are used for this task, their individuals should

1. converge to the Pareto set, and
2. provide a good, representative distribution of solutions.

While the latter aspect is raised only in the multiobjective case by the existence of multiple Pareto-optimal solutions, the first point is an equally important matter in single-objective optimization.

In the research about multiobjective evolutionary algorithms, both of the above requirements – convergence and diversity – have received much attention. Recent studies focus especially on their combination [1], and on the trade-offs between these two goals [2]. However, these investigations almost exclusively concern the selection operators, i.e., the question how to evaluate and compare solutions in the presence of multiple objectives.

On the contrary, the variation operators have so far been of little interest in evolutionary multiobjective optimization. Virtually all algorithms use standard non-adaptive operators from the single objective case. This holds in particular for the mutation operator, where it is common practice to apply fixed mutation rates in binary coded representation, or fixed mutation step sizes for real-coded individuals. Nevertheless, theoretical considerations [3, 4] emphasize the importance of the mutation strength for the convergence properties of multiobjective evolutionary algorithms.

In this chapter, we address the problem of controlling the mutation strength of multiobjective evolutionary algorithms. The study concentrates on the sphere function, a simple continuous model problem, and the standard mutative self-adaptation mechanism. With this adaptation mechanism for the mutation strength, originally proposed in Schwefel [5], evolutionary algorithms achieve linear convergence order on the single-objective sphere model. The major questions of the present study are:

- Can self-adaptive mutations lead to linear convergence order also in the case of multiple objectives?
- How does the choice of the selection operator influence the convergence behavior?

We start by recalling the concepts and different approaches of mutation strength control in the next section. In Section 3.3, the model problem is introduced as well as the algorithm and notion of convergence used in this study. Sections 3.4 to 3.6 examine different selection methods and their influence on the convergence behavior. Two major problems are identified that prevent all selection methods based on the dominance relation from giving the algorithms the desired convergence properties. Finally, an adaptive scalarizing method in combination with a dominance-based archive is proposed, which exhibits linear convergence order on the model problem and is able to approximate solutions from diverse parts of the Pareto set.

## 3.2 Self-adaptive Mutation Control

Evolutionary algorithms contain parameters that can be set by the user to influence or tune the algorithmic behavior. Choosing optimal values for these *strategy parameters* is considered an important – and mainly open – research problem in evolutionary computation. Practitioners often use rules of thumb that are a combination of experience and extrapolation of theoretical results.

### 3.2.1 Methods of Mutation Control

One of the parameterization problems of evolutionary algorithms concerns the *mutation strength*: With too strong variation, the evolution becomes a pure random search; with too weak variation, no real progress can be achieved.

The small region of appropriate mutation strength – sometimes referred to as the "evolution window" – depends on the topology of the objective function, which is usually unknown. Thus, adaptation mechanisms for the mutation strength are a necessity for many optimization problems.

Existing approaches to mutation control can be categorized into three groups of increasing complexity [6]:

- Predefined schedules without feedback (deterministic),
- Feedback-based adaptation with (explicit) external control (adaptive), and
- Internal mechanisms without external control (self-adaptive).

Examples of each class can also be found in multiobjective evolutionary algorithms. All of these, including the present study, consider continuous search spaces and therefore a real-valued representation of the decision variables. For real-valued representations, the term mutation strength, sometimes rephrased as *mutation step size*, refers to the magnitude of change in each variable during mutation. This is different from binary representations, where the term *mutation rate* is used to express how probable it is for a certain binary variable to be changed (inverted) in one mutation operation.

Representatives of the first group of deterministic, predefined control are, for instance, time dependent schedules, as applied in the predator-prey EA of Laumanns et al. [7] in a multiobjective environment. The mutation step sizes are discounted by a constant factor each time an offspring in produced. Convergence to the Pareto set of some simple multiobjective problems can be achieved, if the initial step sizes are big enough and a 'conservative' discount factor is chosen. The disadvantages of this approach is the lack of a possibility to increase step sizes that are too small and the need for new parameters to be set.

A sophisticated explicit control mechanism was proposed in Kahlert [8]. The adaptation rule distinguishes nine different cases depending on the history of the evolution. In each case, the step sizes are altered differently according to heuristics, some of which resemble the so-called 1/5-success rule. This rule is based on the assumption that maximum progress towards the optimum can be achieved through step sizes leading to a success probability of approximately 20%. In the multiobjective case, however, the definition of what constitutes a successful mutation is not as straightforward as in the single-objective case. As discussed in Hanne [4], the probability of making cooperative steps decreases rapidly near the Pareto set, even for small step sizes. This issue will be discussed in detail in Section 3.4.

Self-adaptation of strategy parameters means that these parameters are part of the genetic information encoded in the individuals and subject to the evolutionary optimization process themselves. The self-adaptive mutation step size control of evolution strategies (ES) has been applied to multiobjective optimization problems in [9]. In this algorithm, the selection criterion changes randomly over time, and individuals are supplied with a set of step sizes for each objective function, but the convergence behavior was not investigated.

In the following, we investigate the convergence behavior of the standard isotropic self-adaptive mutation control from evolution strategies [5] in a multiobjective environment. The mechanism and working principle will be explained next.

### 3.2.2 Self-adaptive Mutations

Every individual of an evolutionary algorithm represents a decision alternative, a point in the search space. As we focus on continuous search spaces, an individual contains the $n$ *decision variables* in the decision vector $\boldsymbol{x} = (x_1, x_2, \ldots, x_n) \in \mathbb{R}^n$.

Mutation is carried out by adding a normal distributed random vector. The components of the vector are independent and identically distributed normal random numbers with zero mean and standard deviation $\sigma$. As the same mutation strength is used for all components, this type of mutation is called isotropic.

For the single-objective optimization case, Rudolph [10, p.169] has shown that using a constant mutation strength during the entire run is not a good choice as the convergence rate will decline to the asymptotics of pure random search. Instead, one needs to adapt the support of the mutation distribution depending on the distance to the optimal solution. As this distance is typically not known, the idea of self-adaptive evolution strategies is to let the mutation strength evolve along with the decision variables. Hence, an individual $\boldsymbol{a}^{(t)}$ with index $t$ is given as

$$\boldsymbol{a}^{(t)} = (\boldsymbol{x}^{(t)}, \sigma^{(t)}) \in \mathbb{R}^n \times \mathbb{R}_+ \tag{3.1}$$

The self-adaptation of the mutation strength is conceived by multiplying $\sigma$ with a log-normally distributed random variable. The whole mutation operator can be described according to Rudolph [11] as

$$\sigma^{(t+1)} = \sigma^{(t)} \cdot \exp(\tau \cdot N(0,1)), \quad \tau = n^{-1/2}, \tag{3.2}$$
$$x_i^{(t+1)} = x_i^{(t)} + \sigma^{(t+1)} \cdot N_i(0,1)$$

yielding the offspring individual $\boldsymbol{a}^{(t+1)} = (\boldsymbol{x}^{(t+1)}, \sigma^{(t+1)})$.

For the subsequent investigations, the above self-adaptive mutation operator will be used in different instances of the general multiobjective evolutionary algorithms (MOEA), depicted below as Algorithm 1. The instances differ in the way that fitness assignment and selection is performed.

## 3.3 The Model Problem

All investigations of this study are carried out on the so-called sphere model and its multiobjective extension, the multi-sphere model. The sphere model is defined as follows:

**Algorithm 1** General $(\mu, \lambda)$-MOEA

1: $t := 0$
2: Generate an initial population $Y^{(0)}$ by randomly sampling $\mu$ vectors from the decision space, and set $\sigma^{(0)} := 1$ for all $\mu$ individuals of $Y^{(0)}$.
3: **loop**
4:    $t := t + 1$
5:    *Variation:* Generate an offspring population $Z^{(t)}$ by randomly sampling $\lambda$ individuals from $Y^{(t)}$ (with replacement) and mutate each one according to (3.2).
6:    *Fitness assignment:* Assign each $z \in Z^{(t)}$ the fitness value $|\{z' \in Z^{(t)} : z' \prec z\}|$.
7:    *Selection:* Create $Y^{(t+1)}$ consisting of the best $\mu$ individuals from $Z^{(t)}$ according to their fitness values, ties are broken randomly.
8: **end loop**

$$\text{Minimize} \quad f(\boldsymbol{x}) = \sum_{i=1}^{n} x_i^2 \qquad (3.3)$$

It is a convex function, where the function value only depends on the distance to the optimum. Thus, $f(\boldsymbol{x}) \equiv g(||\boldsymbol{x} - \boldsymbol{x}^*||)$, where $g$ is a function of a single parameter and $\boldsymbol{x}^*$ the optimum, in this case the zero vector.

The sphere model serves as a reference in many theoretic as well as empirical studies, in particular in the context of self-adaptation. Evolutionary algorithms with adaptive mutation strength can achieve linear convergence order on this problem, i.e., the distance to the optimum decreases exponentially [5, 12, 10, 13].

This function can be systematically extended to a multiobjective sphere model by translating the optimum for each component so that the component optima span an $m - 1$-dimensional sub-space in which the Pareto set is located.[1] For this study, let the multi-sphere model problem be defined as

Minimize $\boldsymbol{f} : \mathbb{R}^n \mapsto \mathbb{R}_+^m$
where     $\boldsymbol{f}(\boldsymbol{x}) = (f_1(\boldsymbol{x}), f_2(\boldsymbol{x}), \ldots, f_m(\boldsymbol{x}))$    (3.4)
and       $f_i(\boldsymbol{x}) = 1 + \frac{1}{2}||(\boldsymbol{x} - \boldsymbol{e}_i)||^2 = 1 + \frac{1}{2}(x_i - 1)^2 + \frac{1}{2}\sum_{j=1, j \neq i}^{n} x_j^2$

where $n$ is the number of decision variables, $m$ the number of objectives and $\boldsymbol{e}_i$ denotes the $i$th unit vector.

The multi-sphere model is presumably the most simple multiobjective test function for unbounded search spaces, and the Pareto set, denoted as $X^*$, can be determined analytically: It is the $m - 1$-dimensional polyhedron of the component optima (see Figure 3.1). For $m = 1$, the problem reduces to a (translated) version of (3.3).

As the search space is unbounded, the time to reach the Pareto set depends crucially on the starting point and the (adaptation of the) mutation strength.

---

[1]For the construction principle of this and other multiobjective test functions see [14].

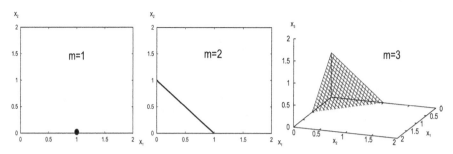

**Figure 3.1.** Pareto set of the multi-sphere model for $m = 1$, $m = 2$ and $m = 3$.

Our aim is to approximate the Pareto set of the given problem with arbitrary precision, and we will empirically investigate the velocity with which this can be achieved.

In mathematical terms, *convergence* refers to the limit behavior of numerical sequences. Here, we are instead dealing with sets (populations), which shall iteratively approach the Pareto set of the given optimization problem. To capture this, we measure the distance of sets of decision vectors (represented by a population of individuals) to the Pareto set.

**Definition 1 (Distance to Pareto set).** *Let $X^* \in \mathbb{R}^n$ be the Pareto set of a given optimization problem, $\boldsymbol{y}$ be a decision vector and $Y$ be a set of decision vectors. The distance of $\boldsymbol{y}$ to the Pareto set is defined as*

$$d(\boldsymbol{y}, X^*) = \min\{\|\boldsymbol{y} - \boldsymbol{y}'\| : \boldsymbol{y}' \in X^*\} \tag{3.5}$$

*and the distance of $Y$ to the Pareto set as*

$$d(Y, X^*) = \max\{d(\boldsymbol{y}, X^*) : \boldsymbol{y} \in Y\} \tag{3.6}$$

Here, $\| \cdot \|$ denotes the Euclidean norm. Now, convergence to the Pareto set can be specified with respect to the stochastic sequence of the population distances.

**Definition 2 (Convergence to the Pareto set).** *Let $(Y^{(t)} : t \geq 0)$ be the sequence of solution sets (populations) generated by a multiobjective evolutionary algorithm. Then the algorithm is said to converge to the Pareto set $X^*$, if the random sequence $(D^{(t)} : t \geq 0)$ with $D^{(t)} = d(Y^{(t)}, X^*)$ converges to zero.*

Different multiobjective evolutionary algorithms with this *global convergence* property have been proposed by Rudolph and Agapie [15]), while the algorithm of Laumanns et al. [1] additionally guarantees a good representation of the whole Pareto set.

Here, our primary concern is the convergence velocity. An appropriate local performance measure is the *progress rate* [16]. The progress rate is defined in the decision space and measures the (expected) distance change from the individuals of a population to a fixed reference point, typically the optimum. In the multiobjective framework, the reference point generalizes to a reference set, the Pareto set.

**Definition 3 (Progress rate).** *Let $Y^{(t)}$ be the current solution set (population) at iteration t and $X^*$ be the Pareto set. Then the progress rate at time t is defined as*

$$\phi = E[d(Y^{(t)}, X^*) - d(Y^{(t+1)}, X^*)].$$  (3.7)

## 3.4 Non-elitist Strategies ("komma" Selection)

As a first experiment, a simple non-elitist $(\mu, \lambda)$-MOEA, Algorithm 1, is run on our model problem. The terminology means that $\mu$ parents are used to create $\lambda > \mu$ offspring by mutation. The best $\mu$ offspring survive to the next generation using the number of individuals by which they are dominated, the dominance grade [17], to rank them.

Figure 3.2 displays the distance $d(Y^{(t)}, X^*)$ of the population to the Pareto set and the expected mutation step length

$$s = \sigma \cdot \sqrt{2} \cdot \frac{\Gamma((n+1)/2)}{\Gamma(n/2)}$$  (3.8)

according to [10, p. 21], where $n = 100$, $\mu = 1$, $\lambda = 10$, and $\Gamma$ denotes the Gamma function.

For $m = 1$, the claimed linear convergence order can easily be noticed. For the multiobjective case, however, this property seems to be valid only for individuals that are "sufficiently far away" from the Pareto-optimal set. After a period of exponentially decreasing population distance to the Pareto set, the solutions suddenly start to oscillate around a small, but fixed final distance.

This mechanism can be explained as follows. For individuals far away from the Pareto set the gradients of the different objective functions are nearly parallel, so the individuals can easily make a cooperative step, i.e., a mutation that improves all objective values simultaneously. This situation changes drastically in the vicinity of the Pareto set. When the individuals move closer to the Pareto set, the angle between the gradients approaches 180°, and the region of cooperative steps shrinks (see Figure 3.3).

To verify this conjecture, we would have to derive the success probability and the progress rate analytically and analogous to the existing theory in the single-objective case. But as in the multiobjective case both terms depend on the exact position of the search point, we only estimate these values by a statistical experiment. The idea is to sample individuals randomly from the search space, mutate them with a certain mutation strength $\sigma$ and record whether this mutation has been successful (leading to a solution that

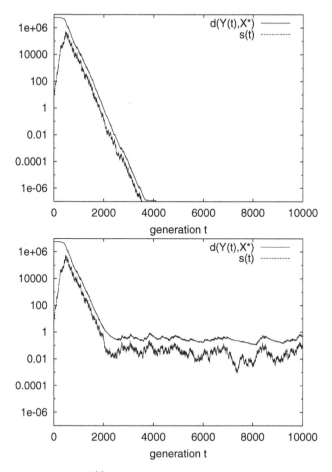

**Figure 3.2.** Distance $d(Y^{(t)}, X^*)$ and expected mutation step length $s$ for the $(1, 10)$-MOEA and $n = 100$ over time. The top graph shows the single-objective case $(m = 1)$ and the bottom graph the multiobjective case with $m = 2$.

dominates the parent) and what progress has been achieved. The results are displayed in Figure 3.4. For $k$ randomly initialized individuals $\boldsymbol{x}_i$ and their mutants $\boldsymbol{x}'_i$, the plots show the success frequency

$$\hat{w} = \frac{1}{k} \sum_{i=1}^{k} \mathbb{1}(\boldsymbol{x}'_i \prec \boldsymbol{x}_i) \tag{3.9}$$

and the average (normalized) progress for successful mutations

$$\hat{\phi}' = \hat{w} \cdot n \cdot \sum_{i=1}^{k} \frac{d(\boldsymbol{x}'_i, X^*) - d(\boldsymbol{x}_i, X^*)}{d(\boldsymbol{x}_i, X^*)} \tag{3.10}$$

over the (normalized) step size

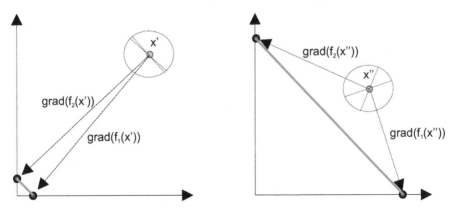

**Figure 3.3.** Success regions of mutations far away and close to the Pareto set. The black circles denote the optima of the individual functions, the line in between the Pareto set.

$$\sigma' = n \cdot \frac{\sigma}{d_0} \qquad (3.11)$$

for mutations of randomly chosen individuals with a fixed expected distance $d_0$ to the Pareto set.

The graphs also indicate that in the single-objective case the success rate and the normalized progress are functions of the normalized mutation strength only and do not depend on the distance to the optimum, as proven by Beyer et al. [12]. A detailed explanation for the working mechanism of the self-adaptation of the mutation strength can be found in Rudolph [10, p. 196f].

In the multiobjective case, the decrease of the success rate close to the Pareto set makes it increasingly difficult to proceed further. The probability that the offspring population contains an individual better than the parent is so low that in many cases the population will move away from the Pareto set. Even raising the number of offspring per parent does not help as the plots in Figure 3.5 show.

In conclusion, it was found that a non-elitist strategy using a fitness assignment based only on the dominance relation does not converge to the Pareto set. It only exhibits a constant progress rate up to a certain distance, after which the average progress rate is zero and the population starts to oscillate. We will investigate next, whether this problem can be solved by introducing elitism into the selection operator.

## 3.5 Pseudo-elitist Strategies ("plus" Selection)

In a $(\mu + \lambda)$-EA the selection operator takes into account both the parent and the offspring population and selects the best $\mu$ individuals out of these $\mu + \lambda$ candidates as the parents of the next generation. Hence, line 6 and 7 of Algorithm 1 must be changed to

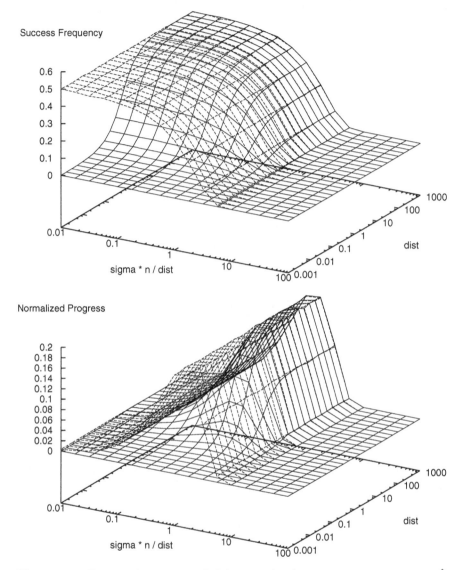

**Figure 3.4.** Estimated success probabilities $\hat{w}$ (top) and normalized progress $\hat{\phi}'$ (bottom) for mutations (step size $\sigma'$) of individuals with distance *dist* to the optimum for $m = 1$ (upper surfaces, dashed lines) and $m = 2$ (lower surfaces, solid lines), $n = 100$.

6:  *Fitness assignment:* Assign each $z \in Y^{(t)} \cup Z^{(t)}$ the fitness value $|\{z' \in Y^{(t)} \cup Z^{(t)} : z' \prec z\}|$.

7:  *Selection:* Create $Y^{(t+1)}$ consisting of the best $\mu$ individuals from $Y^{(t)} \cup Z^{(t)}$ according to their fitness values, ties are broken randomly.

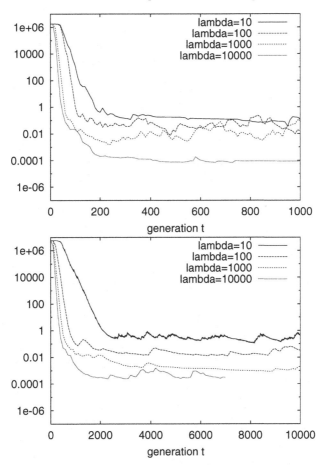

**Figure 3.5.** Distance $d(Y^{(t)}, X^*)$ and for different $\lambda$ values and $m = 2$ over time, $n = 10$ (top) and $n = 100$ (bottom).

The graphs in Figure 3.6 show the same experiment as before, now using a $(1 + 10)$-MOEA. For $m = 1$, stagnation periods are visible, which can be alluded to individuals with good decision variables, but unfavorable large mutation step sizes. In a plus-strategy, such individuals are only replaced if a better individual is found, which might take very long because too large mutation step sizes imply a low success probability. Disappointingly, the results for $m = 2$ are not much different from the previous case with "komma" selection. We even notice an occasional increase in the distance, but how is this possible in an elitist strategy?

The answer is that a "plus"-strategy is no longer an elitist strategy in a multiobjective environment. For $m \geq 2$, the objective space is only partially ordered, and the fitness assignment based on the dominance relation among the individuals is *not* a function of the individuals' decision variables alone,

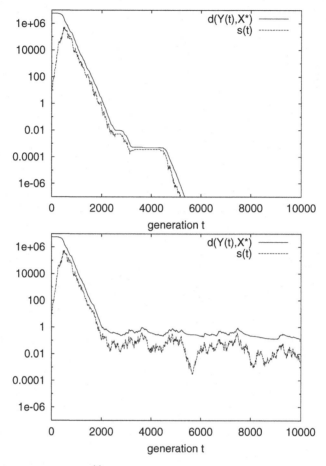

**Figure 3.6.** Distance $d(Y^{(t)}, X^*)$ and expected mutation step length $s$ for the $(1 + 10)$-MOEA and $n = 100$ over time. The top graph shows the single-objective case $(m = 1)$ and the bottom graph the multiobjective case with $m = 2$.

but is relative to all other individuals in the population. Thus, a temporary deterioration of the population can occur, as explained in Figure 3.7.

Zitzler et al. [18] proved that in fact no fitness assignment can be invented that gives a total order on the individuals *and* complies with the dominance relation. Therefore, no "plus"- strategy with dominance-based fitness assignment can be justly called elitist, and we have to consider other selection techniques.

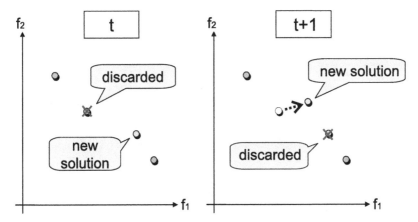

**Figure 3.7.** A possible deterioration of the population from iteration $t$ to $t+2$ of a $(\mu+\lambda)$-MOEA with $\mu=3$ and $\lambda=1$. In iteration $t$, the three individuals in $Y^{(t)}$ plus the new offspring individuals are all mutually non-dominated, and one randomly chosen individual has to be deleted to construct the new population $Y^{(t+1)}$. In iteration $t+1$, another new individual is produced, which is also mutually non-dominated with the three parent individuals in $Y^{(t+1)}$. Again, one individual is chosen at random to be deleted. As a result, one of the surviving individuals at the end of iteration $t+1$ is dominated by another individual that was deleted in the previous iteration. It is noticeable that the resulting population $Y^{(t+2)}$ is obviously worse than $Y^{(t)}$; the deterioration is marked with an arrow.

## 3.6 Elitist Strategies

The use of elitism in multiobjective optimization was found advantageous in many case studies, and several elitist strategies have been proposed [19]. Most of these approaches make use of a secondary population, or archive, in which a certain number of non-dominated solutions can be stored. Nevertheless, it has recently been shown that most of these algorithms, like the "plus"-strategy of the previous section, do *not* preclude the problem of temporary deterioration, and therefore do not converge to the Pareto set [1].

### 3.6.1 An Elitist Strategy Based on Dominance

In Rudolph and Agapie [15] a selection mechanism was proposed that leads to a globally convergent multiobjective EA. Sufficient conditions to fulfill this are:

- A non-dominated parent can only be discarded from the population if it is dominated by an offspring.
- If a previously non-dominated parent is to be removed, at least one of the dominating offspring must in turn be included in the new population.

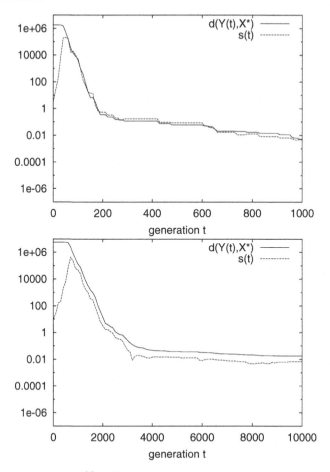

**Figure 3.8.** Distance $d(Y^{(t)}, X^*)$ and expected mutation step length $s$ for the elitist algorithm AR-1 [15], $n = 10$ (top) and $n = 100$ (bottom).

Figure 3.8 displays the results of the elitist algorithm AR-1 from Rudolph and Agapie [15], which fulfills the above criteria. It can be seen that the progress is now always non-negative, and temporary deterioration does not occur. However, the progress rate in the vicinity of the Pareto set is still very low.

These results indicate that it might actually be impossible to achieve linear convergence order with any selection scheme based purely on the dominance relation. In the vicinity of the Pareto set, the probability to produce a dominating individual decreases too rapidly.

Other selection schemes for evolutionary multiobjective optimization are population-based approaches and aggregating approaches [17]. In population- or criterion-based methods, the different objectives determine the selection of different parts of the population (like in VEGA [20]) or, in random succession, of the entire population (as in the algorithms of Kursawe [9] and Laumanns et al.[7]). In Rudolph [3] it was proven that such a $(1+1)$-MOEA with randomly changing selection criterion is able to approach the Pareto set exponentially fast, but only if the mutation strength is chosen proportional to the distance to the Pareto set. As long as these distances are unknown, this strategy is not practicable.

Aggregating approaches combine the objective function values via a scalarizing function. The evolutionary algorithm is allowed to solve a scalar surrogate problem, and it can be expected to exhibit the desired linear convergence order, provided that a usefully parameterized scalarizing function is applied. The disadvantage is that the scalarizing function implicitly defines its optimum, and only this optimum, and no other point on the Pareto set, will be obtained in the end. Multiple runs with different parameters can be applied to reach different points, but for smooth scalarizing functions, it cannot be guaranteed that all parts of the Pareto set are reachable, regardless of its parameterization. Since the self-adaptation mechanism for the mutation strength does not work for non-smooth versions, plain aggregating approaches are not considered here.

### 3.6.2 A Mixed Strategy Using Adaptive Scalarizing Functions

While dominance-based selection strategies enable the algorithm to enter the vicinity of the Pareto set quickly, selection based on scalarizing functions allows for linear convergence order. This raises the question whether both approaches can be combined to fulfill both tasks, and to design an algorithm that is able to converge exponentially fast to any element of the Pareto set.

The idea is to use the dominance-based selection in the first part of the run to locate any arbitrary region of the Pareto set. Thereafter, when this selection method becomes too strong, we switch to an aggregating approach and let the algorithm converge further until the desired precision is reached. For a practical implementation the following questions need to be resolved:

1. How do we determine which selection method to apply, not knowing the current location of the population in the search space?
2. How do we choose an appropriate scalarizing function that lets the algorithm converge locally within the region defined by the first part of the run?

We address the first question by simply applying both selection methods at the same time. While aggregated function values are used to guide the selection of a standard $(1, \lambda)$-EA, all generated solutions are passed to an archive that applies the dominance-based selection and always stores one non-dominated solution off-line (see Figure 3.9). This archive, in turn, provides the (local) reference point that is needed for an adaptive scalarizing function. For this we assume a discretization of the objective space by a hyper-grid, which

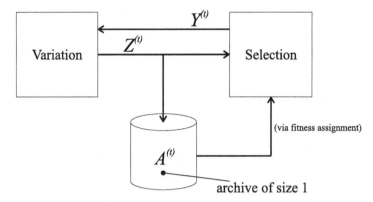

**Figure 3.9.** Generating solutions using aggregation-based selection and together with an archive using dominance-based selection.

has already been used in the archiving method of Laumanns et al. [1]. Given a particular individual $x \in A^{(t)}$, this reference point is calculated as

$$r(x) = (r_1, r_2, \dots, r_m) \qquad (3.12)$$
$$r_i = (1 + \epsilon)^{b_i} \qquad (3.13)$$
$$b_i = \lfloor \frac{\log f_i(x)}{\log (1 + \epsilon)} \rfloor \qquad (3.14)$$

Then, the Euclidean distance to the reference point is used as the selection criterion in the $(1, \lambda)$-EA.

$$\Phi(x) = ||x - r(x)|| \qquad (3.15)$$

This combined strategy is described below as Algorithm 2. Figure 3.10 displays the population distances of several runs of this $(1, 10, \epsilon)$-MOEA for $\epsilon = 0.01$ and $n = 100$. The plots visualize that linear convergence order is achievable even in the critical region close to the Pareto set. The value of $\epsilon$ determines the degree of resolution in the discretization of the objective space and hence the position of possible reference points. Thereby it also fixes the maximum number of different local scalarizing functions available. As each scalarizing function has its own optimum, the $\epsilon$ value can be used to tune the number of different target points in the Pareto set to which the algorithm can converge. Figure 3.11 shows the distribution of the final search points of 100 independent runs in the Pareto set. It can be seen that the algorithm is able not only to converge quickly, but also with a reasonable diversity of the final solutions.

## 3.7 Conclusion

In this chapter, the convergence velocity of multiobjective evolutionary algorithms with different selection methods on a simple continuous model

---

**Algorithm 2** Combined $(1, \lambda, \epsilon)$-MOEA

---
1: $t := 0$
2: Generate an initial individual $y^{(0)}$ by randomly sampling a vector from the decision space, and set $\sigma^{(0)} := 1$.
3: $A^{(0)} := \{y^{(0)}\}$
4: **loop**
5:    $t := t + 1$
6:    *Variation:* Generate an offspring population $Z^{(t)}$ by creating $\lambda$ copies of $y^{(t)}$ and mutating each copy according to (3.2).
7:    **for all** $z \in Z^{(t)}$ **do**
8:       **if** $z \prec a$ **then**
9:          *Archive update:* $A^{(t)} := z$
10:       **end if**
11:    **end for**
12:    *Fitness assignment:* Assign each $z = (x, \sigma) \in Z^{(t)}$ the fitness value $\Phi(x)$ according to (3.15).
13:    *Selection:* Set $y^{(t+1)}$ to the best individual from $Z^{(t)}$ according to their fitness values, ties are broken randomly.
14: **end loop**

---

problem has empirically been investigated. The model problem is a multiobjective generalization of the sphere model, which allows to use the existing theoretical results from the single-objective case as a reference point. As in the single-objective case, an adaptation of the mutation strength is mandatory to achieve linear convergence order on the model problem and to approximate the optimum with arbitrary precision.

It was shown that none of the existing selection methods based on the dominance relation can lead to the desired convergence behavior. This is mainly due to the following two problems that arise in a multiobjective setting, the *low success probability* close to the Pareto set and the *problem of successive deterioration*:

1. The success probability, i.e., the probability to create a dominating individual by mutation, decreases drastically in the vicinity of the Pareto set.
2. The partial order of the objective vectors makes a fitness assignment based on Pareto dominance ambiguous. Selection methods based on such fitness values can lead to a deterioration of the population.

For the different selection methods, the following hierarchy is obtained:

- The non-elitist ("komma") strategy oscillates around a fixed final distance, and the average progress is zero. At this point, many offspring populations are produced, where even the best individuals are farther away from the Pareto set than their parents.
- The "plus" strategies do not significantly improve this situation, although the parents are now included in the selection operation. In case of

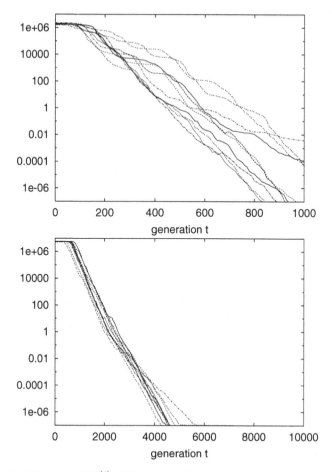

**Figure 3.10.** Distances $d(Y^{(t)}, X^*)$ of 10 independent runs of Algorithm 2, $n = 10$ (top) and $n = 100$ (bottom).

incomparable individuals, the selection operator can pick a random subset of the individuals with the best dominance-based fitness values, so that a non-dominated parent is not guaranteed to be included in the next generation. Thus, successive deterioration can occur, and this strategy cannot be called elitist in a multiobjective context.

- A selection operator that removes a parent individual if and only if a dominating individual is in turn included in the next generation is an elite-preserving strategy also in the multiobjective case. For such an elitist strategy, it is impossible to move farther away from the Pareto set, and hence the progress is always positive. However, the progress also declines to almost zero because of the low success probability.
- Finally, a combined strategy was designed that uses dominance-based selection in the archive and adaptive scalarizing functions to guide the

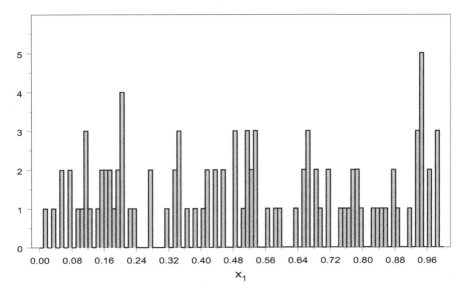

**Figure 3.11.** Histogram of variable $x_1$ of the final solution of 100 independent runs of Algorithm 2 with $n = 2$ and $m = 2$.

selection in the working population. The use of a scalarizing function keeps the success probability constant, even in the vicinity of the Pareto set, and leads to the desired linear convergence order. The dominance-based archive provides the reference points for the constant adaptation of the scalarizing function and ascertains that all regions of the Pareto set are reachable. The number of possible attractors can be tuned by the $\epsilon$ parameter.

The two fundamental problems of dominance-based selection mentioned above form a dilemma: if successive deterioration is to be prevented, only dominating individuals can be accepted, but the probability to produce these individuals declines too rapidly in the vicinity of the Pareto set.

It appears that this dilemma can only be overcome by resorting to the use of scalarizing functions. As plain aggregating approaches are not suitable to find points in any arbitrary regions of the Pareto set, an adaptive scalarizing method in combination with a dominance-based archive provides a viable solution. The single-parent strategy proposed in this study can be used in multiple independent runs to randomly find points in all regions of the Pareto set. It would be worthwhile to investigate a strategy with a multi-membered archive and many $(1, \lambda)$-strategies running concurrently to converge to many different elements of the Pareto set in a single run. Such an archiving method was proposed in Laumanns et al. [1] and could be used to maintain a variety of search directions at the same time.

# Acknowledgments

Parts of this study stem from a joint work with Günter Rudolph and Hans-Paul Schwefel [21, 22]. The author would like to thank the anonymous reviewers for their helpful comments.

# References

1. Laumanns M, Thiele L, Deb K, and Zitzler E, Combining Convergence and Diversity in Evolutionary Multiobjective Optimization. *Evolutionary Computation*, 10(3): 2002; 263-282.
2. Bosman PAN and Thierens D, The Balance Between Proximity and Diversity in Multiobjective Evolutionary Algorithms. *IEEE Transactions on Evolutionary Computation*, 7(2):12003; 74-188.
3. Rudolph G, On a Multi-objective Evolutionary Algorithm and its Convergence to the Pareto set. In *IEEE Int'l Conf. on Evolutionary Computation (ICEC'98)*, pp. 511-516. IEEE Press, 1998.
4. Hanne T, Global Multiobjective Optimization with Evolutionary Algorithms: Selection Mechanisms and Mutation Control. In E. Zitzler et al.(eds), *Evolutionary Multi-Criterion Optimization (EMO 2001)*, Lecture Notes in Computer Science Vol. 1993, pp. 197-212, Berlin, Springer, 2001.
5. Schwefel HP, *Numerische Optimierung von Computer-Modellen mittels der Evolutionsstrategie*. Basel Birkhäuser, 1977.
6. Hinterding R, Michalewicz Z, and Eiben AE, Adaptation in Evolutionary Computation: A Survey. In *IEEECEP: Proceedings of The Forth IEEE Conference on Evolutionary Computation*, pp. 65-69, Piscataway, New Jersey, IEEE Press, 1997.
7. Laumanns M, Rudolph G, and Schwefel HP, A Spatial Predator-Prey Approach to Multi-objective Optimization: A Preliminary Study. In A. E. Eiben et al. (eds), *Parallel Problem Solving from Nature (PPSN V)*, Lecture Notes in Computer Science Vol. 1498, pp. 241-249. Springer, 1998.
8. Kahlert J, *Vektorielle Optimierung mit Evolutionsstrategien und Anwendungen in der Regelungstechnik*. Düsseldorf VDI Verlag, 1991.
9. Kursawe F, A Variant of Evolution Strategies for Vector Optimization. In H.-P. Schwefel and R. Männer (eds), *Parallel Problem Solving from Nature (PPSN)*, pp. 193-197. Springer, 1991.
10. Rudolph G, *Convergence Properties of Evolutionary Algorithms*. Hamburg Verlag Dr. Kovač, 1997.
11. Rudolph G, Evolution Strategies. In Thomas Bäck, D. B. Fogel, and Zbigniew Michalewicz (eds), *Handbook of Evolutionary Computation*, pages B1.3:1-3, Bristol, UK, IOP Publishing and Oxford University Press, 1997.
12. Beyer HG, Toward a Theory of Evolution Strategies: Self-adaptation. *Evolutionary Computation*, 3(3): 1995; 311-347.
13. J. Jägersküpper, Analysis of a Simple Evolutionary Algorithm for Minimization in Euclidian Spaces. In *International Colloquium on Automata, Languages, and Programming (ICALP 2003)*, Lecture Notes in Computer Science Vol. 2719, Springer, 2003.

3 Self-adaptation and Convergence of MOEAs     53

14. Deb K, Thiele L, Laumanns M, and Zitzler E, Scalable Test problems for Evolutionary Multi-objective Optimization. Chapter 6 of this volume.
15. Rudolph G and Agapie A, Convergence Properties of Some Multi-objective Evolutionary Algorithms. In *Congress on Evolutionary Computation (CEC 2000)*, volume 2, pp. 1010-1016. IEEE Press, 2000.
16. Beyer HG and Rudolph G, Local Performance Measures. In Thomas Bäck, D. B. Fogel, and Zbigniew Michalewicz, editors, *Handbook of Evolutionary Computation*, pages C2.4:1-27, Bristol, UK, IOP Publishing and Oxford University Press, 1997.
17. Fonseca CM and Fleming PJ, An Overview of Evolutionary Algorithms in Multiobjective Optimization. *Evolutionary Computation*, 3(1): 1995; 1-16.
18. Zitzler E, Thiele L, Laumanns M, Foneseca CM, and Grunert da Fonseca V, Performance Assessment of Multiobjective Optimizers: An Analysis and Review. *IEEE Transactions on Evolutionary Computation*, 7(2): 2003; 117-132.
19. Deb K, *Multi-objective Optimization Using Evolutionary Algorithms*. Chichester, UK, Wiley, 2001.
20. Schaffer JD, Multiple Objective Optimization with Vector Evaluated Genetic Algorithms. In JJ. Grefenstette (ed), *Proceedings of an International Conference on Genetic Algorithms and Their Applications*, pp. 93-100, 1985.
21. Laumanns M, Rudolph G, and Schwefel HP, Adaptive Mutation Control in Panmictic and Spacially Distributed Multi-objective Evolutionary Algorithms. In *PPSN/SAB Workshop on Multiobjective Problem Solving from Nature (MPSN)*, 2000.
22. Laumanns M, Rudolph G, and Schwefel HP, Mutation Control and Convergence in Evolutionary Multi-objective optimization. In *MENDEL 2001. 7th Int. Conf. on Soft Computing*, pp. 24-29. Brno University of Technology, 2001.

# 4

# A Simple Approach to Evolutionary Multiobjective Optimization

Christine L. Mumford-Valenzuela

**Summary.** This chapter describes a Pareto-based approach to evolutionary multiobjective optimization, that avoids most of the time-consuming global calculations typical of other multi-objective evolutionary techniques. The new approach uses a simple uniform selection strategy within a steady-state evolutionary algorithm (EA) and employs a straightforward elitist mechanism for replacing population members with their offspring. Global calculations for fitness and Pareto dominance are not needed. Other state-of-the-art Pareto-based EAs depend heavily on various fitness functions and niche evaluations, mostly based on Pareto dominance, and the calculations involved tend to be rather time consuming (at least $O(N^2)$ for a population size, $N$). The new approach has performed well on some benchmark combinatorial problems and continuous functions, outperforming the latest state-of-the-art EAs in several cases. In this chapter the new approach will be explained in detail.

## 4.1 Introduction

This chapter concentrates on a simple approach to evolutionary multiobjective optimization that avoids most of the time-consuming global calculations typical of many other Pareto-based evolutionary approaches. The basic algorithm described here is called SEAMO (a Simple Evolutionary Algorithm for Multiobjective Optimization), and although this new technique has not as yet been very widely tested, it has proven successful on some benchmark combinatorial problems and continuous functions, outperforming other state-of-the-art evolutionary algorithms (EAs) in several instances [1]. In addition to fast execution, the simplicity of the new algorithm makes it relatively quick and easy to implement, reducing the development time needed for prototyping and testing new multiobjective applications. If required, more sophisticated Pareto-based evolutionary techniques can be incorporated following an initial proof-of-concept.

The main purpose of the chapter is to introduce and explain the key concepts involved in the new approach using some simple applications as examples. In addition, in order to justify the approach, a summary of some preliminary comparative studies will be included.

The discussion will begin in Section 4.2 with a brief overview of Pareto-based multiobjective optimization, moving on to multiobjective evolutionary techniques in Section 4.3. Section 4.3 also includes a short preview of SEAMO, concentrating on its main features and explaining how it differs from other evolutionary approaches. Following this, Section 4.4 describes the multiple knapsack problem and introduces a sample test problem with two knapsacks. Section 4.5 describes the SEAMO algorithm in detail and this is followed in Section 4.6 by an illustration of SEAMO's operation through the test problem introduced in Section 4.4. Section 4.7 summarizes SEAMO's performance on some large multiple knapsack problems. Having studied a combinatorial application, Section 4.8 will explain how the techniques can be adapted to handle some continuous multiobjective functions. Some results for the continuous functions are summarized in Section 4.9. Full details of the representations and genetic operators are given for the combinatorial and continuous problems.

## 4.2 Pareto-Based Multiobjective Optimization

Many real-world applications require the simultaneous optimization of several (often competing) objectives. For example, in the vehicle routing problem (VRP) the determination of optimum delivery routes to a set of customers can involve a number of different objectives (Figure 4.1), for example the total distance traveled (or time taken), the number of vehicles used, and the number of satisfied customers (i.e. deliveries that have taken place to customers within previously agreed time windows). There are three principal methods of dealing with multiple objectives:

1. Combine all the objectives into a single scalar value, typically as a weighted sum, and optimize the scalar value.
2. Solve for the objectives in a hierarchical fashion, optimizing for a first objective then, if there is more than one solution, optimize these solutions for a second objective, and repeat for a third etc. if appropriate.
3. Obtain a set of alternative, non-dominated solutions, each of which must be considered equivalent in the absence of further information regarding the relative importance of each of the objectives.

The first and the second methods both depend on making a priori assessments to weigh up the relative importance of the various objectives. The third method, on the other hand, involves no such (arbitrary) judgments, and produces a set of viable alternatives from which a decision maker can make an informed selection at a later stage. Ideally each alternative solution produced by method 3 will be optimal in the sense that it will not be possible to improve the value of any one of the objectives, in a given solution vector, without

**Figure 4.1.** Vehicle routing can be a problem.

simultaneously degrading the quality of one or more of the other objectives. Such a solution set is called the *Pareto-optimal set*, and the objective values in the set are located at the *Pareto front*. SEAMO is an evolutionary algorithm that has been designed to produce approximate Pareto sets. Thus method 3 is the way we will deal with multiple objectives in the remainder of this chapter.

## 4.3 An Overview of Evolutionary Techniques for Multiobjective Optimization

Evolutionary algorithms (EAs) are ideally suited for multiobjective optimization problems because they produce many solutions in parallel. However, traditional approaches to EAs require scalar fitness information and converge on a single compromise solution, rather than on a set of viable alternatives. An effective Pareto-based multiobjective EA will converge on a solution set with the following properties:

- solutions that are "good", i.e. close to the Pareto front;
- solutions that are "evenly spread" along the Pareto front;

- solutions that are "widely spread" - i.e. a good range.

To seek solution sets with the above properties, most researchers rely on selection that uses some form of Pareto-based fitness assignment. This idea, which was first proposed by Goldberg [2], is based on dominance ranking and assigns equal probability of reproduction to all non-dominated individuals. Solutions can be further improved using techniques such as fitness sharing [2], niches [3, 4] and auxiliary populations [5, 6]. Unfortunately most of these approaches carry a high computational cost.

The present approach relies on very much simpler techniques. It disposes of all selection mechanisms based on fitness values and instead uses a straightforward uniform selection procedure (i.e. each population member has an equal chance of being selected). Thus no dominance ranking is required. In the new approach improvements to the population and progress of the genetic search depend entirely upon a replacement strategy that follows a few simple rules:

1. parents are (normally) replaced only by their own offspring;
2. offspring only replace parents if the offspring are superior – thus the scheme is elitist;
3. duplicates in the population are deleted.

SEAMO depends on rules 1 and 3 to maintain diversity and prevent premature convergence and on rule 2 to progress the genetic search and also ensure that the best solutions are not lost.

Replacing parents only with their own offspring (rule 1) means that the new individuals tend to be genetically very similar to the population members they are replacing. Alternative replacement schemes, on the other hand (replacing one of the weaker members of the population for example), can lead to a much more rapid propagation of duplicated genetic material, and thus to premature convergence. SEAMO further promotes genetic diversity by deleting duplicates (rule 3) as soon as they arise in the population. Ideally, an EA should discard *genotypic* duplicates. (A genotypic duplicate is an individual with exactly the same genetic makeup as another individual.) Unfortunately the pairwise comparisons between chromosomes needed to detect genotypic duplicates tend to be rather time consuming unless the chromosomes are very short. Current implementations of SEAMO delete *phenotypic* duplicates, i.e. individuals with the same solution vectors as other individuals. As the solution vectors are usually rather shorter than the chromosomes, this tends to be a very much faster process. Deleting phenotypic duplicates will certainly eliminate genotypic copies. Unfortunately it can also lead to the deletion of genetically diverse individuals if, by chance, they produce identical solution vectors. In practice this does not seem to arise very often though.

Rule 2 controls the overall progress of the genetic search, and ensures that the population as a whole improves over time (hence ensuring that solutions are "good"). A "superior" offspring in rule 2 is defined (most of the time) as an offspring that dominates one or other of its parents (i.e. one of the objectives in its solution vectors is better than its parent, and all the other objectives are at least as good). An exception is made when an offspring arises with a new global best value for just one of the objectives in its solution vector. When this occurs, the dominance condition is relaxed, and the new individual is assimilated into the population (hence ensuring that solutions are "widely spread"). The new individual usually replacing one of its parents (this will be explained in Section 4.5). Rule 2 ensures that the EA itself is elitist, thus, unlike Corne et al. [5] and Zitzler and Thiele [6] no archive population is needed.

We shall see later in this chapter that SEAMO's subtle techniques appear to work well in producing solutions that are both "good" and "widely spread", and thus meet two of the three criteria for effective Pareto-based EAs specified at the start of the current section. However, current implementations of SEAMO lack a specific mechanism to ensure that the solutions are "evenly spread", and this can cause difficulties when applying SEAMO to certain functions.

In common with other EAs, successful multiobjective implementations require well-designed representation systems for individual problems and also genetic operators that are appropriate for the task. Recombination (crossover) operators can be particularly problematic. At worst an EA may waste vast quantities of time generating invalid or illegal offspring, and even in a superficially successful system, a crossover may produce an offspring that bears very little phenotypical resemblances to either of its parents. As the similarity between parents and their offspring remains one of the main tenets of evolution, a poorly designed or inappropriate recombination operator can turn an otherwise perfect EA into an implementation that is no more effective than a random search. Unfortunately there does not appear to be a known recipe for producing effective representation schemes, either for single or multiobjective EAs. Experience and intuition can help, but provide no guarantees! Thus the success of SEAMO, or any other EA (multiobjective or otherwise) on a particular application, depends very much on the representation scheme chosen for the application. Additionally it is necessary to tune various parameters of the EA such as population size, crossover and mutation rates, to produce a good performance.

Assessing the performance of EAs can be very difficult in practice. Even when the same data sets are used to compare EAs with each other or with alternative approaches, it can be dangerous to draw firm conclusions as to which algorithm is the best. In addition to making sound (or unsound) choices for representations and genetic operators, there are many other issues to consider, and choices to be made. How long do you let the EAs run? What population sizes and crossover rates do you set? Some EAs converge quickly, while others take longer but produce better results in the end. The algorithms are differently sensitive to parameter settings such as population sizes and crossover rates, so it is not easy to ensure fairness, especially when comparing an unfamiliar EA that somebody else has written with one of your own (that you would obviously like to win). Notwithstanding the difficulties associated with representations, varying convergence rates and parameter settings, comparisons between EAs (or other metaheuristic approaches such as simulated annealing) are frequently based on each algorithm performing an equal number of fitness or objective function evaluations. This is a very crude method, however, as it ignores important run-time issues such as time complexity.

Comparisons between EAs that carry out multiobjective optimizations are even more problematic. Here we have the added difficulty of assessing the quality of each algorithm by examining a set of vectors, instead of examining the single scalar value obtained from a "standard EA". Although a range of performance measures have been derived by various researchers, there is no general agreement upon their usefulness. For vectors consisting of just two objectives it is possible to represent the results quite effectively using 2D plots, and comparisons can be made quite easily if plots for a small number of different algorithms are placed on the same diagram, provided that not too many of the points overlap.

## 4.4 The 0-1 Multiple Knapsack Problem

**Figure 4.2.** The same objects may have different weights in each knapsack.

**Figure 4.3.** The same objects may have different profits in each knapsack.

The 0-1 multiple knapsack problem (0-1 MKP) is a maximization problem. It is a generalization of the 0-1 simple knapsack problem, and is a well-known member of the NP-hard class of problems. In the simple knapsack problem, a set of objects $O = \{o_1, o_2, o_3, ..., o_n\}$ and a knapsack of capacity $C$ are given. Each object $o_i$ has an associated profit $p_i$ and weight $w_i$. The objective is to find a subset $S \subseteq O$ such that the weight sum over the objects in $S$ does not exceed the knapsack capacity and yields a maximum profit. The 0-1 MKP involves $m$ knapsacks of capacities $c_1, c_2, c_3, ..., c_m$. Every selected object must be placed in all $m$ knapsacks, although neither the weight of an object $o_i$ nor its profit is fixed, and will probably have different values in each knapsack (see Figures 4.2 and 4.3). A small problem with 10 objects and two knapsacks is defined in Table 4.1.

A possible solution to the ten object, two knapsack problem from Table 4.1 is $\{2, 3, 4, 5, 6, 7, 9\}$, which involves packing objects number 2, 3, 4, 5, 6, 7 and 9 into the two knapsacks. To evaluate the solution vector for this problem requires that we first ensure that neither knapsack capacity has been exceeded. The total weight of the given objects when packed into knapsack 1 is $8 + 2 + 7 + 3 + 6 + 1 + 9 = 36$ units, and in knapsack 2 they weigh $4+2+4+9+5+4+3 = 31$ units. In neither case is the knapsack capacity (38 and 35) exceeded. We then work out the total profit for each knapsack by adding together the profits for each of the items packed. The total profit in knapsack 1 is $7+4+5+6+2+7+7 = 38$, and in knapsack 2 is $9+1+5+3+8+2+1 = 29$. The solution $\{2, 3, 4, 5, 6, 7, 9\}$ yields a solution vector of $\{38, 29\}$, the profits in knapsacks 1 and 2 respectively. The full Pareto set, for this small problem, is presented in Table 4.2. The solutions were discovered using a simple exhaustive search technique which took only a few seconds to run.

**Table 4.1.** A sample problem with ten objects and two knapsacks.

| | Knapsack 1 | | Knapsack 2 | |
| | Capacity = 38 | | Capacity = 35 | |
| Object number | Weight | Profit | Weight | Profit |
| --- | --- | --- | --- | --- |
| 1 | 9 | 2 | 3 | 3 |
| 2 | 8 | 7 | 4 | 9 |
| 3 | 2 | 4 | 2 | 1 |
| 4 | 7 | 5 | 4 | 5 |
| 5 | 3 | 6 | 9 | 3 |
| 6 | 6 | 2 | 5 | 8 |
| 7 | 1 | 7 | 4 | 2 |
| 8 | 3 | 3 | 8 | 6 |
| 9 | 9 | 7 | 3 | 1 |
| 10 | 3 | 1 | 7 | 3 |

**Table 4.2.** The Pareto set for the sample problem with ten objects and two knapsacks.

| Knapsack 1 Profit | knapsack 2 Profit | Objects in Knapsacks |
| --- | --- | --- |
| 39 | 27 | {2, 3, 4, 5, 7, 8, 9} |
| 38 | 29 | {2, 3, 4, 5, 6, 7, 9} |
| 36 | 30 | {2, 3, 5, 6, 7, 8, 9} |
| 35 | 32 | {2, 3, 4, 6, 7, 8, 9} |
| 34 | 33 | {2, 3, 4, 5, 6, 8, 9} |
| 32 | 34 | {2, 4, 6, 7, 8, 9, 10} |
| 29 | 35 | {1, 2, 3, 4, 5, 6, 8} |
| 27 | 36 | {1, 2, 4, 6, 7, 8, 10} |

## 4.5 An Introduction to SEAMO

The basic SEAMO algorithm is outlined in Figure 4.4. The goal of any Pareto-based multiobjective EA is to breed a widely and evenly spread population of solution vectors, as close to the Pareto front as possible. The dual aims pursued by SEAMO during its search process are: (1) to move the current solutions in the population ever closer to the Pareto front, and (2) to widen the spread of the solution set. Improvements in both (1) and (2) are achieved by the replacement strategy used in SEAMO, and not by the selection process. It was noted previously that SEAMO currently has no specific mechanism for ensuring that the solutions are evenly spread.

The selection procedure for SEAMO is very simple and does not rely on fitness calculations or dominance relationships. The crossover rate is 100%, which means that parents are always selected in pairs. The algorithm sequentially selects every individual in the population to serve as the first parent once, pairing it with a second parent that is selected at random

**Procedure** *SEAMO*
**Begin**
    Generate $N$ random individuals {$N$ is the population size}
    Evaluate the objective vector for each population member and store it
    Record the global *best-so-far* for each objective function in the vector
    **Repeat**
      **For** each member of the population
        This individual becomes the first parent
        Select a second parent at random
        Apply crossover to produce offspring
        Apply a single mutation to the offspring
        Evaluate the objective vector produced by the offspring
        **If** any element of the offspring's objective vector
                improves on a global *best-so-far*
        **Then** the offspring replaces one of the parents
                (or occasionally another individual)
                    and *best-so-far* is updated
        **Else If** offspring dominates one of the parents
           **Then** it replaces it
                (unless it is a duplicate, then it is deleted)
      **Endfor**
    **Until** stopping condition satisfied
    **Print** all non-dominated solutions in the final population
**End**

**Figure 4.4.** Algorithm 1. A Simple Evolutionary Algorithm for Multiobjective Optimization (SEAMO).

(uniformly). A single crossover is then applied that produces one offspring, and this is followed by a single mutation. Objective values and dominance relationships are not considered at this stage. They are applied later, at the replacement stage, and it is here, rather than during selection, that the pressure for improvement is applied.

As explained previously, the replacement of a parent by its offspring is considered whenever an offspring is deemed to be superior to that parent. This idea, called *pre-selection* when it was first suggested by Cavicchio [7], was originally used for EAs with scalar objective functions. The technique easily extends to Pareto-based multiobjective optimization, however. In the SEAMO algorithm, the superiority test is applied first of all to the first parent, and then to the second parent if that fails. Usually superiority is measured as a dominance relationship, i.e. if an offspring dominates its parent, it may replace it in the population. The replacement of population members by dominating offspring ensures that the solution vectors move closer to the Pareto front as the search progresses. To additionally ensure a wider spread of solutions, the dominance condition is relaxed whenever a new global best value is discovered for any of the individual components of the solution vector. In the case of the multiple knapsack problem for example, a global best value will correspond to a maximum profit in one of the $m$ knapsacks. Care has to be taken, however, to ensure that global best values for other components (e.g. maximum profits in other knapsacks) are not lost from the population when a dominance condition is relaxed. Ensuring elitism (i.e. that the best solutions are not lost) at this level is straightforward if multiobjective optimization is restricted to two components in the solution vector. Whenever an offspring produces an improved global best for either of the components, if the global best for the second component happens to occur in one of the parents, the offspring will simply replace the other parent. With three or more components, however, it is possible for global best values to occur in both parents. When this happens SEAMO replaces another population member, chosen at random, provided that the newly selected individual does not itself harbor a global best. If it does, the random selection process is repeated until a suitable individual is found.

As a final precaution, a solution vector for a dominating offspring is compared with all the solution vectors in the current population before a final decision is made on replacement. If the solution vector produced by the offspring is duplicated elsewhere in the population, the offspring dies and does not replace its parent. As previously mentioned, the deletion of duplicates helps maintain diversity in the population and thus avoid the premature convergence of the population to sets of identical, or very similar, individuals. The final action of SEAMO is to save all the non-dominated solutions from the final population to a file.

## 4.6 Illustrating SEAMO Using a Small Multiple Knapsack Problem

Several approaches have been suggested for representing solutions to single objective knapsack problems for EAs. Michalewicz [8] identifies three classes: algorithms based on penalty functions, algorithms based on repair methods, and algorithms based on decoders (i.e. interpreters to convert lists of symbols in the chromosomes into solutions to the required problem). The main challenge with the knapsack problem is to ensure that the EA does not waste vast amounts of its time in generating illegal solutions with over-full knapsacks.

In the present study, SEAMO uses a representation system based on a decoder for the 0-1 MKP. (Experiments with other representations for the 0-1 MKP are documented in a later study by the present author, see [9]). For the decoder scheme MKP solutions are represented as simple permutations of the objects to be packed. The decoder packs the individual objects, one at a time, starting at the beginning of the permutation list, and working through. For each object that is packed, the decoder checks to make sure that none of the

**Figure 4.5.** Packing is discontinued and the final item removed as soon as the weight limit is exceeded for a knapsack.

weight limits is exceeded for any knapsack. Packing is discontinued as soon as a weight limit is exceeded for a knapsack (Figure 4.5) and when this is detected the final object that was packed is removed from all the knapsacks. Thus, each knapsack contains exactly the same objects as required, and each solution that is generated is a feasible solution. Using the ten object problem with two knapsacks given previously as an example, given a permutation of {2,5,1,7,9,8,10,3,4,6}, the decoder would first pack item 2, which weighs 8 units in knapsack 1 and 4 units in knapsack 2. Item 5 would be packed next, weighing 3 units in knapsack 1 and 9 units in knapsack 2, giving total weights of 11 and 13 for the two knapsacks. The decoder would carry on packing items from the permutation list until it had packed item 10, giving total weights of 36 and 39 for knapsacks 1 and 2 respectively. A weight of 39 units in knapsack 2 exceeds the capacity of the knapsack, and so the last item to be packed, which is item 10, is removed from both knapsacks giving final weights of 33 units for knapsack 1 and 31 units for knapsack 2. The profit vector for packing the items 2, 5, 1, 7, 9, and 8 is {32, 24}.

Cycle crossover (CX) [10] is used as the recombination operator with the above permutation representation, and the mutation operator swaps two arbitrarily selected objects within a single permutation list. CX was selected as the recombination operator because it transmits absolute positions of objects in the permutation lists from the parents to the offspring. Neither edge-based nor order-based operators would seem to be appropriate here, for a set membership problem such as this. Some comparative runs shown in Figure 4.6 support the choice of CX as the recombination operator. This figure compares the performance of four different permutation-based operators on a 750 object,

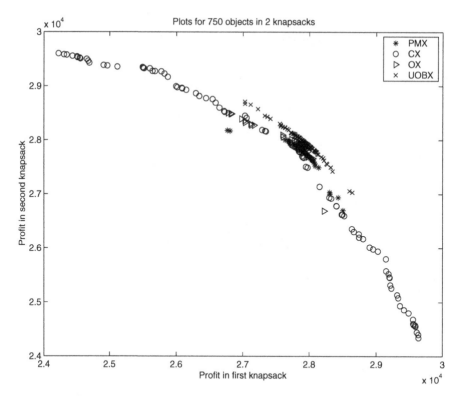

**Figure 4.6.** Non-dominated solutions for different crossovers.

2 knapsack problem (see Section 4.7). The traces on Figure 4.6 are partially matched crossover (PMX) [11], cycle crossover (CX) [10], a version [12] of order crossover (OX) [13] that preserves absolute positions better than the original, and uniform order based crossover (UOBX) [14]. Populations of 250 were used for the test runs, and the EA run for 15,000 generations. Clearly the plot of SEAMO using CX gives a much more diverse set of solutions than any of the other plots. However, the UOBX solutions, although considerably less diverse than the CX solutions, are slightly better in quality.

### 4.6.1 Cycle Crossover

The CX operator ensures that each position in the resulting offspring is occupied by a value occupying the same position in one or other of the parents. As an example, suppose we have strings $A$ and $B$ below as our two parents:

$$A = 8 \quad 7 \quad 6 \quad 4 \quad 1 \quad 2 \quad 5 \quad 3 \quad 9 \quad 10$$
$$B = 2 \quad 5 \quad 1 \quad 7 \quad 3 \quad 8 \quad 4 \quad 6 \quad 10 \quad 9$$

We now start from the left and randomly select an item from string $A$. Suppose we choose item 6 from position 3, this is then copied to position 3 of the offspring we shall call $A'$:

$$A' = - \quad - \quad 6 \quad - \quad - \quad - \quad - \quad - \quad - \quad -$$

In order to ensure that each value in the offspring occupies the same position as it does in either one or other parent, we now look in position 3 of string $B$ and copy item 1 from string $A$ to the offspring:

$$A' = - \quad - \quad 6 \quad - \quad 1 \quad - \quad - \quad - \quad - \quad -$$

Next we look in position 5 of string B and copy item 3 from string $A$:

$$A' = - \quad - \quad 6 \quad - \quad 1 \quad - \quad - \quad 3 \quad - \quad -$$

Looking at position 8 in string B we find item 6. This completes the cycle. We now fill the remaining positions in $A'$ from string $B$ thus:

$$A' = 2 \quad 5 \quad 6 \quad 7 \quad 1 \quad 8 \quad 4 \quad 3 \quad 10 \; 9$$
$$B' = 8 \quad 7 \quad 1 \quad 4 \quad 3 \quad 2 \quad 5 \quad 6 \quad 9 \quad 10$$

The offspring $B'$ is obtained by performing the complementary operations.

## 4.7 A Summary of Results for Multiple Knapsack Problems

The multiple knapsack problems of Zitzler and Thiele [6] were used as the first set of test problems for SEAMO. These were a convenient choice because of the extensive comparative studies that had already been carried out on these problems, covering a wider range of state-of-the-art EAs (see [6] and [15] for details). Furthermore, Zitzler and Thiele have made their test problems and most of their key results available at: http://www.tik.ee.ethz.ch/zitzler/testdata.html

### 4.7.1 Comparisons With Other Evolutionary Algorithms

In Valenzuela [1] SEAMO was compared with SPEA (the strength Pareto evolutionary algorithm) [6], and was found to do better. However, when SEAMO was compared with the more recent EAs covered in Zitzlet et al. [15], PESA (the Pareto envelope-based selection algorithm) [5], NGSA2 (a fast elitist non-dominated sorting genetic algorithm) [16], and SPEA2 an improved version of SPEA, it found these results more difficult to beat. Interestingly, though, SEAMO improved its performance, relative to the other EAs as more knapsacks (i.e. objective functions) were added. For a large problem with 750 objects, for example, SEAMO was easily beaten by some other EAs using the same population sizes and running the algorithms for the same number of generations, when only 2 knapsacks were used. SPEA2 [15] produced particularly impressive results on this problem. When tested on a 750 object problem with 3 knapsacks, SEAMO performed much better, relative to the other EAs, although not quite able to match the other EAs on an evaluation for evaluation basis. For the 750 object problems with either 2 or 3 knapsacks, SEAMO is able to beat its competitors only if it is allowed to perform more evaluations. Given the simplicity of the SEAMO algorithm, however, it may be acceptable that it performs more evaluations, depending on how much faster it runs than its competitors. On the other hand, for the problem with 750 objects and 4 knapsacks, SEAMO was easily able to outperform all its main competitors performing the same number of evaluations.

## 4.7.2 The Effect of Increasing the Population Size

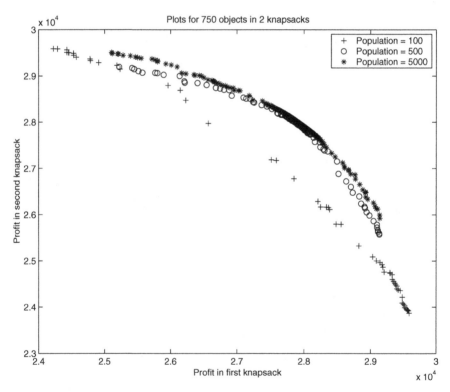

**Figure 4.7.** Non-dominated solutions from single runs of SEAMO showing the effect of increasing the population size.

In order to shed further light on the effect of increasing the number of evaluations performed by SEAMO, a number of single runs were carried out on a 750 object, 2 knapsack problem using various sizes of population. Figure 4.7 illustrates the results of some of these experiments. Population sizes of 100, 200, 500, 1,000, 2,000 and 5,000 were tried and the EA halted after 40 generations had elapsed in which no improvements had been made to the population.

Clearly, increasing the population size produces better results, consisting of a larger quantity of non-dominated solutions which are closer to the Pareto front. However, the improvements are fairly small between population sizes of 500 and 5,000. Surprisingly, perhaps, the SEAMO run with a population of 100 appears to produce a wider spread of results than the runs with the larger populations. Some key features of all the runs are presented in Table 4.3.

**Table 4.3.** The effect on SEAMO of increasing population size.

| Population size | Total evaluations | Run time (secs) | Number of non-dominated solutions | Largest profit 1 | Largest profit 2 |
|---|---|---|---|---|---|
| 100 | 950,900 | 154 | 56 | 29,589 | 29,585 |
| 200 | 2,605,000 | 442 | 79 | 29,543 | 29,555 |
| 500 | 4,154,000 | 777 | 103 | 29,134 | 29,192 |
| 1,000 | 13,956,000 | 2,705 | 176 | 29,255 | 29,318 |
| 2,000 | 32,118,000 | 6,356 | 237 | 29,334 | 29,069 |
| 5,000 | 151,250,000 | 30,603 | 260 | 29,141 | 29,504 |

Columns two and three of Table 4.3 give the total number of evaluations and the run time, respectively. Column four gives the number of non-dominated solutions present in the population at the end of each run. The size of this non-dominated set clearly gets larger as the population is increased. Columns five and six give the smallest and largest profits found in the final non-dominated set for each knapsack. As previously suggested, the range of values would appear to decrease slightly as the population size is increased. A possible explanation for this could be that smaller populations are more focussed towards widening the spread of solutions than larger populations, because the dominance condition for parental replacement is likely to be relaxed, a higher proportion of the time, in order to incorporate new global best-so-far objective values.

### 4.7.3 Investigation of SEAMO's Parental Replacement Strategy

Progress in SEAMO is due entirely to its replacement strategy. Recall from Section 4.5 that an offspring will replace one or other of its parents if it is deemed to be superior to that parent. Most replacements occur when

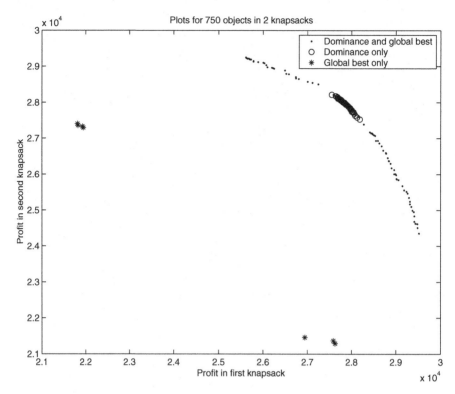

**Figure 4.8.** Results showing the effect of using one or other or both replacement criteria.

an offspring dominates one of its parents. However, in situations where a new global best value is discovered for one of the positions in the solution vector, the dominance condition is relaxed, to encourage a wider spread of approximate Pareto solutions within the population. This section investigates the contribution of each component in the replacement strategy with some experimental runs. In the first run, both replacement components are present. In the second run, parents are replaced only by dominating offspring and not when new global best values are discovered (unless the offspring solution with the new global best also dominates a parental solution). The third run shows the effect of replacing parents only when new global best values are discovered.

The 750 object, 2 knapsack problem is used for the experiments, and the population size set to 500. All three tests are run for 13,504 generations. The results are plotted in Figure 4.8. Clearly, using both the replacement strategies together produces the best results by far. Replacing parents only by dominating offspring appears to produce high quality solutions, but within a very limited range. Replacing parents only with offspring that improve a global best value at any position in the solution vector, produces very poor solutions, and very few of them.

## 4.8 Implementing SEAMO to Solve Continuous Test Problems

**Figure 4.9.** Continuous multiobjective functions.

Having completed some preliminary work testing SEAMO on multiple knapsack problems, SEAMO was tried on some continuous test functions, published in Zitzler et al. [15]. The permutation representation and decoder used for the knapsack problems is not suitable for continuous functions, so a different scheme had to be devised.

The continuous functions and their parameters are summarized in Table 4.4. Each of the test problems in Table 4.4 is a minimization problem consisting of two objectives and 100 variables. For SPH-2 and KUR large domains ($[-10^3, 10^3]$) were selected from Zitzler et al. [15] in order to test the algorithms' ability to locate the Pareto-optimal set in a large objective space.

The function SPH-$m$ is a multiobjective generalization of the Sphere Model, a symmetric unimodal function where the isosurfaces are given by hyperspheres. Only the two objective instance (SPH-2) is covered in the present paper, although Zitzler et al. [15] also included the three objective instance in their experiments.

**Table 4.4.** Continuous test problems used in this study. The objective functions are given by $f_j, 1 \leq j \leq m$, where $m$ denotes the number of objectives and $n$ the number of variables. The type of the objectives is given in the first column (minimization or maximization).

| $n$ Type | Domain | Objective functions |
|---|---|---|
| | SPH-$m$ (Schaffer 1985 [17]; Laumanns, Rudolph and Schwefel 2001 [18]) | |
| 100 min | $[-10^3, 10^3]^n$ | $f_j(x) = \sum_{1 \leq i \leq n, i \neq j} (x_i)^2 + (x_j - 1)^2$ $1 \leq j \leq m, m = 2$ |
| | ZDT6 (Zitzler, Deb and Thiele 2000 [19]) | |
| 100 min | $[0, 1]^n$ | $f_1(x) = 1 - \exp(-4x_1)sin^6(6\pi x_1)$ $f_2(x) = g(x)[1 - (f_1(x)/g(x))^2]$ $g(x) = 1 + 9.((\sum_{i=2}^n x_i/(n-1)))^{0.25}$ |
| | QV (Quagliarella and Vicini 1997 [20]) | |
| 100 min | $[-5, 5]^n$ | $f_1(x) = (1/n \sum_{i=1}^n (x_i^2 - 10\cos(2\pi x_i) + 10))^{1/4}$ $f_2(x) = (1/n \sum_{i=1}^n ((x_i - 1.5)^2 - 10\cos(2\pi(x_i - 1.5)) + 10))^{1/4}$ |
| | KUR (Kursawe 1991 [21]) | |
| 100 min | $[-10^3, 10^3]^n$ | $f_1(x) = \sum_{i=1}^n (|x_i|^{0.8} + 5.\sin^3(x_i) + 3.5828)$ $f_2(x) = \sum_{i=1}^{n-1}(1 - \exp^{-0.2\sqrt{x_i^2 + x_{i+1}^2}})$ |

ZDT6 is also unimodal and has a non-uniformly distributed objective space, both orthogonal and lateral to the Pareto-optimal front. ZDT6 was proposed in Zitzler et al. [15] to test the ability of the various algorithms to find a good distribution of points even in this very difficult case.

The components of the function QV are two multi-modal functions, where the main difficulty, apart from the multi-modality, is the extreme concave Pareto-optimal front together with a diminishing density of solutions towards the extreme points.

Kursawe's function (KUR) finally has a multi-modal function in one component and pair-wise interactions among the variables in the other component. The Pareto-optimal front is not connected and has an isolated point as well as concave and convex regions.

For all of the continuous functions the solutions were coded as real vectors, of length 100, for SEAMO and uniform crossover [22] selected as the recombination operator. Uniform crossover was chosen because the lack of any particular relationship between adjacent variables on the chromosome would seem to reduce any potential advantage that could be obtained by the building blocks created using one or two point crossover (although experiments I carried out later indicate that, in fact, one point crossover produces better results on these continuous functions). For the mutation operator a simple uniform mutation operator was tried initially, but this was found to be much too disruptive, particularly when large objective spaces were used. For ZDT6 and KUR, for example, individual mutated variables could take any value in the range $[-10^3, 10^3]$, and this made convergence of the EA very difficult. To overcome this problem, which is commonplace with real valued representations, a non-uniform mutation based on that described on page 111 of Michalewicz [8] was chosen. The idea of non-uniform mutation is to gradually reduce the magnitude of any change that the operator is allowed to make to the values of the variables as the EA progresses. Non-uniform mutation causes the operator to search the space uniformly initially and very locally at later stages. The non-uniform mutation is defined as follows: if $s_v^t = \langle v_1, \ldots, v_m \rangle$ is a chromosome in the population at time $t$, and the element $v_k$ is selected for this mutation (domain of $v_k$ is $[l_k, u_k]$), the result is a vector $s_v^{t+1} = \langle v_1, \ldots, v_k', \ldots, v_m \rangle$, with $k \in \{1, \ldots, n\}$, and

$$v_k' = \begin{cases} v_k + \Delta(t, u_k - v_k) & \text{if a random digit is 0,} \\ v_k - \Delta(t, v_k - l_k) & \text{if a random digit is 1,} \end{cases}$$

where the function $\Delta(t, y)$ returns a value in the range $[0, y]$ such that the probability of $\Delta(t, y)$ being close to 0 increases as $t$ increases. The following function has been used in the present study:

$$\Delta(t, y) = y.(1 - r^{f(t)})$$

where $r$ is a random number from $[0 \ldots 1]$, $t$ is the number of generations that have elapsed so far. $f(t) = k^t$ is used for these experiments, where $k$ is a constant factor set to 0.999.

An important feature of the SEAMO algorithm is the deletion of duplicates, designed to help maintain diversity and prevent premature convergence. For the knapsack problem, and other combinatorial problems, where the objective functions can take on only a limited number of discrete values, phenotypic duplicates are easily identified as individuals with identical solution vectors. With continuous functions, however, it is sensible to identify duplicates in a rather more flexible manner, because exact duplicates are likely to be rare. To this end, values for component objective functions $x_i$ and $x_i'$ are deemed to be equal if and only if $x_i - \epsilon \leq x_i' \leq x_i + \epsilon$, where $\epsilon$ is an error term, which was set at $0.00001 \times x_i$ for the purpose of these experiments.

## 4.9 Summary of Results for the Continuous Functions

Figures 4.10, 4.11, 4.12 and 4.13 compare the 2D graphical traces of SEAMO with various state-of-the-art EAs on the four continuous problems, respectively SPH-2, ZDT6, QV and KUR. SEAMO's competitors in the 2D plots are PESA, NGSA2, and SPEA2. Population sizes of 100 were used in each case and the algorithms run for 10,000 generations. Each trace is a plot of the non-dominated solutions extracted from the results of 30 replicated runs.

Note that all the function optimization problems used in this study are minimization problems, unlike the multiple knapsack problem. Thus the algorithms producing the lowest traces on these graphs perform best for the continuous functions.

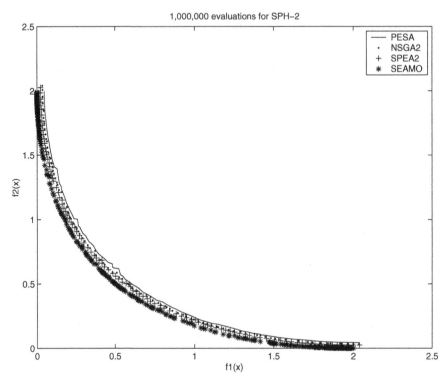

**Figure 4.10.** Non-dominated solutions from 30 runs of PESA, NSGA2, SPEA2 and SEAMO on SPH-2.

The 2D graphical representations indicate that SEAMO performs very well in comparison with its competitors for three out of four of the continuous functions, i.e. SPH-2, QV and KUR. Table 4.5 compares the evolutionary algorithms in pairs using values for the $\mathcal{C}$ metric defined in Zitzler and Thiele [6]. The $\mathcal{C}$ metric measures the coverage of two sets of solution vectors. Let $X', X'' \subseteq X$ be two sets of solutions vectors. The function $\mathcal{C}$ maps the ordered pair $(X', X'')$ to the interval $[0, 1]$

$$\mathcal{C}(X', X'') = \frac{|\{a'' \in X''; \exists a' \in X' : a' \succeq a''\}|}{|X''|} \tag{4.1}$$

The value $\mathcal{C}(X', X'') = 1$ means that all the points in $X''$ are dominated by or equal to points in $X'$, (i.e. all the points in $X''$ are *weakly dominated* by

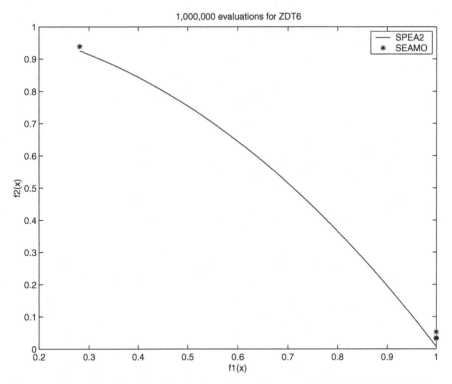

**Figure 4.11.** Non-dominated solutions from 30 runs of SPEA2 and SEAMO on ZDT6.

points in $X'$). The opposite, $\mathcal{C}(X', X'') = 0$, represents the situation when none of the points in $X''$ is weakly dominated by $X'$. Note that both $\mathcal{C}(X', X'')$ and $\mathcal{C}(X'', X')$ have to be considered, since $\mathcal{C}(X', X'')$ is not necessarily equal to $1 - \mathcal{C}(X'', X')$ (i.e. when many solutions in $X'$ and $X''$ neither dominate nor are they dominated by solutions in the alternative set). The $\mathcal{C}$ metric values used in the table indicate superior coverage of the search space by SEAMO for SPH-2, QV and KUR. Single runs of SEAMO on the continuous functions took between 81 secs for SPH-2, and 412 secs for KUR, using a Pentium III processor and 128 MB of memory.

## 4.10 Conclusions

This chapter describes SEAMO, a simple evolutionary algorithm for multiobjective optimization. SEAMO avoids most of the time consuming global calculations typical of other multiobjective evolutionary techniques, using a simple uniform selection strategy within a steady-state evolutionary algorithm (EA) and a straightforward elitist mechanism for replacing

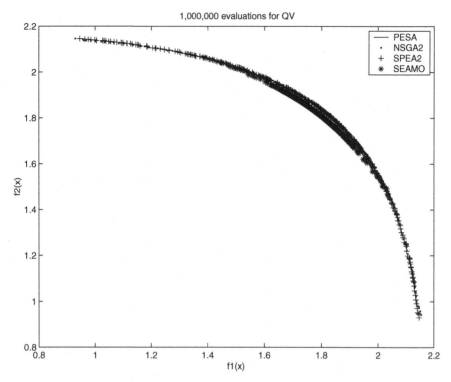

**Figure 4.12.** Non-dominated solutions from 30 runs of PESA, NSGA2, SPEA2 and SEAMO on QV.

**Table 4.5.** $\mathcal{C}$ metrics to compare SEAMO with PESA, NSGA2, and SPEA2. The non-dominated solutions are collected from 30 results files for each algorithm, as before. A population size of 100 is used and a total of 1,000,000 evaluations is carried out for each run of each algorithm.

| $\mathcal{C}$(alg1,alg2) | SPH-2 | ZDT6 | QV | KUR |
|---|---|---|---|---|
| $\mathcal{C}$(SEAMO, PESA) | 99.00 | 00.00 | 94.30 | 54.90 |
| $\mathcal{C}$(PESA, SEAMO) | 00.00 | 93.30 | 0.03 | 04.90 |
| $\mathcal{C}$(SEAMO, NSGA2) | 99.00 | 00.00 | 63.00 | 66.30 |
| $\mathcal{C}$(NSGA2, SEAMO) | 0.00 | 93.30 | 00.60 | 02.00 |
| $\mathcal{C}$(SEAMO, SPEA2) | 99.00 | 00.00 | 58.20 | 70.40 |
| $\mathcal{C}$(SPEA2, SEAMO) | 0.00 | 93.30 | 00.60 | 02.10 |

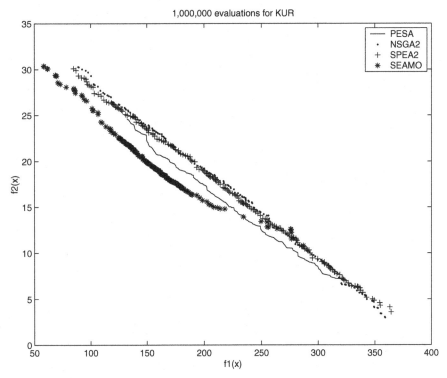

**Figure 4.13.** Non-dominated solutions from 30 runs of PESA, NSGA2, SPEA2 and SEAMO on KUR.

population members with their offspring. Throughout the genetic search, SEAMO's progress depends entirely on the replacement policy, and no global fitness calculations, rankings, sub-populations, niches or auxiliary populations are required. SEAMO has produced some promising results for the multiple knapsack problem, particularly where three or more objectives (knapsacks) are involved. Results are also competitive for several continuous benchmarks, and SEAMO outperforms state-of-the-art Pareto-based EAs compared in Zitzler et al. [15] in many cases. In addition to fast execution, the simplicity of the new algorithm makes it relatively quick and easy to implement, reducing the development time needed for prototyping and testing new multiobjective applications. If required, more sophisticated Pareto-based evolutionary techniques can be incorporated following an initial proof-of-concept. The main weakness identified is SEAMO's current inability to ensure an even spread of Pareto solutions when tackling problems such as ZDT6, where highly non-uniformly distributed objective spaces are involved. Work is currently in progress to address this weakness and generally improve the performance of SEAMO. It remains a challenge to implement improvements without forfeiting the essential simplicity of the SEAMO approach, however.

Additionally, new and better multiple objective techniques are emerging all the time, providing an increasingly difficult challenge for SEAMO. For example, the multiple objective genetic local search of Jaskiewicz [23] has produced some excellent results on the multiple knapsack problem.

This chapter describes the new approach in detail, covering implementations for a combinatorial problem (the 0-1 multiple knapsack problem) and for several continuous functions, and including full details of representations and genetic operators.

## Acknowledgments

I should like to thank my husband, Mark Mumford, for the cartoon illustrations.

## References

1. Valenzuela, CL, A Simple Evolutionary Algorithm for Multi-objective Optimization (SEAMO), *Congress on Evolutionary Computation (CEC)*, Honolulu, Hawaii, 12-17$^{th}$ May 2002, pp. 717-722, 2002.
2. Goldberg, DE, *Genetic Algorithms in Search, Optimization, and Machine Learning*, Addison-Wesley,USA, 1989.
3. Fonseca, CM and Fleming, PJ, Genetic Algorithms for Multiobjective Optimization: Formulation, Discussion and Generalization, *Proceedings of the Fifth International Conference on Genetic Algorithms*, pp. 416-423, Morgan Kaufmann, 1993.
4. Horn, J, Nafpliotis, N and Goldberg, DE, A Niched Pareto Genetic Algorithm for Multiobjective Optimization, *Proceedings of the First IEEE Conference on Evolutionary Computation, IEEE World Congress on Computational Intelligence*, Volume 1, pp. 82-87, IEEE Press, 1994.
5. Corne, DW, Knowles, JD and Oates, MJ, The Pareto Envelope-based Selection Algorithm for Multiobjective Optimization. *Parallel Problem Solving from Nature - PPSN VI*, Lecture Notes in Computer Science 1917, pp. 839-848, Springer, 2000.
6. Zitzler, E and Thiele, L, Multiobjective evolutionary algorithms: A Comparative Case Study and the Strength Pareto Approach, *IEEE Transactions on Evolutionary Computation*, 1999; 3(4)1999: 257-271.
7. Cavicchio, DJ, Adaptive Search Using Simulated Evolution, PhD dissertation, University of Michigan, Ann Arbor, 1970.
8. Michalewicz, Z, *Genetic Algorithms + Data Structures = Evolutionary Programs*, Third, revised and extended edition, Springer,Berlin, 1996.
9. Mumford, CL (Valenzuela), Comparing Representations and Recombination Operators for the Multi-objective 0/1 Knapsack Problem, *Congress on Evolutionary Computation (CEC)*, Canberra, Australia, 2003, pp. 854-861, 2003.

10. Oliver, IM, Smith, DJ and Holland JRC, A Study of Permutation Crossover Operators on the Traveling Salesman Problem, *Genetic Algorithms and their Applications:Proceedings of the Second International Conference on Genetic Algorithms*, pp. 224-230, 1987.
11. Goldberg, DE and Lingle R, Alleles, Loci and the TSP, *Proceedings of an International Conference on Genetic Algorithms and Their Applications*, pp. 154-159, Pittsburgh, PA, 1985.
12. Mühlenbein, H, Gorges-Schleuter, M and Krämer O, Evolution Algorithms in Combinatorial Optimization, *Parallel Computing*, 1988, 7:65-85.
13. Davis, L, Applying Adaptive Algorithms to Epistatic Domains, *Proceedings of the Joint International Conference on Artificial Intelligence*, pp. 162–164, 1985.
14. Davis, L, Order-based Genetic Algorithms and the Graph Coloring problem, *Handbook of Genetic Algorithms* pp. 72-90, New York, Van Nostrand Reinhold, 1991.
15. Zitzler, E, Laumanns, M and Thiele, L, SPEA2: Improving the Strength Pareto Evolutionary Algorithm, TIK-Report 103, Department of Electrical Engineering, Swiss Federal Institute of Technology (ETH), Zurich, Switzerland,2001 {zitzler, laumanns, thiele}@tik.ee.ethz.ch.
16. Deb, K, Agrawal, S, Pratap, A and Meyarivan, T A Fast Elitist Non-dominated Sorting Genetic Algorithm for Mult-objective Optimization: NSGA-II, *Parallel Problem Solving from Nature - PPSN VI*, Lecture Notes in Computer Science 1917, pp. 849-858, Springer, 2000.
17. Schaffer, JD Multiple Objective Optimization with Vector Evaluated Genetic Algorithms, *Proceedings of an International Conference on Genetic Algorithms and Their Applications*, pp. 93-100, Pittsburgh, PA, 1985.
18. Laumanns, M, Rudolph, G and Schwefel, HP Mutation Control and Convergence in Evolutionary Multiobjective Optimization. *Proceedings of the 7th International Mendel Conference on soft Computing (MENDEL 2001)*, Brno, Czech Republic, 2001.
19. Zitzler, E, Deb, K and Thiel, L Comparison of Multiobjective Evolutionary Algorithms: Empirical Results, *Evolutionary Computation*, 2000; 8(2):173-195.
20. Quagliarella, D and Vicini, A Coupling Genetic Algorithms and Gradient Based Optimization Techniques. In D. Quagliarella, J. Périaux, C Poloni, and G. Winter (eds) *Genetic Algorithms and Evolution Strategy in Engineering and Computer Science – Recent Advances and Industrial Applications*, pp. 289–309, Chichester, Wiley, 1997.
21. Kursawe, F A Variant of Evolution Strategies for Vector Optimization. In H. -P. Schewefel and R. Männer (eds), *Parallel Problem Solving from Nature* Berlin, pp. 193-197, Springer, 1991.
22. Syswereda, G Uniform Crossover in Genetic Algorithms, *Genetic Algorithms and their Applications:Proceedings of the Third International Conference on Genetic Algorithms*, pp. 2-9, 1989.
23. Jaskiewicz, A On the Performance of Multiple Objective Genetic Local Search on the 0/1 Knapsack Problem - A Comparative Experiment, *IEEE Transactions on Evolutionary Computation*, 2002, 6(4):402-412.
24. Hajela, P, and Lin, CY Genetic Search Strategies in Multicriterion Optimal Design, *Structural Optimization*, Volume 4, pp. 99-107, New York: Springer, 1992.

# 5

## Quad-trees: A Data Structure for Storing Pareto Sets in Multiobjective Evolutionary Algorithms with Elitism

Sanaz Mostaghim and Jürgen Teich

**Summary.** In multiobjective evolutionary algorithms (MOEAs) with elitism, the data structures for storing and updating archives may have a great impact on the required computational (CPU) time, especially when optimizing higher-dimensional problems with large Pareto sets. In this chapter, we introduce Quad-trees as an alternative data structure to linear lists for storing Pareto sets. In particular, we investigate several variants of Quad-trees and compare them with conventional linear lists. We also study the influence of population size and number of objectives on the required CPU time. These data structures are evaluated and compared on several multiobjective example problems. The results presented show that typically, linear lists perform better for small population sizes and higher-dimensional Pareto fronts (large archives) whereas Quad-trees perform better for larger population sizes and Pareto sets of small cardinality.

## 5.1 Introduction

Multiobjective optimization (MO) has been investigated frequently during the last years [1], and it is proved that stochastic search methods such as evolutionary algorithms (EA) often provide the best solutions for complex optimization problems [2]. Up to now there exist several MOEAs, which can be divided into two groups. The first group contains the MOEAs that always keep the best solutions (non-dominated solutions) of each generation in an *archive*, and they are called MOEAs with elitism. In the second group, there is no archive for keeping best solutions and MOEA may lose them during generations. MOEAs with elitism are studied in several methods like Rudolph's Elitist MOEA, Elitist NSGA-II, SPEA, PAES (see [1] for all) and SPEA2 [3]. Indeed, by using elitism, a good solution will never be lost unless a better solution is discovered. It is proved that MOEAs converge to optimal solutions of some functions in the presence of elitism [4, 5]. Applying the non-dominated solutions in the archive in the selection process, enhances the probability of creating better offsprings, too. Therefore, the archive is playing an important role in MOEAs.

In this chapter, we investigate and compare different data structures for implementing archives such to minimize the CPU time. The motivation of our work comes from the *Quad-tree* data structure proposed by Finkel and Bentley in 1974 [6]. Later, Habenicht [7] adapted Quad-trees to the problem of identifying non-dominated criterion vectors. Finally, Sun and Steuer [8] improved the work of [7] to make the storage more efficient. However, no one so far has investigated Quad-tree data structures in the context of evolutionary algorithms, i.e., MOEAs. For example, the work of Sun and Steuer [8] only considered inserting a randomly generated sequence of test vectors into an empty archive and did not consider the performance of iteratively updated archives like in elitist MOEAs. We will see that a fair comparison of data structures is only possible in case different data structures are tested on (a) equal test problems, and using (b) equal optimization algorithms, e.g., the same MOEA. Up to now, linear lists have been used as the archives for storing non-dominated solutions in MOEAs [1]. Here, we apply the Quad-tree structure from Sun and Steuer [8] to MOEAs (especially SPEA [9]) after treating it for a shortcoming which it had in dealing with some special cases.

In our work, three kinds of Quad-trees are examined which are called Quad-tree1, Quad-tree2 and Quad-tree3. The first data structure called Quad-tree1 is derived from Habenicht [7]. It has two disadvantages: The CPU time depends on the order in which the vectors are added, and deleting a vector means deleting all the subtree and reinserting all vectors again from the root. Therefore, we propose Quad-tree2 as an improved data structure that uses flags to indicate dominated vectors that have to be deleted in the Quad-tree. The third data structure is the implementation of Sun and Steuer's Quad-tree [8]. We have extended this data structure to make it more efficient for MOEA archives, calling it Quad-tree3 in the following.

In this chapter, a comparative study of linear lists with the new Quad-trees data structures is given, i.e., the CPU times are compared for each data structure. We study the influence of population size, archive size and number of objectives on the CPU time for different kinds of test problems. These tests, taken from Zitzler and Thiele [9] and Deb et al. [10], contain 2- to 10-objective test problems. We will see that both linear lists and Quad-trees may be attractive data structures depending on the following three main problem characteristics: (a) dimension $m$ of the objective space, (b) population size, and (c) archive size. As a rule of thumb the presented results indicate that the Quad-tree data structures turn out to be superior for large population sizes and problems with archives of small cardinality.

This chapter consists of five sections. After this introduction, we provide the basic notations and definitions concerning multiobjective optimization. Then the basic structure of MOEAs is studied in Section 5.2. In Section 5.3, different data structures for storing Pareto-points in archives, i.e., linear lists and Quad-trees are proposed. Section 5.4 explains how these data structures are embedded into a MOEA that is used in Section 5.5 where results of experiments are presented using a number of different test functions to evaluate and compare the performance of the different data structures.

### 5.1.1 Multiobjective Optimization

A multiobjective optimization problem has a number of objective functions which are to be minimized or maximized at the same time. In the following, we state the multiobjective optimization problem in its general form:

$$\begin{aligned} \text{minimize} \quad & \mathbf{y} = \mathbf{f}(\mathbf{x}) = (f_1(\mathbf{x}), f_2(\mathbf{x}), \cdots, f_m(\mathbf{x})) \\ \text{subject to} \quad & \mathbf{e}(\mathbf{x}) = (e_1(\mathbf{x}), e_2(\mathbf{x}), \cdot, e_k(\mathbf{x})) \leq \mathbf{0} \\ & \mathbf{x} \in S \end{aligned} \tag{5.1}$$

involving $m (\geq 2)$ conflicting objective functions $f_i : \Re^n \to \Re$ that we want to minimize simultaneously. The *decision vectors* $\mathbf{x} = (x_1, x_2, \cdots, x_n)^T$ belong to the feasible region $S \subset \Re^n$. The feasible region is formed by constraint functions $\mathbf{e}(\mathbf{x})$. We denote the image of the feasible region by $Z \subset \Re^m$ and call it a feasible objective region. The elements of $Z$ are called objective vectors and they consist of objective (function) values $\mathbf{f}(\mathbf{x}) = (f_1(\mathbf{x}), f_2(\mathbf{x}), \cdots, f_m(\mathbf{x}))$.

A decision vector $\mathbf{x}_1 \in S$ is said to *dominate* a decision vector $\mathbf{x}_2 \in S$ if both of the following conditions are true:

1. The decision vector $\mathbf{x}_1$ is not worse than $\mathbf{x}_2$ in all objectives, i.e., $f_i(\mathbf{x}_1) \leq f_i(\mathbf{x}_2)$ for all $i = 1, \cdots, m$.
2. The decision vector $\mathbf{x}_1$ is strictly better than $\mathbf{x}_2$ in at least one objective, i.e., $f_i(\mathbf{x}_1) < f_i(\mathbf{x}_2)$ for at least one $i = 1, \cdots, m$.

A decision vector $\mathbf{x}_1 \in S$ is called *Pareto-optimal* if there does not exist another $\mathbf{x}_2 \in S$ that dominates it. Finally, an objective vector is called Pareto-optimal if the corresponding decision vector is Pareto-optimal.

## 5.2 Multiobjective Evolutionary Algorithms (MOEAs)

Evolutionary algorithms (EAs) are iterative stochastic search methods that are based on the two concepts of generate and evaluate [2]. Multiobjective evolutionary algorithms (MOEAs) with elitism are also based on this idea. Figure 5.1 shows the typical structure of a MOEA with elitism, where $t$ denotes the number of the generation, $P_t$ the population, and $A_t$ the *archive* at generation $t$. The aim of function *Generate* is to generate new solutions in each iteration $t$ which is done through selection, recombination and mutation. The function *Evaluate* calculates the *fitness* value of each individual in the actual population $P_t$. Fitness assignment in MOEA is done in different ways, such as by Pareto ranking [12], non-dominated sorting [11], or by calculating Pareto strengths [9]. Since only the superior solutions must be kept in the archive, it must be updated after each generation. The function *Update*

BEGIN
        Step 1: $t = 0$;
        Step 2: Generate the initial population $P_0$ and initial archive $A_0$
        Step 3: *Evaluate $P_t$*
        Step 4: $A_{t+1} := Update(P_t, A_t)$
        Step 5: $P_{t+1} := Generate(P_t, A_t)$
        Step 6: $t = t + 1$
        Step 7: Unless a *termination criterion* is met, goto Step 3
END

**Figure 5.1.** Typical structure of an archive-based MOEA.

compares whether members of the current population $P_t$ are non-dominated with respect to the members of the actual archive $A_t$ and how and which of such candidates should be considered for insertion into the archive and which should be removed. Thereby, an archive is called *domination-free* if no two solutions in the archive dominate each other. Obviously, during execution of the function *Update*, dominated solutions must be deleted in order to keep the archive domination-free.

These three phases of an elitist MOEA are iteratively repeated until a termination criterion is met, such as a maximum number of generations or when there has been no change in non-dominated solutions found for a given number of generations. The output of an elitist MOEA is the set of non-dominated solutions stored in the final archive. This set is an approximation of the Pareto set and often called *quality set*.

The above algorithm structure is common to most elitist MOEAs. For example, in SPEA [9], newly found non-dominated solutions of the population are compared with the actual archive and the resulting non-dominated solutions are preserved in the updated archive.

## 5.3 Data Structures for Storing Non-dominated Solutions in MOEA

In this section, we propose linear lists and Quad-tree data structures as introduced first by Habenicht [7] and later by Sun and Steuer [8] for the implementation of an archive.

In the following, we assume that at any generation $t$, the archive $A_t$ must always be kept *domination-free*. Also, we assume throughout this chapter that the archive size $|A_t|$ is not a fixed constant, but may grow or decrease at each generation $t$.

### 5.3.1 Linear Lists

A linear list is the most straightforward way to implement an archive. In order to keep an archive domination-free, the following basic operation must be performed, namely *Insertion with Update* of complexity $O(m \cdot |A| \cdot |P|)$: In the worst case, each candidate $\mathbf{x}$ of a population $P$ has to be tested against each member of the archive $A$ for inclusion. In case $\mathbf{x}$ is not dominated by any member of $A$, we assume it is inserted (e.g., at the end), else rejected. On the other hand, if $\mathbf{x}$ dominates members of $A$, these members must be deleted from the archive. Hence, the overall run-time complexity of maintaining a domination-free linear list is $O(m \cdot |A| \cdot |P|)$.

In an MOEA such as SPEA [9], non-dominated solutions (objective vectors) are stored in an array. In this archive, if a candidate $\mathbf{x}$ is not dominated with respect to other members of $P$ and if it also doesn't dominate any vector in the archive $A$, it is added to the end of the array. On the other hand, if the new vector $\mathbf{x}$ is dominated by another vector $\mathbf{y} \in A$, then $\mathbf{x}$ is rejected. If $\mathbf{x}$ dominates $\mathbf{y}$, then $\mathbf{y}$ is deleted.

### 5.3.2 Quad-trees

A Quad-tree [7] is a tree-based data structure for storing objective vectors. Each node is a vector with $m$ elements and can have at most $2^m$ sons which are defined by a successorship. A Quad-tree is a domination-free data structure. In order to explain the data structure, some definitions are necessary. Let $\mathbf{x}$ and $\mathbf{y}$ denote $m$-dimensional objective vectors.

$k$-**Successor:** A node $\mathbf{x}$ is called $k$-successor of node $\mathbf{y}$ where $k$ is a binary string of the form $k = (k_1, \cdots, k_m)_2$ and

$$k_i = \begin{cases} 1 \text{ if } x_i \geq y_i \\ 0 \text{ if } x_i < y_i \end{cases} \tag{5.2}$$

$k$ can also be considered as a scalar value as in [7, 8]:

$$k = \sum_{i=1}^{m} k_i 2^{m-i}$$

$k$-**Son:** Node $\mathbf{x}$ is $k$-son of node $\mathbf{y}$, if $\mathbf{x}$ is a $k$-successor of $\mathbf{y}$ and also the direct son of $\mathbf{y}$.

$k$-**Set:** $S_i(k)$ is a set of $i$ in $k$-successors ($i$ is 0 or 1):

$$S_0(k) = \{i | k_i = 0, k = (k_1, k_2, \ldots, k_m)_2\} \tag{5.3}$$
$$S_1(k) = \{i | k_i = 1, k = (k_1, k_2, \ldots, k_m)_2\} \tag{5.4}$$

As a Quad-tree is a domination-free data structure, there exist no branches with the successorship 0 and $2^m$ because nodes with $k$ equal to 0 will by definition dominate the root and the nodes with $k$ equal to $2^m$ will always be dominated by the root.

**Example 1:**

Figure 5.2 shows an example of a tree for storing non-dominated, $m = 3$ dimensional objective vectors. Each node of this tree has $m = 3$ elements, so each node can have at most 8 sons. The shown tree is not domination-free and, hence, not a Quad-tree because the root (10 10 10) has a (000)-son and a (111)-son. The (000)-son of the root (5 5 5), dominates the root and the (111)-son of the root (12 15 18), is dominated by the root.

□

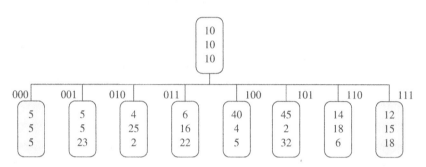

**Figure 5.2.** Example of a tree-structure for storing non-dominated solutions. Node (5 5 5) dominates the root (10 10 10) and node (12 15 18) is dominated by the root.

When processing a vector for possible inclusion into a domination-free Quad-tree, the vector is either discarded as being dominated by a node already in the Quad-tree or it is inserted into the Quad-tree. However, when a vector is inserted, it may dominate other nodes in the Quad-tree. Then, these nodes must be deleted, too. By deleting a node, we obviously destroy the structure of the subtree rooted at the deleted node. This means that all the successors of the deleted node must be considered again for inclusion in the Quad-tree. The corresponding algorithm is shown in Figure 5.3.

The way in which vectors are processed for possible inclusion in the Quad-tree in order to maintain it domination-free is very important to identify all non-dominated vectors. Suppose that we are processing $\mathbf{x} \in \Re^3$ for possible inclusion into a domination-free Quad-tree rooted at $\mathbf{y} \in \Re^3$ and such that $\mathbf{x}$ is a $k$-successor of $\mathbf{y}$. With the definitions of $S_0(k)$ and $S_1(k)$, observe that:

1. The only places in the Quad-tree where there may be vectors that dominate $\mathbf{x}$ are in those subtrees whose roots are sons of $\mathbf{y}$ that have *zeros* in at least all locations that $k$ does. That is the subtree rooted at $l$-sons of $\mathbf{y}$ for which $l < k$ and $S_0(k) \subset S_0(l)$. For example, in the case that $k = (110)$, only the $l = (010)$- and (100)-successors of $\mathbf{y}$ must be checked whether they dominate $\mathbf{x}$ or not.

2. The only places in the Quad-tree where there may be vectors that are dominated by $\mathbf{x}$ are in those subtrees whose roots are sons of $\mathbf{y}$ that have

Algorithm Quad-tree1
<u>BEGIN</u>

Input: $\mathbf{x}$ to be inserted into a Quad-tree rooted at $\mathbf{y}$
Output: Updated (domination-free) Quad-tree

Step 1: Let $\mathbf{y}$ be the root of the tree
Step 2: Calculate $k$ such that $\mathbf{x}$ is the $k$-successor of $\mathbf{y}$
    If $k = 2^m$ or if $x_i = y_i, \forall i \in S_0(k)$, STOP /* $\mathbf{x}$ is dominated by $\mathbf{y}$ */
    If $k = 0$, delete $\mathbf{y}$ and its subtree, /* $\mathbf{y}$ is dominated by $\mathbf{x}$ */
        replace $\mathbf{y}$ by $\mathbf{x}$ and reinsert the subtree of $\mathbf{y}$ from $\mathbf{x}$, STOP
Step 3: For all $\mathbf{z}$ such that $\mathbf{z}$ is a $l$-son of $\mathbf{y}$, $l < k$ and $S_0(k) \subset S_0(l)$:
    TEST1($\mathbf{x}$,$\mathbf{z}$): /* Check if $\mathbf{x}$ is dominated by $\mathbf{z}$ or a son of $\mathbf{z}$ */
        {
        Calculate $k$ such that $\mathbf{x}$ is the $k$-successor of $\mathbf{z}$
        If $x_i = z_i, \forall i \in S_0(k)$, STOP
        For all $\mathbf{v}$ such that $\mathbf{v}$ is a $l$-son of $\mathbf{z}$ and $S_0(k) \subset S_0(l)$:
        execute TEST1($\mathbf{x}$,$\mathbf{v}$)
        }
Step 4: For all $\mathbf{z}$ such that $\mathbf{z}$ is a $l$-son of $\mathbf{y}$, $k < l$ and $S_1(k) \subset S_1(l)$:
    TEST2($\mathbf{x}$,$\mathbf{z}$): /* Check if $\mathbf{x}$ dominates $\mathbf{z}$ or a son of $\mathbf{z}$ */
        {
        Calculate $k$ such that $\mathbf{x}$ is the $k$-successor of $\mathbf{z}$
        If $k = 0$,
                delete $\mathbf{z}$ and reinsert all its subtrees from the global root
        For all $\mathbf{v}$ such that $\mathbf{v}$ is a $l$-son of $\mathbf{z}$ and $S_1(k) \subset S_1(l)$:
        execute TEST2($\mathbf{x}$,$\mathbf{v}$)
        }
Step 5: If a $k$-son of $\mathbf{y}$ already exists, replace $\mathbf{y}$ by the $k$-son, goto Step 2
    else $\mathbf{x}$ is the $k$-son of $\mathbf{y}$, STOP

<u>END</u>

**Figure 5.3.** Quad-tree1 method.

*ones* in at least all locations that $k$ does. That is the subtree rooted at $l$-sons of $\mathbf{y}$ for which $l > k$ and $S_1(k) \subset S_1(l)$. For example, in the case that $k = (100)$, only the $l = (101)$- and $(110)$-successors of $\mathbf{y}$ must be checked whether they are dominated by $\mathbf{x}$ or not.

An objective vector is admitted to a Quad-tree if and only if it is not dominated by any of the vectors already in the Quad-tree. Moreover, when admitted to the Quad-tree, all objective vectors in the Quad-tree dominated by the new entry must be identified and deleted.

**Example 2:**

Figure 5.4 shows a Quad-tree in which we want to insert the vector (4 8 12). According to the Quad-tree algorithm, the $k$-successorship of (4 8 12) to (10 10 10) is calculated in Step 2 as $k$ = (001). In the next step (Step 4), we must look in the (011)- and (101)-successors of (10 10 10) for nodes that are dominated by (4 8 12). The node (6 16 22) is dominated by (4 8 12) and must be deleted. After deleting (6 16 22), we have to reinsert all the nodes in the subtree of (6 16 22), again from the root (10 10 10). Here, (3 25 16) is reinserted as the (011)-successor of (10 10 10), see Figure 5.5. Then, we approach to insert (4 8 12) as a (001)-son of (10 10 10). Since (10 10 10) has already a (001)-son, (5 5 23), we consider (5 5 23) as the new root in the algorithm (Step 5) and we try to insert (4 8 12) in its subtree. (4 8 12) is the (010)-successor of (5 5 23), so the (011)- and (110)-successors of (5 5 23) must be checked whether they are dominated by (4 8 12) or not. (9 8 18) is indeed dominated by (4 8 12), so we delete it, and since (5 5 23) has no other sons, we insert (4 8 12) as the (010)-successor of it. Figure 5.5 shows the Quad-tree after insertion.

□

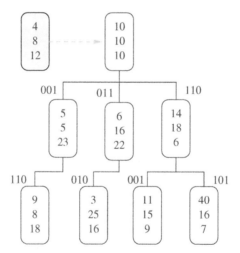

**Figure 5.4.** Domination-free Quad-tree from Example 2.

According to the above algorithm, the data structure Quad-tree1 has two disadvantages: The form and depth of the Quad-tree is dependent on the order of insertion of a given set of vectors. The second disadvantage is that deleting a node destroys the structure of the Quad-tree and requires to reinsert all of the nodes of subtrees of a deleted node. Therefore, deletions combined with reinsertions will be critical and one should carefully avoid having to reinsert

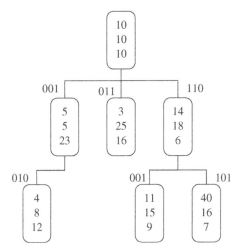

**Figure 5.5.** Domination-free Quad-tree from Example 2 after inserting the vector (4 8 12).

a vector multiple times. Therefore, we propose the following variant called Quad-tree2 in which the deletion process is improved.

In Quad-tree2, a discovered dominated node is not deleted immediately, but it is marked as deleted by a flag. Then, its subtrees are traversed, again setting flags for all encountered dominated nodes instead of reinserting all subtrees immediately. After finishing this recursive descent, we reinsert only those nodes in subtrees that are not marked deleted. The algorithm called Quad-tree2 is shown in Figure 5.6 and Example 3 illustrates it.

**Example 3:**

Consider Figure 5.5 and let us tentatively insert the new vector (12 15 5). (12 15 5) is the (110)-successor of the root (10 10 10). Since (10 10 10) has already a (110)-son, (14 18 6), we consider (14 18 6) as the new root in the algorithm (Step 5) and try to insert (12 15 5) in its subtree. (12 15 5) is the (000)-successor of (14 18 6). It means that (14 18 6) must be deleted. Contrary to algorithm Quad-tree1, we do not delete it and reinsert all nodes of corresponding subtrees immediately. Instead, we only mark it as deleted. Then we look for other dominated nodes in its subtrees. (40 16 7) is also dominated by (12 15 5) and must be deleted. Therefore, we also mark it as deleted. Then, we replace (14 18 6) by (12 15 5). Before finishing Step 2, we clean the subtrees from the marked nodes and reinsert only those nodes that remain un-flagged ,i.e., node (11 15 9). Figures 5.7 and 5.8 show the corresponding Quad-tree2 before and after inserting the vector (12 15 5).

□

Algorithm Quad-tree2
<u>BEGIN</u>

Input: $\mathbf{x}$ to be inserted into a Quad-tree rooted at $\mathbf{y}$
Output: Updated (domination-free) Quad-tree

Step 1: Let $\mathbf{y}$ be the root of the tree
Step 2: Calculate $k$ such that $\mathbf{x}$ is the $k$-successor of $\mathbf{y}$
  If $k = 2^m$ or if $x_i = y_i, \forall i \in S_0(k)$, STOP /* $\mathbf{x}$ is dominated by $\mathbf{y}$ */
  If $k = 0$: { /* $\mathbf{y}$ is dominated by $\mathbf{x}$ */
        Flag $= 0$
        MARK($\mathbf{x}$, $\mathbf{y}$):{
                For all sons $\mathbf{z}$ of $\mathbf{y}$:
                        If $\mathbf{z}$ is a 0-son of $\mathbf{x}$, mark $\mathbf{z}$ as deleted, Flag $= 1$
                        else if Flag $= 1$, mark $\mathbf{z}$ as reinserted
                        MARK($\mathbf{x}$, $\mathbf{z}$) }
        Replace $\mathbf{y}$ by $\mathbf{x}$. Delete all the marked nodes in the subtree of $\mathbf{x}$
        Reinsert the nodes with the reinserted mark in subtrees of $\mathbf{x}$ at $\mathbf{x}$
        STOP
        }
Step 3: For all $\mathbf{z}$ such that $\mathbf{z}$ is a $l$-son of $\mathbf{y}$, $l < k$ and $S_0(k) \subset S_0(l)$:
  TEST1($\mathbf{x},\mathbf{z}$): /* Check if $\mathbf{x}$ is dominated by $\mathbf{z}$ or a son of $\mathbf{z}$ */
        {
        Calculate $k$ such that $\mathbf{x}$ is the $k$-successor of $\mathbf{z}$
        If $x_i = z_i, \forall i \in S_0(k)$, STOP
        For all $\mathbf{v}$ such that $\mathbf{v}$ is a $l$-son of $\mathbf{z}$ and $S_0(k) \subset S_0(l)$:
        execute TEST1($\mathbf{x},\mathbf{v}$)
        }
Step 4: For all $\mathbf{z}$ such that $\mathbf{z}$ is a $l$-son of $\mathbf{y}$, $k < l$ and $S_1(k) \subset S_1(l)$:
  Flag $= 0$
  TEST2($\mathbf{x},\mathbf{z}$): /* Check if $\mathbf{x}$ dominates $\mathbf{z}$ or a son of $\mathbf{z}$ */
        {
        Calculate $k$ such that $\mathbf{x}$ is the $k$-successor of $\mathbf{z}$
        If $k = 0$, mark $\mathbf{z}$ as deleted, Flag $= 1$
        else if Flag $= 1$, mark $\mathbf{z}$ as reinserted
        For all $\mathbf{v}$ such that $\mathbf{v}$ is a $l$-son of $\mathbf{z}$, and $S_1(k) \subset S_1(l)$:
        execute TEST2($\mathbf{x},\mathbf{v}$)
        }
Step 5: If a $k$-son of $\mathbf{y}$ already exists, replace $\mathbf{y}$ by the $k$-son, goto Step 2
        else {
        Place $\mathbf{x}$ as the $k$-son of $\mathbf{y}$
        Delete all the marked nodes in the Quad-tree
        Reinsert the nodes with the reinserted mark from the global root
        STOP
        }
<u>END</u>

**Figure 5.6.** Quad-tree2 method.

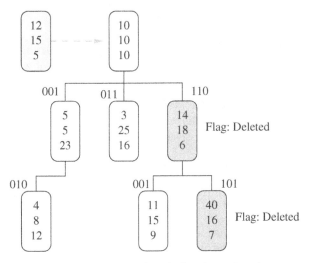

**Figure 5.7.** Quad-tree from Example 3 before inserting the vector (12 15 5).

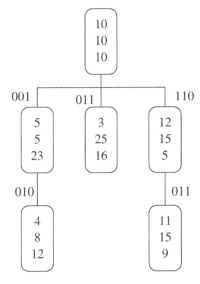

**Figure 5.8.** Quad-tree from Example 3 after inserting the vector (12 15 5).

In our third variant called Quad-tree3 [8], the deletion problem is solved differently. The complete algorithm is shown in Figure 5.9 and the included routines are described as follows.

**DELETE(z):** This routine deletes the node **z**. If **z** has at least one son, then the lowest numbered son of **z** becomes the new root of the subtree. So, only the nodes in the subtrees of the other sons must be considered for reinsertion:

1. Let $k = 1$. Detach the subtree rooted at **z**.

2. If the $k$-son of $\mathbf{z}$ exists, denote it by $\mathbf{t}$, move $\mathbf{t}$ to the position of $\mathbf{z}$ in the Quad-tree and goto 4.
3. Let $k = k + 1$. If $k > 2^m - 2$, RETURN. Otherwise goto 2.
4. For each $k$ such that $k + 1 \leq k \leq 2^m - 2$, if the $k$-son of $\mathbf{z}$ exists, denote it by $\mathbf{s}$ and execute REINSERT($\mathbf{t}$, $\mathbf{s}$).

**REPLACE(c, s):** In this routine, we replace $\mathbf{c}$ with $\mathbf{s}$ because $\mathbf{c}$ is dominated by $\mathbf{s}$. So, the successorships in the subtrees of $\mathbf{c}$ are not valid any more and corresponding nodes must be reconsidered again:

1. Detach the subtree rooted at $\mathbf{c}$. Replace $\mathbf{c}$ by $\mathbf{s}$.
2. For each $k$ such that $1 \leq k \leq 2^m - 2$, if the $k$-son of $\mathbf{c}$ exists in the detached subtree, denote it by $\mathbf{t}$ and execute RECONSIDER($\mathbf{s}$, $\mathbf{t}$).
3. Discard $\mathbf{c}$.

**REINSERT(c, s):** This routine finds the right position in the subtree rooted at $\mathbf{c}$ at which to insert $\mathbf{s}$ and its successors. This routine is just called when we are sure that there is no need for domination test. This case happens, for example, in the routine DELETE where we take the lowest successor of the deleted root and make it the new root. Since all other vectors in the detached subtree are non-dominated with respect to the new root, these vectors need only be reinserted into the subtree without any dominance tests:

1. For each $k$ such that $1 \leq k \leq 2^m - 2$, if the $k$-son of $\mathbf{s}$ exists, denote it by $\mathbf{t}$ and execute REINSERT($c$, $t$);
2. Determine $l$ such that $\mathbf{s}$ is a $l$-successor of $\mathbf{c}$. If the $l$-son of $\mathbf{c}$ exists, denote it by $\mathbf{t}$ and execute REINSERT($\mathbf{t}$, $\mathbf{s}$). If the $l$-son of $\mathbf{c}$ does not exist, move $\mathbf{s}$ to the position of the $l$-son of $\mathbf{c}$.

**RECONSIDER(c, s):** This routine is called in the REPLACE routine, when a deleted root is replaced directly by a new vector. In this case, the successors $\mathbf{s}$ of the deleted root may also be dominated by the new vector $\mathbf{c}$. This means that each successor $\mathbf{s}$ of the deleted root must be tested for dominance before being inserted into the new subtree rooted at $\mathbf{c}$:

1. For each $k$ such that $1 \leq k \leq 2^m - 2$, if the $k$-son of $\mathbf{s}$ exists, denote it by $\mathbf{t}$ and execute RECONSIDER($c$, $t$);
2. Determine $l$ such that $\mathbf{s}$ is a $l$-successor of $\mathbf{c}$
3. If $l = 2^m$, discard $\mathbf{s}$, RETURN.
4. If the $l$-son of $\mathbf{c}$ exists, denote it by $\mathbf{t}$ and execute REINSERT($\mathbf{t}$, $\mathbf{s}$), else move $\mathbf{s}$ to the position of $l$-son of $\mathbf{c}$ in the Quad-tree.

**Example 4:**

In this example, we illustrate the routine DELETE of the Quad-tree3 algorithm. Consider the Quad-tree in Figure  5.10 and let us insert the node (12 8 4). As it was explained throughout previous examples and in the corresponding algorithms, it is obvious that node (14 18 6) is dominated by

Algorithm Quad-tree3
<u>BEGIN</u>

    Input: $\mathbf{x}$ to be inserted into a Quad-tree rooted at $\mathbf{y}$
    Output: Updated (domination-free) Quad-tree

    Step 1: Let $\mathbf{y}$ be the root of the tree
    Step 2: Calculate $k$ such that $\mathbf{x}$ is the $k$-successor of $\mathbf{y}$
      If $k = 2^m$ or if $x_i = y_i, \forall i \in S_0(k)$, STOP. /* $\mathbf{x}$ is dominated by $\mathbf{y}$ */
      If $k = 0$, REPLACE($\mathbf{y}, \mathbf{x}$). STOP. /*$\mathbf{y}$ is dominated by $\mathbf{x}$ */
    Step 3: For all $\mathbf{z}$ such that $\mathbf{z}$ is a $l$-son of $\mathbf{y}$, $l < k$ and $S_0(k) \subset S_0(l)$:
    TEST1($\mathbf{x}$,$\mathbf{z}$): /* Check if $\mathbf{x}$ is dominated by $\mathbf{z}$ or a son of $\mathbf{z}$ */
        {
      Calculate $k$ such that $\mathbf{x}$ is the $k$-successor of $\mathbf{z}$
      If $x_i = z_i, \forall i \in S_0(k)$, STOP
      For all $\mathbf{v}$ such that $\mathbf{v}$ is a $l$-son of $\mathbf{z}$, and $S_0(k) \subset S_0(l)$:
      execute TEST1($\mathbf{x}$,$\mathbf{v}$)
        }
    Step 4: For all $\mathbf{z}$ such that $\mathbf{z}$ is a $l$-son of $\mathbf{y}$, $k < l$ and $S_1(k) \subset S_1(l)$:
    TEST2($\mathbf{x}$,$\mathbf{z}$): /* Check if $\mathbf{x}$ dominates $\mathbf{z}$ or a son of $\mathbf{z}$ */
        {
      Calculate $k$ such that $\mathbf{x}$ is the $k$-successor of $\mathbf{z}$
      If $k = 0$, DELETE($\mathbf{z}$)
      For all $\mathbf{v}$ such that $\mathbf{v}$ is a $l$-son of $\mathbf{z}$, and $S_1(k) \subset S_1(l)$:
      execute TEST2($\mathbf{x}$,$\mathbf{v}$)
        }
    Step 5: If a $k$-son of $\mathbf{y}$ already exists, replace $\mathbf{y}$ by the $k$-son, goto Step 2
      else $\mathbf{x}$ is the $k$-son of $\mathbf{y}$, STOP

<u>END</u>

**Figure 5.9.** Quad-tree3 method.

(12 8 4) and must be deleted. In the routine DELETE of Quad-tree3, node (14 18 6) is deleted. Since the node (11 14 9) is the (001)-son of (14 18 6), it is moved to its place and the node (40 12 3) in reinserted again from (11 14 9). The result of this insertion is shown in Figure 5.11.

□

## 5.4 Use of Quad-trees in MOEA

We have integrated the Quad-tree variants into the SPEA (Strength Pareto Evolutionary Algorithm) [9]. In this algorithm, there is an external set (archive) for storing non-dominated solutions of each generation. Updating the archive in SPEA is done as follows: In each generation, non-dominated solutions of the actual population are marked first. Then, only these non-

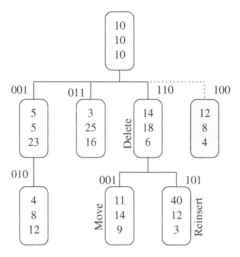

**Figure 5.10.** Example 4 - Quad-tree by inserting (12 8 4).

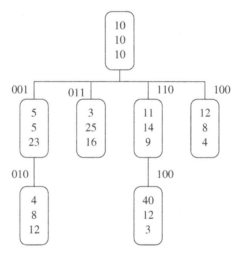

**Figure 5.11.** Example 4 - Quad-tree.

dominated solutions are considered for insertion into the actual archive. The archive is always kept domination-free.

In the experiments presented in the next section, the linear list as well as the three Quad-tree implementations are evaluated using different test functions and compared. In the three Quad-tree implementations, Quad-trees are used as the data structure for the archive only but not for the population. Each individual of the actual population is tentatively inserted into the archive in each generation. It is obvious that only non-dominated solutions do remain in the Quad-tree because the Quad-tree is domination-free.

In SPEA, the archive as well as the population undergo selection and tournament selection is applied to individuals of the archive and the actual population. In order to have equal behavior in our Quad-tree MOEA, we have therefore implemented a routine that is able to randomly select individuals for tournament selection in the union of individuals of the population and the tree archive.

## 5.5 Experiments

In this section, we introduce different test functions first. Then, experiments of running the three Quad-tree algorithms and the linear list implementation for different test functions are presented. In particular, we investigate the influence of the three parameters of (a) population size $|P|$, (b) archive size $|A|$, and (c) dimension $m$ of the objective space on the CPU time for the linear list and the three Quad-tree implementations.

### 5.5.1 Test Functions

There exist many test functions that are used for testing MOEAs, e.g., those introduced in Deb et al. [10] and Zitzler et al. [9]. They are built with consideration to difficulties in MO like converging to the true Pareto-optimal front and maintaining diversity within the archive. For the following experiment, we have also used these functions which are 2- to 10-objective minimization problems. Table 5.1 shows the used test functions. Tests TF1 to TF6 are optimization problems with 2 objectives:

$$\text{minimize } \mathbf{f}(\mathbf{x}) = (f_1(x_1), f_2(\mathbf{x}))$$
$$\text{subject to } f_2(\mathbf{x}) = g(x_2, \cdots, x_n) \cdot h(f_1(x_1), g(x_2, \cdots, x_n))$$
$$\text{where } \mathbf{x} = (x_1, \cdots, x_n)$$

DTLZ$m$ denotes a class of test problems where $m = 1, \cdots, 10$ indicates the number of objectives.

**Influence of Population size $|P|$ on CPU time for test functions with $m = 2$**

The first experiments were performed using the two-objective test functions TF1, TF2, $\cdots$, TF6 with $m = 2$ dimensions and unbounded archive size. So, the free parameter is the size $|P|$ of the population. Figure 5.12 and Table 5.2 present and compare the average CPU times over different runs when running each algorithm for 400 generations and for different population sizes. The recorded archive sizes for different test functions have ranged depending on initial seed between 110-127 for TF1, 20-30 for TF2, 190-215 for TF3, 25-33 for TF4, 10-15 for TF5 and 29-38 for TF6 independent on the use of linear

**Table 5.1.** Test functions.

| Test | Function | $x_i$ |
|------|----------|-------|
| TF1 | $f_1(x_1) = x_1$ <br> $g(x_2, \cdots, x_n) = 1 + 9(\sum_{i=2}^{n} x_i)/(n-1)$ <br> $h(f_1, g) = 1 - \sqrt{f_1/g}$ | $n = 30,$ <br> $x_i \in [0,1]$ |
| TF2 | $f_1(x_1) = x_1$ <br> $g(x_2, \cdots, x_n) = 1 + 9(\sum_{i=2}^{n} x_i)/(n-1)$ <br> $h(f_1, g) = 1 - (f_1/g)^2$ | $n = 30,$ <br> $x_i \in [0,1]$ |
| TF3 | $f_1(x_1) = x_1$ <br> $g(x_2, \cdots, x_n) = 1 + 9(\sum_{i=2}^{n} x_i)/(n-1)$ <br> $h(f_1, g) = 1 - \sqrt{f_1/g} - (f_1/g)\sin(10\pi f_1)$ | $n = 30,$ <br> $x_i \in [0,1]$ |
| TF4 | $f_1(x_1) = x_1$ <br> $g(x_2, \cdots, x_n) = 1 + 9(\sum_{i=2}^{n} x_i)/(n-1)$ <br> $h(f_1, g) = 1 - (f_1/g)^2 - (f_1/g)\sin(10\pi f_1)$ | $n = 30,$ <br> $x_i \in [0,1]$ |
| TF5 | $f_1(x_1) = x_1$ <br> $g(x_2, \cdots, x_n) =$ <br> $1 + 10(n-1)\sum_{i=2}^{n} (x_i^2 - 10\cos(4\pi x_i))$ <br> $h(f_1, g) = 1 - \sqrt{f_1/g} - (f_1/g)\sin(10\pi f_1)$ | $n = 10,$ <br> $x_1 \in [0,1],$ <br> $x_2, \cdots, x_n \in$ <br> $[-5,5]$ |
| TF6 | $f_1(x_1) = 1 + u(x_1)$ <br> $g(x_2, \cdots, x_n) = \sum_{i=2}^{n} v(u(x_i))$ <br> $h(f_1, g) = 1/f_1$ | $n = 11,$ <br> $x_1 \in \{0,1\}^{30},$ <br> $x_2, \cdots, x_n \in$ <br> $\{0,1\}^5$ |
| DTLZm | $f_1(\mathbf{x}) = (1 + x_n^2)\cos(x_1\pi/2)\cos(x_2\pi/2)\cdots\cos(x_n\pi/2)$ <br> $f_2(\mathbf{x}) = (1 + x_n^2)\cos(x_1\pi/2)\cos(x_2\pi/2)\cdots\sin(x_n\pi/2)$ <br> $\vdots$ <br> $f_M(\mathbf{x}) = (1 + x_n^2)\sin(x_1\pi/2)$ | $n = m,$ <br> $x_i \in [0,1]$ <br><br> $m = 3 - 10$ |

lists or Quad-trees. Therefore, all these experiments have this property that the archive size $|A|$ is rather small as compared to the population size $|P|$, i.e., $|A| \ll |P|$ in common. Also, the archive sizes did not grow with increasing population size (between 100 and 5,000).

*Discussion:*

- Comparison of Quad-tree1, Quad-tree2, and Quad-tree3: In Figure 5.12, it can be seen that for large population sizes, there is almost no difference in CPU time between the three different Quad-tree variants. However, for

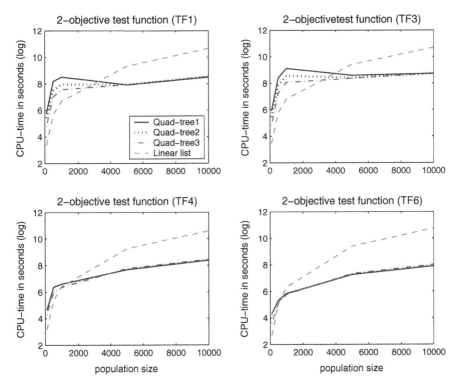

**Figure 5.12.** Average CPU time for different 2-objective test functions for different population sizes $|P|$.

small population sizes, the Quad-tree3 is always the faster implementation among the three.

- Comparison of Quad-tree and linear list archives: In Figure 5.12, one can also see that linear list archives perform better for small population sizes, and depending on the test function, there is a certain population size in the range of 1,000-5,000 for which the Quad-tree approach becomes faster. For example, we see in Table 5.2 that Quad-tree3 is almost 10 times faster than the linear list implementation for larger population sizes.

As a summary, we can conclude that for small dimensions ($m$) of the objective space and for problems with $|A| \ll |P|$, Quad-trees are the better data structure for large population sizes.

### Influence of number of objectives $m$ and population size $|P|$ on CPU time

The second set of experiments involve the test of the influence of the dimensionality $m$ of the objective space and archive size $|A|$ on the CPU time, again compared for the linear list and the three Quad-tree implementations.

**Table 5.2.** Average CPU times in seconds for different population sizes of the six 2-objective test functions TF1 to TF6 (from top to bottom) ($T_i/L$ is the ratio of Quad-tree$_i$'s CPU time to the CPU time when using linear lists.)

| $|P|$ | linear list | Quad-tree1 | Quad-tree2 | Quad-tree3 | T1/L | T2/L | T3/L |
|---|---|---|---|---|---|---|---|
| 100 | 30.68 | 332.90 | 232.83 | 118.99 | 10.85 | 7.59 | 3.88 |
| 500 | 294.71 | 3629.58 | 1859.02 | 1133.81 | 12.32 | 6.31 | 3.85 |
| 1000 | 818.54 | 4952.93 | 2840.45 | 1937.81 | 6.05 | 3.47 | 2.37 |
| 5000 | 11299.92 | 2774.41 | 2826.68 | 2794.71 | 0.25 | 0.25 | 0.25 |
| 10000 | 42274.91 | 4898.97 | 5100.49 | 5160.54 | 0.12 | 0.12 | 0.12 |
| 100 | 24.21 | 120.60 | 91.05 | 74.68 | 4.98 | 3.76 | 3.08 |
| 500 | 186.61 | 244.68 | 253.87 | 234.20 | 1.31 | 1.36 | 1.26 |
| 1000 | 537.58 | 418.46 | 446.45 | 456.18 | 0.78 | 0.83 | 0.85 |
| 5000 | 10328.27 | 2066.73 | 2218.92 | 2326.68 | 0.20 | 0.21 | 0.23 |
| 10000 | 40091.71 | 4142.21 | 4385.24 | 4517.08 | 0.10 | 0.11 | 0.11 |
| 100 | 31.82 | 370.47 | 234.36 | 126.56 | 11.64 | 7.37 | 3.98 |
| 500 | 318.48 | 4389.25 | 2515.66 | 1387.84 | 13.78 | 7.90 | 4.36 |
| 1000 | 916.46 | 9097.29 | 5283.90 | 3178.60 | 9.93 | 5.77 | 3.47 |
| 5000 | 12234.25 | 5383.50 | 4484.65 | 4300 | 0.44 | 0.37 | 0.35 |
| 10000 | 44055.57 | 6163.18 | 6212.26 | 6195.52 | 0.14 | 0.14 | 0.14 |
| 100 | 23.35 | 105.75 | 99.50 | 75.45 | 4.53 | 4.26 | 3.23 |
| 500 | 216.72 | 586.77 | 363.53 | 387.83 | 2.71 | 1.68 | 1.79 |
| 1000 | 626.88 | 745.08 | 640.92 | 580.44 | 1.19 | 1.02 | 0.93 |
| 5000 | 10524.19 | 2176.9 | 2336.12 | 2393.23 | 0.21 | 0.22 | 0.23 |
| 10000 | 40317.49 | 4355.43 | 4707.76 | 4655.86 | 0.11 | 0.12 | 0.12 |
| 100 | 20.20 | 41.66 | 44.25 | 45.80 | 2.06 | 2.19 | 2.27 |
| 500 | 176.19 | 207.11 | 216.82 | 228.72 | 1.18 | 1.23 | 1.30 |
| 1000 | 546.19 | 417 | 437.26 | 459.84 | 0.76 | 0.80 | 0.84 |
| 5000 | 10415.29 | 2104.20 | 2223.27 | 2375.99 | 0.20 | 0.21 | 0.23 |
| 10000 | 40410.43 | 4244.57 | 4454.04 | 4632.82 | 0.11 | 0.11 | 0.11 |
| 100 | 14.50 | 76.92 | 69.04 | 36.82 | 5.30 | 4.76 | 2.54 |
| 500 | 161.50 | 209.84 | 201.86 | 165.53 | 1.30 | 1.25 | 1.02 |
| 1000 | 555.29 | 345.70 | 342.95 | 324.13 | 0.62 | 0.62 | 0.58 |
| 5000 | 12090.32 | 1430.13 | 1451.23 | 1543.43 | 0.12 | 0.12 | 0.13 |
| 10000 | 47489.3 | 2728.1 | 2819.97 | 3038.54 | 0.06 | 0.06 | 0.06 |

Figure 5.13 shows the measured CPU times of different test functions for a different number of objectives, and again for different population sizes. As the results of Quad-tree3 were also better than the two other Quad-tree implementations (this will be discussed later), we just compare Quad-tree3 as Quad-tree with linear list archives.

*Discussion:*

• Influence of $m$ on CPU time: In Figure 5.13, we can see that for the 3-objective test function, the Quad-tree can be up to 10 times slower than the linear list archive with the break-even point of equal CPU time shifted here

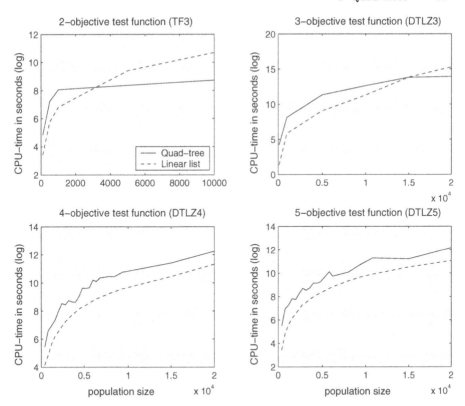

**Figure 5.13.** Average CPU time of $m$-objective test functions for different population sizes.

up to a population size of $|P| = 15,000$. Only for larger population sizes is the Quad-tree faster here. For the even higher-dimensional test functions (4 and 5), the linear list implementation is faster than the Quad-tree for population sizes of up to 20,000 individuals.

- Influence of archive size $|A|$ on CPU time: Contrary to the test functions with only 2 objectives, we found out that in all of these higher-dimensional test functions, the archive size increased also with increasing population size. Figure 5.14 shows the recorded archive sizes for different population sizes for the 4-objective test function DTLZ4. The archive size of this test function contains more than 60000 vectors when the population size has been chosen to 20,000. As it seems that it is not the number $m$ of objectives alone but the dimensionality of the approximated Pareto-front, and as a consequence, the archive size $|A|$ that must be taken into account in order to compare linear lists with Quad-trees, we need to take a deeper look at the number of reinsertions that must be performed that might become the bottleneck in performance for problems with large archive sizes.

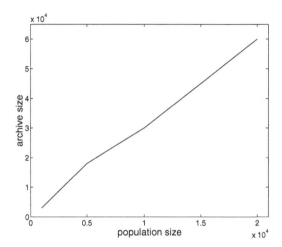

**Figure 5.14.** Archive sizes of the 4-objective test function according to different population sizes.

**Influence of archive size $|A|$ and $m$ on CPU time for large constant population size $|P|$**

Figure 5.15 shows the CPU times of the Quad-tree and the linear list implementations for different archive size bounds and a fixed population size of $|P| = 20,000$ for the four test functions DTLZ$m$ with $m = 3, 4, 5, 6$. It can be seen that the Quad-tree algorithm is faster when the archive size is less than about 2,000 for the 3-objective test function, 3,000 for the 4-objective test, 6000 for the 5-objective test and 7,000 for the 6-objective test function.

*Discussion:*

- The above observation confirms that for increasing archive sizes, the Quad-tree implementation becomes less competitive than the linear list implementation. This may be related to the fact that for larger archive sizes, the number of costly reinsertions of already inserted points can destroy the advantage gained when not having to walk through the whole list of Pareto points. Reinsertion takes place for all nodes of subtrees when their root node is dominated and must be deleted. Therefore, we also record the number of deletions and reinsertions depending on the archive size.

Table 5.3 lists the number of recorded deletions and reinsertions in a Quad-tree for different population and archive sizes and test functions with different number of objectives.

*Discussion:*

- We can see that the above test functions and SPEA behave such that when the population size increases, the archive size increases, too.

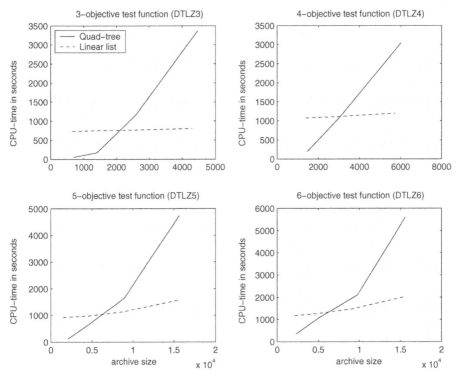

**Figure 5.15.** Average CPU time of $m$-objective test functions DTLZ$m$, $m = 3, 4, 5, 6$ according to different archive size bounds $|A|$ and fixed population size $|P| = 20000$.

**Table 5.3.** Number of deletions and reinsertions in the Quad-tree archive for the $m$-objective test functions DTLZ$m$ (T is the CPU time in seconds).

| $m$ | $|P|$ | $|A|$ | Deletions | Reinsertions | T |
|-----|-------|-------|-----------|--------------|-----|
| 4 | 100 | 290 | 1111 | 2600 | 22 |
|   | 500 | 1180 | 6080 | 15600 | 432 |
|   | **1000** | **3300** | **12200** | **36150** | **1280** |
|   | 2000 | 7150 | 22050 | 49500 | 3235 |
|   | 5000 | 16350 | 68650 | 149770 | 17200 |
| 5 | **1000** | **4200** | **12500** | **30400** | **1830** |
|   | 5000 | 19950 | 50071 | 105600 | 17850 |
| 6 | **1000** | **3800** | **12710** | **29000** | **2280** |
|   | 5000 | 18750 | 57488 | 127750 | 30500 |
| 7 | **1000** | **5200** | **10000** | **23000** | **4240** |
|   | 5000 | 23400 | 56400 | 117650 | 56700 |
| 10 | **1000** | **5150** | **3170** | **11245** | **17400** |
|   | 5000 | 23542 | 33216 | 88074 | 314131 |

- The archive size can be much larger than the population size ($|P| \ll |A|$).
- Consider now all rows of equal population size 1,000 in Table 5.3. We observe that for a certain archive size, higher values of $m$ reduce the number of reinsertions and deletions. This is because each node in the tree can have at most $2^m - 2$ sons, and for higher values of $m$, the width of the tree is considerably higher whereas for smaller values of $m$, the depth is considerably higher. For example, for $m = 10$, each node can have up to 1,022 sons whereas for $m = 4$, it can have only up to 14 sons. Hence, for a given archive size and large $m$, the tree won't have a large depth but rather a large width.
- For lower values of $m$ and certain archive size, the deletion of a dominated node therefore requires in average a large number of reinsertions because the subtrees will be larger on average than for archive trees for higher values of $m$.
- Finally, the CPU time increases with increasing $m$ because the number of required comparison increases. For each insertion, at most $2^m/2 - 1$ nodes must be checked if they are dominated by the new vector.

All the above experiments present average values obtained from several runs of the MOEA with different seeds and equal number of generations. The values of crossover and mutation probabilities have also been kept constant.

### 5.5.2 Comparison

From the results and the discussion in the previous section, we can conclude that the number of comparisons and CPU times depend on three factors: number of objectives ($m$), archive size ($|A|$) and the population size ($|P|$).

It is recorded by Sun and Steuer [8] that Quad-trees have always better CPU times than linear lists for storing non-dominated solutions, especially for large number of points to insert. They have studied 2- to 8-objective tests with 100-10,000 randomly generated vectors to be considered for inclusion into an initially empty tree. Hence, they never obtained a tree of size larger than this number of points. Indeed, with randomly generated sequences, the archive size in their experiments was always much smaller. The experiments therefore are only valid in our context for optimization problems with only 1 generation. As our results of implementing the archive data structure into a MOEA and dynamically updating the archive with elements of the actual population from generation to generation have shown, the archive size can grow much larger than the population size. In that case, we found out that Quad-trees can become slower than linear list implementations. For example, in Sun and Steuer's tests, the archive size for an example with 8-objective and 10,000 vectors for inclusion has been about 2,400 (when the search space is [0,1]). In the DTLZ test functions that we have chosen, the archive size can become even as big as 60,000. This was the reason why we were able to discover that Quad-trees can be worse than linear list implementations.

Unfortunately, little is known about the average height of a tree, e.g. binary trees, when both insertion and deletion are used [13]. So as a rule of thumb, we can say that Quad-trees are more efficient than linear list archives when used in MOEAs when the archive sizes are small and the population sizes are large. When we are dealing with smaller population sizes and larger archive sizes, our experiments indicate that linear lists take less CPU time than Quad-trees. Figure 5.16 tries to identify regions of better usefulness of both kinds of data structures. Therefore, if Quad-trees are used, the size of the archive should be rather small. Keeping the size of archive as a fixed value is also a desired property of the MOEA methods, like SPEA, PAES, and others. Under this restriction we are able to conclude that Quad-trees take less CPU time than linear lists when used inside MOEAs with restricted archive size.

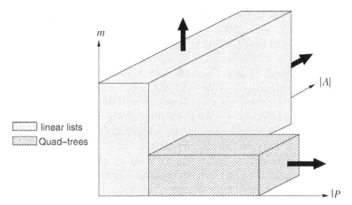

**Figure 5.16.** Regions of applicability of linear list and Quad-tree as archive data structures within MOEA depending on the archive size $|A|$, population size $|P|$ and number of objectives $m$.

## 5.6 Conclusion and Future Work

We have studied and compared Quad-trees as a data structure for the archive of elitist MOEAs with linear list implementations. It has been shown that Quad-trees take less computational (CPU) time in comparison to linear lists for large population sizes and small archive sizes. Hence, as a rule of thumb, we recommend the use of Quad-trees for problems with large populations but small archive sizes. This is the case for problems with large search spaces but where the Pareto fronts are non-continuous curves or just point sets of small cardinality.

In the future, we would like to investigate and compare other alternative data structures. Thereby, we will consider also the complexity of other operations apart from insertion and deletion, such as fitness computation.

Obviously, this operation might also influence the choice of the data structure used.

## Acknowledgment

We would like to thank Ambrish Tyagi for implementing the three Quad-tree algorithms and integrating them into the SPEA multiobjective evolutionary algorithm.

## References

1. Deb, K, Multi-Objective Optimization Using Evolutionary Algorithms. John Wiley & Sons,Chichester, 2001.
2. Corne, D, Dorigo, M and Glover, F, New Ideas in Optimization. UK, Mc Graw Hill, 1999.
3. Zitzler, E, Laumanns, M and Thiele, L, SPEA2: Improving the Strength Pareto Evolutionary Algorithm. In EUROGEN 2001, Evolutionary Methods for Design, Optimisation and Control with Applications to Industrial Problems, 2001.
4. Rudolph, G, On a Multi-Objective Evolutionary Algorithm and Its Convergence to the Pareto Set. In Proceedings of the 5th IEEE Conference on Evolutionary Computation, pp. 511-516, IEEE Press, 1998.
5. Rudolph, G and Agapie, A, Convergence Properties of Some Multi-Objective Evolutionary Algorithms. In Proceedings of the 2000 Congress on Evolutionary Computation, pp. 1010-1016, Piscataway, NJ, 2000. IEEE Service Center, 2000.
6. Finkel, RA and Bentley, JL, Quad Trees: A Data Structure for Retrieval on Composite Keys, Acta Informatica, 1974;4: 1-9.
7. Habenicht, W, Quad Trees, a Data Structure for Discrete Vector Optimization Problems. In Lecture Notes in Economic and Mathematical Systems, pp. 136-145, Springer-Verlag, 1983.
8. Sun, M and Steuer, RE, Quad Trees and Linear List for Identifying Nondominated Criterion Vectors. In INFORM Journal on Computing, 1996; 8(4): pp. 367-375.
9. Zitzler, E and Thiele, L, Multiobjective Evolutionary Algorithms: A Comparative Case Study and the Strength Pareto Approach. In IEEE Transactions on Evolutionary Computation, 1999; 3(4): pp. 257-271.
10. Deb, K, Thiele, L, Laumanns, M and Zitzler, E, Scalable Multi-objective Optimization Test Problems. In IEEE Proceedings, World Congress on Computational Intelligence (CEC02), USA, 2002.
11. Deb, K, Agrawal, S, Pratap, A and Meyarivan, T, A Fast Elitist Non-dominated Sorting Genetic Algorithm for Multi-objective Optimization: NSGA II. In Parallel Problem Solving from Nature VI (PPSN VI), pp. 849-858, 2000.
12. Goldberg, DE, Genetic Algorithms in Search, Optimization and Machine Learning. Reading, MA: Addison-Wesley, 1989.
13. Cormen, TH, Leiserson, CE and Rivest, RL, *Introduction to Algorithms*. The MIT Press - Mc Graw Hill, 1990.

# 6

## Scalable Test Problems
## for Evolutionary Multiobjective Optimization

Kalyanmoy Deb, Lothar Thiele, Marco Laumanns and Eckart Zitzler

**Summary.** After adequately demonstrating the ability to solve different two-objective optimization problems, multiobjective evolutionary algorithms (MOEAs) must demonstrate their efficacy in handling problems having more than two objectives. In this study, we have suggested three different approaches for systematically designing test problems for this purpose. The simplicity of construction, scalability to any number of decision variables and objectives, knowledge of the shape and the location of the resulting Pareto-optimal front, and introduction of controlled difficulties in both converging to the true Pareto-optimal front and maintaining a widely distributed set of solutions are the main features of the suggested test problems. Because of the above features, they should be found useful in various research activities on MOEAs, such as testing the performance of a new MOEA, comparing different MOEAs, and better understanding of the working principles of MOEAs.

## 6.1 Introduction

Most earlier studies on multi-objective evolutionary algorithms (MOEAs) introduced test problems which were either too simple or not scalable in terms of number of objectives and decision variables. Some test problems were too complicated to visualize the exact shape and location of the resulting Pareto-optimal front. Schaffer's [1] study introduced two single-variable test problems (SCH1 and SCH2), which have been widely used as test problems. Kursawe's test problem [2], KUR, was scalable to any number of decision variables, but was not scalable in terms of the number of objectives. The same is true with Fonseca and Fleming's test problem [3], FON. Poloni et al.'s test problem [4], POL used only two decision variables. Although the mathematical formulation of the problem is non-linear, the resulting Pareto-optimal front corresponds to an almost linear relationship among decision variables. Viennet's test problem [5], VNT, has a discrete set of Pareto-optimal fronts, but was designed for three objectives only. Similar simplicity prevails in the existing constrained test problems [6, 7].

However, in 1999, the first author, for the first time, introduced a systematic procedure of designing two-objective test problems which are simple to construct and are scalable to the number of decision variables [8]. In these problems, the exact shape and location of the Pareto-optimal front are also known. The basic construction used two functionals, $g$ and $h^*$, with non-overlapping sets of decision variables to introduce difficulties towards the convergence to the true Pareto-optimal front and to introduce difficulties along the Pareto-optimal front for an MOEA to find a widely distributed set of solutions, respectively. The construction procedure adopted in that study is not the only alternative for the test problem design and certainly many other principles are possible. In the absence of any other systematic construction procedure, those test problems have been used by many researchers since then. However, they have also been somewhat criticized for the relative independence feature of the functionals in achieving both the tasks. Such critics have overlooked an important aspect of that study. The non-overlapping property of the two key functionals in the test problems was introduced for ease of the construction procedure. That study also suggested the use of a procedure to map the original variable vector (say $\mathbf{y}$) on which an MOEA works to a different decision variable vector (say $\mathbf{x}$) with a transformation matrix: $\mathbf{x} = \mathcal{M}\mathbf{y}$. This way, although test problems are constructed for two non-overlapping sets from $\mathbf{x}$, each dependent variable $x_i$ involves a correlation of all (or many) variables of $\mathbf{y}$. Such a mapping couples both aspects of convergence and maintenance of diversity and makes the problem harder to solve. However, Zitzler et al. [9] showed that six test problems designed based on an uncorrelated version of Deb's construction procedure were even difficult to solve exactly using the then-known state-of-the-art MOEAs.

In the recent past, many MOEAs have adequately demonstrated their ability to solve two-objective optimization problems by including three basic operators: (1) an elite-preserving operator, (2) a niche-preserving operator, and (3) a non-domination based selection operator. With the suggestion of a number of such MOEAs, it is time that they must be investigated for their ability to solve problems with more than two objectives. In order to help achieve such studies, it is therefore necessary to develop scalable test problems for a larger number of objectives. Besides testing an MOEA's ability to solve problems with a large number of objectives, the proposed test problems may also be used for systematically comparing two or more MOEAs. Since one such test problem can be used to test a particular aspect of multiobjective optimization, such as for convergence to the true Pareto-optimal front or maintenance of a good spread of solutions, etc., the test problems can be used to identify MOEAs which are better in terms of that particular aspect. For these reasons, these test problems may help provide a better understanding of the working principles of MOEAs, thereby allowing a user to develop better and more efficient MOEAs.

In the remainder of the study, we first describe the desired features needed in a test problem and then suggest three approaches for systematically designing test problems for multiobjective optimization algorithms. Although most problems are illustrated for three objectives (for ease of illustration), the test problems are generic and scalable to an arbitrary number of objectives. Finally, we suggest a set of nine test problems based on the suggested construction procedures and show the difficulties faced by two MOEAs (NSGA-II and SPEA2) in solving these problems.

A short version of this study appeared elsewhere [10],but this study describes different test problem design procedures in a more systematic manner and presents more simulation results. Hopefully, the techniques suggested in this study would be useful in designing further test problems for multiobjective optimization.

## 6.2 Desired Features of Test Problems

The ultimate goal of developing any optimization algorithm is to solve real-world optimization problems reliably and efficiently. However, since in real-world optimization problems the nature of landscape and optimum solution(s) are not usually known beforehand, at the end of a simulation run, it becomes difficult to test how well an algorithm has performed. For this purpose, there is a need to develop test problems for testing optimization algorithms. Since the landscape and corresponding optimum solution(s) of such problems will be known, they allow to test an algorithm's ability to overcome the difficulties posed by the landscape and ability to converge near the optimum solution(s). Keeping in mind the ultimate goal of solving real-world problems, it then becomes important to construct test problems which are representative to real-world problems. However, since real-world problems can be very different from each other and since their landscapes may not be known a priori, it is essential to design a test suite, instead of a single test problem, for the task. This way, various complexities which may be present in real-world problems may be introduced systematically in a number of test problems.

Besides handling different landscape complexities, algorithms should be scalable to the problem size. An algorithm which is efficient in solving a problem with a few decision variables may not work well (or may work with exponentially more computations) in higher problem sizes. Therefore, it is desirable that a test suite, containing test problems each of which is capable of testing an algorithm's ability to handle different aspects of landscape complexity, is also scalable to the problem size. This way, a test problem not only allows to study a particular landscape complexity, but also allows to test how that landscape complexity scales with increased problem sizes. Based on this discussion, we suggest the following features that a test problem suite should have for adequately testing an MOEA:

1. Test problems should introduce controllable hindrance to converge to the true Pareto-optimal front and also to find a widely distributed set of

Pareto-optimal solutions. This is because convergence near to the Pareto-optimal front and maintenance of a diverse set of solutions are two basic goals in multiobjective optimization.

2. Test problems may be scalable to have any number of decision variables. This is because many real-world problems usually involve a large number of decision variables. For all practical purposes, test problems involving a few hundred variables may be included in the test suite.

3. Test problems should be scalable to have any number of objectives. Although in most real-world problems the number of objectives can be reduced to four or five, test problems involving as large as 15 to 20 objectives may be included in the test suite.

4. Test problems may be simple to construct. This may not be an essential matter for constructing test problems, but if desired features can be incorporated in test problems with a simple construction procedure, it is always desirable.

5. The resulting Pareto-optimal front (continuous or discrete) may be easy to comprehend, and its shape and location may be exactly known. The corresponding decision variable values may also be easy to find.

6. To make the test problems useful in practice, they should exhibit difficulties similar to those present in most real-world problems.

It is important to mention that the fifth feature described above may not be of much importance for comparing two or more MOEAs. But for evaluating an MOEA's performance in convergence and maintenance of diversity, knowledge of the exact Pareto-optimal set is essential.

Along with the test problems designed by keeping the above features in mind, it does not do any harm to keep a few additional real-world problems in the test suite. Such problems can be treated as a black-box with a clearly defined set of input decision variables (and their possible ranges) and corresponding objective values and constraints (if any). Many such real-world problems [6, 11] have been already solved using MOEAs and some representative of them can be included in the test suite. A network design application problem along with a number of MOEAs already exist on the PISA [12] web page (http://www.tik.ee.ethz.ch/pisa) for this purpose.

The popularity of two-objective test problems suggested earlier [8] in many research studies is partly because of the ease of constructing the test problems and the ease of illustrating the obtained non-dominated solutions against the true Pareto-optimal solutions in two dimensions. Visually comparing the obtained set of solutions against the true Pareto-optimal front provides a clear idea of the performance of an MOEA. This can somewhat be achieved even for three objectives, with such a comparison shown in three dimensions. But for problems with more than three objectives, it becomes difficult to illustrate such a plot. Thus, for higher-objective test problems, it may be wise to have some regularity in the search space so that the Pareto-optimal surface is easily comprehensible. One of the ways to achieve this would be to have a Pareto-optimal surface symmetric along interesting hyper-planes, such as $f_1 = f_2 = \cdots = f_{M-1}$ (where $M$ is the number of objectives). This only requires a user to comprehend the interaction between $f_M$ and $f_1$, and the rest of the problem can be constructed by using symmetry. Another interesting approach would be to construct a problem for which the Pareto-optimal surface is a symmetric curve or at most a three-dimensional surface. Although $M$-dimensional, the obtained solutions can be easily illustrated parametrically in a two-dimensional plot in the case of a curve and in a three-dimensional plot in the case of the three-dimensional surface.

It is now well established that MOEAs have two tasks to achieve: converging as close to the Pareto-optimal front and finding as diverse a set of solutions on the entire Pareto-optimal front as possible. An MOEA therefore, should be tested for each of the two tasks. Thus, some test problems should test an MOEA's ability to negotiate artificial hurdles which hinder MOEA's progress towards converging to the true Pareto-optimal front. This can be achieved by placing some local Pareto-optimal attractors or biased density of solutions away from the Pareto-optimal front. Test problems must also test an MOEA's ability to find a diverse set of solutions. This can be achieved by making the Pareto-optimal front non-convex, discrete, and having variable density of solutions along the front. Although these features of test problems were also suggested for two-objective problems earlier [8], the technique can be extended to more than two objectives. In any case, the increased dimensionality associated with a large number of objectives may cause added difficulties to MOEAs.

In the following sections, we suggest different approaches of designing test problems for multiobjective optimization.

## 6.3 Different Methods of Test Problem Design

Although the main focus of the above discussion is based on solving real-world problems, there is a need to develop simple-to-understand scalable test problems for theoretical studies, such as studies for analyzing the running time complexity of MOEAs. Keeping in mind all the above issues which may be present in a test problem suite, a number of different construction procedures can be adopted for multiobjective optimization. Here we discuss three different methods:

1. Multiple single-objective functions approach,
2. Bottom-up approach,
3. Constraint surface approach.

The first approach is the most intuitive one and has been implicitly used by early MOEA researchers to construct test problems. In this approach, $M$ different single-objective functions are used to construct a multiobjective test problem. To simplify the construction procedure, in many cases, different objective functions are simply used as different translations of a single objective function. For example, the problem SCH1 uses the following two single-objective functions for minimization [1]:

$$f_1(x) = x^2, \quad f_2(x) = (x-2)^2.$$

Since the optimum $x^{*(1)}$ for $f_1$ is not the optimum for $f_2$ and vice versa, the Pareto-optimal set consists of more than one solution, including the individual minimum of each of the above functions. All other solutions which make trade-offs between the two objective functions with themselves and with the above two solutions become members of the Pareto-optimal set. In the above problem, all solutions $x^* \in [0, 2]$ become members of the Pareto-optimal set. Similarly, the problem FON shown below

$$\begin{cases} \text{Minimize } f_1(\mathbf{x}) = 1 - \exp\left(-\sum_{i=1}^{n}(x_i - \frac{1}{\sqrt{n}})^2\right), \\ \text{Minimize } f_2(\mathbf{x}) = 1 - \exp\left(-\sum_{i=1}^{n}(x_i + \frac{1}{\sqrt{n}})^2\right), \\ \qquad -4 \le x_i \le 4 \quad i = 1, 2, \ldots, n. \end{cases} \tag{6.1}$$

has $x_i^* = -1/\sqrt{n}$ for all $i$ as the minimum solution for $f_1$ and $x_i^* = 1/\sqrt{n}$ for all $i$ as the minimum solution for $f_2$. The Pareto-optimal set is constituted with all solutions in $x_i^* \in [-1/\sqrt{n}, 1/\sqrt{n}]$ for all $i$. Veldhuizen [7] lists a number of other test problems, which follow this construction principle. It is interesting to note that such a construction procedure can be extended to problems having more than two objectives as well [13]. In a systematic procedure, each optimum may be assumed to lie on each of $M$ (usually $< n$) coordinate directions. The main advantage of this procedure is its simplicity and ease of construction. However, the Pareto-optimal set resulting from such a construction depends on the chosen objective functions, thereby making it difficult to comprehend the true nature of the Pareto-optimal front. Moreover, even in simple objective functions (such as in SCH2 [1]), the Pareto-optimal front may be a combination of disconnected fronts. Thus, a test problem constructed using this procedure must be carefully analyzed to find the true Pareto-optimal set of solutions. For running time complexity analysis, a two-objective leading-ones-trailing-zeros (LOTZ) problem was designed recently [14].

The latter two approaches of test problem design mentioned above directly involve the Pareto-optimal front, thereby making them convenient to be used in practice. Since they require detailed discussions, we devote two separate sections to describing them.

## 6.4 Bottom-up Approach

In this approach, a mathematical function describing the Pareto-optimal front is assumed in the objective space and an overall objective space is constructed

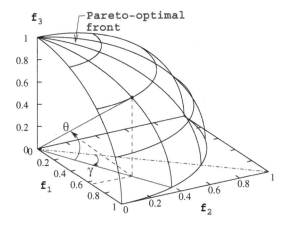

**Figure 6.1.** First quadrant of a unit sphere as a Pareto-optimal front.

from this front to define the test problem. For two objectives, one such construction was briefly suggested earlier [8] and was extended for higher objectives elsewhere [6]. Here we outline the generic procedure through a three-objective example problem:

Step 1: Choose a Pareto-optimal front. The first task in the bottom-up approach is to choose the Pareto-optimal front. For $M$ objectives, this means designing a parametric surface involving $(M-1)$ variables. For illustration purposes, let us assume that we would like to have a Pareto-optimal front in a three-objective problem, where all objective functions take non-negative values and the desired front is the surface of an octant of a sphere of radius one (as shown in Figure 6.1). With the help of spherical coordinates (we call them *parametric* variables) $\theta$, $\gamma$, and $r$ ($= 1$ here), the front can be described as follows:

$$\left.\begin{array}{l} f_1(\theta, \gamma) = \cos\theta\cos(\gamma + \pi/4), \\ f_2(\theta, \gamma) = \cos\theta\sin(\gamma + \pi/4), \\ f_3(\theta, \gamma) = \sin\theta, \\ \text{where} \quad 0 \le \theta \le \pi/2, \\ \qquad\qquad -\pi/4 \le \gamma \le \pi/4. \end{array}\right\} \qquad (6.2)$$

It is clear from the construction of the above surface that if all three objective functions are minimized, any two points on this surface are non-dominated to each other.

Step 2: Build the objective space. Using the chosen Pareto-optimal surface, we construct the complete objective space. A simple way to construct the rest of the objective space is to construct an extreme boundary surface parallel to the Pareto-optimal surface, so that the hyper-volume bounded by these two surfaces constitute the entire objective space. This can be achieved by introducing an additional variable in the parametric

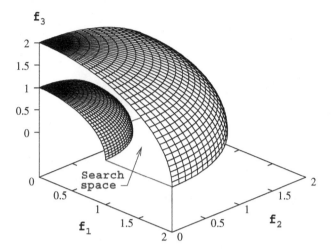

**Figure 6.2.** Overall search space is bounded by the two spheres.

equations. For the example problem, this can be achieved by multiplying the above three functions with a radius term, which takes a value greater than or equal to one. Different values of the third independent variable $r$ (besides $\theta$ and $\gamma$) will construct different layers of spherical surfaces on top of the Pareto-optimal sphere. Thus, the overall problem with the above three variables is as follows:

$$\left.\begin{array}{l} \text{Minimize } f_1(\theta, \gamma, r) = (1 + g(r)) \cos \theta \cos(\gamma + \pi/4), \\ \text{Minimize } f_2(\theta, \gamma, r) = (1 + g(r)) \cos \theta \sin(\gamma + \pi/4), \\ \text{Minimize } f_3(\theta, \gamma, r) = (1 + g(r)) \sin \theta, \\ \quad 0 \leq \theta \leq \pi/2, \\ \quad -\pi/4 \leq \gamma \leq \pi/4, \\ \quad g(r) \geq 0. \end{array}\right\} \quad (6.3)$$

As described earlier, the Pareto-optimal solutions for the above problem are as follows:

$$0 \leq \theta^* \leq \pi/2, \quad -\pi/4 \leq \gamma^* \leq \pi/4, \quad g(r^*) = 0.$$

Figure 6.2 shows the overall objective space with any function for $g(r)$ with $0 \leq g(r) \leq 1$. We shall discuss more about different $g(r)$ functions a little later. The above construction procedure illustrates how easily a multiobjective test problem can be constructed from an initial choice of a Pareto-optimal surface.

Step 3: Construct the decision space. The above construction of the objective space requires exactly $M$ variables, describing an objective vector anywhere in the objective space. The final task is to map each decision variable vector to an objective vector. This mapping provides an additional flexibility in constructing a test problem. For this mapping, any number of decision variables ($n$) can be chosen. If $n < M$, not all parametric variables are independent, thereby causing a reduction in dimensionality of the Pareto-optimal surface. For the three-objective example problem, the three parametric variables used earlier ($\theta$, $\gamma$, and $r$) can each be considered as a function of $n$ decision variables of the underlying problem:

$$\theta = \theta(x_1, x_2, \ldots, x_n), \tag{6.4}$$

$$\gamma = \gamma(x_1, x_2, \ldots, x_n), \tag{6.5}$$

$$r = r(x_1, x_2, \ldots, x_n). \tag{6.6}$$

The functions must be so chosen that they satisfy the lower and upper bounds of $\theta$, $\gamma$ and $g(r)$ mentioned in Equation 6.3.

Although the above construction procedure is simple, it can be used to introduce different modes of difficulty described earlier. In the following, we describe a few such extensions of the above construction.

### 6.4.1 Difficulty in Converging to the Pareto-optimal Front

The difficulty of a search algorithm to progress towards the Pareto-optimal front from the interior of the objective space can be introduced by simply using a difficult $g$ function. It is clear that the Pareto-optimal surface corresponds to the minimum value of function $g$. A multi-modal $g$ function with a global minimum at $g^* = 0$ and many local minima at $g^* = \nu_i$ value will introduce global and local Pareto-optimal fronts, where a multiobjective optimizer can get stuck to.

Moreover, even using a unimodal $g$ function, variable density of solutions can be introduced in the search space. For example, for the three-objective example problem, if $g(r) = r^{10}$ is used, denser solutions exist away from the Pareto-optimal front. Figure 6.3 shows 15,000 solutions, which are randomly created in the decision variable space of the above problem. On the objective space, they are shown to be biased away from the Pareto-optimal front. For such a biased search space away from the Pareto-optimal front, multiobjective optimizers may have difficulties in converging quickly to the desired front.

### 6.4.2 Difficulties Across the Pareto-optimal Front

By using a non-linear mapping between parametric and decision variables, some portion of the search space can be made to have more dense solutions than the rest of the search space. For example, in the three-objective problem a variable density of solutions can be created on the Pareto-optimal front by choosing non-linear expressions for the parametric variables $\theta$ and $\gamma$ in Equations 6.4 to 6.5. For example, Figures 6.4 and 6.5 show the problem stated in Equation 6.3 with

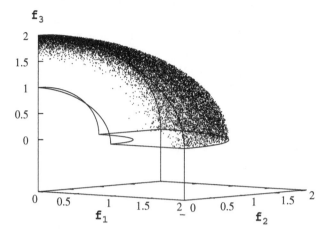

**Figure 6.3.** The effect of a non-linear $g$ function.

$$\theta(x_1) = \tfrac{\pi}{2}x_1, \qquad \theta(x_1) = \tfrac{\pi}{2}0.5\left(1 + [2(x_1 - 0.5)]^{11}\right),$$
$$\gamma(x_2) = \tfrac{\pi}{2}x_2 - \tfrac{\pi}{4}. \quad \text{and} \quad \gamma(x_2) = \tfrac{\pi}{2}0.5\left(1 + [2(x_2 - 0.5)]^{11}\right) - \tfrac{\pi}{4}.$$

respectively. In both cases, $g(r) = r = x_3$ is chosen. In order to satisfy the bounds in Equation 6.3, we have chosen $0 \le x_1, x_2, x_3 \le 1$ and 15,000 randomly created points (in the decision space) are shown in each figure showing the objective space. The figures show the density of solutions in the search space gets affected by the choice of mapping of the parametric variables. In the second problem, there is a natural bias for an algorithm to find solutions in middle region of the search space[1]. In trying to solve such test problems, the task of an MOEA would be to find a widely distributed set of solutions on the entire Pareto-optimal front despite the natural bias of solutions in certain regions on the Pareto-optimal front.

### 6.4.3 Generic Sphere Problem

The following is a generic problem to that described in Equation 6.3, having $M$ objectives.

$$
\begin{aligned}
&\text{Minimize } f_1(\boldsymbol{\theta}, \mathbf{r}) = (1 + g(\mathbf{r})) \cos \theta_1 \cos \theta_2 \cdots \cos \theta_{M-2} \cos \theta_{M-1},\\
&\text{Minimize } f_2(\boldsymbol{\theta}, \mathbf{r}) = (1 + g(\mathbf{r})) \cos \theta_1 \cos \theta_2 \cdots \cos \theta_{M-2} \sin \theta_{M-1},\\
&\text{Minimize } f_3(\boldsymbol{\theta}, \mathbf{r}) = (1 + g(\mathbf{r})) \cos \theta_1 \cos \theta_2 \cdots \sin \theta_{M-2},\\
&\qquad \vdots \qquad\quad \vdots\\
&\text{Minimize } f_{M-1}(\boldsymbol{\theta}, \mathbf{r}) = (1 + g(\mathbf{r})) \cos \theta_1 \sin \theta_2,\\
&\text{Minimize } f_M(\boldsymbol{\theta}, \mathbf{r}) = (1 + g(\mathbf{r})) \sin \theta_1,\\
&\qquad 0 \le \theta_i \le \pi/2, \quad \text{for } i = 1, 2, \dots, (M-1),\\
&\qquad g(\mathbf{r}) \ge 0.
\end{aligned}
\right\} \tag{6.7}
$$

---

[1] In three-objective knapsack problems, such a biased search space is observed elsewhere [15].

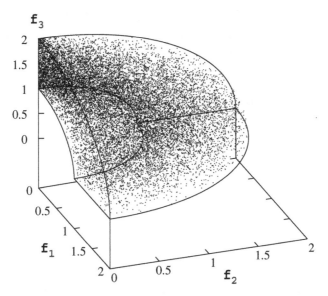

**Figure 6.4.** Linear mapping (15,000 points).

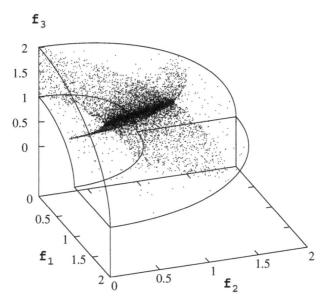

**Figure 6.5.** Non-linear mapping introduces bias in the search space (15,000 points).

Note that the variables are mapped in a different manner here. The decision variables are mapped to the parametric variable vector $\boldsymbol{\theta}$ (of size $(M-1)$) as follows:

$$\theta_i = \frac{\pi}{2}x_i, \quad \text{for } i = 1, 2, \ldots, (M-1). \tag{6.8}$$

The above mapping and the condition on $\theta_i$ in Equation 6.7 restrict each of the above $x_i$ to lie within $[0, 1]$. The rest $(n - M + 1)$ of the decision variables are defined as the $\mathbf{r}$ vector (or $r_i = x_{M+i-1}$ for $i = 1, 2, \ldots, (n - M + 1)$) and a suitable $g(\mathbf{r})$ is chosen. It is clear that the above generic sphere function is defined for $n \geq M$.

The Pareto-optimal surface always occurs for the minimum of $g(\mathbf{r})$ function. For example, if the function $g(\mathbf{r}) = \|\mathbf{r}\|^2$ with $r_i \in [-1, 1]$ is chosen, the Pareto-optimal surface corresponds to $r_i = 0$ and the optimal function values must satisfy the following condition:

$$\sum_{i=1}^{M} (f_i^*)^2 = 1. \tag{6.9}$$

As mentioned earlier, the difficulty of the above test problem can also be varied by using different functionals for $f_i$ and $g$.

### 6.4.4 Curve Problem

Instead of having a complete $M$-dimensional surface as the Pareto-optimal surface, a lower-dimensional surface can also be chosen as the Pareto-optimal front to the above problem. We realize that in this case not all $\theta_i$ variables will be independent to each other. For example, in the case of an $M$-dimensional curve as the Pareto-optimal front, there would be only one independent variable describing the Pareto-optimal front. A simple way to achieve this would be to use the following mapping of variables:

$$\theta_i = \frac{\pi}{4(1 + g(\mathbf{r}))} (1 + 2g(\mathbf{r})x_i), \quad \text{for } i = 2, 3, \ldots, (M - 1), \tag{6.10}$$

The above mapping ensures that the curve is the only non-dominated region in the entire search space. Since $g(\mathbf{r}) = 0$ corresponds to the Pareto-optimal front, $\theta_i = \pi/4$ for all but the first variable. The advantage of this problem over the generic sphere problem as a test problem is that a two-dimensional plot of Pareto-optimal points with $f_M$ and any other $f_i$ will mark a curve (circular or elliptical). A plot with any two objective functions (other than $f_M$) will show a straight line. Figure 6.6 shows a sketch of the objective space and the resulting Pareto-optimal curve for a three-objective version of the above problem. One drawback with this formulation is that the density of solutions closer to the Pareto-optimal curve is more than anywhere else in the search space. In order to make the problem more difficult, a non-linear $g(\mathbf{r})$ function with a higher density of solutions away from $g(\mathbf{r}) = 0$ (such as $g(\mathbf{r}) = 1/\|\mathbf{r}\|^\alpha$, where $\alpha \gg 1$) can be used. Using a multi-modal $g(\mathbf{r})$ function will also cause multiple local Pareto-optimal surfaces to exist. Interestingly, this drawback of the problem can be used to create a hard maximization problem. If all the objectives are maximized in the above problem, the top surface becomes the desired Pareto-optimal front. Since there exist less dense

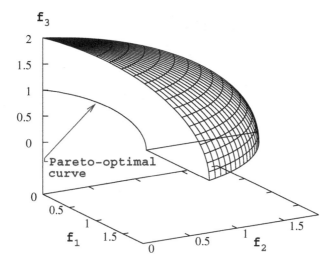

**Figure 6.6.** The search space and the Pareto-optimal curve.

solutions on this surface, this problem may be a difficult maximization test problem.

Degeneration of the Pareto-optimal front to a low-dimensional surface (such as a curve) is not a mere fantasy. This can happen in problems where some objectives are likely to be non-conflicting to each other. For example, in a recent gearbox design problem having three objectives of minimizing overall volume of the gearbox, maximizing power delivered, and minimizing distance between input-output shafts, a three-dimensional curve appeared as the obtained non-dominated front [16]. This is because of the fact that minimization of the first and the third objectives are not intuitively contradictory to each other.

### 6.4.5 Test Problem Generator

The earlier study [6] suggested a generic multiobjective test problem generator, which belongs to this bottom-up approach. For $M$ objective functions, with a complete decision variable vector partitioned into $M$ non-overlapping groups

$$x \equiv (\mathbf{x}_1, \mathbf{x}_2, \ldots, \mathbf{x}_{M-1}, \mathbf{x}_M)^T,$$

the following function was suggested:

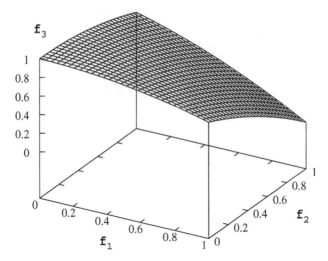

**Figure 6.7.** A non-convex Pareto-optimal front.

Minimize $f_1(\mathbf{x}_1)$,
Minimize $f_2(\mathbf{x}_2)$,

$$\vdots \quad \vdots$$

Minimize $f_{M-1}(\mathbf{x}_{M-1})$,
Minimize $f_M(\mathbf{x}) = g(\mathbf{x}_M)h(f_1(\mathbf{x}_1), f_2(\mathbf{x}_2), \ldots, f_{M-1}(\mathbf{x}_{M-1}), g(\mathbf{x}_M))$,
subject to $\mathbf{x}_i \in \mathbb{R}^{|\mathbf{X}_i|}, \quad$ for $i = 1, 2, \ldots, M$.

$$(6.11)$$

Here, the Pareto-optimal front is described by solutions which are global minimum of $g(\mathbf{x}_M)$ (with $g^*$). Thus, the Pareto-optimal front is described as

$$f_M = g^* h(f_1, f_2, \ldots, f_{M-1}). \qquad (6.12)$$

Since $g^*$ is a constant, the $h$ function (with a fixed $g = g^*$) describes the Pareto-optimal surface. In the bottom-up approach of test problem design, the user can first choose an $h$ function in terms of the objective function values, without caring about the decision variables at first. For example, for constructing a problem with a non-convex Pareto-optimal front, a non-convex $h$ function can be chosen, such as the following:

$$h(f_1, f_2, \ldots, f_{M-1}) = 1 - \left( \frac{\sum_{i=1}^{M-1} f_i}{\beta} \right)^{\alpha}, \qquad (6.13)$$

where $\alpha > 1$. Figure 6.7 shows a non-convex Pareto-optimal front with $\alpha = 2$ for $M = 3$ and $\beta = 0.5$.

A disjoint set of Pareto-optimal fronts can be constructed by simply choosing a multi-modal $h$ function as done in the case of two-objective test problem design [8]. Figure 6.8 illustrates a disconnected set of Pareto-optimal

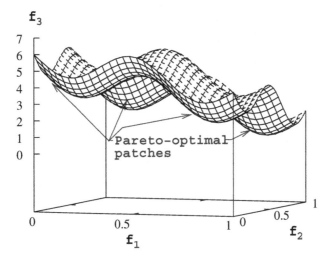

**Figure 6.8.** A disjoint set of Pareto-optimal regions.

surfaces (for three objectives), which can be generated from the following generic $h$ function:

$$h(f_1, f_2, \ldots, f_{M-1}) = 2M - \sum_{i=1}^{M-1} (2f_i + \sin(3\pi f_i)). \qquad (6.14)$$

Once the $h$ function is chosen, a $g$ function can be chosen to construct the entire objective space. It is important to note that the $g$ function is defined over a set of decision variables. Recall also that the Pareto-optimal front corresponds to the global minimum value of the $g$ function. Any other values of $g$ will represent a surface parallel to the Pareto-optimal surface. All points in this parallel surface will be dominated by some solutions in the Pareto-optimal surface. As mentioned earlier, the $g$ function can be used to introduce complexities in approaching towards the Pareto-optimal region. For example, if $g$ has a local minimum, a local Pareto-optimal front exists on the corresponding parallel surface.

Once appropriate $h$ and $g$ functions are chosen, $f_1$ to $f_{M-1}$ can be chosen as functions of different non-overlapping sets of decision variables. Using a non-linear objective function introduces a variable density of solutions along that objective. The non-linearity in these functions will test an MOEA's ability to find a good distribution of solutions, despite the natural non-uniform density of solutions in the objective space. Another way to make the density of solutions non-uniform is to use an overlapping set of decision variables for objective functions. To construct more difficult test problems, the procedure of mapping the decision variables to an intermediate variable vector, as suggested earlier [8] can also be used here.

The recently suggested two-objective counting-ones-counting-zeros problem (COCZ problem) is a test problem developed using the bottom-up approach for running time complexity analysis [17].

### 6.4.6 Advantages and Disadvantages of the Bottom-up Approach

The advantage of using the above bottom-up approach is that the exact form of the Pareto-optimal surface can be controlled by the developer. The number of objectives and the variability in density of solutions can all be controlled by choosing appropriate functions.

Since the Pareto-optimal front must be expressed mathematically, some complicated Pareto-optimal fronts can be difficult to write mathematically. Like the two-objective problems suggested in Deb [8], these problems may also be criticized because of their variable-wise decomposable nature, but we would like to emphasize that this feature is primarily used to facilitate the introduction of different problem difficulties in a simple manner. As before, the problems can be made more complex by using the variable mapping $(\mathbf{x} = \mathcal{M}\mathbf{y})$ discussed in Section 6.1. Nevertheless, the ability to control different features of the problem is the main strength of this approach.

## 6.5 Constraint Surface Approach

Unlike starting from a pre-defined Pareto-optimal surface in the bottom-up approach, the constraint surface approach begins by predefining the overall search space. In the following, we describe the construction procedure.

Step 1: Choose a basic objective space. First, a simple $M$-dimensional bounded region, such as a rectangular hyper-box or an $M$-dimensional hyper-sphere, is assumed. We illustrate the construction principle here with a hyper-box. Each objective function value is restricted to lie within a predefined lower and a upper bound. The resulting problem is as follows:

$$\left. \begin{array}{l} \text{Minimize} \quad f_1(\mathbf{x}), \\ \text{Minimize} \quad f_2(\mathbf{x}), \\ \quad\vdots \qquad\qquad \vdots \\ \text{Minimize} \quad f_M(\mathbf{x}), \\ \text{Subject to } f_i^{(L)} \le f_i(\mathbf{x}) \le f_i^{(U)} \quad \text{for } i = 1, 2, \ldots, M. \end{array} \right\} \qquad (6.15)$$

It is intuitive that the Pareto-optimal set of the above problem has only one solution (the solution with the lower bound of each objective $(f_1^{(L)}, f_2^{(L)}, \ldots, f_1^{(L)})^T$. Figure 6.9 shows this problem for three objectives (with $f_i^{(L)} = 0$ and $f_i^{(U)} = 1$) and the resulting singleton Pareto-optimal solution $\mathbf{f} = (0, 0, 0)^T$) is also marked.

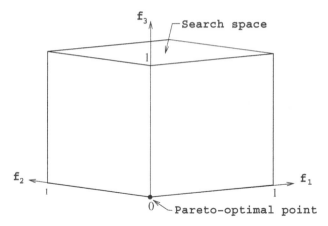

**Figure 6.9.** Entire cube is the search space. The origin is the sole Pareto-optimal solution.

Step 2: Eliminate part of the objective space. Next, a number of constraints (linear or non-linear) involving the objective function values are added:

$$g_j(f_1, f_2, \ldots, f_M) \geq 0, \quad \text{for } j = 1, 2, \ldots, J. \tag{6.16}$$

This is done to chop off portions of the original bounded region systematically. Figure 6.10 shows the resulting feasible region after adding the following two linear constraints on the originally chosen three-objective rectangular box:

$$g_1 \equiv f_1 + f_3 - 0.5 \geq 0,$$
$$g_2 \equiv f_1 + f_2 + f_3 - 0.8 \geq 0.$$

What remains is the feasible search space. The objective of the above problem is to find the non-dominated portion of the boundary of the feasible search space. Figure 6.10 also marks the Pareto-optimal surface of the above problem. For simplicity and easier comprehension, each constraint involving at most two objectives (similar to the first constraint above) can be used.

Step 3: Map decision variable space to objective space. The final task is to map each decision variable vector to the objective space. This can be achieved by choosing each objective function $f_i$ as a linear or non-linear function of $n$ decision variables.

Interestingly, there exist two-variable and three-variable constrained test problems TNK [18] and problems [19] in the literature using the above concept. In these problems, only two objectives (with $f_i = x_i$) and two constraints were used. The use of $f_i = x_i$ made a uniform density of solutions in the search space. As an illustration of further difficulties through non-linear

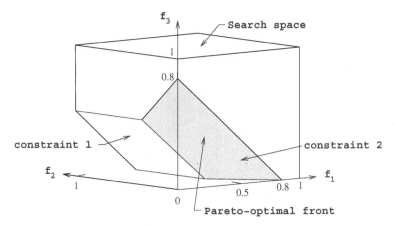

**Figure 6.10.** Two constraints are added to eliminate a portion of the cube, thereby resulting in a more interesting Pareto-optimal front.

$f_i$, we construct the following three-objective problem with a bias in the search space:

$$\begin{aligned}
\text{Minimize} \quad & f_1(x_1) = 1 + (x_1 - 1)^5, \\
\text{Minimize} \quad & f_2(x_2) = x_2, \\
\text{Minimize} \quad & f_3(x_3) = x_3, \\
\text{Subject to} \quad & g_1 \equiv f_3^2 + f_1^2 - 0.5 \geq 0, \\
& g_2 \equiv f_3^2 + f_2^2 - 0.5 \geq 0, \\
& 0 \leq x_1 \leq 2, \\
& 0 \leq x_2, x_3 \leq 1.
\end{aligned} \right\} \quad (6.17)$$

Figure 6.11 shows 25,000 feasible solutions randomly generated in the decision variable space. The Pareto-optimal curve and the feasible region are shown in the figure. Because of the non-linearity in the functional $f_1$ with $x_1$, the search space results in a variable density of solutions along the $f_1$ axis. Solutions are more dense near $f_1 = 1$ than any other region in the search space. Although this apparent plane ($f_1 = 1$) is not a local Pareto-optimal front, an MOEA may get attracted here simply because of the sheer density of solutions near it.

It is clear that by choosing complicated functions of $f_1$ to $f_M$, more complicated search spaces can be created. Since the task of an MOEA is to reach the Pareto-optimal region (which is located at one end of the feasible search space), interesting hurdles in the search space can be placed to provide difficulties to an MOEA to reach the desired Pareto-optimal front.

### 6.5.1 Advantages and Disadvantages

The construction process here is simpler compared to the bottom-up approach. Simple geometric constraints can be used to construct the feasible search

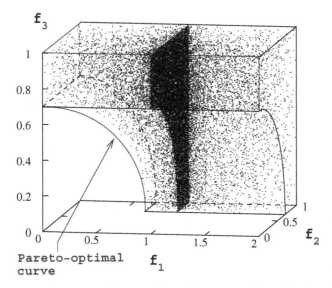

**Figure 6.11.** Non-linearity in functionals produces non-uniform density of solutions.

space. Using this procedure, different shapes (convex, non-convex, or discrete) of the Pareto-optimal region can be generated. Using a systematic choice of constraint surfaces, scalable test problems can be constructed. Unlike the bottom-up approach, here the feasible search space is not constructed by layer-wise construction from the Pareto-optimal front. Since no particular structure is used, the feasible objective space can be derived with any non-linear mapping of the decision variable space.

However, the resulting Pareto-optimal front will, in general, be hard to express mathematically. Moreover, although the constraint surfaces can be simple, the shape and continuity of the resulting Pareto-optimal front may not be easy to visualize. Another difficulty is that since the Pareto-optimal front will lie on one or more constraint boundaries, a good constraint-handling strategy must be used with an MOEA. Thus, this approach may be ideal for testing MOEAs for their ability to handle constraints.

## 6.6 Difficulties with Existing MOEAs

Most MOEA studies up until now have considered two objectives, except a few application studies where more than two objectives are used. This is not to say that the existing MOEAs cannot be applied to problems having more than two objectives. Developers of the state-of-the-art MOEAs (such as PAES [20], SPEA [15], NSGA-II [21] and others) have all considered the scalability aspect while developing their algorithms. The domination principle, non-dominated sorting algorithms, elite-preserving and other EA operators can all be extended for handling more than two objectives. Although the niching operator can also be applied in most cases, their computational issues and ability in maintaining a good distribution of solutions need to be investigated in higher-objective problems. For example, a niching operator may attempt to maintain a good distribution of solutions by replacing a crowded solution with a less crowded one and the crowding of a solution may be determined by the distance from its neighbors. For two objectives, the definition of a neighbor along the Pareto-optimal curve is clear and involves only two solutions (left and right solutions). However, for more than two objectives, when the Pareto-optimal front is a higher-dimensional surface, it is not clear which (and how many) solutions are neighbors of a solution. Even if a definition can be made, calculation of a metric to compute distances from all neighbors gets computationally expensive because of the added dimensionality. Although a widely distributed set of solutions can be found, as using NSGA-II or SPEA2, the obtained distribution can be far from being a uniformly distributed set of points on the Pareto-optimal surface. Niching methods are usually designed to attain a uniform distribution (provided that the EA operators are able to generate the needed solutions), the overall process may be much slower in problems with a large number of objectives. The test problems suggested in this study will certainly enable researchers to make such a complexity study for the state-of-the-art MOEAs.

Although the distribution of solutions is a matter to test for problems with a large number of objectives, it is also important to keep track of the convergence to the true Pareto-optimal front. Because of sheer increase in the dimensionality in the objective space, interactions among decision variables may produce difficulties in terms of having local Pareto-optimal fronts and variable density of solutions. An increase in dimensionality of the objective space also causes a large proportion of a random initial population to be non-dominated to each other [6], thereby reducing the effect of the selection operator in an MOEA. Thus, it is also important to test if the existing domination-based MOEAs can reach the true Pareto-optimal front in such test problems. Since the desired front will be known in test problems, a convergence metric (such as average distance to the front) can be used to track the convergence of an algorithm.

## 6.7 Test Problem Suite

Using the latter two approaches of test problem design discussed in this study, we suggest here a representative set of test problems – DTLZ problems named with the first letter of the last names of the authors. In all cases, the problem can be made more difficult by using a different set of variables $\mathbf{y}$ obtained from the decision variable vector $\mathbf{x}$ by a transformation: $\mathbf{y} = \mathcal{M}\mathbf{x}$ (where $\mathcal{M}$ is a $n \times n$ transformation matrix). However, other more interesting and useful test problems can also be designed using the techniques of this study.

### 6.7.1 Test Problem DTLZ1

As a simple test problem, we construct an $M$-objective problem with a linear Pareto-optimal front:

$$\left.\begin{array}{l} \text{Minimize } f_1(\mathbf{x}) = \frac{1}{2}x_1 x_2 \cdots x_{M-1}(1 + g(\mathbf{x}_M)), \\ \text{Minimize } f_2(\mathbf{x}) = \frac{1}{2}x_1 x_2 \cdots (1 - x_{M-1})(1 + g(\mathbf{x}_M)), \\ \quad \vdots \quad \vdots \\ \text{Minimize } f_{M-1}(\mathbf{x}) = \frac{1}{2}x_1(1 - x_2)(1 + g(\mathbf{x}_M)), \\ \text{Minimize } f_M(\mathbf{x}) = \frac{1}{2}(1 - x_1)(1 + g(\mathbf{x}_M)), \\ \text{subject to } 0 \le x_i \le 1, \quad \text{for } i = 1, 2, \ldots, n. \end{array}\right\} \quad (6.18)$$

The last $k = (n - M + 1)$ variables are represented as $\mathbf{x}_M$. The functional $g(\mathbf{x}_M)$ requires $|\mathbf{x}_M| = k$ variables and must take any function with $g \ge 0$. We suggest the following:

$$g(\mathbf{x}_M) = 100 \left[ |\mathbf{x}_M| + \sum_{x_i \in \mathbf{X}_M} (x_i - 0.5)^2 - \cos(20\pi(x_i - 0.5)) \right]. \quad (6.19)$$

The Pareto-optimal solution corresponds to $x_i = 0.5$ (for all $x_i \in \mathbf{x}_M$) and the objective function values lie on the linear hyper-plane: $\sum_{m=1}^{M} f_m^* = 0.5$. The only difficulty provided by this problem is the convergence to the Pareto-optimal hyper-plane. The search space contains $(11^k - 1)$ local Pareto-optimal fronts, where an MOEA can get attracted before reaching the global Pareto-optimal front.

To demonstrate how a couple of state-of-the-art MOEAs perform on this and other test problems suggested in this study, we have applied NSGA-II and SPEA2 to the three-objective ($M = 3$) version of the problems. In all cases, a population of size 100 is used. Since all test problems involve real parameters, the SBX recombination operator (with $\eta_c = 15$) and a variable-wise polynomial mutation operator (with $\eta_m = 20$) [6] are used in all cases. The crossover probability of 1.0 and mutation probability of $1/n$ are used.

The performances of NSGA-II and SPEA2 on DTLZ1 after 300 generations are shown in Figures 6.12 and 6.13, respectively. The figure shows that both NSGA-II and SPEA2 come close to the Pareto-optimal front and the distributions of solutions over the Pareto-optimal front are also not bad. In this problem and in most of the latter problems, we observed a better distribution of solutions with SPEA2 compared to NSGA-II. However, the better distributing ability of SPEA2 comes with a larger computational complexity in its selection/truncation approach compared to that needed in the objective-wise crowding approach of NSGA-II. The problem can be made more difficult by using a more difficult $g$ function or a variable transformation technique suggested earlier. By merely increasing the number of decision variables used in $\mathbf{x}$, the problem can be made harder.

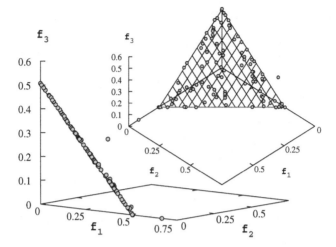

**Figure 6.12.** The NSGA-II population on test problem DTLZ1.

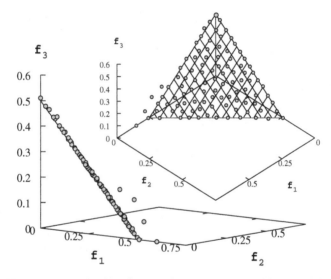

**Figure 6.13.** The SPEA2 population on test problem DTLZ1.

## 6.7.2 Test Problem DTLZ2

This test problem is identical to the problem described in Section 6.4.3:

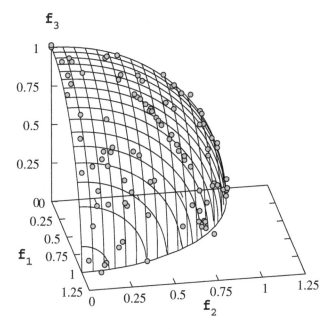

**Figure 6.14.** The NSGA-II population on test problem DTLZ2.

$$
\left.
\begin{aligned}
&\text{Min. } f_1(\mathbf{x}) = (1 + g(\mathbf{x}_M)) \cos(x_1\pi/2) \cdots \cos(x_{M-2}\pi/2) \cos(x_{M-1}\pi/2),\\
&\text{Min. } f_2(\mathbf{x}) = (1 + g(\mathbf{x}_M)) \cos(x_1\pi/2) \cdots \cos(x_{M-2}\pi/2) \sin(x_{M-1}\pi/2),\\
&\text{Min. } f_3(\mathbf{x}) = (1 + g(\mathbf{x}_M)) \cos(x_1\pi/2) \cdots \sin(x_{M-2}\pi/2),\\
&\ \vdots \qquad \vdots\\
&\text{Min. } f_M(\mathbf{x}) = (1 + g(\mathbf{x}_M)) \sin(x_1\pi/2),\\
&\text{with } g(\mathbf{x}_M) = \sum_{x_i \in \mathbf{x}_M} (x_i - 0.5)^2,\\
&\qquad 0 \le x_i \le 1, \quad \text{for } i = 1, 2, \ldots, n.
\end{aligned}
\right\}
$$

$$(6.20)$$

Once again, the $\mathbf{x}$ vector is constructed with $k = n - M + 1$ variables. The Pareto-optimal solutions corresponds to $x_i = 0.5$ for all $x_i \in \mathbf{x}_M$ and all objective function values must satisfy Equation 6.9. NSGA-II and SPEA2 with identical parameter setting as in DTLZ1 simulation runs and with $k = 10$ find Pareto-optimal solutions very close to the true Pareto-optimal front after 300 generations, as shown in Figures 6.14 and 6.15, respectively.

This function can also be used to investigate an MOEA's ability to scale up its performance in a large number of objectives. Like in DTLZ1, for $M > 3$, the Pareto-optimal solutions must lie inside the first octant of the unit sphere in a three-objective plot with $f_M$ as one of the axes. Since all Pareto-optimal solutions need to satisfy $\sum_{m=1}^{M} f_m^2 = 1$, the difference between the left term with the obtained solutions and one can be used as a metric for convergence as well. Besides the suggestions given in DTLZ1, the problem can be made

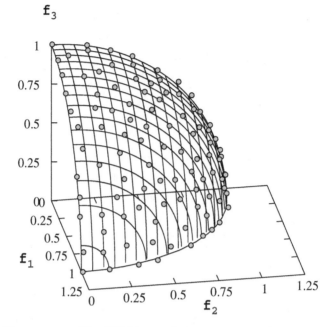

**Figure 6.15.** The SPEA2 population on test problem DTLZ2.

more difficult by replacing each variable $x_i$ (for $i = 1$ to $(M - 1)$) with the mean value of $p$ variables: $x_i = \frac{1}{p} \sum_{k=(i-1)p+1}^{ip} x_k$.

### 6.7.3 Test Problem DTLZ3

In order to investigate an MOEA's ability to converge to the global Pareto-optimal front, we suggest using the above problem with the $g$ function given in Equation 6.19:

$$
\left.
\begin{aligned}
&\text{Min. } f_1(\mathbf{x}) = (1 + g(\mathbf{x}_M)) \cos(x_1\pi/2) \cdots \cos(x_{M-2}\pi/2) \cos(x_{M-1}\pi/2), \\
&\text{Min. } f_2(\mathbf{x}) = (1 + g(\mathbf{x}_M)) \cos(x_1\pi/2) \cdots \cos(x_{M-2}\pi/2) \sin(x_{M-1}\pi/2), \\
&\text{Min. } f_3(\mathbf{x}) = (1 + g(\mathbf{x}_M)) \cos(x_1\pi/2) \cdots \sin(x_{M-2}\pi/2), \\
&\quad\vdots \qquad \vdots \\
&\text{Min. } f_M(\mathbf{x}) = (1 + g(\mathbf{x}_M)) \sin(x_1\pi/2), \\
&\text{with } g(\mathbf{x}_M) = 100 \left[|\mathbf{x}_M| + \sum_{x_i \in \mathbf{x}_M} (x_i - 0.5)^2 - \cos(20\pi(x_i - 0.5))\right], \\
&\quad 0 \le x_i \le 1, \quad \text{for } i = 1, 2, \ldots, n.
\end{aligned}
\right\}
$$

(6.21)

The above $g$ function introduces $(3^k - 1)$ local Pareto-optimal fronts and one global Pareto-optimal front. All local Pareto-optimal fronts are parallel to the global Pareto-optimal front and an MOEA can get stuck at any of these local Pareto-optimal fronts, before converging to the global Pareto-optimal front (at $g^* = 0$). The global Pareto-optimal front corresponds to $x_i = 0.5$

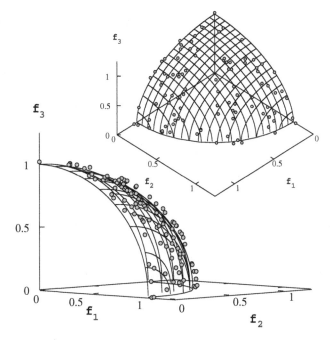

**Figure 6.16.** The NSGA-II population on test problem DTLZ3.

for $x_i \in \mathbf{x}_M$. The next local Pareto-optimal front is at $g^* = 1$. NSGA-II and SPEA2 populations (using $k = 10$) after 500 generations are shown in the true Pareto-optimal fronts in Figures 6.16 and 6.17. It is seen that both algorithms could not quite converge on to the true front, however both algorithms have maintained a good diversity of solutions on the true front. The problem can be made more difficult by using a larger $k$ or a higher-frequency cosine function.

### 6.7.4 Test Problem DTLZ4

In order to investigate an MOEA's ability to maintain a good distribution of solutions, we modify problem DTLZ2 with a different parametric variable mapping:

$$
\left.
\begin{aligned}
&\text{Min. } f_1(\mathbf{x}) = (1 + g(\mathbf{x}_M)) \cos(x_1^\alpha \pi/2) \cdots \cos(x_{M-2}^\alpha \pi/2) \cos(x_{M-1}^\alpha \pi/2), \\
&\text{Min. } f_2(\mathbf{x}) = (1 + g(\mathbf{x}_M)) \cos(x_1^\alpha \pi/2) \cdots \cos(x_{M-2}^\alpha \pi/2) \sin(x_{M-1}^\alpha \pi/2), \\
&\text{Min. } f_3(\mathbf{x}) = (1 + g(\mathbf{x}_M)) \cos(x_1^\alpha \pi/2) \cdots \sin(x_{M-2}^\alpha \pi/2), \\
&\quad\vdots \quad\quad \vdots \\
&\text{Min. } f_M(\mathbf{x}) = (1 + g(\mathbf{x}_M)) \sin(x_1^\alpha \pi/2), \\
&\text{with } g(\mathbf{x}_M) = \sum_{x_i \in \mathbf{x}_M} (x_i - 0.5)^2, \\
&\quad\ 0 \le x_i \le 1, \quad \text{for } i = 1, 2, \dots, n.
\end{aligned}
\right\}
$$

$$(6.22)$$

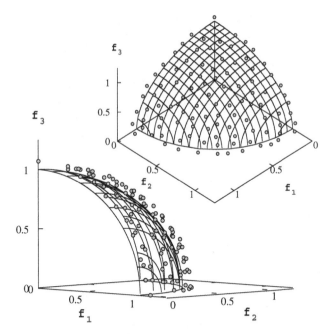

**Figure 6.17.** The SPEA2 population on test problem DTLZ3.

The parameter $\alpha = 100$ is suggested here. This modification allows a dense set of solutions to exist near the $f_M$-$f_1$ plane (as in Figure 6.5). NSGA-II and SPEA2 populations (using $k = 10$) at the end of 200 generations are shown in Figures 6.18 and 6.19, respectively. For this problem, the final population is found to be dependent on the initial population. But in both methods, we have obtained either of the three different outcomes: (1) all solutions are in the $f_3$-$f_1$ plane, (2) all solutions are in the $f_1$-$f_2$ plane, or (3) solutions are on the entire Pareto-optimal surface. Since the problem has more dense solutions near the $f_3$-$f_1$ and $f_1$-$f_2$ planes, some simulation runs of NSGA-II and SPEA2 get attracted to these planes. Problems with a biased density of solutions at other regions in the search space may also be created using the mapping suggested in Section 6.4.2. It is interesting to note that although the search space has a variable density of solutions, the classical weighted-sum approaches or other directional methods may not have any added difficulty in solving these problems compared to DTLZ2. Since MOEAs attempt to find multiple and well-distributed Pareto-optimal solutions in one simulation run, these problems may hinder MOEAs to achieve a well-distributed set of solutions.

### 6.7.5 Test Problem DTLZ5

The mapping of $\theta_i$ in the test problem DTLZ2 can be replaced with that given in Equation 6.10:

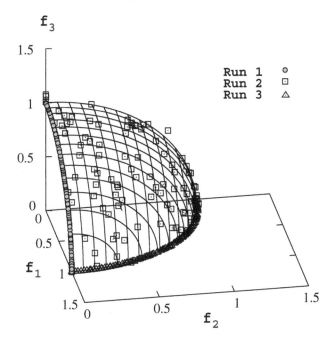

$\mathbf{f}_3$

**Figure 6.18.** The NSGA-II population on test problem DTLZ4. Three different simulation runs are shown.

Min. $f_1(\mathbf{x}) = (1 + g(\mathbf{x}_M)) \cos(\theta_1 \pi/2) \cdots \cos(\theta_{M-2} \pi/2) \cos(\theta_{M-1} \pi/2),$
Min. $f_2(\mathbf{x}) = (1 + g(\mathbf{x}_M)) \cos(\theta_1 \pi/2) \cdots \cos(\theta_{M-2} \pi/2) \sin(\theta_{M-1} \pi/2),$
Min. $f_3(\mathbf{x}) = (1 + g(\mathbf{x}_M)) \cos(\theta_1 \pi/2) \cdots \sin(\theta_{M-2} \pi/2),$

$\vdots \qquad \vdots$

Min. $f_M(\mathbf{x}) = (1 + g(\mathbf{x}_M)) \sin(\theta_1 \pi/2),$
with $\theta_i = \frac{\pi}{4(1+g(\mathbf{x}_M))} (1 + 2g(\mathbf{x}_M)x_i),$ for $i = 2, 3, \ldots, (M-1),$
$g(\mathbf{x}_M) = \sum_{x_i \in \mathbf{x}_M} (x_i - 0.5)^2,$
$0 \le x_i \le 1,$ for $i = 1, 2, \ldots, n.$

(6.23)

The Pareto-optimal front corresponds to $x_i = 0.5$ for all $x_i \in \mathbf{x}_M$ and function values satisfy $\sum_{m=1}^{M} f_m^2 = 1$. This problem will test an MOEA's ability to converge to a curve and will also allow an easier way to visually demonstrate (just by plotting $f_M$ with any other objective function) the performance of an MOEA. Since there is a natural bias for solutions close to this Pareto-optimal curve, this problem may be easy for an algorithm to solve, as shown in Figure 6.20 and 6.21 obtained using NSGA-II and SPEA2 after 200 generations and with other parameter settings as before and with $k = 10$.

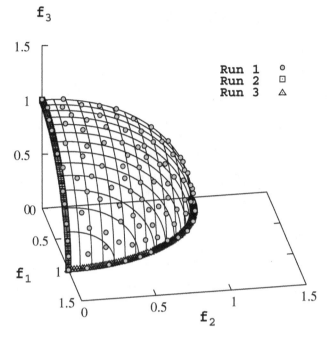

**Figure 6.19.** The SPEA2 population on test problem DTLZ4. Three different simulation runs are shown.

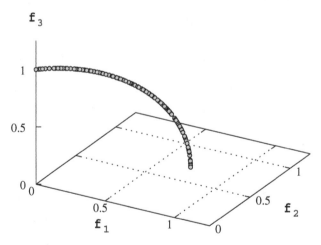

**Figure 6.20.** The NSGA-II population on test problem DTLZ5.

## 6.7.6 Test Problem DTLZ6

The above test problem can be made harder by making a similar modification to the $g$ function in DTLZ5, as done in DTLZ3. However, in DTLZ6, we use

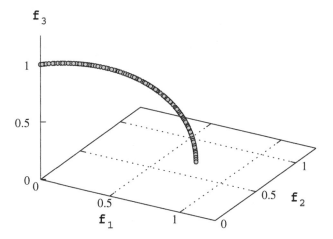

**Figure 6.21.** The SPEA2 population on test problem DTLZ5.

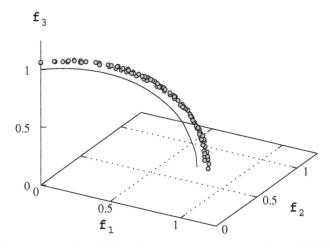

**Figure 6.22.** The NSGA-II population on test problem DTLZ6.

a different $g$ function:

$$g(\mathbf{x}_M) = \sum_{x_i \in \mathbf{X}_M} x_i^{0.1}. \tag{6.24}$$

Here, the Pareto-optimal front corresponds to $x_i = 0$ for all $x_i \in \mathbf{x}_M$. The size of $\mathbf{x}_M$ vector is chosen as 10 and the total number of variables is identical as in DTLZ5. The above change in the problem makes NSGA-II and SPEA2 difficult to converge to the true Pareto-optimal front as in DTLZ5. The population after 500 generations of both algorithms are shown in Figures 6.22 and 6.23, respectively. The Pareto-optimal curve is also marked on the plots.

It is clear from the figures that both NSGA-II and SPEA2 do not quite converge to the true Pareto-optimal curve. The lack of convergence to the

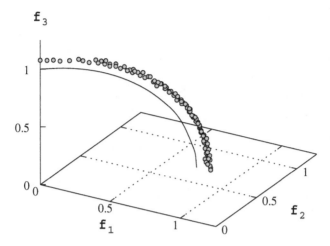

**Figure 6.23.** The SPEA2 population on test problem DTLZ6.

true front in this problem causes these MOEAs to find a dominated surface as the obtained front, whereas the true Pareto-optimal front is a curve. In real-world problems, this aspect may provide misleading information about the properties of the Pareto-optimal front, a matter which we discuss more in Section 6.8.

### 6.7.7 Test Problem DTLZ7

This test problem is constructed using the problem stated in Equation 6.11. This problem has a disconnected set of Pareto-optimal regions:

$$
\left.
\begin{aligned}
&\text{Minimize } f_1(\mathbf{x}_1) = x_1, \\
&\text{Minimize } f_2(\mathbf{x}_2) = x_2, \\
&\qquad \vdots \quad \vdots \\
&\text{Minimize } f_{M-1}(\mathbf{x}_{M-1}) = x_{M-1}, \\
&\text{Minimize } f_M(\mathbf{x}) = (1 + g(\mathbf{x}_M))h(f_1, f_2, \ldots, f_{M-1}, g), \\
&\quad \text{where } g(\mathbf{x}_M) = 1 + \frac{9}{|\mathbf{x}_M|}\sum_{x_i \in \mathbf{x}_M} x_i, \\
&\qquad h(f_1, f_2, \ldots, f_{M-1}, g) = M - \sum_{i=1}^{M-1}\left[\frac{f_i}{1+g}(1 + \sin(3\pi f_i))\right], \\
&\text{subject to } 0 \le x_i \le 1, \quad \text{for } i = 1, 2, \ldots, n.
\end{aligned}
\right\}
$$
(6.25)

This test problem has $2^{M-1}$ disconnected Pareto-optimal regions in the search space. The functional $g$ requires $k = |\mathbf{x}_M| = n - M + 1$ decision variables. The Pareto-optimal solutions corresponds to $\mathbf{x}_M = \mathbf{0}$. This problem will test an algorithm's ability to maintain subpopulation in different Pareto-optimal regions. For a problem with $k = 20$ and $M = 3$, Figures 6.24 and 6.25 show the NSGA-II and SPEA2 populations after 200 generations. It is clear that both algorithms are able to find and maintain stable and distributed subpopulations

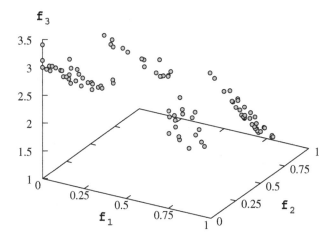

**Figure 6.24.** The NSGA-II population on test problem DTLZ7.

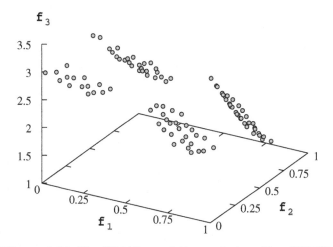

**Figure 6.25.** The SPEA2 population on test problem DTLZ7.

in all four disconnected Pareto-optimal regions. The problem can be made harder by using a higher-frequency sine function or using a multi-modal $g$ function as described in Equation 6.19.

### 6.7.8 Test Problem DTLZ8

Here, we use the constraint surface approach to construct the following test problem:

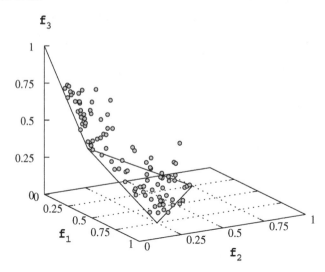

**Figure 6.26.** The NSGA-II population of non-dominated solutions on test problem DTLZ8.

$$
\left.
\begin{array}{l}
\text{Minimize} \quad f_j(\mathbf{x}) = \frac{1}{\lfloor \frac{n}{M} \rfloor} \sum_{i=\lfloor (j-1)\frac{n}{M}\rfloor}^{\lfloor j \frac{n}{M} \rfloor} x_i, \quad j = 1, 2, \ldots, M, \\[2mm]
\text{Subject to } g_j(\mathbf{x}) = f_M(\mathbf{x}) + 4f_j(\mathbf{x}) - 1 \geq 0, \quad \text{for } j = 1, 2, \ldots, (M-1), \\[2mm]
\qquad\qquad g_M(\mathbf{x}) = 2f_M(\mathbf{x}) + \min_{\substack{i,j=1 \\ i \neq j}}^{M-1} \left[ f_i(\mathbf{x}) + f_j(\mathbf{x}) \right] - 1 \geq 0, \\[2mm]
\qquad 0 \leq x_i \leq 1, \quad \text{for } i = 1, 2, \ldots, n.
\end{array}
\right\}
$$

$$(6.26)$$

Here, the number of variables is considered to be larger than the number of objectives or $n > M$. We suggest $n = 10M$. In this problem, there are a total of $M$ constraints. The Pareto-optimal front is a combination of a straight line and a hyper-plane. The straight line is the intersection of the first $(M-1)$ constraints (with $f_1 = f_2 = \cdots = f_{M-1}$) and the hyper-plane is represented by the constraint $g_M$. MOEAs may find difficulty in finding solutions in both the regions in this problem and also in maintaining a good distribution of solutions on the hyper-plane. Figures 6.26 and 6.27 show NSGA-II and SPEA2 populations after 500 generations. The Pareto-optimal region (a straight line and a triangular plane) is also marked in the plots. Although some solutions on the true Pareto-optimal front are found, there exist many other non-dominated solutions in the final population. These *redundant* solutions lie on the adjoining surfaces to the Pareto-optimal front. Their presence in the final non-dominated set is difficult to eradicate in real-parameter MOEAs, a matter which we discuss in Section 6.8.

### 6.7.9 Test Problem DTLZ9

This final test problem is also created using the constraint surface approach:

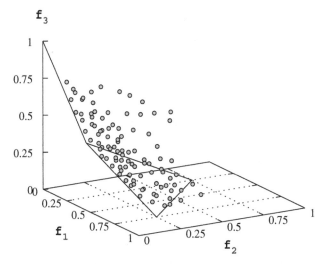

**Figure 6.27.** The SPEA2 population of non-dominated solutions on test problem DTLZ8.

$$
\left.
\begin{array}{l}
\text{Minimize} \quad f_j(\mathbf{x}) = \sum_{i=\lfloor(j-1)\frac{n}{M}\rfloor}^{\lfloor j\frac{n}{M}\rfloor} x_i^{0.1}, \quad j = 1, 2, \ldots, M, \\
\text{Subject to } g_j(\mathbf{x}) = f_M^2(\mathbf{x}) + f_j^2(\mathbf{x}) - 1 \geq 0, \quad \text{for } j = 1, 2, \ldots, (M-1), \\
\quad 0 \leq x_i \leq 1, \quad \text{for } i = 1, 2, \ldots, n.
\end{array}
\right\}
$$
$$(6.27)$$

Here too, the number of variables is considered to be larger than the number of objectives. For this problem, we also suggest $n = 10M$. The Pareto-optimal front is a curve with $f_1 = f_2 = \cdots = f_{M-1}$, similar to that in DTLZ5. However, the density of solutions gets thinner towards the Pareto-optimal region. The Pareto-optimal curve lies on the intersection of all $(M-1)$ constraints. This feature of this problem may cause MOEAs difficulty in solving this problem. However, the symmetry of the Pareto-optimal curve in terms of $(M-1)$ objectives allows an easier way to illustrate the obtained solutions. A two-dimensional plot of the Pareto-optimal front with $f_M$ and any other objective function should represent a circular arc of radius one. A plot with any two objective functions except $f_M$ should show a 45° straight line. Figures 6.28 and 6.29 show NSGA-II and SPEA2 populations after 500 generations on a $f_3$-$f_1$ plot of the 30-variable, three-objective DTLZ9 problem. The Pareto-optimal circle is also shown in the plots. It is clear that both algorithms could not cover the entire range of the circle and there exist many non-dominated solutions away from the Pareto-optimal front.

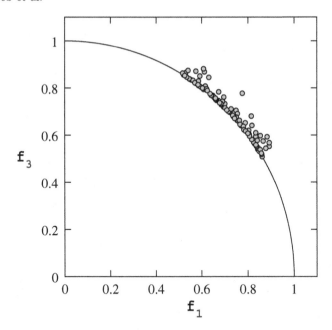

**Figure 6.28.** The NSGA-II population on test problem DTLZ9.

## 6.8 Redundant Solutions

Many of the above test problems (such as DTLZ6, DTLZ8, and DTLZ9) introduce a different kind of difficulty to multiobjective real-parameter optimization techniques. In these problems, the Pareto-optimal front is weakly non-dominated with the adjoining surfaces (whose intersections give rise to the Pareto-optimal front). If a good representative set of solutions is not found on the true Pareto-optimal front, an MOEA which works with the domination concept can find a set of non-dominated solutions all of which may not be on the true Pareto-optimal front. Figures 6.30 and 6.31 demonstrate this matter, for two and three-objective minimization problems, respectively.

With respect to two Pareto-optimal solutions A and B in the figure, any other solution in the shaded region is non-dominated to both A and B. That is, if no other Pareto-optimal solutions within the line joining A and B are found, any solution from the shaded region would be non-dominated with both A and B and may exist in an MOEA population. In such cases, the obtained set of solutions may wrongly depict a higher-dimensional surface or a redundant surface as the obtained Pareto-optimal front. Another study [22] has also recognized that this feature of problems can cause domination-based MOEAs difficulty in finding the true Pareto-optimal solutions. It is worth highlighting here that with the increase in the dimensionality of the objective space, the probability of occurrence of such redundant solutions is more. Figures 6.30 and 6.31 illustrate that the region containing such redundant

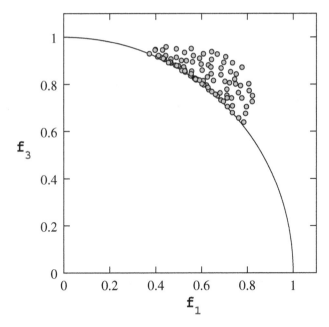

**Figure 6.29.** The SPEA2 population on test problem DTLZ9.

solutions would in general be more for a problem having more objectives. We term this difficulty associated with the dimension of the objective space as the problem of 'redundancy' in the context of multiobjective optimization. In handling such problems, MOEAs with the newly suggested $\epsilon$-dominance concept [23] introduced by the authors may be found useful. A recent study [24] has demonstrated that the use of $\epsilon$-dominance concept is one way to reduce the redundancy problem. However, this is a serious difficulty in the context to multiobjective optimization and must be addressed further.

## 6.9 Conclusions

In this study, we have suggested three approaches for systematically designing scalable test problems for multiobjective optimization. The first approach simply uses a translated set of single-objective functions. Although the construction procedure is simple, the resulting Pareto-optimal front may be difficult to comprehend. The second approach (we called a bottom-up approach) begins the construction procedure by assuming a mathematical formulation of the Pareto-optimal front. Such a function is then embedded in the overall test problem design so that two different types of difficulties of converging to the Pareto-optimal front and maintaining a diverse set of solutions can also be introduced. The third approach (we called the constraint surface approach) begins the construction process by assuming the overall

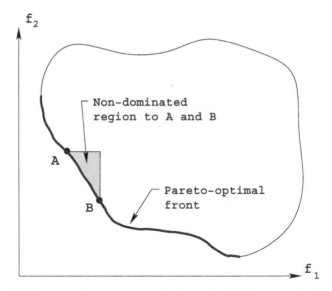

**Figure 6.30.** The shaded region is non-dominated with Pareto-optimal solutions A and B (for two objectives).

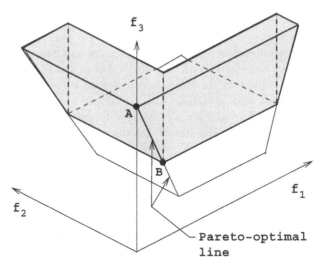

**Figure 6.31.** The shaded region is non-dominated with Pareto-optimal solutions A and B (for three objectives).

search space to be a rectangular hyper-box. Thereafter, a number of linear or non-linear constraint surfaces are added one by one to eliminate some portion of the original hyper-box. The remaining enclosed region becomes the feasible search space. A few three-objective test problems are constructed illustrating the latter two approaches to demonstrate their relative advantages and disadvantages. Finally, a number of test problems have been suggested and attempted to solve using two popular state-of-the-art MOEAs (NSGA-II and SPEA2) for their systematic use in practice.

In this study, we have not suggested any explicit constrained test problem, although problems constructed using the constraint surface approach can be treated as constrained test problems. However, other difficulties pertinent to the constrained optimization suggested in a two-objective constrained test problem design elsewhere [25] can also be used with the proposed procedures for constrained test problem design.

## Acknowledgments

This study originated during the first author's visit to ETH Zurich. The authors acknowledge the support from the Swiss National Science Foundation under the ArOMA project 2100-057156.99/1.

## A Appendix: Another Test Problem Using the Bottom-up Approach: The Comet Problem

To demonstrate the ease of using the bottom-up approach to design test problems further, we create one more problem which has a comet-like Pareto-optimal front. Starting from a widely spread region, the Pareto-optimal front continuously reduces to a thinner region. Finding a wide variety of solutions in both broad and thin portions of the Pareto-optimal region simultaneously becomes a challenging task for any multiobjective optimizer, including classical methods:

$$\left. \begin{array}{l} \text{Minimize } f_1(\mathbf{x}) = (1 + g(x_3))(x_1^3 x_2^2 - 10x_1 - 4x_2), \\ \text{Minimize } f_2(\mathbf{x}) = (1 + g(x_3))(x_1^3 x_2^2 - 10x_1 + 4x_2), \\ \text{Minimize } f_3(\mathbf{x}) = 3(1 + g(x_3))x_1^2, \\ \qquad 1 \le x_1 \le 3.5, \\ \qquad -2 \le x_2 \le 2, \\ \qquad g(x_3) \ge 0. \end{array} \right\} \qquad (6.28)$$

Here, we have chosen $g(x_3) = x_3$ and $0 \le x_3 \le 1$. The Pareto-optimal surface corresponds to $x_3^* = 0$ and for $-2 \le x_1^{*3} x_2^* \le 2$ with $1 \le x_1^* \le 3.5$. Figure 6.32 shows the Pareto-optimal front on the $x_3 = 0$ surface. For better illustration purposes, the figure is plotted with negative $f_i$ values. This problem illustrates that the entire $g = g^*$ surface need not correspond to the Pareto-optimal front. Only the region which dominates the rest of the $g = g^*$ surface belongs to the Pareto-optimal front.

We have designed this function and the curve function for a special purpose. Because of the narrow Pareto-optimal region in both problems, we

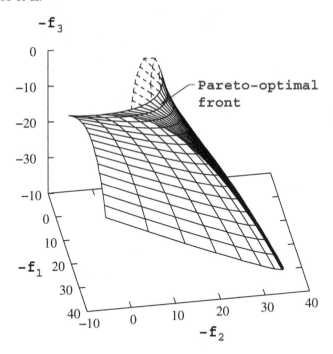

**Figure 6.32.** The comet problem.

argue that the classical generating methods will require a large computational overhead in solving the above problems. Figure 6.33 shows the projection of the Pareto-optimal region in the $f_1$-$f_2$ space of the comet problem. For the use of the $\epsilon$-constraint method [6, 26] as a method of generating Pareto-optimal solutions (usually recommended for its convergence properties), the resulting single-objective optimization problem, which has to be solved for different combinations of $\epsilon_1$ and $\epsilon_2$, is as follows:

$$\left.\begin{array}{r} \text{Minimize}\ \ f_3(\mathbf{x}), \\ \text{subject to}\ f_2(\mathbf{x}) \leq \epsilon_2, \\ f_1(\mathbf{x}) \leq \epsilon_1, \\ \mathbf{x} \in \mathcal{D}, \end{array}\right\} \tag{6.29}$$

where $\mathcal{D}$ is the feasible decision space. It is well known that the minimum solution for the above problem for any $\epsilon_1$ and $\epsilon_2$ $(\geq 0)$ is either a Pareto-optimal solution or is infeasible [26]. The figure illustrates a scenario with $\epsilon_2 = -30$. It can be seen from the figure that the solution of the above single-objective optimization problem for $\epsilon_1 = -15$ is not going to produce any new Pareto-optimal solution other than that obtained for $\epsilon_1 = -20$ (for example) or for $\epsilon_1$ set to get the Pareto-optimal solution at A. Thus, the above generating method will resort to solving many redundant single-objective optimization problems. By calculating the area of the projected Pareto-

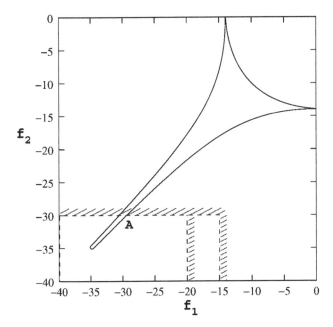

**Figure 6.33.** Classical generating method with the $\epsilon$-constraint method will produce redundant single-objective optimization problems.

optimal region, it is estimated that about 88% of single-objective optimization problems are redundant in the above three-objective optimization problem, if a uniform set of $\epsilon$ vectors is chosen in the generating method. Compared to classical generating methods, MOEAs may show superior performance in these problems in terms of overall computational effort needed in finding multiple and well distributed Pareto-optimal solutions. This is mainly because of their implicit parallel processing, which enables them to quickly settle to feasible regions of interest, and due to their population approach, which allows them to find a wide variety of solutions simultaneously with the action of a niche-preserving operator.

# References

1. Schaffer, JD *Some Experiments in Machine Learning Using Vector Evaluated Genetic Algorithms.* PhD thesis, Nashville, TN: Vanderbilt University, 1984.
2. Kursawe, F A Variant of Evolution Strategies for Vector Optimization. In *Parellel Problem Solving from Nature I (PPSN-I)*, pp. 193-197, 1990.
3. Fonseca, CM and Fleming, PJ An Overview of Evolutionary Algorithms in Multi-objective Optimization. *Evolutionary Computation Journal*, 1995; 3(1): 1-16.
4. Poloni, C, Giurgevich, A, Onesti, L and Pediroda, V Hybridization of a Multiobjective Genetic Algorithm, a Neural Network and a Classical Optimizer

for Complex Design Problem in Fluid Dynamics. *Computer Methods in Applied Mechanics and Engineering*, 2000; 186(2–4): 403-420.

5. Viennet, R Multicriteria Optimization Using a Genetic Algorithm for Determining the Pareto Set. *International Journal of Systems Science*, 1996; 27(2): 255-260.

6. Deb, K *Multi-objective Optimization Using Evolutionary Algorithms*. Chichester, UK: Wiley, 2001.

7. Van Veldhuizen, D *Multiobjective Evolutionary Algorithms: Classifications, Analyses, and New Innovations*. PhD Thesis, Dayton, OH: Air Force Institute of Technology, 1999. Technical Report No. AFIT/DS/ENG/99-01.

8. Deb, K Multi-objective Genetic Algorithms: Problem Difficulties and Construction of Test Problems. *Evolutionary Computation Journal*, 1999; 7(3): 205-230.

9. Zitzler, E, Deb, K and Thiele, L Comparison of Multiobjective Evolutionary Algorithms: Empirical Results. *Evolutionary Computation Journal*, 2000; 8(2): 125-148.

10. Deb, K, Thiele, L, Laumanns, M and Zitzler, E Scalable Multi-objective Optimization Test Problems. In *Proceedings of the Congress on Evolutionary Computation (CEC-2002)*, pp. 825-830, 2002.

11. Coello, CAC, VanVeldhuizen, DA, and Lamont G *Evolutionary Algorithms for Solving Multi-Objective Problems*. Boston, MA: Kluwer Academic Publishers, 2002.

12. Bleuler, S, Laumanns, M, Thiele, L and Zitzler, E PISA - A Platform and Programming Language Independent Interface for Search Algorithms. In *Evolutionary Multi-Criterion Optimization (EMO 2003)*, Lecture Notes in Computer Science, Berlin, 2003. Springer.

13. Laumanns, M, Rudolph, G and Schwefel, HP A Spatial Predator-prey Approach to Multi-objective Optimization: A Preliminary Study. In *Proceedings of the Parallel Problem Solving from Nature, V*, pp. 241-249, 1998.

14. Laumanns, M, Thiele, L, Ziztler, E, Welzl, E and Deb, K Running Time Analysis of Multi-objective Evolutionary Algorithms on a Simple Discrete Optimization Problem. In *Proceedings of the Seventh Conference on Parallel Problem Solving from Nature (PPSN-VII)*, pp. 44-53, 2002.

15. Zitzler, E and Thiele, L Multiobjective Evolutionary Algorithms: A Comparative Case Study and the Strength Pareto Approach. *IEEE Transactions on Evolutionary Computation*, 1999; 3(4): 257-271.

16. Deb, K and Jain, S Multi-speed Gearbox Design Using Multi-objective Evolutionary Algorithms. *ASME Transactions on Mechanical Design*, 2003; 125(3): 609-619.

17. Laumanns, M, Thiele, L and Zitzler, E Running Time Analysis of Multiobjective Evolutionary Algorithms on Pseudo-boolean Functions. *IEEE Transactions on Evolutionary Computation*, 2004. Accepted for publication.

18. Tanaka, M GA-based Decision Support System for Multi-criteria Optimization. In *Proceedings of the International Conference on Systems, Man and Cybernetics*, Volume 2: pp. 1556-1561, 1995.

19. Tamaki, H Multi-objective Optimization by Genetic Algorithms: A Review. In *Proceedings of the Third IEEE Conference on Evolutionary Computation*, pp. 517-522, 1996.

20. Knowles, JD and Corne, DW Approximating the Non-dominated Front Using the Pareto Archived Evolution Strategy. *Evolutionary Computation Journal*, 2000; 8(2): 149-172.

21. Deb, K, Agrawal, S, Pratap, A and Meyarivan, T A Fast and Elitist Multi-objective Genetic Algorithm: NSGA-II. *IEEE Transactions on Evolutionary Computation*, 2002; 6(2):182-197.

22. Kokolo, I, Kita, H, and Kobayashi, S Failure of Pareto-based Moeas: Does Non-dominated Really Mean Near to Optimal? In *Proceedings of the Congress on Evolutionary Computation 2001*, pp. 957-962, 2001.

23. Laumanns, M, Thiele, L, Deb, K and Zitzler, E Combining Convergence and Diversity in Evolutionary Multi-objective Optimization. *Evolutionary Computation*, 2002; 10(3): 263-282.

24. Deb, K, Mohan, M, and Mishra, S Towards a Quick Computation of Well-spread Pareto-optimal Solutions. In *Proceedings of the Second Evolutionary Multi-Criterion Optimization (EMO-03) Conference (LNCS 2632)*, pp. 222-236, 2003.

25. Deb, K, Pratap, A and Meyarivan, T Constrained Test Problems for Multi-objective Evolutionary Optimization. In *Proceedings of the First International Conference on Evolutionary Multi-Criterion Optimization (EMO-01)*, pp. 284-298, 2001.

26. Miettinen, K, *Nonlinear Multiobjective Optimization*, Boston, Kluwer, 1999.

# Particle Swarm Inspired Evolutionary Algorithm (PS-EA) for Multi-Criteria Optimization Problems

Dipti Srinivasan and Tian Hou Seow

**Summary.** This chapter presents a synergistic combination of particle swarm optimization and evolutionary algorithm for optimization problems. The performance of the hybrid algorithm is bench-marked against conventional genetic algorithm and particle swarm optimization algorithm. Finally, the hybrid algorithm is illustrated as a multiobjective optimization algorithm using the Fonseca 2-objective function.

## 7.1 Introduction

Population-based stochastic search algorithms have been very popular in recent years in the research arena of computational intelligence. Some of the well established search algorithms such as Genetic Algorithm (GA)[1-3], Evolutionary Strategies (ES) [4], Evolutionary Programming (EP) [5] and Artificial Immune Systems [6], have been successfully implemented to solve a range of problems from functions optimization to complex real world problems like scheduling [7-9] and complex network routing problems [3].

In recent years, swarm intelligence has become a research interest to many research scientists of related fields. The main algorithm for swarm intelligence is Particle Swarm Optimization (PSO)[10-14], which is inspired by the paradigm of birds flocking. PSO is successfully implemented in various optimization problems like weight training in Neural Networks [12] and functions optimization [10-11,13-14]. PSO is very popular because of the simplicity in its implementation, as it requires only the tuning of a few parameters. As the core updating mechanism in the algorithm relies only on two simple PSO self-updating equations, the process of updating the individuals per iteration is fast as compared to the computationally expensive reproduction mechanism using mutation or crossover operations in typical EA.

The manner in which PSO searches for solutions in the solution space is also different from a typical EA. An EA iteratively searches for several good individuals in the population, and tries to make the population emulate the best solutions found in that generation through crossover operation, while the mutation operation tries to introduce diversity to the population. Very often, premature convergence occurs when all individuals in the solutions become very similar to each other. This results in the population getting stuck in local optima, if the initial best individual as found by the EA is very near to a local optima. In contrast, the PSO maintains a memory to store the elite individuals of the best global individual (*gbest*) found, as well as the best solutions as found by each individual particle (*pbest*). The population is not required to contain any of the elite individuals already found, but each individual in the population tries to emulate the *gbest* and *pbest* solutions in the memory through the updating process governed by PSO weight update equations. The random element in the PSO equations introduces diversity around the elite individuals found.

While PSO is a good and fast search algorithm, it has its limitations should it be used to solve real world problems. PSO relies heavily on the two PSO equations such that additional domain-specific heuristics related to the real-world problems cannot be easily incorporated in the algorithm; while in an EA, heuristics can be easily incorporated in the population generator and mutation operator to prevent leading the individuals to infeasible solutions. Therefore, PSO does not perform well in its search in complex multi-constrained solution spaces, which are the case for many complex real world problems.

To overcome the limitations of PSO and EA, a hybridized evolutionary algorithm, Particle Swarm Inspired Evolutionary Algorithm (PS-EA), is proposed to use a synergistic combination of PSO and EA. In the following sections, a description of the PS-EA algorithm is presented. The algorithm is benchmarked against Genetic Algorithm (GA) and PSO. It is found that PS-EA provides an advantage over typical GA and PSO for complex multi-modal functions like Rosenbrock, Schwefel and Rastrigrin functions. An application of PS-EA to minimize the classic Fonseca 2-objective functions is also described to illustrate the feasibility of PS-EA as a multiobjective search algorithm.

## 7.2 Particle Swarm Optimization

PSO is an optimization technique developed by Russell C. Eberhart [10-11]and James Kennedy [10] in 1995, inspired by the paradigm of birds flocking. It is similar to evolutionary algorithms in the population generation, in that the initialization is done with a swarm of random particles. For every updating cycle, each particle is updated such that it tries to emulate the global best particle, known as *gbest*, or the particle best, known as *pbest*. The *gbest* particle is the best particle found so far in the swarm of particles, while *pbest[k]* is the best solution so far as found by particle $k$. The number of *pbest* particles stored in the memory of the algorithm is equivalent to the number of particles in the swarm. No selection scheme is incorporated in PSO, since the updating of the particles is done by the self-updating equations, and the elite particles (*pbest[]* and *gbest[]*) are stored in the memory, to prevent the degeneration of the overall fitness of the particle swarm. The self-updating equations of PSO are as follows:

$$v[] = v[] + c1.rand().\{pbest[]\text{-}present[]\} + c2.rand().\{gbest[]\text{-}present[]\} \quad (7.1)$$

$$present[] = present[]+v[] \quad (7.2)$$

Where *v[]* is the particle velocity, *present[]* is the current particle, *rand ()* is a random number between 0 and 1, and *c1* and *c2* are the learning factors. In an unconstrained solution space, the particles are allowed to take any values, and Equations 7.1 and 7.2 would work perfectly well. In a semi-constrained solution space as exemplified in Figure 7.1, there will be upper and/or lower limits that the value of *present[]* can have. Defining *present_UPPER[]* and *present_LOWER[]* as the upper and lower limits solves the problem of maneuvering the particle to non-feasible solution spaces. In a multi-constrained solution space as exemplified in Figure 7.2, the PSO equations can pose a problem as the equations may maneuver the *present[]* values to the restricted solution space. To solve this problem in a simple way without

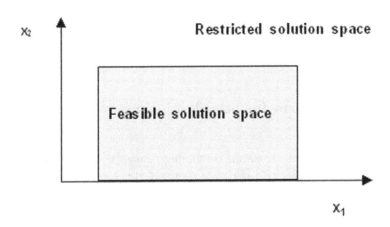

**Figure 7.1.** A 2-dimensional semi-constrained solution space.

modifying the PSO equations, we can simply issue a huge penalty if *present[]* lies in the restricted solution space. However, this is not a good solution, as it will slow down the rate of convergence. This is because if *present[]* can be moved to the restricted region, the probability of *present[]* to be placed in the correct position, which is in the feasible region, will be reduced, resulting in a slower convergence and a poorer performance. Furthermore, it is very difficult to include any heuristic in the PSO equations, due to the limitation as posed by the mathematical format of the equations, to avoid *present[]*

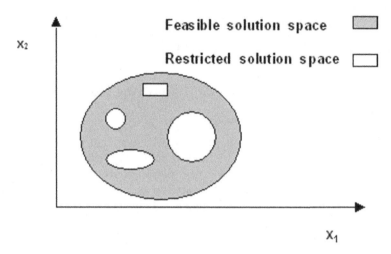

**Figure 7.2.** A 2-dimensional multi-constrained solution space.

to be placed in the restricted solution space. To implement heuristics after the PSO equations have updated the individual defeats the purpose of the updating equations of PSO. There is a need to provide an extension to the PSO updating mechanism in order to be able to include the heuristics for the avoidance of wrong maneuver to the restricted region.

## 7.3 Particle Swarm Inspired Evolutionary Algorithm (PS-EA)

PS-EA is a hybridized algorithm combining concepts of PSO and EA. As discussed in Section 7.2, PS-EA aims to overcome the limitations of PSO and EA, while building on their strengths. The core intelligence of PS-EA is incorporated in the Self-Updating Mechanism (SUM) module, which makes use of the Inheritance Probability Tree (PIT) to perform the updating operation of each individual in the population. A Dynamic Inheritance Probability Adjuster (DIPA) is incorporated in SUM to dynamically adjust the inheritance probabilities in PIT based on the convergence rate or status of the algorithm in a particular iteration.

### 7.3.1 Flow of PS-EA

The general flow of PS-EA is shown in Figure  7.3. Although this hybrid algorithm is similar to population-based stochastic search algorithms in some ways, it has several unique features. The algorithm has a memory to store the elite particles or individuals, and there is no reproduction of offspring.

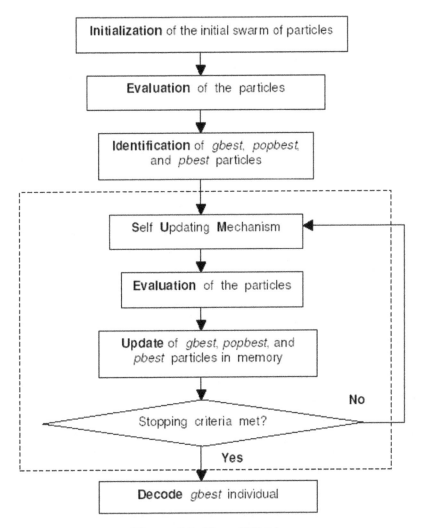

**Figure 7.3.** Flow of PS-EA.

All particles in the swarm or population undergo modifications by SUM, irrespective of whether they are the elite particles or not. It is noted that *popbest* is included as one of the elite particles. The *popbest* particle is the best particle in the current population. More details will be discussed in the next sub-section on SUM.

## 7.3.2 Self-updating Mechanism (SUM)

The SUM functions as an emulator of the PSO self-updating Equations 7.1and 7.2. The functioning of this mechanism can be described as follows.

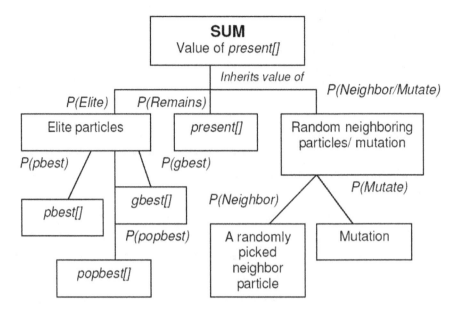

**Figure 7.4.** The probability inheritance tree (PIT) of SUM.

If we analyze the PSO Equations 7.1and 7.2, we can deduce the following possible results:

- *present[]* becomes *gbest[]*
- *present[]* becomes *pbest[]*
- *present[]* remains as *present[]*
- *present[]* is assigned a value near *gbest[]* or *pbest[]*

Thus, it is possible to use the operators of EA to emulate the workings of PSO equations. Replacing the PSO equations, we introduce a probability inheritance tree (PIT) as illustrated in Figure 7.4.

The end branches at the bottom of the probability inheritance tree show all the possible values that a parameter value of a particle can take. A parameter value of the present particle, *present[]*, can inherit the parameter values from the elite particles or any random neighboring particles, undergo mutation operation or retain its original value. The mutation operation in SUM emulates the random element in the PSO equation as in Equation (7.1). An additional elite particle *popbest[]*, which is the best particle of a current swarm, is introduced to SUM for faster convergence. To introduce more diversity in the swarm of particles, we allow *present[]* to inherit parameter values of a randomly selected neighbor particle.

The SUM process can be illustrated by considering the updating of the first parameter of a *particle k*. When the first parameter value of *particle k* undergoes the SUM, the parameter has the probability $P(Elite)$ to inherit the value of one of the elite particles, probability $P(Remains)$ to retain its original value and probability $P(Neighbor/Mutation)$ to inherit the value from one of its neighboring particles or undergo a mutation operation. If it chooses to inherit from one of the elite particles, it still has to choose whether it will inherit from the global best particle *gbest*, the current population best particle *popbest*, or the best particle that *particle k* has in its memory *pbest[k]*. The probabilities that it will choose to inherit from *gbest*, *popbest* and *pbest[k]* are $P(gbest)$, $P(popbest)$ and $P(pbest)$ respectively. Similarly, if it chooses to inherit from a neighbor particle or undergoes mutation operation, it will again need to choose from two options. The probabilities that it will choose to inherit from a randomly selected neighbor particle in the current population and undergo mutation operation are $P(Neighbor)$ and $P(Mutate)$ respectively.

### 7.3.3 Dynamic Inheritance Probability Adjuster (DIPA)

By introducing the probability inheritance tree in the self-updating mechanism, the total number of parameters to be set increases to nine, considering the eight inheritance probabilities and the population size. It presents a challenge for the algorithm designer to determine the correct values of inheritance probabilities. A DIPA is therefore incorporated in the algorithm to automatically adjust the inheritance probabilities.

The DIPA obtains feedback regarding the convergence status from the convergence rate feedback mechanism, in order to detect whether the algorithm is converging well. This information is obtained based on the cost of the *gbest* particle, which is logged in each iteration. For every even-numbered iteration, the feedback mechanism will calculate the difference of the costs of the *gbest* particle in the odd-numbered and even-numbered iterations. If it is detected that the cost of the *gbest* particle is not converging well, this information is fed back to DIPA, which carries out the necessary adjustment to the inheritance probabilities. It also samples the cost of the *gbest* particle in long iteration intervals and checks whether the cost of the *gbest* particle has decreased. DIPA does the necessary adjustment based on this information regarding the convergence status from the feedback mechanism. Thus, the algorithm designer can set any arbitrary set of the initial inheritance probabilities, which are dynamically adjusted by DIPA to find the optimum values.

## 7.4 Benchmarking Experiments

Five numerical experiments are conducted to compare the performance of PS-EA with GA and PSO in minimizing five popular test functions.

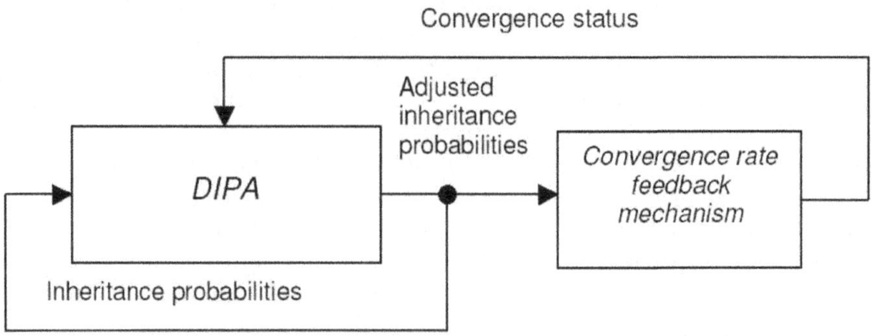

Convergence status

**Figure 7.5.** DIPA flow diagram.

## 7.4.1 Benchmarking Test Functions

The algorithms were tested on five test functions that are widely used for benchmarking purposes of optimization algorithms. These functions involve many local optima and/or saddles in their solution spaces. The amount of local optima and saddles increases with increasing complexity of the functions, i.e. with increasing dimension.

### Griewank Function

Griewank function (Figure 11.4) can be represented by:

$$f_1 = \frac{1}{4000} \sum_{d=1}^{D} x_d^2 - \prod_{d=1}^{D} \cos(\frac{x_d}{\sqrt{d}}) + 1 \tag{7.3}$$

The global minimum of $f_1$ is zero, and it occurs when $x_d = 0$ for all $d = 1, 2, ...D$. It has many widespread local minima. The locations of the minima are, however, regularly distributed.

### Rastrigrin Function

The second test function is the Rastrigrin function (Figure 11.5) given by:

$$f_2 = \sum_{d=1}^{D} (x_d^2 - 10 \cos(2\pi x_d) + 10) \tag{7.4}$$

The global minimum of $f_2$ is zero, and it occurs when $x_d = 0$ for all $d = 1, 2, ...D$. It is highly multi-modal and, similar to Griewank, it has widespread local minima which are regularly distributed.

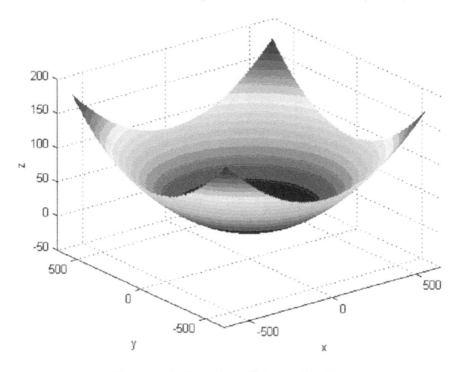

**Figure 7.6.** Generalised Griewank function.

## Rosenbrock Function

The third test function is Rosenbrock function (Figure 11.6) given by:

$$f_3 = \sum_{d=1}^{D-1} (100(x_{d+1} - x_d^2)^2 + (x_d - 1)^2) \tag{7.5}$$

The global minimum of $f_3$ is zero, and it occurs when $x_d = 1$ for all $d = 1, 2, ...D$. It is a classic unimodal optimization problem. The global optimum is inside a long, narrow, parabolic shaped flat valley, popularly known as Rosenbrock's valley. To find the valley is trivial, but to achieve convergence to the global optimum is difficult task.

## Ackley Function

The fourth test function is the Ackley function (Figure 7.9) given by:

$$f_4 = 20 + e - 20e^{(-0.2\sqrt{\frac{1}{D}\sum_{d=1}^{D} x_d^2})} - e^{\frac{1}{D}\sum_{d=1}^{D} \cos(2\pi x_d)} \tag{7.6}$$

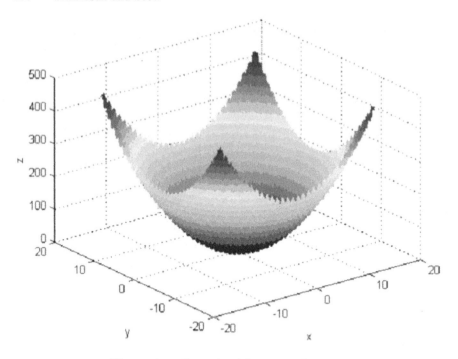

**Figure 7.7.** Generalized Rastrigrin function.

The global minimum of $f_4$ is zero, and it occurs when $x_d = 0$ for all $d = 1, 2, ...D$. It is a highly multi-modal function, similar to the Griewank and Rastrigrin functions.

**Schwefel Function**

The fifth test function is the Schwefel function (Figure 7.10) given by

$$f_5 = D \times 418.9829 + \sum_{d=1}^{D} -x_d \sin(\sqrt{|x_d|}) \qquad (7.7)$$

The global minimum of $f_5$ is zero, and it occurs when $x_d = 420.9867$ for all $d = 1, 2, ...D$. The Schwefel function is deceptive in that the global minimum is geometrically distant, over the parameter space, from the next best local minima. The solution space is wickedly irregular with many local optima. The search algorithms are potentially prone to convergence in the wrong direction in the optimization of this function.

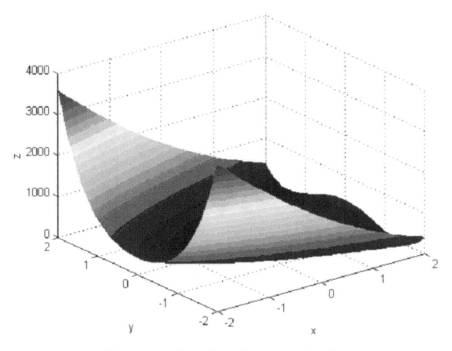

**Figure 7.8.** Generalized Rosenbrock function.

## 7.4.2 GA Parameters

The GA scheme used in the comparison experiment is used as suggested in Digalakis and Margaritis [2]. The scheme is shown in Table 7.1.

**Table 7.1.** GA scheme.

| | |
|---|---|
| **Crossover probability** | 0.95 |
| **Crossover scheme** | Single point crossover |
| **Crossover parent selection scheme** | Random selection (no elitism) |
| **Mutation probability** | 0.1 |
| **Child production scheme** | A child chromosome is added to the population from any crossover or mutation operation |
| **New generation selection scheme** | Best fixed number of chromosomes are selected from the "expanded" population of parent and child chromosomes for the next GA operations |

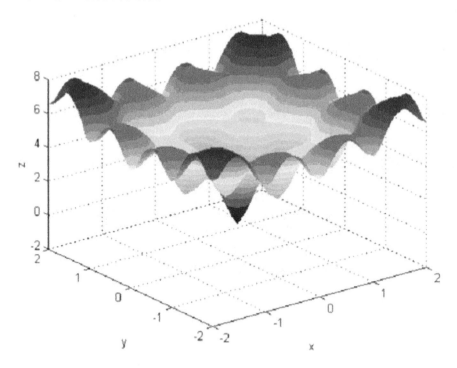

**Figure 7.9.** Generalized Ackley function.

### 7.4.3 PSO Scheme

The PSO scheme used in the experiment is used as suggested in Lvbjerg et al. [14]. The PSO used Equations 7.1 and 7.2, except that 7.1 is modified to as follows:

$$v[] =$$
$$w \ x \ v[] + c1 \ x \ rand() \ x \ (pbest[] - present[]) + c2 \ x \ rand() \ x \ (gbest[] - present[])$$
(7.8)

where $w$ is the additional initial weight, which varies from 0.9 to 0.7 linearly with the iterations. The learning factors, $c1$ and $c2$, are set to be 2 and. The upper and lower bounds for $v[]$, $(V_{min}, V_{max})$ are set to be the maximum upper and lower bounds of $present[]$, i.e. $(V_{min}, V_{max}) = (present\_MIN \ and \ present\_MAX)$. If the sum of accelerations would cause the velocity on that dimension to exceed $Vmax$ or $Vmin$, then the velocity on that dimension is limited to $Vmax$ or $Vmin$ respectively.

### 7.4.4 PS-EA Parameter settings

Three different sets of initial inheritance probabilities are used to test the performance of the DIPA module of PS-EA. The purpose of setting the

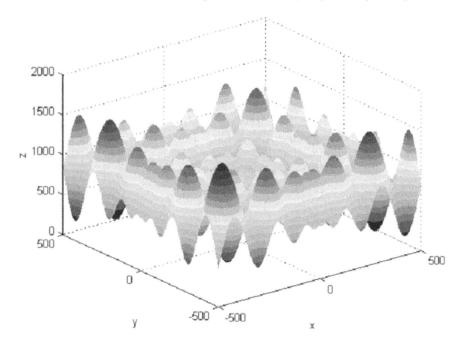

**Figure 7.10.** Generalised Schwefel function.

initial inheritance probabilities differently is to observe whether DIPA works properly and how a different initial set of inheritance probabilities will affect the performance of the algorithm. The sets are shown in Table 7.2.

**Table 7.2.** The three sets of initial inheritance probabilities.

| Inheritance probabilities | Set 1 | Set 2 | Set 3 |
|---|---|---|---|
| $P(Elite)$ | 4/10 | 1/12 | 1/3 |
| $P(Neighbor/Mutate)$ | 3/10 | 1/12 | 1/3 |
| $P(Remains)$ | 3/10 | 10/12 | 1/3 |
| $P(gbest)$ | 0.16 | 1/144 | 1/9 |
| $P(popbest)$ | 0.12 | 1/144 | 1/9 |
| $P(pbest)$ | 0.12 | 10/144 | 1/9 |
| $P(Neighbor)$ | 0.273 | 1/132 | 1/6 |
| $P(Mutate)$ | 0.027 | 10/132 | 1/6 |

Having the inheritance probabilities to be set fixed as according to Set 2 will result in slow/no convergence or even deterioration in the overall fitness of the swarm population. Thus, initial inheritance probabilities are purposely set as Set 2 so as to verify whether DIPA is able to adjust the set of inheritance probabilities for effective search. Set 3 is an arbitrary set by setting all inheritance probabilities to be equal.

### 7.4.5 Common Experimental Settings

In order to have a consistent set of initial settings for the experiments, the population size was set as 125. The range of values used for initialization for these test functions is shown in Table 7.3. The corresponding maximum generation for each dimension of the test function is shown in Table 7.4.

Table 7.3. Initialization range for the test functions.

| Function | Initialization range |
|----------|---------------------|
| $f_1$ | $(-600, 600)^n$ |
| $f_2$ | $(-15, 15)^n$ |
| $f_3$ | $(-15, 15)^n$ |
| $f_4$ | $(-32.768, 32.768)^n$ |
| $f_5$ | $(-500, 500)^n$ |

Table 7.4. Maximum generation for each dimension of the test function.

| Dimension | 10 | 20 | 30 |
|-----------|-----|-----|------|
| Maximum Generation | 500 | 750 | 1000 |

To compare the performance of these algorithms, tests were conducted to run each algorithm for various dimensions (10, 20 and 30) for each test function. A total of 30 runs were carried out for each, and the mean best and standard deviation (unbiased) for runs were collected for comparison, as shown later in this chapter

## 7.5 Simulation Results and Discussion

The results on the best mean values and standard deviations were obtained and tabulated after performing 30 trial runs of each algorithm for the five test functions. The best mean values provide a good indication regarding the convergence of the algorithm, while the standard deviations obtained indicate the stability of the algorithms. The best results of PS-EA, which are obtained using Set 2 probabilities, are compared with GA and PSO.

### 7.5.1 Optimization of Test Functions with Increasing Function Dimension

Table 7.5 shows the results of the simulation for the performance of each algorithm in optimizing the various functions of dimension 10 and maximum generation of 500 after running 30 trials. From these results, it is evident that PS-EA outperforms GA and PSO in the optimization of Rastrigrin and Schwefel functions, which are highly multi-modal. PS-EA has performed particularly well in the optimization of the Schwefel function, which is wickedly irregular with many local optima.

**Table 7.5.** Mean best costs and standard deviation (unbiased) obtained from 30 trials for function dimension 10 and maximum generation of 500.

| Function | GA | | PSO | | PS-EA | |
|---|---|---|---|---|---|---|
| | Mean best cost | Standard deviation | Mean best cost | Standard deviation | Mean best cost | Standard deviation |
| $f_1$ | 0.050228 | 0.029523 | 0.079393 | 0.033451 | 0.2223 | 0.0781 |
| $f_2$ | 1.3928 | 0.76319 | 2.6559 | 1.3896 | 0.43404 | 0.2551 |
| $f_3$ | 46.3184 | 33.8217 | 4.3713 | 2.3811 | 25.303 | 29.7964 |
| $f_4$ | 0.59267 | 0.22482 | $9.8499 \times 10^{-13}$ | $9.6202 \times 10^{-13}$ | 0.19209 | 0.1951 |
| $f_5$ | 1.9519 | 1.3044 | 161.87 | 144.16 | 0.32037 | 1.6185 |

Table 7.6 shows the results of the simulation for the performance of each algorithm in optimizing the various functions of dimension 20 and maximum generation of 750 after running 30 trials. It is observed that PS-EA outperforms GA and PSO in the optimization of Rastrigrin, Rosenbrock and Schwefel functions. It is noted for the optimization of Rosenbrock function, PS-EA has overtaken PSO as the best convergence performer at a higher dimension of 20 by a small margin. This suggests that PS-EA performs better when the problem becomes more complex. On Griewank and Ackley functions, PS-EA remains as the middle performer, with PSO and GA as the best and worst performers respectively.

**Table 7.6.** Mean best costs and standard deviation (unbiased) obtained from 30 trials for function dimension 20 and maximum generation of 750.

| Function | GA | | PSO | | PS-EA | |
|---|---|---|---|---|---|---|
| | Mean best cost | Standard deviation | Mean best cost | Standard deviation | Mean best cost | Standard deviation |
| $f_1$ | 1.0139 | 0.026966 | 0.030565 | 0.025419 | 0.59036 | 0.2030 |
| $f_2$ | 6.0309 | 1.4537 | 12.059 | 3.3216 | 1.8135 | 0.2551 |
| $f_3$ | 103.93 | 29.505 | 77.382 | 94.901 | 72.452 | 27.3441 |
| $f_4$ | 0.92413 | 0.22599 | $1.1778 \times 10^{-8}$ | $1.5842 \times 10^{-8}$ | 0.32321 | 0.097353 |
| $f_5$ | 7.285 | 2.9971 | 543.07 | 360.22 | 1.4984 | 0.84612 |

Table 7.7 shows the results of the simulation for the performance of each algorithm in optimizing the various functions of dimension 30 and maximum generation of 1,000 after running 30 trials. It is observed that PS-EA maintains itself as the best performer in the optimization of Rastrigrin, Rosenbrock and Schwefel functions, and a middle-performer in the optimization of Griewank and Ackley functions. Generally, PS-EA performs particularly well on functions of high dimension and complexity.

**Table 7.7.** Mean best costs and standard deviation (unbiased) obtained from 30 trials for function dimension 30 and maximum generation of 1,000.

| Function | GA | | PSO | | PS-EA | |
|---|---|---|---|---|---|---|
| | Mean best cost | Standard deviation | Mean best cost | Standard deviation | Mean best cost | Standard deviation |
| $f_1$ | 1.2342 | 0.11045 | 0.011151 | 0.014209 | 0.8211 | 0.1394 |
| $f_2$ | 10.4388 | 2.6386 | 32.476 | 6.9521 | 3.0527 | 0.9985 |
| $f_3$ | 166.283 | 59.5102 | 402.54 | 633.65 | 98.407 | 35.5791 |
| $f_4$ | 1.0989 | 0.24956 | $1.4917 \times 10^{-6}$ | $1.8612 \times 10^{-6}$ | 0.3771 | 0.098762 |
| $f_5$ | 13.5346 | 4.9534 | 990.77 | 581.14 | 3.272 | 1.6185 |

PS-EA has experimentally proven to be a good optimization algorithm for multi-model test functions of Rastrigrin and Schwefel, as well as the unimodal function of Rosenbrock. In the optimization of Griewank and Ackley functions, it middle-performs between GA and PSO. It is also observed that PS-EA performs exceedingly well when the function dimension increases, as shown in its optimization of Rastrigrin, Rosenbrock and Schwefel functions for function dimension of 30 in Table 7.7, where the results obtained by PS-EA are much better than GA and PSO.

### 7.5.2 Multiobjective Function Optimization

PS-EA can be applied to solve multiobjective problems. The results on Fonseca 2-objective minimization problem, defined as follows, are shown in this section.
    Minimize:

$$f_1(x_1, x_2, ...x_8) = 1 - exp(-\sum_{i=1}^{8}(x_i - \frac{1}{\sqrt{8}})^2) \qquad (7.9)$$

$$f_1(x_1, x_2, ...x_8) = 1 - exp(-\sum_{i=1}^{8}(x_i + \frac{1}{\sqrt{8}})^2) \qquad (7.10)$$

where $-2 \leq x_i \leq 2, \forall i = 1, 2, ...8$.
The true Pareto-optimal set for this problem is $x_1 = x_2 = ... = x_8, -\frac{1}{\sqrt{8}} \leq$

---

1.  Initialization of swarm

2.  Evaluation of particles (based on shared fitness and Pareto ranking).

3.  While (NOT maximum generation)

     a.   Identify pbest

     b.   PS-EA operations

     c.   Evaluation of extended population

     d.   Selection for next generation

4.  Use either the final population of particles or pbest as the final solutions for the Pareto front.

---

**Figure 7.11.** The flow of multiobjective PS-EA (MOPS-EA).

$x_i \leq \frac{1}{\sqrt{8}}, i = 1, 2, ..., 8$. To apply PS-EA in this multiobjective problem, the algorithm is modified as in Figure 7.11.

With MOPS-EA as modified from PS-EA, simulation tests were conducted to solve the Fonseca's problem. A sample objective curve, as shown in Figure 7.12 is plotted at the 100th generation, showing the objective positions of *pbest* particles.

It can be seen that the final solution of *pbest* particles (as denoted by +) converges closely to the true Pareto front. This application establishes the applicability of this algorithm for searching in multi-modal as well as multiobjective problem domains.

## 7.6 Conclusions

This chapter describes Particle Swarm Inspired Evolutionary Algorithm (PS-EA), which is a hybridized Evolutionary Algorithm (EA) that combines the concepts of EA and Particle Swarm Theory. The Self-updating Mechanism (SUM) developed in this chapter overcomes the inherent limitations of PSO and promises drastic performance improvement for multi-modal functions. Another important element of this hybrid algorithm is the Dynamic Inheritance Probability Adjuster (DIPA), an autonomous module which dynamically adjusts the inheritance probabilities of the probability inheritance tree based on the convergence rate of the algorithm. DIPA greatly reduces the need for the algorithm designers to experimentally determine the best set of parameter values for a given optimization task. A comparison of results between PS-EA, and previously reported best methods such as Genetic Algorithm (GA) and PSO, demonstrates that PS-EA outperforms

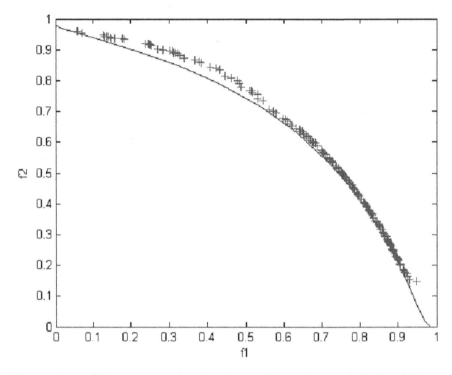

**Figure 7.12.** Objective curve showing the true Pareto front and the found Pareto optimal set (+) at the 100th generation of PS-EA.

these methods on challenging benchmark functions in terms of both its convergence and stability. These favorable results render PS-EA an attractive candidate algorithm to solve difficult real-world optimization problems of high dimensions.

## References

1. Hondroudakis, A, Malard, J and Wilson, GV, An Introduction to Genetic Algorithms Using RPL2: The EPIC Version, Computer Based Learning Unit, University of Leeds, 1995.
2. Digalakis, JG, and Margaritis, KG, An Experimental Study of Benchmarking Functions for Genetic Algorithms, 2000 IEEE International Conference on Systems, Man, and Cybernetics, Nashville, vol. 5, pp. 3810 -3815, 2000.
3. Sinclair, MC, The application of a genetic algorithm to trunk network routing table optimization," 10th.Performance Engineering in Telecommunications Network Teletraffic Symposium, pp. 2/1 -2/6, 1993.

4. Greenwood, GW, Lang, C, and Hurley, S, Scheduling Tasks in Real-time Systems Using Evolutionary Strategies, Proceedings of the Third Workshop on Parallel and Distributed Real-Time Systems, pp. 195 -196, 1995.
5. Fogel, D, and Sebald, AV, Use of Evolutionary Programming in the Design Of Neural Networks For Artifact Detection," Proceedings of the Twelfth Annual International Conference of the IEEE Engineering in Medicine and Biology Society, pp. 1408 -1409, 1990.
6. Meshref, H, and VanLandingham, H, Artificial Immune Systems: Application to Autonomous Agents, 2000 IEEE International Conference on Systems, Man, and Cybernetics, Nashville, Vol. 1, pp. 61 -66, 2000.
7. Di Stefano, C and Tettamanzi, AGB, An Evolutionary Algorithm for Solving the School Time-Tabling Problem, Proceedings of Applications of Evolutionary Computing, pp. 452-462, 2001.
8. Srinivasan, D, Seow, TH, and Xu, JX, Automated Time Table Generation Using Multiple Context for University Modules,Proceedings of IEEE Congress of Evolutionary Computation, vol. 2, pp. 1751-1756, 2002.
9. Srinivasan, D, Seow, TH, and Xu, JX, Constraint-Based University Time-Tabling Using Evolutionary Algorithm,Proceedings of the 4th Asia-Pacific Conference on Simulated Evolution And Learning, Singapore, vol. 2, pp. 252-256, 2002.
10. Kennedy, J, Eberhart, RC, and Shi, Y, Swarm Intelligence, San Francisco, Morgan Kaufman Publishers, 2002.
11. Eberhart, RC, and Shi, Y, Particle Swarm Optimization: Developments, Applications and Resources, Proceedings of the 2001 Congress on Evolutionary Computation, Seoul, vol. 1, pp. 81-86, 2001.
12. Zhang, C, Shao, H, and Li, Y, Particle Swarm Optimisation for Evolving Artificial Neural Network, 2000 IEEE International Conference on Systems, Man, and Cybernetics, vol. 4, pp. 2487-2490 ,2000.
13. Angeline, PJ, Using Selection to Improve Particle Swarm Optimization, The 1998 IEEE International Conference on IEEE World Congress on Computational Intelligence Evolutionary Computation Proceedings, Alaska, pp. 84 -89, 1998.
14. Lvbjerg, M, Rasmussen, T, and Krink, T, Hybrid Particle Swarm Optimiser with Breeding and Subpopulations, Proceedings of the Genetic and Evolutionary Computation Conference, 2001.
15. Tan, KC, Lee, TH, and Khor, EF, Evolutionary Algorithms with Goal and Priority Information for Multiobjective Optimzation," In Proceedings of the Congress in Evolutionary Computation, Washington, DC, vol. 1, pp. 106-113, 1999.

# 8

# Evolving Continuous Pareto Regions

D. Dumitrescu, Crina Groşan, and Mihai Oltean

**Summary.** In this chapter we propose a new evolutionary elitist approach combining a non-standard solution representation and an evolutionary optimization technique. The proposed method permits detection of continuous decision regions. In our approach an individual (a solution) is either a closed interval or a point. The individuals in the final population give a realistic representation of the Pareto-optimal set. Each solution in this population corresponds to a decision region of the Pareto-optimal set. The proposed technique is an elitist one. It uses a unique population. The current population contains non-dominated solutions already computed.

## 8.1 Introduction

Several evolutionary algorithms for solving multiobjective optimization problems have been proposed [1-14]; see also the reviews [15-17].

Usually Pareto evolutionary algorithms aim to give a discrete picture of the Pareto-optimal set (and of the corresponding Pareto frontier), but generally the Pareto-optimal set is a continuous region in the search space. Therefore a continuous region is represented by a discrete set. When continuous decision regions are represented by discrete solutions there is loss of information. Moreover reconstructing a continuous Pareto set from a discrete picture is not an easy task [16].

In Dumitrescu et al. [4] an evolutionary algorithm for detecting continuous Pareto-optimal sets has been proposed. The method proposed there uses a Genetic Chromodynamics evolutionary technique [18] to maintain population diversity.

In this chapter a new evolutionary approach, combining a non-standard solution representation and a Genetic Chromodynamics optimization technique, is considered. Within the proposed approach continuous decision regions may be detected. A solution (individual) is either a closed interval or a point (considered as a degenerated interval). Mutation is the unique search operator considered.

The mutation operator idea is to expand each individual towards the left and towards the right. In this respect both interval extremities are mutated. The left extremity is mutated towards the left and the right extremity is mutated towards the right.

To reduce population size and to obtain the correct number of solutions within the final population the *merging* operator introduced in the context of Genetic Chromodynamics is used.

The solutions in the final population supply a realistic representation of the Pareto-optimal set. Each solution in this population corresponds to a decision region (a subset of Pareto set). A decision region will also be called a *Pareto region.*

The solutions are detected in two stages. In the first stage a Genetic Chromodynamics technique is used to detect all (local and global) Pareto solutions. In the second stage the solutions are refined. During the fine tuning the sub-optimal regions are removed.

The evolutionary multiobjective technique proposed in this chapter is called the *Pareto Evolutionary Continuous Regions*(PECR) algorithm.

## 8.2 Problem statement

Let $\Omega$ be the search space. Consider $n$ objective functions $f_1, f_2, \ldots f_n$, $f_i : \Omega \to \Re$, where $\Omega \subset \Re$. Consider the multiobjective optimization problem:

$$\begin{cases} \text{optimize } f(x) = (f_1(x), ..., f_n(x)) \\ \text{subject to } x \in \Omega. \end{cases}$$

The key concept in determining solutions of multiobjective optimization problems is that of Pareto optimality. In what follows we recall some basic definitions.

**Definition 1.** (*Pareto dominance*)
Consider a maximization problem. Let $x$, $y$ be two decision vectors (solutions) from $\Omega$.

Solution $x$ *dominate* $y$ (also written as $x \succ y$) if and only if the following conditions are fulfilled:

(1) $f_i(x) \geq f_i(y)$, $\forall i = 1, 2, \ldots, n$,
(2) $\exists j \in \{1, 2, \ldots, n\}$: $f_j(x) > f_j(y)$.

**Definition 2.**
Let $S \subseteq \Omega$ be a subset of the search space. All solutions, which are not dominated by any vector of $S$, are called *non-dominated* with respect to $S$.

**Definition 3.**
Solutions that are non-dominated with respect to $S$, $S \subset \Omega$, are called *local Pareto* solutions or *local Pareto regions*.

**Definition 4.**
Solutions that are non-dominated with respect to the entire search space $\Omega$ are called *Pareto-optimal* solutions.

Let us note that when the search space is a subset of $\Re$, then the Pareto-optimal set may be represented as:

*(1)* a set of points;
*(2)* a set of disjoint intervals;
*(3)* a set of disjoint intervals and a set of points.

**Remark**
In each of the cases *(1)*, *(2)* and *(3)* a point or an interval represents a Pareto region.

Evolutionary multiobjective optimization algorithms are intended for supplying a discrete picture of the Pareto-optimal set and of the Pareto frontier. But the Pareto set is usually a union of continuous set. When continuous decision regions are represented by discrete solutions there is some information loss. The resulting sets are but a discrete representation of their continuous counterparts.

Methods for finding the Pareto-optimal set and Pareto-optimal front using discrete solutions are computationally very difficult. However, the results may be accepted as the best possible at a given computational resolution.

The evolutionary method proposed in this chapter directly supply the true (i.e. possibly continuous) Pareto-optimal set.

## 8.3 Solution Representation and Domination

In this chapter we consider solutions are represented as intervals in the search space $\Omega$.

Each interval-solution $k$ is encoded by an interval $[x_k, \ y_k] \subset \Re$. Degenerated intervals are allowed. Within degenerate case $(y_k = x_k)$ the solution is a point.

In order to deal with the proposed representation a new domination concept is needed. This domination concept is given by the next definition.

**Definition 5.**
An interval-solution $[x, y]$ is said to be *interval-nondominated* if and only if all points of that interval $[x, y]$ are non-dominated point-wise solutions. An interval-nondominated solution will be called a *Pareto-interval*.

**Remarks**

1. If $x = y$ this concept reduced towards the ordinary non-domination notion.
2. If no ambiguity arises we will use *non-dominated* instead of *interval-nondominated*.

## 8.4 ε−dominance

A true Pareto set may comprise well-separated points which do not dominate each other. However, due to the representation capabilities these points could be represented by different numbers. For instance the number $x = 0.17$ may be represented either as $x' = 0.1$ or as $x" = 0.2$, for a particular parameter representation setting. Let us consider that $x$ represent a non-dominated solution. It is possible that $x'$ or $x"$ are dominated solutions.

Therefore representation limitations may induce a falsification of domination relationship. As a consequence some points belonging to the true Pareto set could be lost during the search process based on domination.

A procedure for avoiding the loss of some solutions is highly needed. Such a procedure may be based on a new concept of dominance that takes into account the representation precision.

We propose to use the notion of $\varepsilon$-*dominance*.

**Definition 6.** (ε-*dominance*)
Consider a maximization problem. Let $x$, $y$ be two decision vectors (solutions) from $\Omega$.

Solution $x$ $\varepsilon$-*dominate* $y$ if and only if the following conditions are fulfilled:

(i) $f_1(x) \geq f_i(y), \forall \quad i = 1, 2, \ldots, n,$
(2) $\exists j \in \{1, 2, \ldots, n\}: f_j(x) > f_j(y) + \varepsilon.$

The concept of $\varepsilon$-dominance will be used for the fine tuning process.

## 8.5 Mutation

Problem solutions are detected in two stages. In the first stage a Genetic Chromodynamics technique is used to detect all (global and local) solutions. This represents the *evolution stage.*

In the second stage (*fine tuning* or *refinement stage*) solutions that have been detected in the first stage are refined. By using the refinement procedure sub-optimal Pareto regions are removed from the final population.

Most of the multiobjective optimization techniques based on Pareto ranking use a secondary population (an archive) denoted $P_{second}$ for storing nondominated individuals. Archive members may be used to guide the search process. As dimension of secondary population may dramatically increase several mechanisms for reducing archive size have been proposed. In Knowles and Corne [10] and Schaffer [11] a population decreasing technique based on a clustering procedure is considered. We may observe that preserving only one individual from each cluster implies a loss of information.

In our approach the population size does not increase during the search process even if the number of Pareto-optimal points increase. The population size is kept low due to the special representation we consider.

When a new non-dominated point is found it replaces another point solution in the population or it is used for building a new interval solution with another point in the population. This does not cause any information loss concerning the Pareto-optimal set during the search process.

The algorithm starts with a population of degenerated intervals (i.e. a population of points). The unique variation operator is mutation. It consists of normal perturbation of interval extremities. Mutation can also be applied to point-solutions (considered as degenerated intervals). Each interval extremity is mutated. The left extremity of an interval is always mutated towards the left and the right interval extremity is mutated only towards the right.

For mutation two cases are to be considered.

1. *Degenerated interval.*
   First, the individual is mutated towards the left. The obtained point represents the offspring. Parent and offspring compete for survival.
   If the offspring dominates its parent it will be added to the new population. If the parent dominates the offspring then the parent is mutated towards the right. The best, in the sense of domination, enter the new population. If parent and offspring are not comparable with respect to domination relation then the two points define an interval solution. The new interval solution is included in the new generation. The point solution representing the parent is discarded.

2. *Non-degenerated interval.*
   (a) First, the left extremity of the interval $[u, v]$ is mutated towards the left. A point-offspring $u'$ is obtained. Consider the case when the offspring $u'$ and the parent $u$ do not dominate each other. In this situation a new interval solution $[u', v]$ is generated. The new solution has the offspring $u'$ as its left extremity and $v$ as its right extremity.
   If the offspring $u'$ dominates the parent $u$, then the interval solution $[u, v]$ enters the new population.
   (b) A similar mutation procedure is applied to the right interval extremity of the solution ($[u, v]$ or $[u', v]$) previously obtained.

## 8.6 Population Model

For each generation every individual in the current population is mutated. Parents and offspring directly compete for survival. The domination relation guides this competition.

For detecting the correct number of Pareto-optimal regions it is necessary to have, in the final population, only one solution per Pareto-optimal region.

In this chapter we consider the merging operator of Genetic Chromodynamics for implementing the population decreasing mechanism. Very close solutions are fused and population size decreases accordingly.

In the framework of this chapter the merging operator is described as bellow:

- If two interval solutions overlap the shortest interval solution is discarded.
- Degenerated interval-solutions included in non-degenerated interval-solutions are removed too;
- If two degenerated solutions are closer than a fixed threshold $r$ then the worst solution is discarded.

The merging operator is applied each time a new individual enters the population.

The method allows a natural termination condition. The algorithm stops when there is no improvement of the solutions for a fixed number of generations. Each solution in the last population supplies a Pareto-optimal region contributing to the picture of the Pareto-optimal set.

### 8.6.1 Fine Tuning

For this reason final solutions may consist from inhomogeneous sub-solutions representing global and local optima. Some sub-solutions may correspond to optimal Pareto regions.

It is desirable to eliminate sub-solutions (segments) corresponding to local optima. This elimination may be considered as a fine tuning process. Solutions closer to the true Pareto set are expected to be obtained. Other sub-solutions may represent to local Pareto regions.

The idea of fine-tuning is to isolate and discard from each final solution sub-intervals representing local optima. For accomplishing the fine tuning task each final solution is discretized.

Let $D$ be the set of points obtained by discretizing the solution $[x, y]$. Domination of each member of $D$ is tested against the other points from $D$. The proposed model is based on local domination (only pairs of individuals are compared with respect to domination relation). The discretized solutions are compare by using the $\varepsilon$-dominance concept.

During the fine tuning stage sub-optimal solutions (regions) are removed. For this aim each continuous Pareto region is transformed into a discrete set. Discretized version is obtained considering points within each interval solution at a fixed step size.

Let us denote by $ss$ the step size. Consider an interval solution $[x, y]$. From this solution consider the points $x_j$ fulfilling the conditions:

$(1)\, x_j = x + j \cdot ss,\ j = 0,\ 1,\ \ldots$
$(2)\, x_j \leq y.$

These points represent the discretized version (denoted $D$) of the interval solution $[x, y]$.

Each point $x_j$ within the interval solutions is checked. If a point from the discretized set $D$ dominates the point $x_j$ then $x_j$ is removed from the Pareto interval $[x, y]$ together with a small neighboring region. The size of the removed region is equal with $ss$.

The intervals obtained after this stage are considered as the true Pareto sets.

## 8.7 Algorithm Complexity

The complexity of the proposed algorithm is low. Let $m$ be the number of objectives and $N$ the population size. The first stage requires

$$K_1 = O(m \cdot N \cdot \textit{IterationNumber}) \quad \text{operations.}$$

Consider $I_{max}$ as the longest interval solution in the population. Consider a function

$$F : \Re \times \Re \to N.$$

Admit that $F$ fulfills the following conditions:

*(1)* $F$ is a linear function,
*(2)* $F([a, a]) = 1$,
    for each $a \in (-\infty, \infty)$.

Second stage (fine tuning) requires

$$K_2 = O(N^2 \cdot F(I_{max})^2) \quad \text{operations.}$$

## 8.8 PECR Algorithm

Using the previous considerations we are ready to design a new multiobjective optimization algorithm.

The evolution stage of the PECR algorithm is outlined as below:

```
generates an initial population P(0). {all intervals are degenerated i.e. xk = yk}
   t = 0;
   while not (Stop_Condition) do
   begin
     for each individual k in P(t) do
     begin
       Left_offspr = MutateTowardsLeft(xk);
       if dominate(Left_offspr, xk)
       then
         if xk = yk
         then xk = yk = Left_offspr;
       else
         if nondominated(Left_offspr, xk)
         then xk= Left_offspr;
       Right_offspr = MutateTowardsRight(yk);
```

    **if** dominate(Right_offspr, $y_k$)
    **then**
      **if** $x_k = y_k$
      **then** $x_k = y_k = $ Right_offspr;
    **else**
      **if** nondominated(Right_offspr, $y_k$)
      **then** $y_k = $ Right_offspr;
    **endif**
    **endfor**
    Remove_Overlaping_Intervals;
    Remove_Similar_Degenerated_Intervals;
    $t = t + 1$
   **endwhile**

Fine tuning part of PECR algorithm is obvious.

## 8.9 Numerical Experiments

Several numerical experiments using PECR algorithm have been performed. For all examples the detected solutions gave correct representations of Pareto set with an acceptable accuracy degree. Some particular examples are given below.

### 8.9.1 Example 1

Consider the functions $f_1, f_2 : [-9, 9] \to \Re$ defined as

$$f_1(x) = x^2,$$
$$f_2(x) = 9 - \sqrt{81 - x^2},$$

and the multiobjective optimization problem:

$$\begin{cases} \text{minimize } f(x) = (f_1(x), f_2(x)) \\ \text{subject to} \\ x \in [-9, 9]. \end{cases}$$

The initial population is depicted in Figures 8.1 and 8.2.
Consider the standard deviation parameter value

$$\sigma = 0.1.$$

In this case population obtained after 10 generations is depicted in Figures 8.3 and 8.4. The final population, obtained after 70 generations, is depicted in Figures 8.5 and 8.6.

The final population obtained at convergence after 70 generations contains only one individual represented as degenerated interval (i.e. a point)

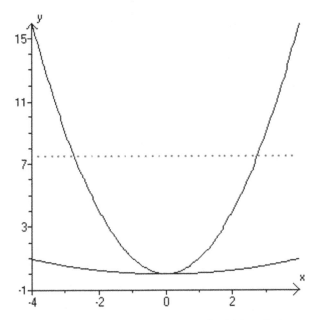

**Figure 8.1.** Initial population represented within solution space.

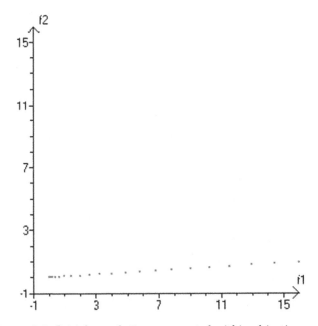

**Figure 8.2.** Initial population represented within objective space.

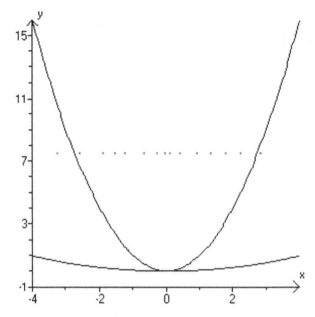

**Figure 8.3.** Population obtained after 10 generations represented within solution space.

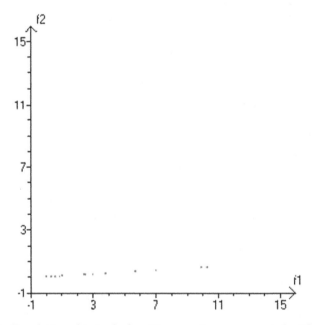

**Figure 8.4.** Population obtained after 10 generations represented within objective space.

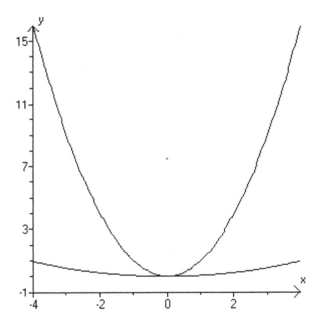

**Figure 8.5.** Final population obtained after 70 generations represented within solution space.

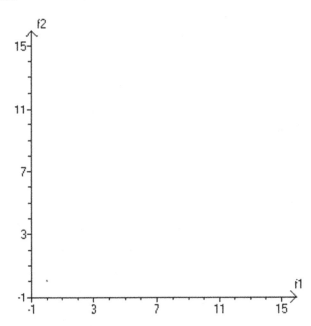

**Figure 8.6.** Final population obtained after 70 generations represented within objective space.

$$s = -0.001.$$

Therefore, the detected Pareto-optimal set consists from a single point:

$$P_{detect} = \{-0.001\}.$$

We may remark that the detected Pareto set represents a good estimation of the correct Pareto-optimal set

$$P_c = \{0\}.$$

Accuracy of this estimation can be easily improved by using smaller values of the parameter $\sigma$ (standard deviation). In this case a larger number of generations are needed for convergence. For instance, if we put

$$\sigma = 0.01,$$

the obtained solution is

$$s = 0.0008.$$

## 8.9.2 Example 2

Consider the functions $f_1, f_2 : [-4, 6] \to \Re$ defined as

$$f_1(x) = x^2,$$

$$f_2(x) = (x - 2)^2.$$

Consider the multiobjective optimization problem:

$$\begin{cases} \text{minimize } f(x) = (f_1(x), f_2(x)) \\ \text{subject to } x \in [-4, 6]. \end{cases}$$

The initial population represented within solution space is depicted in Figure 8.7. The initial population represented within objective space is depicted in Figure 8.8.

For the value

$$\sigma = 0.1$$

of the standard deviation parameter solutions obtained after 5 generations are depicted in Figures 8.9 and 8.10.

The final population, obtained after 35 generations, is depicted in Figures 8.11 and 8.12.

The final population contains only one individual. This individual is:

$$s = [0.01, 1.98],$$

and represents a continuous Pareto optimal solution.

The obtained solution accuracy may be increased, if necessary, by decreasing the parameter standard deviation of normal perturbation. Of course, the number of iterations needed for convergence increases this case.

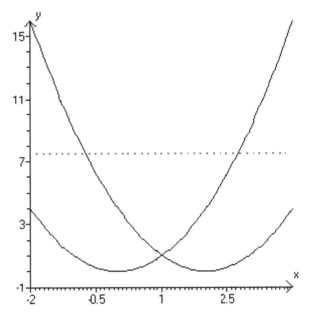

**Figure 8.7.** Initial population represented within solution space.

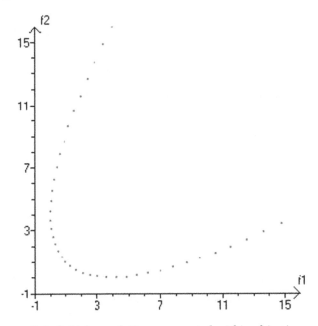

**Figure 8.8.** Initial population represented within objective space.

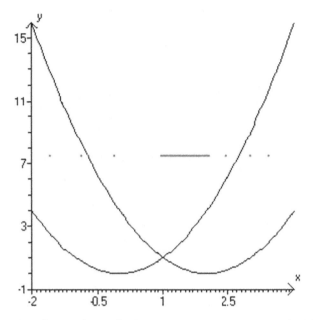

**Figure 8.9.** Population obtained after 5 generations represented within solution space.

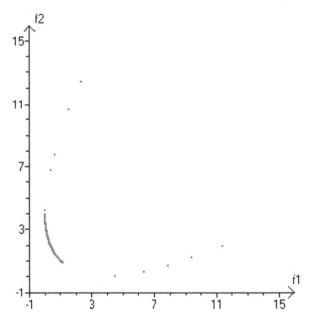

**Figure 8.10.** Population obtained after 5 generations represented within objective space.

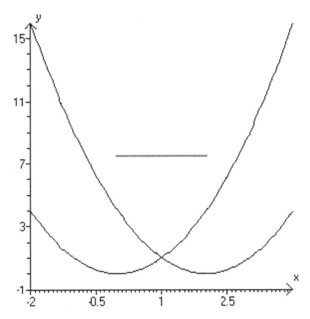

**Figure 8.11.** Final population obtained after 35 generations represented within solution space.

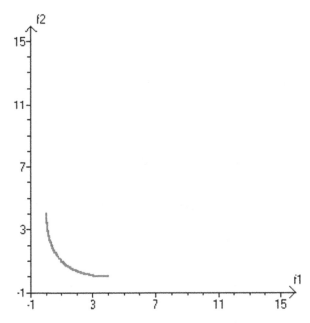

**Figure 8.12.** Final population obtained after 35 generations represented within objective space.

### 8.9.3 Example 3

Consider the functions $f_1, f_2 : [-10, 13] \rightarrow \Re$ defined as

$$f_1(x) = sin(x),$$

$$f_2(x) = sin(x + 0.7).$$

Consider the multiobjective optimization problem:

$$\begin{cases} \text{minimize } f(x) = (f_1(x), f_2(x)) \\ \text{subject to } x \in [-10, 13] \end{cases}$$

The initial population is depicted in Figures 8.13 and 8.14.
Consider the value

$$\sigma = 0.1$$

for the standard deviation of mutation operator. Solutions obtained after 3 generations are depicted in Figures 8.15 and 8.16.

The final population, obtained after 42 generations, is depicted in Figures 8.17 and 8.18.

The final population after the refinement stage is depicted in Figures 8.19 and 8.20.

Solutions in the final population are:

$$\begin{aligned} s_1 &= [-8.47, -7.86], \\ s_2 &= [-2.26, -1.56], \\ s_3 &= [4.01, 4.69], \\ s_4 &= [10.29, 10.99]. \end{aligned}$$

### 8.9.4 Example 4

Consider the functions $f_1, f_2 : [-10, 20] \rightarrow \Re$ defined as

$$f_1(x) = sin(x),$$

$$f_2(x) = 2 \cdot sin(x) + 1.$$

Consider the multiobjective optimization problem:

$$\begin{cases} \text{minimize } f(x) = (f_1(x), f_2(x)) \\ \text{subject to } x \in [-10, 20] \end{cases}$$

The initial population is depicted in Figures 8.21 and 8.22.
For the value

$$\sigma = 0.1$$

solutions obtained after 14 generations are depicted in Figures 8.23 and 8.24.

The final population, obtained after 70 generations, is depicted in Figures 8.25 and 8.26.

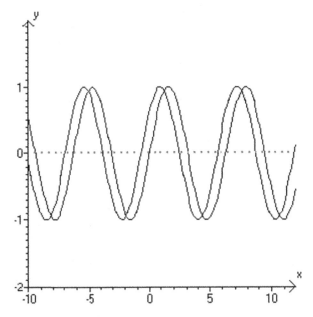

**Figure 8.13.** Initial population represented within solution space.

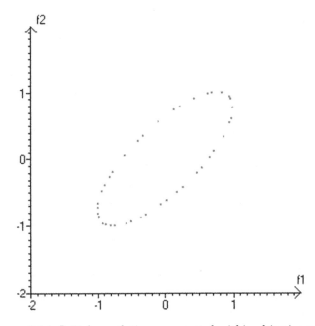

**Figure 8.14.** Initial population represented within objective space.

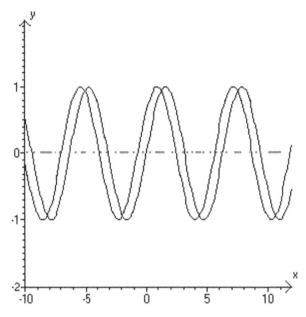

**Figure 8.15.** Population obtained after 3 generations represented within solution space.

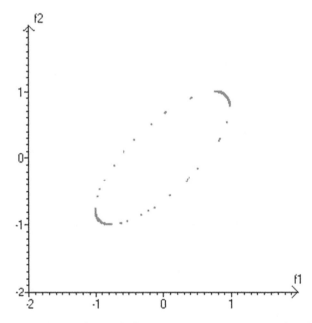

**Figure 8.16.** Population obtained after 3 generations represented within objective space.

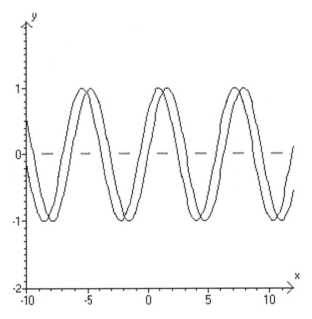

**Figure 8.17.** Population obtained at convergence (after 42 generations) represented within solution space.

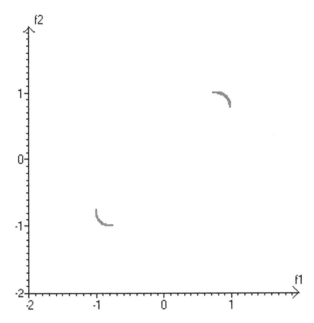

**Figure 8.18.** Population obtained at convergence (after 42 generations) represented within objective space.

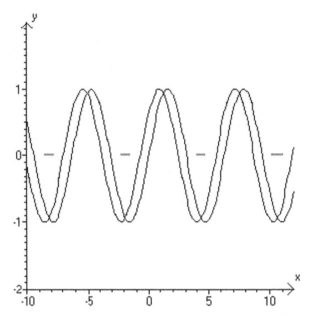

**Figure 8.19.** Final population obtained after fine tuning stage represented within solution space.

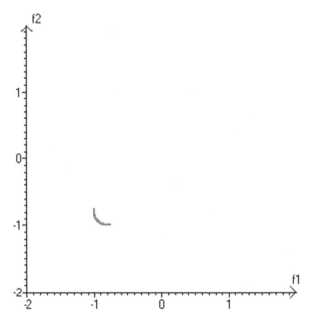

**Figure 8.20.** Final population obtained after fine tuning stage represented within objective space.

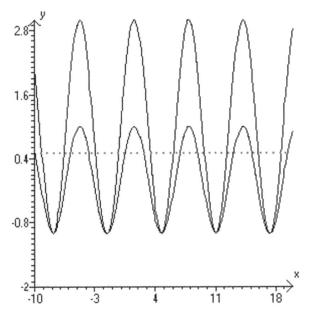

**Figure 8.21.** Initial population represented within solution space.

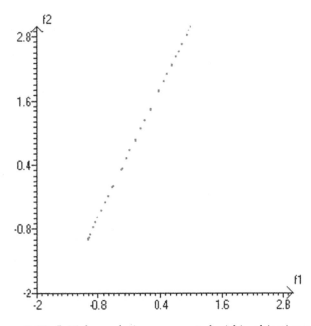

**Figure 8.22.** Initial population represented within objective space.

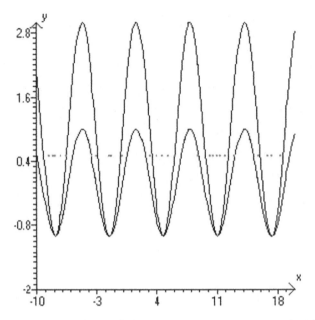

**Figure 8.23.** Population obtained after 14 generations represented within solution space.

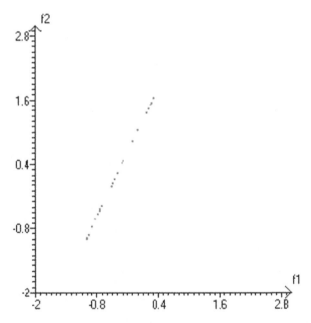

**Figure 8.24.** Population obtained after 14 generations represented within objective space.

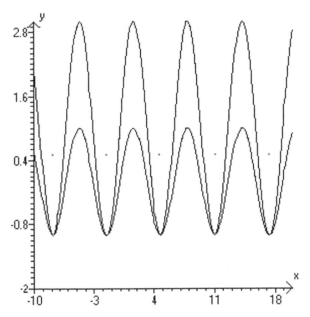

**Figure 8.25.** Final population obtained after 70 generations represented within solution space.

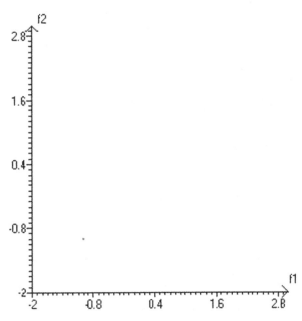

**Figure 8.26.** Final population obtained after 70 generations represented within objective space.

**8.9.5 Example 5**

Consider the functions $f_1, f_2 : [0, 24] \to \Re$ defined as

$$f_1(x) = sin(x),$$

$f_2(x) =$

$$\begin{cases} \frac{-4 \cdot x}{\pi} + 8 \cdot k, & 2 \cdot k \cdot \pi \le x < 2 \cdot k \cdot \pi + \frac{\pi}{2}, \\ \frac{4 \cdot x}{\pi} - 4 \cdot (2 \cdot k + 1), & 2 \cdot k \cdot \pi + \frac{\pi}{2} \le x < (2 \cdot k + 1) \cdot \pi, \\ \frac{-2 \cdot x}{\pi} + 2 \cdot (2 \cdot k + 1), & (2 \cdot k + 1) \cdot \pi \le x < (2 \cdot k + 1) \cdot \pi + \frac{3 \cdot \pi}{2}, \\ \frac{2 \cdot x}{\pi} - 4 \cdot (k + 1), & 2 \cdot k \cdot \pi + \frac{3 \cdot \pi}{2} \le x < 2 \cdot (k + 1) \cdot \pi. \end{cases} \quad k \in Z^+.$$

Consider the multiobjective optimization problem:

$$\begin{cases} \text{minimize } f(x) = (f_1(x), f_2(x)) \\ \text{subject to } x \in [0, 24] \end{cases}$$

The initial population is depicted in Figure 8.27 and 8.28.
For the value

$$\sigma = 0.1$$

solutions obtained after 4 generations are depicted in Figures 8.29 and 8.30.

The final population, obtained after 60 generations, is depicted in Figures 8.31 and 8.32.

The final population after the refinement stage is depicted in Figures 8.33 and 8.34.

## 8.10 Comparison of Several Multiobjective Evolutionary Algorithms

Here we show a comparison of various evolutionary algorithms for multiobjective optimization using five test functions. The functions were provided in the previous section.

We compared four algorithms on each test function.

NSGA II: The Nondominated Sorting Genetic Algorithm II [3]

PAES: The Pareto Archived Evolution Strategy [9, 10]

SPEA: The Strength Pareto Evolutionary Algorithm [13]

PECR: The Pareto Evolutionary Continuous Regions

The multiobjective EAs were executed once on each test problem. In what follows we provide parameters used for each algorithm.

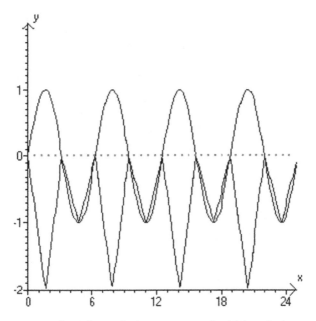

**Figure 8.27.** Initial population represented within solution space.

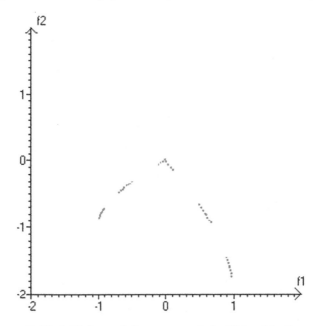

**Figure 8.28.** Initial population represented within objective space.

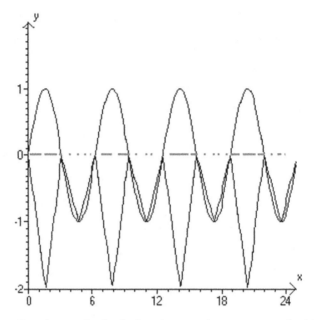

**Figure 8.29.** Population obtained after 4 generations represented within solution space.

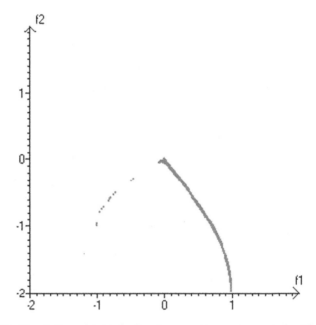

**Figure 8.30.** Population obtained after 4 generations represented within objective space.

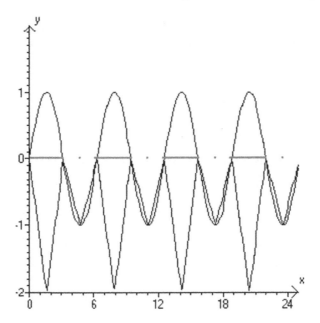

**Figure 8.31.** Population obtained at convergence (after 60 generations) represented within solution space.

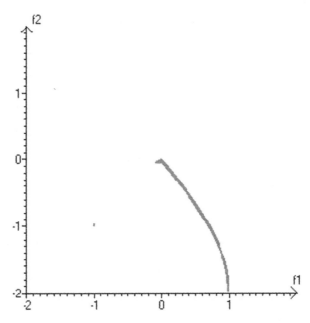

**Figure 8.32.** Population obtained at convergence (after 60 generations) represented within objective space.

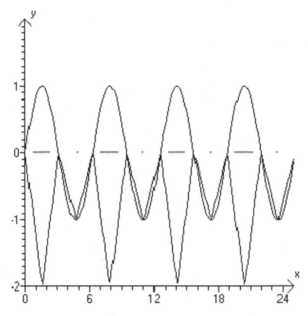

**Figure 8.33.** Final population obtained after fine tuning stage represented within solution space.

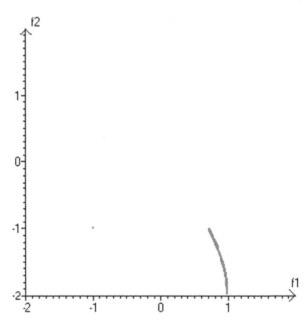

**Figure 8.34.** Final population obtained after fine tuning stage represented within objective space.

NSGA II:

Individual representation: binary encoding
Selection strategy: binary tournament
Chromosome length: 10
Crossover type: 1 cut-point
Crossover probability: 0.8
Mutation probability: 0.1
Generations: 250
Population size: 100

SPEA

Individual representation: binary encoding
Selection strategy: binary tournament
Chromosome length: 10
Crossover type: 1 cut-point
Mutation probability: 0.1
Generations: 250
Population size: 100

PAES

Individual representation: binary encoding
Chromosome length: 10
Division depth: 6
Mutation probability: 0.2
Number of function evaluations: 25000
Archived size: 100

PECR

Individual representation: Real
Population size: 40
Sigma: 0.03
Similarity distance: 0.1
$\varepsilon-$dominance value: 0.003

The results of the comparison are depicted in Figures 8.35, 8.36, 8.37, 8.38, 8.39. Solutions obtained by the first three algorithms are drawn as vertical segments in order to obtain a true representation.

## 8.11 Concluding Remarks and Further Research

A new evolutionary technique for solving multiobjective optimization problems involving one variable functions is proposed. A new solution representation is used. Standard search (variation) operators are modified accordingly. The proposed evolutionary multiobjective optimization technique

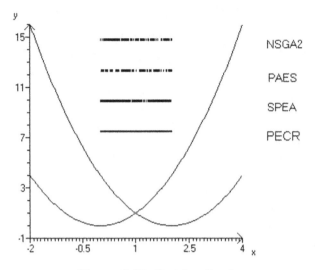

**Figure 8.35.** Test function 1.

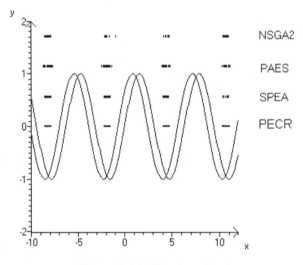

**Figure 8.36.** Test function 2.

uses only one population. This population consists of non-dominated solutions already computed.

All known standard or recent multiobjective optimization techniques supply a discrete picture of Pareto-optimal solutions and of the Pareto frontier. But the Pareto optimal set is usually non-discrete. Finding the Pareto-optimal set and Pareto-optimal frontiers using a discrete representation is not a very easy task computationally (see [16]).

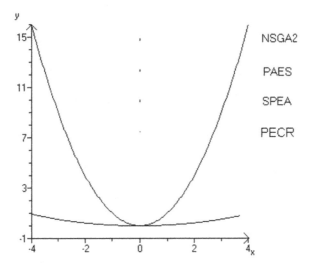

**Figure 8.37.** Test function 3.

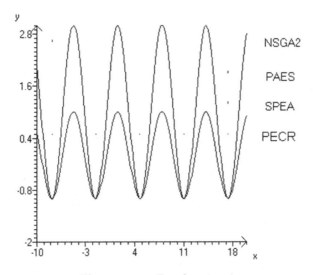

**Figure 8.38.** Test function 4.

The evolutionary technique proposed in this chapter supplies directly a continuous picture of the Pareto-optimal set and of the Pareto frontier. This makes our approach very appealing for solving problems where very accurate solutions detection is needed.

Another advantage is that the PECR technique has a natural termination condition derived from the nature of the evolutionary method used for

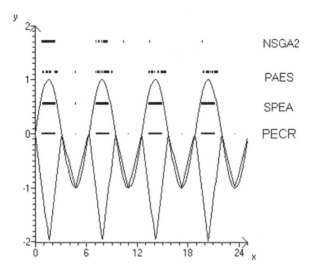

**Figure 8.39.** Test function 5.

preserving population diversity. Experimental results suggest that the PECR algorithm supplies correct solutions after few generations.

Further research will focus on the possibilities to extend the proposed technique to deal with multidimensional domains. Another research direction is to exploit the solution representation as intervals for solving inequality systems and other problems for which this representation seems to be natural.

# References

1. Corne, DW and Knowles, JD., The Pareto-Envelope Based Selection Algorithm for Multiobjective Optimization. In Proceedings of the Sixth International Conference on Parallel Problem Solving from Nature, Springer-Verlag, pp. 839-848, Berlin, 2000
2. Deb, K, (1999) Multiobjective Evolutionary Algorithms: Problem Difficulties and Construction of Test Problems. Evolutionary Computation 1999; 7: 205-230.
3. Deb, K, Agrawal, S, Pratap, A and Meyarivan, T, A Fast Elitist Non - dominated Sorting Genetic Algorithm for Multi-objective Optimization: NSGA II. In Schoenauer, M, et al. (eds), Parallel Problem Solving From Nature - PPSN VI, Springer-Verlag, pp. 849-858, Berlin, 2000.
4. Dumitrescu, D, Grosan, C and Oltean M, An Evolutionary Algorithm for Detecting Continuous Pareto Regions. Studia Babes-Bolyai University, Ser. Informatica, 2000; 45: 51-68.
5. Goldberg, DE, Evolutionary Algorithms in Search, Optimization and Machine Learning. Reading, Addison Wesley, 1989.

6. Grosan, C, A New Evolutionary Technique for Detecting Pareto Continuos Regions, Proceedings of Genetic and Evolutionary Computation Conference (GECCO-2003), Workshop Program, Barry, A (ed), pp. 304 -307, 2003.

7. Horn, J and Nafpliotis, N, Multiobjective Optimization Using Niched Pareto Evolutionary Algorithms. IlliGAL Report 93005, Illinois Evolutionary Algorithms Laboratory, University of Illinois, Urbana Champaign, 1993.

8. Horn, J, Nafpliotis, N and Goldberg, DE, A Niche Pareto Evolutionary Algorithm for Multiobjective Optimization. In Proc. 1st IEEE Conf. Evolutionary Computation, Piscataway, 1: pp. 82-87, 1994.

9. Knowles, JD and Corne, DW, Approximating the Nondominated Front Using the Pareto Archived Evolution Strategies. Evolutionary Computation 2000; 8(2): 149-172.

10. Knowles, JD and Corne, DW, The Pareto Archived Evolution Strategy: A New Baseline Algorithm for Pareto Multiobjective Optimization. In Congress on Evolutionary Computation (CEC 99), Piscataway, NJ, 1: pp. 98-105, 1999.

11. Schaffer, JD, Multiple Objective Optimization with Vector Evaluated Evolutionary Algorithms. Evolutionary Algorithms and Their Applications, In Grefenstette, JJ, (ed.), pp. 93-100, Hillsdale, NJ, Erlbaum, 1985.

12. Srinivas, N and Deb, K, Multiobjective Function Optimization Using Nondominated Sorting Evolutionary Algorithms. Evolutionary Computing 1994; 2: 221-248.

13. Zitzler, E, Evolutionary Algorithms for Multiobjective Optimization: Methods and Applications. Doctoral Dissertation, Swiss Federal Institute of Technology Zurich, 1999.

14. Zitzler, E, Laumanns, M and Thiele, L, SPEA 2: Improving the Strength Pareto Evolutionary Algorithm, TIK Report 103, Computer Engineering and Networks Laboratory (TIK), Department of Electrical Engineering, Swiss Federal Institute of Technology (ETH) Zurich, 2001.

15. Coello, CAC, A Comprehensive Survey of Evolutionary- based Multiobjective Optimization Techniques. Knowledge and Information Systems, 1999; 1(3): 269-308.

16. Veldhuizen, DAV, Multiobjective Evolutionary Algorithms: Classification, Analyses and New Innovations. Ph.D Thesis, Graduated School of Engineering of the Air Force Institute of Technology, Air University, 1999.

17. Veldhuizen, DAV and Lamont, GB, Multiobjective Evolutionary Algorithms: Analyzing the State-of-the-art. Evolutionary Computation, 2000; 8: 125-147.

18. Dumitrescu, D, Genetic Chromodynamics. Studia, Babes-Bolyai University, Ser. Informatica, 2000; 45: 39-50.

# MOGADES: Multi-Objective Genetic Algorithm with Distributed Environment Scheme

Tomoyuki Hiroyasu, Mitsunori Miki, Jiro Kamiura, Shinya Watanabe, and Hiro Hiroyasu

**Summary.** This chapter proposes a Multi-Objective Genetic Algorithm with Distributed Environment Scheme (MOGADES). The performance of MAGADES is compared with SPEA2 and NSGA-II. Further a Distributed Cooperation Model of Multi-Objective Genetic Algorithm (DEMOGA) is introduced. The effectiveness of DCMOGA is illustrated by comparing with SPEA2 and other multiobjective optimization algorithms. Finally MOGADES and DCMOGA are combined into a hybrid algorithm called Distributed Cooperation Model of Multi-Objective Genetic Algorithm with Environmental Scheme (DCMOGADES) and applied to some test problems. Performance of MOGADES is also illustrated by applying to some real world problems.

## 9.1 Introduction

Recently, computers have made rapid progress in hardware and software. As a result, designers of cars, airplanes, electric circuit devices, controllers, etc. have begun to use computer simulations for decision-making. In these cases, optimization techniques are often utilized. However, especially in real-world problems, not only one objective but also several objectives exist. As a result, multiobjective optimization problems should be solved. One of the goals of multiobjective optimization problems is to obtain a set of Pareto-optimal solution. Pareto optimal sets are an assembly of the solutions from genetic algorithms (GA), which is one of the multi-point search methods suitable to derive Pareto-optimal sets [1]. In the following years, several new algorithms for finding good Pareto-optimal solutions with small calculation costs were developed [2]. These are NSGA-II [3], SPEA-2 [4], and NPGA-II [5]. These algorithms treat Pareto-optimal concepts explicitly.

One disadvantage of these methods is a high calculation cost [6] for which a solution is the performing of GA on parallel computers. Evolutionary algorithms (EAs) are genetic algorithms that have implicit parallelism [7]. Therefore, algorithms of parallel EAs are very important. Previous studies have examined parallel algorithms of GAs for multi objective optimization problems (MOPs). In this study, we propose a parallel genetic algorithm for MOPs called Multi-Objective Genetic Algorithm with Distributed Environment Scheme (MOGADES). This is an expanded algorithm of distributed GA (DGA) and it also uses the concept of environment DGA [6]. This algorithm is based on the algorithm that treats Pareto-optimal concepts implicitly. To clarify the characteristics and the effectiveness of MOGADES, we apply MOGADES to some test functions. Through the comparison of MOGADES to SPEA2 [4] and NSGA-II [3], the advantages and disadvantages of MOGADES are illustrated.

Good Pareto-optimal solutions should have the following characteristics: solutions should be close to the real Pareto front, solutions should not be concentrated but distributed, and solutions should have the optimum solution of every single-objective function. In this study, a new mechanism is added to multiobjective GAs called "Distributed Cooperation Model of Multi-Objective Genetic Algorithm (DCMOGA)." In DCMOGA, there are not only individuals for searching Pareto-optimal solutions but also individuals for searching the solution of one object. This mechanism of DCMOGA helps to derive distributed Pareto solutions. In this study, DCMOGA was applied to MOGA [8] and SPEA2. Through numerical examples, the effectiveness of the proposed algorithm was illustrated.

After illustrating MOGADES and DCMOGA, these two algorithms were combined. This hybrid algorithm is called "Distributed Cooperation Model of Multi-Objective Genetic Algorithm with Environmental Scheme (DCMOGADES)." DCMOGADES was also applied to test functions that demonstrated its high searching ability.

Finally, in this study, MOGADES was applied to real-world problems. GA can be applied to several types of problems and have the robustness to find solutions. Therefore, it is viable that GA is suitable to find solutions to real-world problems. For example, the MOPs of diesel engine emissions were dealt with in this study. In this problem, the amount of Nitrogen Oxide (NOx) and soot of engines was minimized and fuel efficiency maximized.

## 9.2 Genetic Algorithms for Multiobjective Optimization Problems

### 9.2.1 Multiobjective Optimization Problems

In optimization problems when there are several objective functions, the problems are called Multiobjective Optimization Problems (MOPs)[1]. MOPs are formulated as follows:

$$\begin{cases} minimize \quad \mathbf{f}(\mathbf{x}) = (f_1(\mathbf{x}), f_2(\mathbf{x}), \ldots, f_k(\mathbf{x}))^T \\ subject \quad to \quad the \quad constraints \quad g_j(\mathbf{x}) \leq 0, (j = 1, \ldots, m) \end{cases} \quad (9.1)$$

Usually these objectives cannot minimize or maximize at the same time due to a trade-off relationship between the objectives. As a result, one of the goals of the MOPs is to find a set of Pareto-optimal solutions. Several algorithms were proposed and applied to MOPs [1]. Recently, several good algorithms have been developed, most of which have similar mechanisms as recent GA approaches. The followings mechanisms are:

- Reservation mechanism of the excellent solutions
- Reflection to search solutions mechanism of the reserved excellent solutions
- Cut down (sharing) method of the reserved excellent solutions
- Assignment method of fitness function
- Unification mechanism of values of each objective
- Selection methods.

Those algorithms are roughly divided into two categories: the algorithms that either treat Pareto optimal solutions implicitly or explicitly. Most multiobjective GAs treat Pareto-optimal solutions explicitly. Among those algorithms, SPEA2 [4] and NSGA-II [3] have powerful search mechanisms and derive good results.

On the other hand, VEGA [9] is a traditional GA for multiobjective problems and an algorithm that treats Pareto optimal solutions implicitly. MOGLS [10] is also an algorithm that treats Pareto optimal solutions implicitly. MOGLS has several important mechanisms. It also has a Pareto archive where Pareto solutions are reserved from not only the genetic search but also the local search. The weights that are used when the objectives are combined are varied randomly.

MOGADES, which is proposed in this chapter, is an algorithm based on the GA that treats Pareto optimal solutions implicitly.

### 9.2.2 Parallelization of Multiobjective Genetic Algorithms

GAs are optimization algorithms that mimic the process of evolution [8,11]. Due to GA being one of the multi-point search methods, several types of parallel methods exist. Parallel GAs are roughly classified into three categories: a master-slave population model, an island model, and a cellular model [12].

In the island model, also called Distributed GA (DGA), a population is divided into sub-populations. In each island, a conventional GA is performed for several iterations in which some individuals are chosen and moved to other islands. This operation is called migration. After a migration, GA operations are started again in each island. As the network traffic is not huge and each island has a small number of individuals, an island model can gain high parallel efficiency [12]. In a single-objective problem, it is reported that DGA can find a good solution with a small calculation cost [13]. However, because the number of individuals is small in an island, DGA cannot find good Pareto-optimal solutions in multiobjective problems. Therefore, to find good solutions in an island model, some mechanisms to find solutions should be included. In a previous study, we developed an island model that is called a Divided Range Multi Objective Genetic Algorithm (DRMOGA) [14]. This is an algorithm that treats Pareto optimal solutions explicitly. However, the searching ability of DRMOGA is not good compared to SPEA2 [4] and NSGA-II [3].

### 9.2.3 Environment Distributed Genetic Algorithms

Usually each island of DGAs is assigned to one processor of parallel computers [7]. Since the network cost is not high in DGAs, a high parallel efficiency can be derived. It is also reported that DGAs can find optimum solutions with smaller calculation costs than that of the simple GA. As a result, DGAs provide many advantages.

Generally, every island has the same environment: population size, crossover rate, mutation rate and so on. However, the environment can be different in each island. For example, when the crossover rate and mutation rate are different in each island, the searching ability of DGA is increased. We named this DGA Environment Distributed Genetic Algorithm (EDGA) [14].

This scheme can also be applied to other problems. In the following section, the proposed algorithm, MOGADES, is explained. MOGADES is an algorithm where the EDGA is extended for MOPs.

### 9.2.4 Evaluation Methods

To compare the results derived by each algorithm, the following evaluation methods were used in this study.

### Ratio of Non-dominated Individuals (RNI)

This performance measure is obtained by comparing two solutions which are derived by two methods. RNI is derived from the following steps. First, two populations from different methods are mixed. Second, the solutions that are non-dominated are chosen. Finally, the RNI of each method is determined as the ratio of the number of the solutions from chosen solutions and derived by the method and the total number of the solutions. With RNI, the accuracy of the solutions can be compared.

Figure 9.1 shows an example of RNI. In this figure, method A and B are compared. This case suggests that A and B are almost the same.

### Maximum, Minimum and Average Values of Each Object of Derived Solutions (MMA)

To evaluate the derived solutions, not only the accuracy but also the expanse of the solutions is important. To discuss the expanse of the solutions, the maximum, minimum and average values of each object are considered.

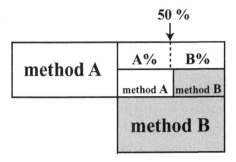

Figure 9.1. Example of RNI.

**Cover Rate (CR)**

Cover rate is the index for the coverage of the Pareto optimum individuals. It indicates the diversity of the solutions. We derive the cover rate from the division space of objective domain. The division space is derived as follows: the area between the minimum and the maximum values of each objective function is divided into certain number N. The number of the division spaces containing an individual is counted. The cover rate is the average of this number. Therefore, the solution whose cover rate is close to 1.0 has a high diversity. In the following simulations, $N = 50$ was used.

## 9.3 Multiobjective Genetic Algorithm with Distributed Environment Scheme (MOGADES)

### 9.3.1 Algorithm of MOGADES

In the previous section, EDGA was explained. In this section, EDGA is extended for MOPs. The proposed algorithm is called "Multi-Objective Genetic Algorithm with Distributed Environment Scheme (MOGADES)".

A MOP can be changed into a single objective optimization using weighted parameters $w_i$ as follows:

$$\min_{x \in X} \quad f(x) = \sum_{i=1}^{k} w_i f_i(x) \tag{9.2}$$

$$where \quad w_i \geq 0, \quad \sum_{i=1}^{k} w_k = 1 \tag{9.3}$$

To derive Pareto-optimal solutions, several simulations with different weight parameters are needed. Because MOGADES is one of the EDGAs, there are several islands with each island having a different weighted parameter. This is the basic concept of MOGADES. At the same time, the search mechanisms of SPEA2 and NSGA-II are included in MOGADES. The overall process of MOGADES is summarized as follows. In this case, the problem that has two objectives is explained. Each island has its own weighted value, an elite archive and a Pareto archive. The weighted value is used when the fitness value is derived. During a search, the solutions that have the best fitness values are preserved in an elite archive. Similarly, the solutions that are non-dominated to the other solutions are also stored in a Pareto archive.

1. Initialization: Generate new individuals. Those individuals are divided into islands $P_i^0$ $(i = 1, 2, \ldots M)$. Set the weight value $w_i$ of $i$th island. At first, the weight values are arranged equally from 0.0 to 1.0. For example, when $M = 5$, the weights are 0, 0.25, 0.5, 0.75 and 1.0. In this time, the elite archive $EA_i^0$ and Pareto archive $PA_i^0$ are empty. Set generation $t = 0$. Calculate the values of function 1, 2 and the fitness value of each individual.
2. Starting new generation: Set $t = t + 1$.
   The Steps from 3 to 9 are performed in an island independently.
3. Crossover and mutation: Perform crossover and mutation operations.
4. Evaluation: Calculate the values of function 1 and 2. Normalize the values of functions by the maximum value of each function. Calculate the fitness value of each individual. The fitness value is derived from Equation 9.3.
5. Selection: Perform selection operation to $P_i^t$.
6. Terminal check: When the terminal condition is satisfied, terminate the simulation. Otherwise, the simulation is continued.
7. Pareto reservation: Choose the individuals of $P_i^t$ and $PA_i^{t-1}$ that are non-dominated and copy them into $PA_i^t$. When the number of $PA_i^t$ overcomes the maximum number of the Pareto archive, the sharing operation is performed. The sharing method of MOGADES is carried out as follows. The individuals of $P_i^t$ are sorted with along to the fitness value. Calculate the distance of the fitness value between the neighborhood individuals. Truncate the individual who has the smallest distance.
8. Elite reservation: According to the fitness values, reserve the individuals who have good fitness values into $EA_i^t$.
9. Renewal of the search individuals: $P_i^t = P_i^{t-1} + PA_i^t + EA_i^t$.
10. Migration: Choose some individuals and move to the other island. In MOGADES, migration topology is fixed. When migration is performed, the weight value of the island is changed in the following equation:

$$w_i(new) = w_{i+1} \frac{d_{(i+1,i)}}{d_{(i,i-1)} + d_{(i+1,i)}} + w_{i-1} \frac{d_{(i,i-1)}}{d_{(i,i-1)} + d_{(i+1,i)}} \qquad (9.4)$$

    In this equation, $w_i$ is the weight value of $i$th island, $d_{(i+1,i)}$ the distance between the individuals who has the best value in $i + 1$th island and $i$th island.
11. Return to Step 2.

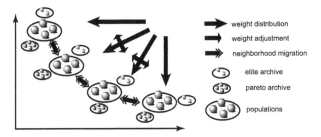

Figure 9.2. MOGADES.

## 9.3.2 Numerical Examples

This section discusses the effectiveness of MOGADES. MOGADES was applied to find Pareto-optimal solutions of test functions. The results are compared with those of SPEA2 and NSGA-II.

### Test Functions

In this paper, we use a continuous function and a knapsack problem. These problems are explained as follows. In these equations, $f$ denotes an objective function and $g(g \geq 0)$ indicates a constraint.

$$KUR : \begin{cases} \min f_1 = \sum_{i=1}^{n}(-10\exp \\ \qquad\qquad (-0.2\sqrt{x_i^2 + x_{i+1}^2})) \\ \min f_2 = \sum_{i=1}^{n}(|x_i|^{0.8} + 5\sin(x_i)^3) \\ x_i[-5,5], \ i = 1, \ldots, n, \ n = 100 \end{cases}$$

$$KP750 - 2 : \begin{cases} \min f_i(x) = \sum_{i=1}^{n} x_i \cdot p_{i,j} \\ s.t. \\ \qquad g(x) = \sum_{i=1}^{n} x_i \dot{w}_{i,j} \leq W_j \\ \qquad p_{i,j}(\text{profit value}) \\ \qquad w_{i,j}(\text{weight value}) \\ \qquad 1 \leq j \leq 2 \end{cases}$$

KUR was used by Kursawa [15]. It has a multi-modal function in one component and pair-wise interactions among the variables in the other component. As there are 100 design variables, a high calculation cost is needed to derive solutions. KP750-2 is a 0/1 knapsack problem and it is a combinatorial problem [4,16]. There are 750 items and two objects. The profit and weight values are the same as those in Zitzler [17].

### Parameters of GAs

In this study, in order to discuss the effectiveness of the algorithm, a bit coding is applied for all the problems. It is known that good results are derived when real value coding is applied. Similarly, one point crossover and bit flip are used for crossover and mutation. The length of the chromosome is 20 bit per one design variable for the continuous problems and 750 bit for the knapsack problems. In continuous problems, population size is 100 and the simulation is terminated when the generation is over 250. In the knapsack problems, population size is 250 and the simulation is terminated when the generation exceeds 2000.

## KUR

In this problem, there are 100 design variables and a lot of generations are needed to derive the solutions. The results of RNI and MMA are shown in Figures 9.3 and 9.4.

In this case, the RNI of MOGADES is superior to the other methods. Since MOGADES has islands searching the edges of Pareto-optimal solutions, it can derive diverse solutions especially in difficult problems.

## KP-2

KP-2 is the knapsack problem. It is very difficult to search real Pareto-optimal solutions. The results of RNI, MMA and CR are shown in Figures 9.5 - 9.7.

In this case, MOGADES obtained very good results. Because this problem is very difficult, the factor of MOGADES that derives the diverse solutions is efficient.

### 9.3.3 Conclusion of this Section

In this section, a new algorithm of GA for MOPs was explained. The proposed algorithm is called MOGADES. Through the comparison of NSGA-II and SPEA2 with test functions, MOGADES was found to have the better searching ability.

As MOGADES is based on distributed GAs, MOGADES is a very suitable model for parallel computers.

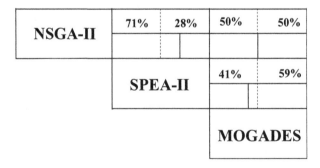

**Figure 9.3.** Results of KUR (RNI).

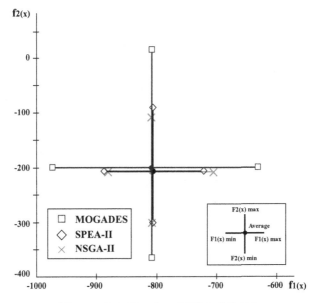

**Figure 9.4.** Results of KUR (MMA).

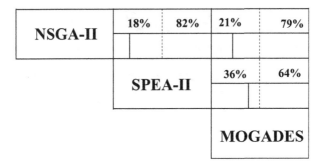

**Figure 9.5.** Results of KP750 (RNI).

## 9.4 Distributed Cooperation Model of Multiobjective Genetic Algorithm (DCMOGA)

### 9.4.1 Algorithm of DCMOGA

In good Pareto-optimal solutions, an optimum solution that gives a minimum/maximum value for each objective should be included. In DCMOGA, there are $N + 1$ islands when there are $N$ objects. One island is the group for finding the Pareto-optimal solutions. This group is called the MOGA group. One of the other groups is a group for finding the optimum of the $i$th objective function. These groups are called SOGA groups. After some iterations, the solutions are exchanged between the MOGA group and SOGA

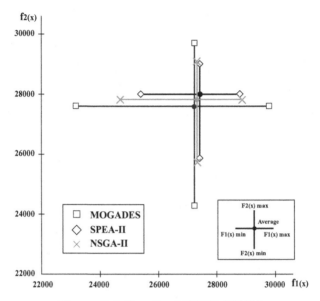

**Figure 9.6.** Results of KP750 (MMA).

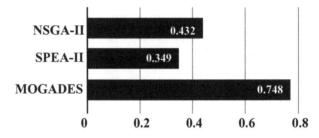

**Figure 9.7.** Results of KP750 (Cover Rate).

group for the $i$th objective function. From the MOGA group, the solutions whose value of the $i$th objective function is the best is sent to the SOGA group for the $i$th objective function. From the SOGA group, for each $i$th objective function, the best solution at that iteration is sent to the MOGA group. In this way, the solutions are derived with the cooperation of MOGA and SOGA groups.

1. All of the individuals are initialized.
2. These individuals are divided into $n + 1$ groups. $n$ of them are SOGA groups and each group has its own objective function. One of them is a MOGA group that searches Pareto-optimal solutions.
3. In each group, the solution search has been performed for several iterations.
4. In every iteration, the elite archive and the Pareto archive are renewed.

5. After certain iterations, solutions are transformed between MOGA and SOGA groups. In this step, the solution $M_i$ whose value of the $i$th objective function $F_i$ is best in the MOGA group is chosen. The solution $M_i$ is sent to the group whose target objective function is the $i$th objective function.

6. On the other hand, the best solution $S_i$ in the $i$th group of SOGA is sent to the MOGA group.

7. The solutions $M_i$ and $S_i$ are compared. When $S_i > M_i$, some individuals of MOGA are added and SOGA are decreased. When $S_i < M_i$, some individuals of MOGA are deceased and SOGA are added.

8. The terminal condition is checked. If the condition is not satisfied, the process is back to Step 3.

### 9.4.2 Numerical Examples

In this section, in order to discuss the effectiveness of DCMOGA, MOGA and SPEA2 are combined into DCMOGA. Then DCMOGA is applied to solve a knapsack problem.

### Test Functions

The knap sack problem is a discrete problem for which it is very difficult to find a real Pareto front. In this paper, the problem that has 750 items and 2 objectives is treated and it is called KP750-2. The equations are explained in Section 9.3.2.

### GA Parameters

To solve the test functions, a bit coding is used for representing the individual. A 750 bit length is used for the knapsack problem. In GA, two point crossover and bit flip mutation is applied. In the knapsack problem, there are 250 individuals. The simulation is terminated when the number of evaluations is over 500,000. All the results are the average of 10 trials.

### Results

The derived Pareto fronts are shown in Figures 9.8 - 9.11. In these figures, DC/MOGAs means that MOGA is used in DCMOGA. Similarly, DC/SPEA2 means that SPEA2 is combined into DCMOGA.

There is a big difference between the solutions of DCMOGA where MOGA is implemented with MOGA versus the solutions of MOGA itself. The solutions of MOGA are concentrated on one part. On the other hand, DCMOGA can find widespread solutions.

When DCMOGA is combined with SPEA2, the solutions are also widespread. However, the accuracy of the solutions is lost. Therefore, the RNI

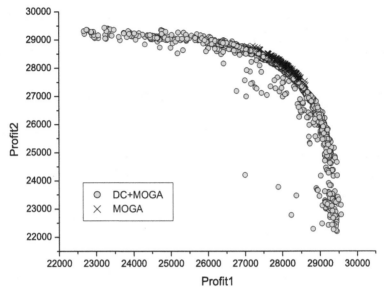

**Figure 9.8.** Plot of Pareto Solutions (DC/MOGAs).

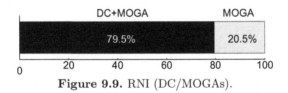

**Figure 9.9.** RNI (DC/MOGAs).

of DCMOGA is not good in the comparison with SPEA2. Even in this case, the real accuracy is not so different. Thus, it is concluded that DCMOGA is an efficient mechanism for GAs in multiobjective problems.

## 9.5 Distributed Cooperation model of MOGA with Environmental Scheme (DCMOGADES)

### 9.5.1 Flow of DCMOGADES

In the previous sections, two algorithms of GAs for MOP, MOGADES and DCMOGA are explained. In this section, MOGADES and DCMOGA are combined. The algorithm is called DCMOGADES.

DCMOGADES has the mechanism to find the Pareto-optimal solutions that are close to the real Pareto front, widespread, and the same as the solutions that maximize/minimize each objective. The following steps are the procedures.

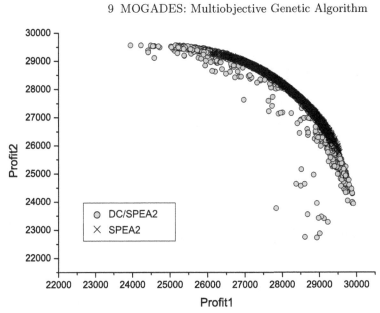

**Figure 9.10.** Plot of Pareto Solutions (DC/SPEA2).

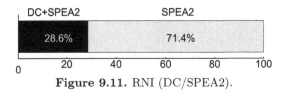

**Figure 9.11.** RNI (DC/SPEA2).

1. There are $m$ islands. These islands are divided into $n+1$ groups, since there are N objective functions. One is the group for finding the Pareto-optimal solutions. This group is the MOGA group. One of the other groups is the group for finding the optimum of the $i$th objective function. These groups are called the SOGA groups.
2. Initialize all of the individuals in the islands.
3. In the MOGA group, the Pareto-optimal solutions are searched by MOGADES. In SOGA groups, each optimum solution is searched by DGA.
4. At every generation, the elite archive and the Pareto archive are renewed in the MOGA group. The elite archive is renewed in the SOGA groups.
5. After some iterations, individuals are chosen randomly and moved to the other islands in every group.
6. After some iterations, the solutions are exchanged between the MOGA group and the SOGA group for the $i$th objective function. From the MOGA group, the solutions whose value of $i$th objective function is the best is sent to the SOGA group for the $i$th objective function. This solution

is $M_i$. From the SOGA group for the $i$th objective function, the best solution at that iteration is sent to the MOGA group. This solution is $S_i$.

7. $M_i$ and $S_i$ are compared. When $M_i > S_i$, one of the islands from the MOGA group is moved to the SOGA group for the $i$th objective function. When $M_i ¡ S_i$, one of the islands of the SOGA group for the $i$th objective function is moved to the MOGA group.

8. The terminal criterion is checked. If the criterion is not satisfied, the simulation returns to Step 3.

The concept of DCMOGADES is summarized in Figure 9.12.

## 9.5.2 Numerical Examples

In this section, in order to discuss the effectiveness of DCMOGA, DCMOGA is applied to test functions. The results are compared with those of SPEA2 and NSGA-II.

### Test Functions

In this section, we use a knapsack problem for a discrete problem and KUR for a continuous problem. The problems are shown in Section 9.3.2.

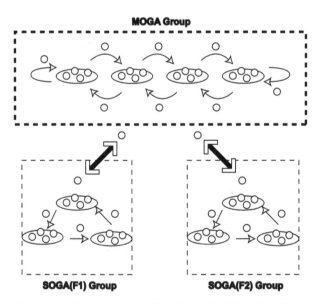

**Figure 9.12.** Distributed Cooperation Model of Multiobjective Genetic Algorithm with Environmental Scheme (DCMOGADES).

## GA Parameters

To solve the test functions, a bit coding was used for representing the individuals. A 750 bit length was used for the knapsack problem and a 20 bit length was used for each design variable of the KUR. In GA, two-point crossover and bit-flip mutation was applied. In the knapsack problem, there were 250 individuals. The simulation was terminated when the number of evaluations was over 500,000. In the KUR problem, there were 100 individuals. The simulation was terminated when the generation was over 1,000. In the following section, the results of DCMOGADES are compared with those of NSGA-II and SPEA2. All the results are the average of 10 trial runs.

### KP750-2

The derived Pareto fronts are shown in Figure 9.13 (all-in-one) and in Figures 9.15 to 9.17 (individual comparisons). The RNI of KP750-2 is shown in Figure 9.14.

From the results, it is obvious that the solution set of DCMOGADES is more diverse than that of the other algorithms. The figure of RNI illustrates the superiority of DCMOGADES to the MOGADES. These results illustrate the effectiveness of DCMOGA.

### KUR

The derived Pareto fronts are shown in Figure 9.18 (all-in-one) and in Figures 9.20 to 9.22 (individual comparisons). In the KUR problem, DCMOGADES

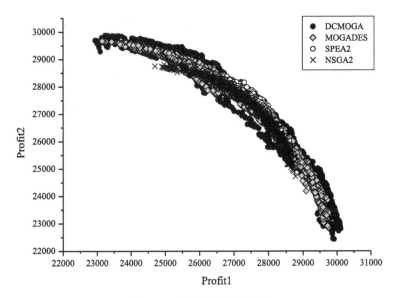

**Figure 9.13.** KP750 (all).

and MOGADES derived the Pareto front whose solutions are widespread. On the other hand, some solutions of SPEA2 and NSGA-II are concentrated around the center of the figure. This figure also indicates that MOGADES has higher searching ability compared to the SPEA2 and NSGA-II in this problem. In the comparison of DCMOGADES with MOGADES, the results of DCMOGADES are superior to MOGADES. Therefore, in this problem, the factor of DCMOGA works well.

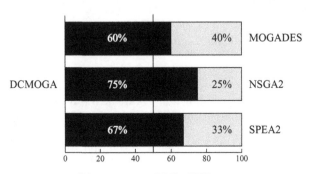

**Figure 9.14.** RNI of KP750.

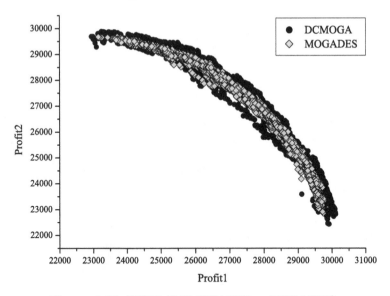

**Figure 9.15.** KP750 (DCMOGADES vs MOGADES).

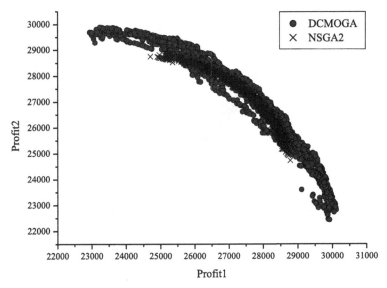

**Figure 9.16.** KP750 (DCMOGADES vs NSGA2).

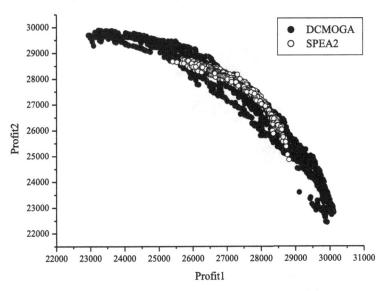

**Figure 9.17.** KP750 (DCMOGADES vs SPEA2).

## 9.6 Multiobjective Optimization of Diesel Engine Emissions and Fuel Economy by MOGADES

### 9.6.1 Introduction

This section discusses the application of MOGADES to real-world problems. The MOPs of diesel engine emissions are also discussed in this section.

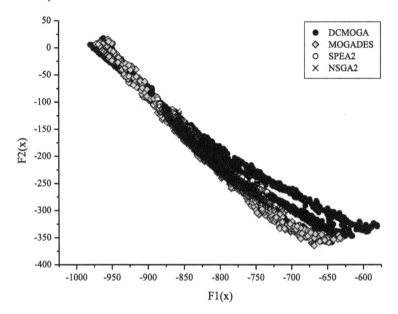

Figure 9.18. KUR (all).

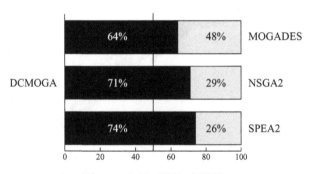

Figure 9.19. RNI of KUR.

Because of the merit of the durability and fuel efficiency, a diesel engine is loaded from small to large vehicles. However, with increasing environmental concerns and legislated emissions standards, current engine research is focused on simultaneous reduction of soot and NOx while maintaining reasonable fuel economy. The combustion improvement can be achieved by designing a good injection system with characteristics of spray combustion. To develop a good injection system, the parameter search for determining the influence of an organization performance and an exhaust performance should be performed. However, when this parameter search is performed experimentally, large amounts of expense and time are incurred. For this reason, optimization of the parameter by the simulation on a computer is very useful.

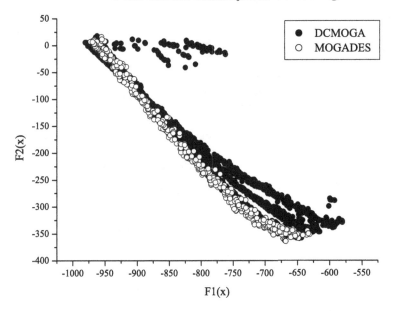

**Figure 9.20.** KUR (DCMOGADES vs MOGADES).

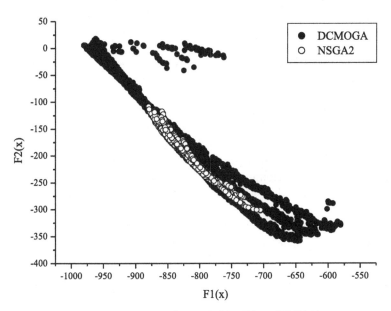

**Figure 9.21.** KUR (DCMOGADES vs NSGA2).

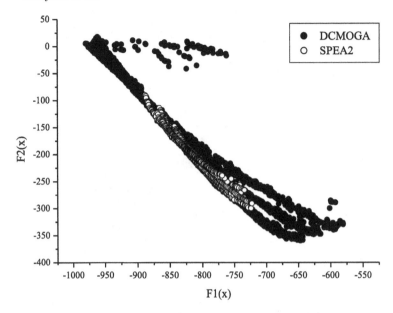

**Figure 9.22.** KUR (DCMOGADES vs SPEA2).

When optimizing the parameter by the simulation to minimize the fuel efficiency, the amount of NOx discharge and the amount of soot discharge have been made into the objective functions. However, in previous studies [18, 19] these problems are treated as single-objective problems. As there is a trade-off relationship between the fuel efficiency, NOx and soot, it is natural to treat these problems as multi-objective optimization problems.

In this study, the minimization of fuel efficiency, the amount of NOx discharge, and the amount of soot discharge are simultaneously performed by using the concept of multiple-purpose optimization. It is then shown that multiobjective optimization is very useful in real-world problems. At the same time, it is also shown that MOGADES can find reasonable solutions in the problems of diesel engine emission.

### 9.6.2 Diesel Engine Combustion Models

The process of combustion in diesel engines is very complicated. There are many required items for models such as the prediction of the heat generation rate, the prediction of exhaust ingredients, the heat distribution, the density distribution, and so on. As a result, it is almost impossible to build the model of diesel combustion with numerical expressions. On the other hand, several types of the models of diesel combustion have been proposed [20-23]. Those are roughly divided into three categories.

- Thermodynamic model: This model only predicts the heat generation ratio.
- Phenomenological model: In this model, the prediction of equation which is derived by the experience is used.
- Detailed multidimensional model: This model predicts several items by solving differential equations with small time steps.

In this section, the HIDECS code [21] was used for a diesel engine simulation. HIDECS is based on the phenomenological model.

In the detailed multidimensional model [20], the heat and density distribution of the engine is predicted. However, it takes a large amount of computational time to derive the value of the fuel efficiency, the amount of NOx and soot. This is the very big disadvantage for solving optimization problems by GAs. On the other hand, the phenomenological model is suitable for the optimization by GAs. The phenomenological model does not need a high calculation cost to derive the values of the fuel efficiency, the amount of NOx and soot with a high degree of accuracy.

HIDECS can deal with several types of diesel engines. In this simulation, the following items are the specifications of the target diesel engine: bore diameter is 102.0 mm, stroke is 52.5 mm, connecting rod is 165.0 mm, and compression ratio is 17.0, cylinder pressure is 101.3 kPa, number of holes is 4, and injector hole diameter is 0.2 mm, The included spray angle is 32 degrees, the start of the fuel injection is -5 degree, and the amount of fuel is 40.0 mg/st.

In diesel engines, the connecting rod is rotating in the cylinder. In HIDECS, these rotations are expressed as the connecting rod angle from -180 to 180 degree in a stroke. When the connecting rod angle equals 0, a piston is located in the highest place.

In a simulation of this engine, the fuel injection starts at -5.0 degree and the injection lasts for 32 degrees.

The total amount of fuel injection is constant, but the shape of the fuel injection can be changed. The shape of the fuel injection is a design variable in this simulation.

HIDECS can derive several characteristics of engines. In this simulation, specefic fuel consumption (SFC), the amount of NOx, and the amount of soot were focused. SFC indicates fuel efficiency. A smaller value of SFC means a better fuel efficiency.

### 9.6.3 System Construction

In the proposed system, MOGADES was used as an optimizer and HIDECS was used as an analyzer. Between the optimizer and analyzer, text files were exchanged. Basically, several types of GAs and analyzers were used in this system.

In this simulation, the amount of SFC, the amount of NOx and the amount of soot are the objectives. The split injection rate-shape is a design variable.

The total amount of fuel injection, the start of the injection and the duration of the injection are fixed while the injection rate is variable. The shape of the injection rate can be defined as follows.

The duration of the injection is divided into six blocks. Each block has its own width and height. When these widths and heights are determined, the shape of the injection rate is determined. Therefore, MOGADES decides these values.

In Figure 9.23, the concept of the coding method is summarized. There are 12 variables (6 blocks have widths and heights). These are real values and coded into 8 bits by gray coding.

Because the amount of fuel and the duration of injection are fixed, the total area of 6 blocks is also fixed.

### 9.6.4 GA Parameters

In these simulations, the following parameters are used. The length of the chromosome is 8 bit per one design variable, while the total length of the chromosome is 96. The population size is 100 and the number of subpopulations is 10. The crossover rate and mutation rate are 1.0 and 1/96 respectively. At the same time, migration rate and migration interval are 0.4 and 10 respectively. We use two-point crossover and tournament selection. The simulation is terminated when the generation is over 100.

### 9.6.5 Results

In Figure 9.24, the derived Pareto solutions are plotted. In the figure, all the plotted solutions are dominant and there are no non-dominant solutions that are derived during the search.

In Figure 9.25, the derived solutions are projected on the SFC-NOx, SFC-soot and NOx-soot surfaces respectively.

From these figures, it is found that the Pareto solutions are derived.

In Figure 9.26, the solutions with the best value for each objective function are illustrated.

From Figure 9.26, the following points are clarified.

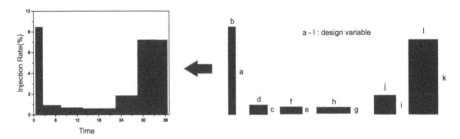

**Figure 9.23.** Coding method.

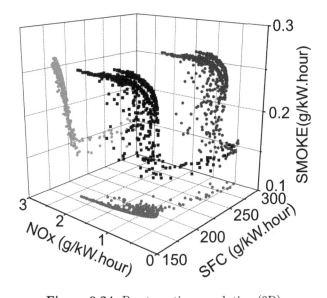

**Figure 9.24.** Pareto optimum solution (3D).

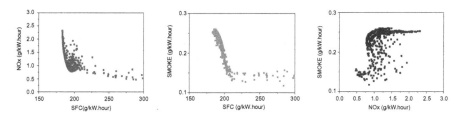

**Figure 9.25.** Pareto optimum solution (2D).

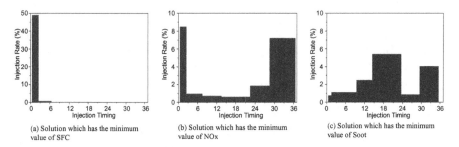

(a) Solution which has the minimum value of SFC

(b) Solution which has the minimum value of NOx

(c) Solution which has the minimum value of Soot

**Figure 9.26.** Solutions which have the minimum value of each objective function.

- It is confirmed that there are trade-off relationships between NOx and SFC, soot and SFC, and NOx and soot.
- In the solution with the best value of SFC, all of the fuel evaporated at once at the beginning of the injection.
- In the solution with the best value of NOx, some of the fuel evaporated at the beginning of the injection while the rest evaporated at the end of the injection.
- A double step injection is used to reduce the amount of NOx. It is known as a pilot projection.

From the results, the following advantages of GAs for MOPs are confirmed.

- GAs can find Pareto-optimal solutions with one trial. In a single-objective optimization problem, GAs need a high calculation cost compared to gradient search methods. On the other hand, in a MOP, gradient search methods also need much iteration to find Pareto-optimal solutions. It is very easy to apply GAs to several types of problems. GAs also have the robustness for finding the optimum solution in a global area. Thus, GAs are very useful tools for finding Pareto-optimum solutions.
- Usually, a multi-objective problem is turned into a single objective problem by setting an evaluation function when the solutions are derived by gradient search method. However, it is very difficult to set up an evaluation function because it affects the results. On the other hand, GAs can find the Pareto optimum solutions without setting up the excess evaluation function.
- From the results of this section, the solutions that minimize each objective are different since there are trade-off relations between the objective functions and because designers do not know the relationship between the objectives early in the design stage. Therefore, it is very useful for designers to show the Pareto-optimal solutions. Designers can find solutions with their preferences.
- Even when the problems are at the bottom stage of design and designers know the relationship between the objective functions, it is useful to derive the solutions by GAs. To solve the problem, the designers have to define the objective function and the constraints and the values of the constraints. Usually the solutions are on the constraints. Therefore, the designers should be careful in deciding the value of the constraints. When the designers set these constraints as objective functions, they can find several solutions around the constraints. Therefore, the information of the Pareto solutions is useful for the designers.

### 9.6.6 Summary of this Section

In this section, MOGADES was applied to optimization problems of diesel engine emissions. In this simulation, the amount of SFC, NOx and soot were minimized by changing the rate of fuel injection. As there is a trade-off relationship between SFC, NOx and soot, this problem becomes a multiobjective optimization problem. From this simulation, MOGADES can successfully derive Pareto solutions. It is also concluded that MOGADES can derive good solutions in real-world problems and GAs are very powerful tools for MOPs in real-world problems.

## 9.7 Conclusion

In this study, a new GA for MOPs was illustrated called "Multi-Objective Genetic Algorithm with Distributed Environment Scheme (MOGADES)". MOGADES is based on an algorithm that treats Pareto optimality implicitly. However, MOGADES includes other mechanisms from recent methods that are based on algorithms that also treat Pareto optimality explicitly, such as NSGA-II or SPEA2.

In this study, other mechanisms of GA for MOPs were introduced called "Distributed Cooperation Model of Multi-Objective Genetic Algorithm (DCMOGA)". DCMOGA searches not only Pareto solutions but also solutions that minimize/maximize each objective function. Using DCMOGA, widespread Pareto solutions can be derived.

Finally, MOGADES was applied to optimization problems of diesel engine emissions. From this simulation, it is found that MOGADES can derive good solutions in real-world problems. GAs are very powerful tools for MOPs found in real-world problems.

## References

1. Deb, K, Multi-Objective Optimization Using Evolutionary Algorithms, Chichester, UK: Wiley, 2001
2. Coello, CA, (2000), Handling Preferences in Evolutionary Multiobjective Optimization: A Survey, 2000 Congress on Evolutionary Computation, vol.1: 30-37, 2000.
3. Pratab, A, Deb, K, Agrawal, S, and Meyarivan, T, A Fast Elitist Non-dominated Sorting Genetic Algorithm For Multi-objective Optimization: NSGA-II, KanGAL report 200001 Indian Institute of Technology, Kanpur, India, 2000.
4. Zitzler, E, Laumanns, M, and Thiele, L, SPEA2: Improving the Performance of the Strength Pareto Evolutionary Algorithm. In Technical Report 103, Computer Engineering and Communication Networks Lab (TIK), Swiss Federal Institute of Technology (ETH), Zurich, 2001.
5. Mayer, A, Erickson, M, and Horn, J, The Niched Pareto Genetic Algorithm Applied to the Design of Groundwater Remediation Systems, First International Conference on Evolutionary Multi-Criterion Optimization, Lecture Notes in Computer Science No. 1993, pp. 681-695, Springer Verlag, 2000.

6. Hiroyasu, T, Miki, M, and Watanabe, S, The New Model of Parallel Genetic Algorithm in Multi-objective Optimization Problems -Divided Range Multi-objective Genetic Algorithms, IEEE Proceedings of the 2000 Congress on Evolutionary Computation, pp. 333-340, 2000.

7. Hiroyasu, T, Miki, M, and Tanimura, Y, Characteristics of models of parallel genetic algorithms on pc cluster systems, Proceedings of 1st International Workshop on Cluster Computing (IWCC'E9), CD-ROM, 1999.

8. Fonseca, CM, and Fleming, PJ, Genetic Algorithms for Multiobjective Optimization: Formulation, Discussion and Generalization, Proceedings of the 5th International Conference on Genetic Algorithms, pp. 416-423, 1993.

9. Sawa, G, Long, YH, and Hiroyasu, H, The Simulation of the Distribution of Temperature and Mass of Liquid and Vapor Fuels, and the Wall Implinging Spray Pattern in a Diesel Combustion Chamber, SAE Techinical Paper Series, (2000-01-1887), 2000.

10. Murata, T, and Ishibuchi, H, Moga: Multi-Objective Genetic Algorithms, Proceedings of the 2nd IEEE International Conference on Evolutionary Computing, pp. 289-294, 1995.

11. Goldberg, DE, Genetic Algorithms in Search, Optimization and Machine Learning, Addison-Wesly, USA, 1989.

12. Cantu-Paz, E, A Survey of Parallel Genetic Algorithms, Calculateurs Paralleles, 10(2), 1998.

13. Tanese, R, Distributed Genetic Algorithms, Proceedings of 3rd International Conference on Genetic Algorithms, 1989.

14. Miki, M, Hiroyasu, T, and Kaneko, M, A Parallel Genetic Algorithm with Distributed Environment Scheme, Proceedings of the International Conference on Parallel and Distributed Processing Techiniques and Applications, vol.2, pp. 619-625, 2000.

15. Frank, L, A variant of evolution strategies for vector optimization, PPSN I, Lecture Notes in Computer Science: 496, pp. 193-197, 1991.

16. Zitzler, E, and Thiele, L, Multiobjective Evolutionary Algorithms: A Comparative Case Study and the Strength Pareto Approach, IEEE Transactions on Evolutionary Computation, 1999; 3(4): 257-271.

17. Zitzler, E, Test Problems for Multiobjective Optimizers, http://www.tik.ee.ethz .ch/~zitzler/testdata.html accessed on 19 March 2004.

18. Montgomery, DT, Senecal, PK, and Reitz, RD, A Methodology for Engine Design Using Multi-dimensional Modeling and Genetic Algorithms with Validation Through Experiments, International Journal of Engine Research, 2000.

19. Senecal, PK, and Reitz, RD, Simultaneous Reduction of Emissions and Fuel Consumption Using Genetic Algorithms and Multi-dimensional Spray and Combustion Modeling, SAE Paper, (2000-01-1890), 2000.

20. Amsden, AA, Kiva-3v: A Block-structured Kiva Program for Engines with Vertical or Canted Valves, Los Alamos National Labs (LA-13313-MS), 1997.

21. Hiroyasu, H, and Kadota, T, Phenomenologocal Model of Diesel Combustion, hidecs, SAE Technical Paper Series, (760129), 1976.

22. Nishida, K, Yoshizaki, T, and Hiroyasu, H, Approach to Low NOx and Smoke Emission Engines by Using Phenomenological Simulation, SAE Techinical Paper Series, (930612), 1993.

23. Nishida, K, Yoshizaki, T, and Hiroyasu, H, Three-dimensional Spray Distributions in a Direct Injection Diesel Engine, SAE Techinical Paper Series, (941693)Schafer J. D., (1985), Multiple Objective Optimization with Vector Evaluated Genetic Algorithms, Proceedings of 1st International Conference on Genetic Algorithms and Their Applications, pp. 93-100, 1994.

# 10

# Use of Multiobjective Optimization Concepts to Handle Constraints in Genetic Algorithms

Efrén Mezura-Montes and Carlos A. Coello Coello

**Summary.** This chapter describes the general multiobjective optimization concepts that can and have been used to incorporate constraints of any type (linear, non-linear, equality and inequality) into the fitness function of a genetic algorithm used for global optimization. Several approaches reported in the literature are also described and four of them are compared using several test functions. The results obtained are discussed and further ideas about how to devise new approaches are also briefly analyzed.

## 10.1 Introduction

Evolutionary Algorithms (EAs) are heuristics that have been successfully applied in a wide set of areas [1-11], both in single- and in multiobjective optimization. However, EAs lack a mechanism able to bias efficiently the search towards the feasible region in constrained search spaces. This has triggered a considerable amount of research and a wide variety of approaches have been suggested in the last few years to incorporate constraints into the fitness function of an evolutionary algorithm [12,13].

The most common approach adopted to deal with constrained search spaces is the use of penalty functions. When using a penalty function, the amount of constraint violation is used to punish or "penalize" an infeasible solution so that feasible solutions are favored by the selection process. Despite the popularity of penalty functions, they have several drawbacks from which the main one is that they require a careful fine tuning of the penalty factors that can bias the search in an appropriate way [12,14].

Among the several approaches that have been proposed as an alternative to the use of penalty functions, there is a group of techniques in which the constraints of a problem are handled as objective functions (i.e., a single-objective constrained problem is restated as an unconstrained multiobjective problem). This chapter focuses on these techniques.

This chapter is organized as follows. Section 10.2 presents the basic concepts both from global optimization and from multiobjective optimization that are going to be used in the remainder of this chapter. In Section 10.3, the most popular multiobjective-based constraint-handling techniques are discussed. Section 10.4 presents a small comparative study in which four of the techniques discussed in the previous section are tested on four benchmark problems taken from the standard constraint-handling literature [13]. Section 10.5 discusses the results obtained, and Section 10.6 concludes and presents some possible paths of future research in this area.

## 10.2 Basic Concepts

We are interested in the general non-linear programming problem in which we want to:

$$\text{Find } \mathbf{x} \text{ which optimizes } f(\mathbf{x}) \tag{10.1}$$

subject to:

$$g_i(\mathbf{x}) \leq 0, \quad i = 1, \ldots, n \tag{10.2}$$

$$h_j(\mathbf{x}) = 0, \quad j = 1, \ldots, p \tag{10.3}$$

where $\mathbf{x}$ is the vector of solutions $\mathbf{x} = [x_1, x_2, \ldots, x_r]^T$, $n$ is the number of inequality constraints and $p$ is the number of equality constraints (in both cases, constraints could be linear or non-linear).

If we denote with $\mathcal{F}$ to the feasible region and with $\mathcal{S}$ to the whole search space, then it should be clear that $\mathcal{F} \subseteq \mathcal{S}$.

For an inequality constraint that satisfies $g_i(\mathbf{x}) = 0$, then we will say that $\mathcal{F}$ is active at $\mathbf{x}$. All equality constraints $h_j$ (regardless of the value of $\mathbf{x}$ used) are considered active at all points of $\mathcal{F}$.

Now, we will define some basic concepts from multiobjective optimization.

**Definition 1    (General Multiobjective Optimization Problem):** *Find the vector* $\mathbf{x}^* = [x_1^*, x_2^*, \ldots, x_n^*]^T$ *which will satisfy the* $m$ *inequality constraints:*

$$g_i(\mathbf{x}) \geq 0 \quad i = 1, 2, \ldots, m \tag{10.4}$$

*the* $p$ *equality constraints*

$$h_i(\mathbf{x}) = 0 \quad i = 1, 2, \ldots, p \tag{10.5}$$

*and will optimize the vector function*

$$\mathbf{f}(\mathbf{x}) = [f_1(\mathbf{x}), f_2(\mathbf{x}), \ldots, f_k(\mathbf{x})]^T \tag{10.6}$$

*where* $\mathbf{x} = [x_1, x_2, \ldots, x_n]^T$ *is the vector of decision variables.*    □

Having several objective functions, the notion of "optimum" changes, because in multiobjective optimization problems, the aim is to find good compromises (or "trade-offs") rather than a single solution as in global optimization. The notion of "optimum" that is most commonly adopted is that originally proposed by Francis Ysidro Edgeworth in 1881 [15]and later generalized by Vilfredo Pareto (in 1896) [16]. This notion is normally referred to as "Pareto optimality" and is defined next.

**Definition 2  (Pareto Optimality:):**  *A point* $\mathbf{x}^* \in \mathcal{F}$ *is* **Pareto optimal** *if for every* $\mathbf{x} \in \mathcal{F}$ *and* $I = \{1, 2, \dots, k\}$ *either,*

$$\forall_{i \in I}(f_i(\mathbf{x}) = f_i(\mathbf{x}^*)) \tag{10.7}$$

*or, there is at least one* $i \in I$ *such that*

$$f_i(\mathbf{x}) > f_i(\mathbf{x}^*) \tag{10.8}$$

$\square$

In words, this definition says that $\mathbf{x}^*$ is Pareto optimal if there exists no feasible vector $\mathbf{x}$ which would decrease some criterion without causing a simultaneous increase in at least one other criterion. The phrase "Pareto optimal" is considered to mean with respect to the entire decision variable space unless otherwise specified.

Other important definitions associated with Pareto optimality are the following:

**Definition 3  (Pareto Dominance):**  *A vector* $\mathbf{u} = (u_1, \dots, u_k)$ *is said to dominate* $\mathbf{v} = (v_1, \dots, v_k)$ *(denoted by* $\mathbf{u} \preceq \mathbf{v}$*) if and only if u is partially less than v, i.e.,* $\forall i \in \{1, \dots, k\}$, $u_i \leq v_i \wedge \exists i \in \{1, \dots, k\} : u_i < v_i$.  $\square$

**Definition 4     (Pareto-optimal Set):**  *For a given multiobjective optimization problem,* $\mathbf{f}(x)$*, the Pareto optimal set* $(\mathcal{P}^*)$ *is defined as:*

$$\mathcal{P}^* := \{x \in \mathcal{F} \mid \neg \exists \, x' \in \mathcal{F} \;\; \mathbf{f}(x') \preceq \mathbf{f}(x)\}. \tag{10.9}$$

$\square$

## 10.3 Multiobjective-based Constraint Handling Techniques

The main idea behind using multiobjective techniques to handle constraints is to redefine the single-objective optimization of $f(\mathbf{x})$ as a multiobjective optimization problem in which we will have $m + 1$ objectives, where $m$ is the total number of constraints. Then, we can apply any multiobjective optimization technique [1] to the new vector $\bar{v} = (f(\mathbf{x}), f_1(\mathbf{x}), \dots, f_m(\mathbf{x}))$, where $f_1(\mathbf{x}), \dots, f_m(\mathbf{x})$ are the original constraints of the problem. An ideal solution $\mathbf{x}$ would thus have $f_i(\mathbf{x})=0$ for $1 \leq i \leq m$ and $f(\mathbf{x}) \leq f(\mathbf{y})$ for all feasible $\mathbf{y}$ (assuming minimization).

There are three mechanisms taken from evolutionary multiobjective optimization that are more frequently incorporated into constraint-handling techniques:

1. Use of Pareto dominance as a selection criterion.
2. Use of Pareto ranking [17] to assign fitness in such a way that nondominated individuals (i.e., feasible individuals in this case) are assigned a higher fitness value.
3. Split the population in subpopulations that are evaluated either with respect to the objective function or with respect to a single constraint of the problem. This is the selection mechanism adopted in the Vector Evaluated Genetic Algorithm (VEGA) [18].

We will now proceed to discuss the different approaches that have been proposed adopting the three main ideas previously indicated.

### 10.3.1 COMOGA

Surry and Radcliffe [19] used a combination of the Vector Evaluated Genetic Algorithm (VEGA)[18] and Pareto Ranking to handle constraints in an approach called COMOGA (Constrained Optimization by Multi-Objective Genetic Algorithms).

In this technique, individuals are ranked depending on their sum of constraint violation (number of individuals dominated by a solution). However, the selection process is based not only on ranks, but also on the fitness of each solution. COMOGA uses a non-generational GA and extra parameters defined by the user (e.g., parameter called $\epsilon$ is used to define the change rate of $P_{cost}$). One of these parameters is $P_{cost}$, that sets the rate of selection based on fitness. The remaining $1 - P_{cost}$ individuals are selected based on ranking values. $P_{cost}$ is defined by the user at the beginning of the process and it is adapted during the run using as a basis the percentage of feasible individuals that one wishes to have in the population.

COMOGA was applied on a gas network design problem and it was compared against a penalty function approach. Although COMOGA showed a slight improvement in the results with respect to a penalty function, its main advantage is that it does not require a fine tuning of penalty factors or any other additional parameter. The main drawback of COMOGA is that it requires several extra parameters, although its authors argue that the technique is not particularly sensitive to their values [19].

The algorithm of COMOGA is as follows [19]:

**Begin**
1. Calculate constraint violation for all solutions.
2. Rank solutions based on constraint violation (nondominance checking).
3. Evaluate the fitness of solutions.
4. Select a $P_{cost}$ proportion of parents based on fitness and the remaining $1 - P_{cost}$ based on constraint ranking.
5. Apply genetic operators

6. Adjust $P_{cost}$: Decreasing it favors feasible solutions; Increasing it favors lower cost solutions (high fitness)
**End**

## 10.3.2 VEGA

Parmee and Purchase [20] proposed to use VEGA [18] to guide the search of an evolutionary algorithm to the feasible region of an optimal gas turbine design problem with a heavily constrained search space. After having a feasible point, they generated an optimal hypercube around it in order to avoid leaving the feasible region after applying the genetic operators. Note that this approach does not really use Pareto dominance or any other multiobjective optimization concepts to exploit the search space. Instead, it uses VEGA just to reach the feasible region. The use of special operators that preserve feasibility make this approach highly specific to one application domain rather than providing a general methodology to handle constraints.

Coello [21] used a population-based approach similar to VEGA [18] to handle constraints in single-objective optimization problems. At each generation, the population was split into $m + 1$ subpopulations of equal fixed size, where $m$ is the number of constraints of the problem. The additional subpopulation handles the objective function of the problem and the individuals contained within it are selected based on the unconstrained objective function value. The $m$ remaining subpopulations take one constraint of the problem each as their fitness function. The aim is that each of the subpopulations tries to reach the feasible region corresponding to one individual constraint. By combining these different subpopulations, the approach will reach the feasible region of the problem considering all of its constraints.

The algorithm of this approach is as follows:

**Begin**
Create $M$ random solutions for the initial population.
Split the population into $m + 1$ subpopulations
Evaluate all $M$ individuals
Assign a fitness value to all $M$ individuals depending on their corresponding subpopulation.
**While** stopping criterion is not satisfied **Do**
Insert the best individual of the current population into the next population
**While** the next population is not full **Do**
Select 2 parents $p_1$ and $p_2$ based on **tournament selection with n candidates** from all the $M$ individuals of the main population
Apply crossover to $p_1$ and $p_2$ to generate 2 offspring $c_1$ and $c_2$
Apply mutation to offspring $c_1$ and $c_2$

    Insert $c_1$ and $c_2$ into the next population
   **End While**
   Split the population into $m + 1$ subpopulations
   Evaluate all $M$ new individuals
   Assign a fitness value to all $M$ individuals depending of their
   corresponding subpopulation.
  **End While**
 **End**

The fitness assignment scheme of the approach is as follows:

   **if** $g_j(\mathbf{x}) < 0.0$   **then**   fitness $= g_j(\mathbf{x})$
   **else if** $v \neq 0$    **then**   fitness $= -v$
   **else**           fitness $= f(\mathbf{x})$

where $g_j(\mathbf{x})$ refers to the $j$th constraint of the problem, $v$ is the number of violated constraints ($v \leq m$) and $f(\mathbf{x})$ is the value of the objective function of the individual.

As can be seen above, each subpopulation tries to satisfy one single constraint. If the encoded solution does not violate the constraint of its corresponding subpopulation, then the fitness of an individual will be determined by the total number of constraints violated. Finally, if the solution is feasible, then the feasible criterion is to optimize the objective function. Therefore, any feasible individuals will be merged with the subpopulation on charge of optimizing the original (unconstrained) objective function.

The genetic operators are applied to the entire population and it is allowed for every individual in a subpopulation to mate with any other in any subpopulation (including its own, of course). In this way, individuals who satisfy constraints are combined with individuals with a good fitness value. At the end, it is expected to have a population of feasible individuals with high fitness values.

This approach was tested with some engineering problems [21] in which it produced competitive results. It has also been successfully used to solve combinational circuit design problems [22]. The main drawback of this approach is that the number of subpopulations required increases linearly with the number of constraints of the problem. This has some obvious scalability problems. Furthermore, it is not clear how to determine appropriate sizes for each of the subpopulations used.

### 10.3.3 MOGA

Coello [23] proposed the use of Pareto dominance selection to handle constraints in EAs. This is an application of Fonseca and Fleming's Pareto ranking process [24] (called Multi-Objective Genetic Algorithm, or MOGA) to constraint-handling. In this approach, feasible individuals are always ranked higher than infeasible ones. Based on this rank, a fitness value is assigned to each individual. This technique also includes a self-adaptation mechanism that avoids the usual empirical fine-tuning of the main genetic operators.

Coello's approach uses a real-coded GA with universal stochastic sampling selection (to reduce the selection pressure caused by the Pareto ranking process).

The algorithm of this approach is as follows:

**Begin**
    Create $M$ random solutions for the initial population.
    Evaluate the $M$ individuals in the population.
    Calculate the rank for each of the $M$ individuals in the population.
    Assign a fitness value to all $M$ individuals depending on rank
    **While** stopping criterion is not satisfied **Do**
      Insert the best individual of the current
      population into the next population
      **While** the next population is not full **Do**
        Select 2 parents $p_1$ and $p_2$ using **Universal Stochastic Sampling**
        Apply crossover to $p_1$ and $p_2$ to generate 2 offspring $c_1$ and $c_2$
        Apply mutation to offspring $c_1$ and $c_2$
        Insert $c_1$ and $c_2$ into the next population
      **End While**
      Evaluate the $M$ new individuals in the population
      Calculate the rank for each one of the $M$ individuals in the
      population.
      Assign a fitness value to all $M$ individuals depending on rank
    **End While**
  **End**

To compute the **rank** of an individual $x_i$ this approach uses the following procedure:
Evaluate:

$$\text{rank}(\mathbf{x}_i) = \text{count}(\mathbf{x}_i) + 1 \qquad (10.10)$$

where $\text{count}(\mathbf{x}_i)$ is computed according to the following rules:

1. Compare $\mathbf{x}_i$ against every other individual in the population. Assuming pairwise comparisons, we will call $\mathbf{x}_j$ $(j = 1, \ldots, pop\_size$ and $j \neq i)$ the other individual against which $x_i$ is being compared at any given time.
2. Initialize $\text{count}(\mathbf{x}_i)$(for $i = 1, \ldots, pop\_size$) to zero.
3. If both $\mathbf{x}_i$ and $\mathbf{x}_j$ are feasible, then both are given a rank of zero and $\text{count}(\mathbf{x}_i)$ remains without changes.
4. If $\mathbf{x}_i$ is infeasible and $\mathbf{x}_j$ is feasible, then $\text{count}(\mathbf{x}_i)$ is incremented by one.
5. If both $\mathbf{x}_i$ and $\mathbf{x}_j$ are infeasible, but $\mathbf{x}_i$ violates more constraints than $\mathbf{x}_j$, then $\text{count}(\mathbf{x}_i)$ is incremented by one.

6. If both $\mathbf{x}_i$ and $\mathbf{x}_j$ are infeasible, and both violate the same number of constraints, but $\mathbf{x}_i$ has a total amount of constraint violation larger than the constraint violation of $\mathbf{x}_j$, then count($\mathbf{x}_i$) is incremented by one.
   If any constraint $g_k(\mathbf{x})$ ($k = 1, \ldots, m$, where $m$ is the total amount of constraints) is considered satisfied if $g_i(\mathbf{x}) \leq 0$, then the total amount of constraint violation for an individual $\mathbf{x}_i$ (denoted as coef($\mathbf{x}_i$)) is given by:

$$\text{coef}(\mathbf{x}_i) = \sum_{k=1}^{p} g_k(\mathbf{x}_i) \quad \text{for all } g_k(\mathbf{x}_i) > 0 \qquad (10.11)$$

To compute **fitness**, the following rules are adopted:

1. If $\mathbf{x}_i$ is feasible, then rank($\mathbf{x}_i$) = $fitness(\mathbf{x}_i)$, else
2. rank($\mathbf{x}_i$) = $\frac{1}{\text{rank}(\mathbf{x}_i)}$

Then, individuals are selected based on rank($\mathbf{x}_i$) (stochastic universal sampling is used). Note that the values produced by $fitness(\mathbf{x}_i)$ must be normalized to ensure that the rank of feasible individuals is always higher than the rank of infeasible ones.

This approach has been used to solve some engineering design problems [23] in which it produced very good results. Furthermore, the approach showed great robustness and a relatively low number of fitness function evaluations with respect to traditional penalty functions. Additionally, it does not require any extra parameters. Its main drawback is the computational cost ($O(M^2)$, where $M$ is the population size) derived from the Pareto ranking process.

### 10.3.4 NPGA

Coello and Mezura [25] implemented a version of the Niched-Pareto Genetic Algorithm (NPGA) [26] to handle constraints in single-objective optimization problems. The NPGA is a multiobjective optimization approach in which individuals are selected through a tournament based on Pareto dominance. However, unlike the NPGA, Coello and Mezura's approach does not require niches (or fitness sharing [27]) to maintain diversity in the population. The NPGA is a more efficient technique than traditional multiobjective optimization algorithms, since it does not compare every individual in the population with respect to each other (as in traditional Pareto ranking), but uses only a sample of the population to estimate Pareto dominance. This is the main advantage of this approach with respect to Coello's proposal [23].

Note, however, that Coello and Mezura's approach requires an additional parameter called $S_r$ that controls the diversity of the population. $S_r$ indicates the proportion of parents selected by four comparison criteria described below. The remaining $1 - S_r$ parents will be selected by a pure probabilistic approach. Thus, this mechanism is responsible for keeping infeasible individuals in the population (i.e., the source of diversity that keeps the algorithm from converging to a local optimum too early in the evolutionary process).

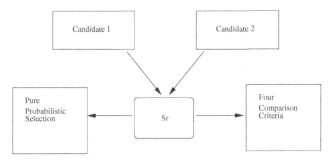

**Figure 10.1.** Diagram that illustrates the role of $S_r$ in the selection process of Coello and Mezura's algorithm.

A graphical illustration of the role of the parameter $S_r$ is shown in Figure 10.1.

Tournaments in this approach are decided using as a basis for comparison criteria. If:

1. both individuals are feasible, the individual with the higher fitness wins.
2. one is feasible and the other is infeasible, the feasible individual wins.
3. both are infeasible: non-dominance checking is applied (tournament selection as in the NPGA [26].
4. both are non-dominated or dominated, the individual with the lowest amount of constraint violation wins.

The algorithm of this approach is as follows:

**Begin**
    Create $M$ random solutions for the initial population.
    Evaluate the $M$ individuals in the population.
    **While** stopping criterion is not satisfied **Do**
      Insert the best individual of the current
      population into the next population
      **While** the next population is not full **Do**
        Select 2 parents $p_1$ and $p_2$ based on $\mathbf{S_r}$ value
        Apply crossover to $p_1$ and $p_2$ to generate 2 offspring $c_1$ and $c_2$
        Apply mutation to offspring $c_1$ and $c_2$
        Insert $c_1$ and $c_2$ into the next population
      **End While**
      Evaluate the $M$ new individuals in the population
    **End While**
**End**

This approach has been tested with several benchmark problems and was compared against several types of penalty functions [28]. Results indicated that the approach was robust, efficient, and effective. However, it was also found that the approach had scalability problems (its performance degrades as the number of decision variables increases).

### 10.3.5 Pareto Set and Line Search

Camponogara and Talukdar [29] proposed an approach in which a global optimization problem was transformed into a bi-objective problem where the first objective is to optimize the original objective function and the second is to minimize:

$$\Phi(\mathbf{x}) = \sum_{i=1}^{n} \max(0, g_i(\mathbf{x})) \qquad (10.12)$$

Equation 10.12 tries to minimize the total amount of constraint violation of a solution (i.e., it tries to make it feasible). At each generation of the process, several Pareto sets are generated. An operator that substitutes crossover takes two Pareto sets $S_i$ and $S_j$ where $i < j$ and two solutions $x_i \in S_i$ and $x_j \in S_j$ where $x_i$ dominates $x_j$. With these two points a search direction is defined using:

$$d = \frac{(x_i - x_j)}{|x_i - x_j|} \qquad (10.13)$$

Line search begins by proyecting $d$ over one variable axis on decision variable space in order to find a new solution $x$ which dominates both $x_i$ and $x_j$. At pre-defined intervals, the worst half of the population is replaced with new random soutions to avoid premature convergence. This indicates some of the problems of the approach to maintain diversity. Additionally, the use of line search within a GA adds some extra computational cost.

The algorithm is as follows [29]:

**Begin**
    Let $S$ be a random initial population.
    Let $F = \{f_0(), \ldots, f_k()\}$ be a set of objectives to be minimized.
    **While** stopping criterion is not satisfied **Do**
        Let $L = \{S_1, \ldots, S_t\}$ be the Pareto list for $S$ with respect to $F$
        **If** $t = 1$ **Then**
            Replace half of the points in $S$ by random points
            Rebuild the Pareto List $L$
        **End If**
        Let $N = \emptyset$ be the set of new points to be generated
        **While** $|N| < m$ **Do**
            Choose two Pareto sets $S_i$ and $S_j$ with $i < j$
            Choose two points sets $x_i \in S_i$ and $x_j \in S_j$ with $i < j$
            Let $d = \frac{(x_i - x_j)}{|x_i - x_j|}$ be the search direction
            With probability $\alpha$ project $d$ onto the axis of one variable $j$ in the solution space
            Execute line search through the line defined by the point $x_i$ and

by the direction $d$
Let $U = \{u_o, \ldots, u_k\}$ be the set of points obtained in the line
search such that $u_j$ is the best point with
evaluation $f_j()$
Let $N = N \bigcup U$
**End While**
Let $S = S \bigcup N$
Let $L = \{S_1, \ldots, S_l\}$ be the Pareto list for $S$
Remove $|N|$ points from the last Pareto sets in List L
**End While**
**End**

The authors of this approach validated it using a benchmark consisting of
five test functions. The results obtained were either optimal or very close to
it. The main drawback of this approach is its additional computational cost.
Also, it is not clear what is the impact of the segment chosen to search in the
overall performance of the algorithm.

### 10.3.6 Min-max

An approach similar to a min-max formulation used in multiobjective
optimization [30] combined with tournament selection was proposed by
Jiménez and Verdegay [31].
    The algorithm is as follows:

**Begin**
Create $M$ random solutions for the initial population.
Evaluate the $M$ individuals in the population.
**While** stopping criterion is not satisfied **Do**
Insert the best individual of the current
population into the next population
**While** the next population is not full **Do**
Select 2 parents $p_1$ and $p_2$ based on **tournament selection** and
based on the criteria shown below
Apply crossover to $p_1$ and $p_2$ to generate 2 offspring $c_1$ and $c_2$
Apply mutation to offspring $c_1$ and $c_2$
Insert $c_1$ and $c_2$ into the next population
**End While**
Evaluate the $M$ new individuals in the population
**End While**
**End**

The selection criteria is based on the following rules:

- Between two feasible individuals, the one with a higher fitness wins.
- A feasible individual wins over an infeasible individual.

- Between two infeasible individuals, the one with the lowest amount of constraint violation wins.

This approach was validated using four test functions, and the results obtained in most cases were very close to the optima. A subtle problem with this approach is that the evolutionary process first concentrates only on the constraint satisfaction problem and therefore it samples points in the feasible region essentially at random [42]. This means that in some cases (e.g., when the feasible region is disjoint) we might land in an inappropriate part of the feasible region from which we will not be able to escape. However, this approach (as in the case of Parmee and Purchase's [20] technique) may be a good alternative to find a feasible point in a heavily constrained search space. The relative simplicity of this approach is another advantage of this technique.

### 10.3.7 Pareto Ranking and Domain Knowledge

Ray et al. [33] proposed the use of a Pareto ranking approach that operates on three spaces: objective space, constraint space and the combination of the two previous spaces. This approach also uses mating restrictions to ensure better constraint satisfaction in the offspring generated and a selection process that eliminates weaknesses in any of these spaces. To maintain diversity, a niche mechanism based on Euclidean distances is used. This approach can solve both constrained or unconstrained optimization problems with one or several objective functions.

The algorithm is as follows [33]:

**Begin**
    Let $M$ be a random initial population.
    **Do**
        Compute Pareto Ranking based on objective matrix to yield
        a vector **RankObj**
        Compute Pareto Ranking based on constraint matrix to yield
        a vector **RankCon**
        Compute Pareto Ranking based on the combined matrix to yield
        a vector **RankCom**
        **If** problem is multiobjective optimization **Then**
            Select individuals from the population in this generation if
            **RankCom**=1 and Feasible and put them into the population for
            the next generation
        **End If**
        **If** problem is single objective optimization **Then**
            Select individuals from the population in this generation if
            **RankCom** is better than allowable rank and Feasible
            and put them into the population for the next generation
        **End If**

**Do**

　Select an individual $A$ and its partner from the population at
　this generation
　Mate $A$ with its partner
　Put parents and children into the population of the next
　generation
**While** the population is not full
Remove duplicate points in parametric space and shrink population
　**While** the maximum number of generations is not attained
**End**

From the previous pseudo-code, it can be seen that three different matrices must be computed: the objective matrix (containing the objective function values of each solution), the constraint matrix (that contains the constraint values of each individual), and a matrix that combines the two previous. These matrices are illustrated in Equations 10.14 - 10.16.

$$\begin{pmatrix} f_{11} & f_{12} & \cdots & f_{1k} \\ f_{21} & f_{22} & \cdots & f_{2k} \\ \vdots & \vdots & \ddots & \vdots \\ f_{M1} & f_{M2} & \cdots & f_{Mk} \end{pmatrix} \tag{10.14}$$

$$\begin{pmatrix} c_{11} & c_{12} & \cdots & c_{1s} \\ c_{21} & c_{22} & \cdots & c_{2s} \\ \vdots & \vdots & \ddots & \vdots \\ c_{M1} & c_{M2} & \cdots & c_{Ms} \end{pmatrix} \tag{10.15}$$

$$\begin{pmatrix} f_{11} & f_{12} & \cdots & f_{1k} & c_{11} & c_{12} & \cdots & c_{1s} \\ f_{21} & f_{22} & \cdots & f_{2k} & c_{21} & c_{22} & \cdots & c_{2s} \\ \vdots & \vdots & \ddots & \vdots & \vdots & \vdots & \ddots & \vdots \\ f_{M1} & f_{M2} & \cdots & f_{Mk} & c_{M1} & c_{M2} & \cdots & c_{Ms} \end{pmatrix} \tag{10.16}$$

The mating restrictions used by this method are based on the information that each individual has about its own feasibility. Such a scheme is based on an idea proposed by Hinterding and Michalewicz [34].

The main advantage of this approach is that it requires a very low number of fitness function evaluations (between 2% and 10% of the number of evaluations required by the homomorphous maps of Koziel and Michalewicz [35], which is one of the best constraint-handling techniques known to date). The technique has some problems to reach the global optima, but it produces very good approximations considering its low computation cost. The main drawback of the approach is that its implementation is considerably more complex than any of the other techniques previously discussed.

### 10.3.8 Pareto Dominance and Preselection

Jiménez et al. [36] proposed an algorithm that uses Pareto dominance inside a preselection scheme to solve several types of optimization problems (multiobjective, constraint satisfaction, global optimization, and goal programming problems). The approach redefines the problem as an unconstrained multiobjective optimization problem in which objectives are given priorities. Feasible solutions with a good objective function value are given the highest priority. The authors use a real-coded non-generational GA with two types of crossover operators (uniform and arithmetic) and two mutation operators (uniform and non-uniform).

The preselection scheme of this approach works as follows [36]:

**Begin**
    At each iteration of the algorithm
    select two parents $p_1$ and $p_2$ at random.
    Apply the crossover operators $NC$ times to produce $NC$ offspring
    Apply the mutation operators to produce a total of $2 \times NC$ offspring
    Obtain the best $c_1$ individuals of the first $NC$
    offspring based on Pareto dominance
    Obtain the best $c_2$ individuals of the second $NC$
    (mutated) offspring based on Pareto dominance
    **If** $c_1$ dominates $p_1$ **Then**
        $c_1$ replaces $p_1$ in the population
    **EndIf**
    **If** $c_2$ dominates $p_2$ **Then**
        $c_2$ replaces $p_2$ in the population
    **EndIf**
**End**

The authors argue that this preselection mechanism is an implicit niche formation technique because individuals are replaced only by similar ones (i.e., their offspring). As only the best individuals are inserted into the new population, this scheme is also an elitist strategy.

This approach was validated with eleven test functions, producing very good results. Note, however, that the authors do not specify the computational cost of the approach and it is not clear if the approach is competitive with other techniques in that regard.

### 10.3.9 Pareto Ranking and Robust Optimization

Ray [37] explored an extension of his previous work on constraint-handling [33] in which the emphasis was robustness. A robust optimized solution is not sensitive to parametric variations due to incomplete information of the problem or to changes on it. This approach is capable of handling constraints and finds feasible solutions that are robust to parametric variations produced over time. This is achieved using the individual's self-feasibility and its neighborhood feasibility. Thus, a new matrix called "modified constraint matrix" is used to replace both the constraint matrix and the combined matrix of Ray's original proposal (see Equations 10.15 and 10.16). An example of this modified constraint matrix is the following:

$$
\begin{pmatrix}
c_{11} & c_{12} & \cdots & c_{1s} & c_{1s+1} & c_{1s+2} & \cdots & c_{12s} \\
c_{21} & c_{22} & \cdots & c_{2s} & c_{2s+2} & c_{2s+2} & \cdots & c_{22s} \\
\vdots & \vdots & \ddots & \vdots & \vdots & \vdots & \ddots & \vdots \\
c_{M1} & c_{M2} & \cdots & c_{Ms} & c_{Ms+1} & c_{Ms+2} & \cdots & c_{M2s}
\end{pmatrix}
\tag{10.17}
$$

where $c_{is+1}, c_{is+2} \cdots c_{i2s}$ denotes the number of violations of the first constraint among $k$ neighbors and so on. A mechanism based on ranking values in both spaces (objective space and constraint space) is used to select the best individuals and copy them into the next population. The remaining portion of the new population is filled by mating two parents $p_1$ and $p_2$. One parent $(p_1)$ is selected based on a crowding factor using roulette wheel selection. The partner of this individual $(p_2)$ is the result of the competition between two individuals ($A$ and $B$) picked up by a roulette wheel selection process. To decide between $A$ and $B$ in order to obtain $p_2$ the following criteria are adopted:

1. If $A$ is feasible and $B$ is not: Select $A$ as the partner $p_2$.
2. If $B$ is feasible and $A$ is not: Select $B$ as the partner $p_2$.
3. If both $A$ and $B$ are feasible: Select one with a minimum **Rank Objective**. If the **Rank Objective** of $A$ and $B$ are the same, select one with the minimum number of neighbors in the parametric space as a mate.
4. If both $A$ and $B$ are infeasible: Select $A$ or $B$ with a minimum **Rank Constraint**. If the **Rank Constraints** are the same, randomly select between $A$ and $B$.

The general algorithm is as follows [37]:

**Begin**
    Let $M$ be a random initial population.
    **Do**
        Generate the Objective and Constraint matrices
        Rank individuals based on these matrices
        Select elite solutions and copy them into the population
        to be used in the next generation
        Pick an elite individual
        Choose its partner
        Mate them and generate two children
        Put these children into the population
        to be used in the next generation

     **While** termination condition=true
**End**

A real-coded GA with Simulated Binary Crossover [38] was used to implement this technique. The results reported in two well-known design problems [37] showed that the proposed approach did not reach solutions as good as the other techniques against which it was compared, but it turned out to be less sensitive to parametric variations, which was the main goal of the approach. In contrast, the other techniques analyzed showed significant changes when the parameters were perturbed. The main drawback of this approach is, again, its relative complexity (i.e., its difficulty to implement it), and it would also be desirable that the approach is further refined so that it can get closer to the global optimum than the current available version.

## 10.4 A Small Comparative Study

Four techniques were selected from those discussed before to perform a small comparative study that aims to illustrate some practical issues of constraint-handling techniques. The techniques selected are the following: COMOGA [19], the use of VEGA proposed by Coello [21], the NPGA to handle constraints [25] and the approach that uses MOGA [23]. In order to simplify our notation, the last three techniques previously indicated will be called HCVEGA, HCNPGA, and HCMOGA, respectively.

    To evaluate the performance of the techniques selected, we decided to use two of the well-known benchmarks proposed in Michalewicz and Schoenauer [13] plus two engineering design problems used in Coello [23]. The full description of the four test functions is as follows:

1. **g04**:
   Minimize:

$$f(\mathbf{x}) = 5.3578547x_3^2 + 0.8356891x_1x_5 + 37.293239x_1 - 40792.141 \quad (10.18)$$

   subject to:

   $g_1(\mathbf{x})= 85.334407+0.0056858x_2x_5+0.0006262x_1x_4-0.0022053x_3x_5-92\leq 0$
   $g_2(\mathbf{x})= -85.334407 - 0.0056858x_2x_5 - 0.0006262x_1x_4 + 0.0022053x_3x_5 \leq 0$
   $g_3(\mathbf{x})= 80.51249 + 0.0071317x_2x_5 + 0.0029955x_1x_2 + 0.0021813x_3^2 - 110 \leq 0$
   $g_4(\mathbf{x})= -80.51249 - 0.0071317x_2x_5 - 0.0029955x_1x_2 - 0.0021813x_3^2 + 90 \leq 0$
   $g_5(\mathbf{x})= 9.300961 + 0.0047026x_3x_5 + 0.0012547x_1x_3 + 0.0019085x_3x_4 - 25 \leq 0$
   $g_6(\mathbf{x})= -9.300961-0.0047026x_3x_5-0.0012547x_1x_3-0.0019085x_3x_4+20\leq 0$

   where: $78 \leq x_1 \leq 102$, $33 \leq x_2 \leq 45$, $27 \leq x_i \leq 45$ $(i = 3, 4, 5)$.

2. **g11**

Minimize:

$$f(\mathbf{x}) = x_1^2 + (x_2 - 1)^2 \qquad (10.19)$$

subject to:

$$h(\mathbf{x}) = x_2 - x_1^2 = 0$$

where: $-1 \le x_1 \le 1,\ -1 \le x_2 \le 1$.

3. **Design of a Pressure Vessel**

A cylindrical vessel is capped at both ends by hemispherical heads as shown in Figure 10.2. The objective is to minimize the total cost, including the cost of the material, forming, and welding. There are four design variables: $T_s$ (thickness of the shell), $T_h$ (thickness of the head), $R$ (inner radius) and $L$ (length of the cylindrical section of the vessel, not including the head). $T_s$ and $T_h$ are integer multiples of 0.0625 in., which are the available thicknesses of rolled steel plates, and $R$ and $L$ are continuous. Using the same notation given by Kannan and Kramer [39], the problem can be stated as follows:

Minimize :

$$F(\mathbf{x}) = 0.6224x_1x_3x_4 + 1.7781x_2x_3^2 + 3.1661x_1^2x_4 + 19.84x_1^2x_3 \quad (10.20)$$

Subject to :

$$g_1(\mathbf{x}) = -x_1 + 0.0193x_3 \le 0 \qquad (10.21)$$

$$g_2(\mathbf{x}) = -x_2 + 0.00954x_3 \le 0 \qquad (10.22)$$

$$g_3(\mathbf{x}) = -\pi x_3^2 x_4 - \frac{4}{3}\pi x_3^3 + 1{,}296{,}000 \le 0 \qquad (10.23)$$

$$g_4(\mathbf{x}) = x_4 - 240 \le 0 \qquad (10.24)$$

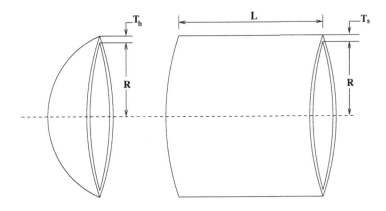

**Figure 10.2.** Center and end section of the pressure vessel used for the third example.

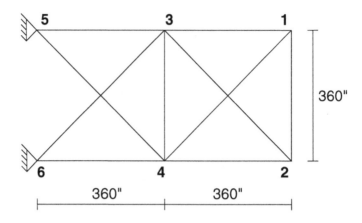

**Figure 10.3.** 10-bar plane truss used for the fourth example.

4. **Design of a 10-bar plane truss**
   Consider the 10-bar plane truss shown in Figure 10.3 [40]. The problem is
   to find the moment of inertia of each member of this truss, such that we
   minimize its weight, subject to stress and displacement constraints. The
   weight of the truss is given by:

$$f(x) = \sum_{j=1}^{10} \rho A_j L_j \tag{10.25}$$

   where $x$ is the candidate solution, $A_j$ is the cross-sectional area of the $j$th
   member, $L_j$ is the length of the $j$th member, and $\rho$ is the weight density
   of the material.
   The assumed data are: modulus of elasticity, $E = 1.0 \times 10^4$ ksi 68965.5
   MPa), $\rho = 0.10$ lb/in.$^3$ (2768.096 kg/m$^3$), and a load of 100 kips (45351.47
   Kg) in the negative y-direction is applied at nodes 2 and 4. The maximum
   allowable stress of each member is called $\sigma_a$, and it is assumed to be $\pm 25$
   ksi (172.41 MPa). The maximum allowable displacement of each node
   (horizontal and vertical) is represented by $u_a$, and it is assumed to be 2
   ins. (5.08 cm).
   There are 10 stress constraints, and 12 displacement constraints (we
   can really assume only 8 displacement constraints because there are two
   nodes with zero displacement, but they will nevertheless be considered
   as additional constraints). The moment of inertia of each element can be
   different, thus the problem has 10 design variables.

   To get a measure of the difficulty of solving each of these problems, a $\rho$
   metric (as suggested by Koziel and Michalewicz [35]) was computed using the

following expression:

$$\rho = |F|/|S| \qquad (10.26)$$

where $|F|$ is the number of feasible solutions and $|S|$ is the total number of solutions randomly generated. In this work $S = 1,000,000$ random solutions. The different values of $\rho$ for each of the functions chosen are shown in Table 10.1, where $n$ is the number of decision variables, LI is the number of linear inequalities, NI the number of non-linear inequalities, LE is the number of linear equalities and NE is the number of non-linear equalities. It can be clearly seen that the second test function should be the most difficult to solve since it presents the lowest value of $\rho$.

In our comparative study, we used a binary-coded GA with two-point crossover and uniform mutation. Equality constraints were transformed into inequalities using a tolerance value of 0.001 (see Coello [12] for details of this transformation). The number of fitness function evaluations is the same for all the approaches under study $(80,000)$. The parameters adopted for each of the methods were as follows:

- **COMOGA:**
  - Population size = 200
  - Crossover rate = 1.0
  - Mutation rate = 0.05
  - Desired proportion of feasible solutions = 10%
  - $\epsilon = 0.01$
- **HCVEGA:**
  - Population Size = 200
  - Number of generations = 400
  - Crossover rate = 0.6
  - Mutation rate = 0.05
  - Tournament size = 5
- **HCNPGA:**
  - Population Size = 200
  - Number of generations = 400
  - Crossover rate = 0.6
  - Mutation rate = 0.05
  - Size of sample of the population = 10
  - Selection ratio = 0.8

**Table 10.1.** Values of $\rho$ for the four test problems chosen.

| Problem | n | Type of function | $\rho$ | LI | NI | LE | NE |
|---------|-----|------------------|----------|----|----|----|----|
| 1 | 5 | quadratic | 27.0079% | 0 | 0 | 4 | 2 |
| 2 | 2 | quadratic | 0.0973% | 0 | 1 | 0 | 0 |
| 3 | 4 | quadratic | 39.6762% | 0 | 0 | 3 | 1 |
| 4 | 10 | non linear | 46.8070% | 0 | 0 | 0 | 22 |

- **HCMOGA**:
  - Population size = 200
  - Number of generations = 400
  - Crossover rate = 0.6
  - Mutation rate = 0.05

A total of 100 runs per technique per problem were performed. Statistical results are presented in Tables 10.2- 10.5, where $P_i$ refers to the problem solved ($1 \leq i \leq 4$), $0.0 \leq F_p \leq 1.0$ is the average rate of feasible solutions found during a single run (with respect to the full population).[1]

## 10.5 Discussion of Results

Although this study is too limited to derive general conclusions, there are a few interesting issues that deserve discussion. First, it is important to emphasize that all of the approaches tested were able to reach the feasible region in all of the test functions. We also found that HCNPGA was the most robust approach. This technique was able to find the best results in all of the test functions, except for **g11** in which there was a tie with HCMOGA. Note that the mean values obtained by the HCNPGA is not always the best of all the approaches in all of the test functions (see for example **g04** and **g11**), but it tends to have the lowest standard deviations, which is indicative of a more robust performance.

**Table 10.2.** Experimental results using COMOGA with the four test problems.

| P | Optimal | Best | Median | Mean | St. Dev. | Worst | $F_p$ |
|---|---------|------|--------|------|----------|-------|-------|
| | | | COMOGA | | | | |
| $P_1$ | -30665.539 | -30533.057 | -30328.199 | -30329.563 | 74.793290 | -30141.033 | 0.002358 |
| $P_2$ | 0.750 | 0.749058 | 0.749787 | 0.749829 | 0.000495 | 0.751753 | 0.000286 |
| $P_3$ | 6059.9463 | 6369.4282 | 7889.8389 | 7795.4115 | 701.36397 | 9147.5205 | 0.003989 |
| $P_4$ | 5152.6361 | 6283.1987 | 6675.1267 | 6660.4556 | 126.28925 | 6968.6274 | 0.006516 |

**Table 10.3.** Experimental results using HCVEGA to handle constraints with the four test problems.

| P | Optimal | Best | Median | Mean | St. Dev. | Worst | $F_p$ |
|---|---------|------|--------|------|----------|-------|-------|
| | | | HCVEGA | | | | |
| $P_1$ | -30665.539 | -30647.246 | -30628.588 | -30628.469 | 7.877054 | -30607.240 | 0.408108 |
| $P_2$ | 0.750 | 0.749621 | 0.812369 | 0.798690 | 0.025821 | 0.847242 | 0.011206 |
| $P_3$ | 6059.9463 | 6064.7236 | 6238.4897 | 6259.9637 | 170.25402 | 6820.9448 | 0.425354 |
| $P_4$ | 5152.6361 | 5327.4185 | 5453.4460 | 5455.8719 | 56.744241 | 5569.2407 | 0.676408 |

---

[1]Due to format limitations the performance values are rounded off to at most eight significant digits.

COMOGA presented its best performance in function **g11**, which is the one with the most heavily constrained search space. HCMOGA normally presented the best statistical performance (i.e., lowest standard deviations) of all the approaches. HCVEGA presented its best performance in **g04** but its best result was still relatively far from the global optimum.

The high selection pressure of the non-generational GA used in COMOGA made it difficult to avoid premature convergence. This is reflected by the $F_p$ values produced by this approach, which are lower than those generated by the three other approaches.

The population-based approach used by the HCVEGA was the most robust in the test function with the highest number of decision variables. This seems to suggest that this sort of approach may be more effective in problems with high dimensionality. In fact, we have found in other studies that most constraint-handling techniques based on Pareto dominance tend to degrade their performance as the number of decision variables increases.

HCMOGA performed well in all four problems but its overall performance was not as good as that of the HCNPGA. However, in problem 4 (**g11**) the HCMOGA presented the most consistent behavior and the best solution that it found was the same as the one produced by the HCNPGA. This seems to suggest that ranking all the population may be useful to deal with highly constrained spaces. The obvious drawback is its computational cost.

Dealing with a high number of constraints (e.g., problem 4) was not difficult for any of the approaches, except for COMOGA which could not find good results.

Although not conclusive, this study seems to indicate that Pareto dominance, Pareto ranking and population-based mechanisms are promising

**Table 10.4.** Experimental results using HCNPGA to handle constraints with the four test problems.

| P | | | | HCNPGA | | | |
|---|---|---|---|---|---|---|---|
| | Optimal | Best | Median | Mean | St. Dev. | Worst | $F_p$ |
| $P_1$ | -30665.539 | -30661.033 | -30635.347 | -30630.883 | 20.466057 | -30544.324 | 0.345432 |
| $P_2$ | 0.750 | 0.749001 | 0.749613 | 0.753909 | 0.012147 | 0.832940 | 0.025842 |
| $P_3$ | 6059.9463 | 6059.9263 | 6127.6184 | 6172.5274 | 123.89755 | 6845.7705 | 0.330693 |
| $P_4$ | 5152.6361 | 5179.7407 | 5256.1082 | 5259.0132 | 37.658930 | 5362.8906 | 0.503566 |

**Table 10.5.** Experimental results using HCMOGA to handle constraints with the four test problems.

| P | | | | HCMOGA | | | |
|---|---|---|---|---|---|---|---|
| | Optimal | Best | Median | Mean | St. Dev. | Worst | $F_p$ |
| $P_1$ | -30665.539 | -30649.959 | -30570.755 | -30568.918 | 53.531272 | -30414.773 | 0.344896 |
| $P_2$ | 0.750 | 0.749001 | 0.749155 | 0.749393 | 0.000595 | 0.752445 | 0.016913 |
| $P_3$ | 6059.9463 | 6066.9697 | 6561.4832 | 6629.0640 | 385.11074 | 7547.4033 | 0.452672 |
| $P_4$ | 5152.6361 | 5336.6187 | 5745.2383 | 5748.8395 | 210.69610 | 6474.0420 | 0.603598 |

approaches to handle constraints. These results also seem to suggest that a traditional (i.e., generational) GA performs better in optimization problems than non-generational GAs.

Regarding diversity, the four approaches exhibited a good performance, which seems to indicate that the search space is well sampled by all of them. However, note that none of the four approaches could reach the global optimum. This indicates that further refinements are required to improve the effectiveness of these approaches.

The use of a sample of the population to determine the Pareto dominance of an individual was found to be appropriate in this context. This is consistent with the behavior reported for the NPGA in multiobjective optimization problems [41]. However, in problems with highly constrained search spaces, Pareto ranking of the entire population seems to be advantageous. On the other hand, population-based approaches seem to be less sensitive to scalability of the decision variable space. An open question is if the advantages of each of these techniques can be combined into a single approach.

## 10.6 Conclusions and Future Work

A set of constraint-handling techniques based on multiobjective concepts were presented in this chapter. In each case, advantages and disadvantages were discussed. We also presented a small comparative study in which four of the techniques discussed were implemented and evaluated using four test functions. Our results provided some insights regarding the behavior of each type of technique. Note, however, that comparisons with respect to traditional penalty functions [14,42] and with the most competitive constraint-handling techniques used with EAs (e.g., stochastic ranking [43], the homomorphous maps [35], and the adaptive segregational constrained handling evolutionary algorithm (ASCHEA) [44] are still lacking.

The results obtained seem to indicate that techniques based on multiobjective optimization can properly deal with constrained search spaces. However, such results also seem to indicate that additional mechanisms should be used to improve the effectiveness of these approaches, since they had obvious difficulties to reach the global optimum in all the test functions used.

Some of the most promising paths of future research in this area are the following:

- Incorporation of self-adaptation or on-line adaptation to make unnecessary the fine tuning of additional parameters.
- Exploitation of domain knowledge extracted from the evolutionary process to improve the results obtained by the EA.
- Hybridization with classical global optimization techniques and/or with other heuristics.

# Acknowledgments

This work is representative of the research performed by the Evolutionary Computation Group at CINVESTAV-IPN (EVOCINV). The first author acknowledges support from the Mexican Consejo Nacional de Ciencia y Tecnología (CONACyT) through a scholarship to pursue graduate studies at CINVESTAV-IPN's Electrical Engineering Department. The second author acknowledges support from (CONACyT) through project number 32999-A.

# References

1. Coello Coello, CA, Van Veldhuizen, DA and Lamont, GB, *Evolutionary Algorithms for Solving Multi-Objective Problems*. New York, Kluwer Academic Publishers, 2002.
2. Michalewicz, Z, *Genetic Algorithms + Data Structures = Evolution Programs*. Springer-Verlag, Third edition, 1996.
3. Arnold, DV, *Noisy Optimization with Evolution Strategies*. New York, Kluwer Academic Publishers, 2002.
4. Butz, MV, *Anticipatory Learning Classifier Systems*. New York, Kluwer Academic Publishers, 2001.
5. Goldberg, D, *The Design of Innovation*. Kluwer Academic Publishers, New York, June 2002.
6. Cant-Paz, E, *Efficient and Accurate Parallel Genetic Algorithms*. New York, Kluwer Academic Publishers, 2000.
7. Branke, J, *Evolutionary Optimization in Dynamic Environments*. New York, Kluwer Academic Publishers, 2001.
8. Obayashi, S, Pareto Solutions of Multipoint Design of Supersonic Wings using Evolutionary Algorithms. In IC Parmee (ed.), *Adaptive Computing in Design and Manufacture V*, pp. 3-15, London, Springer-Verlag, 2002.
9. Tesh, K, Atherton, MA, and Collins, MW, Genetic Algorithms Search for Stent Design Improvements. In IC Parmee (ed.), *Adaptive Computing in Design and Manufacture V*, pp. 99-107, London, Springer-Verlag, 2002.
10. Tan, KC, Lee, TH, Cai, J, and Chew, YH, Automating the Drug Scheduling of Cancer Chemotherapy via Evolutionary Computation. In *Proceedings of the Congress on Evolutionary Computation 2001 (CEC'2001)*, vol. 2, pp. 908–913, Piscataway, 2001, IEEE Service Center.
11. Majumdar, NS, and Dasgupta, D, Determining Optimal Configuration for Turbine Generator Cooler. In *Proceedings of the Congress on Evolutionary Computation 2001 (CEC'2001)*, vol. 2, pp. 1009-1014, Piscataway, 2001, IEEE Service Center.
12. Coello Coello, CA, Theoretical and Numerical Constraint Handling Techniques used with Evolutionary Algorithms: A Survey of the State of the Art. *Computer Methods in Applied Mechanics and Engineering*, 2002; 191(11-12): 1245–1287.
13. Michalewicz, Z and Schoenauer, M, Evolutionary Algorithms for Constrained Parameter Optimization Problems. *Evolutionary Computation*, 1996; 4(1): 1–32.
14. Smith, AE, and Coit, DW, Constraint Handling Techniques—Penalty Functions. In Thomas Bäck, DB, Fogel and Michalewicz, Z (eds.) *Handbook

*of Evolutionary Computation*, Chapter C 5.2. Oxford University Press and Institute of Physics Publishing, 1997.

15. Edgeworth, FY, *Mathematical Physics*. P. Keagan, London:1881.

16. Pareto, V, *Cours D'Economie Politique*, vol. I and II. Lausanne, F. Rouge: 1896.

17. Goldberg, DE, *Genetic Algorithms in Search, Optimization and Machine Learning*. Reading, MA, Addison-Wesley, 1989.

18. Schaffer, JD, Multiple Objective Optimization with Vector Evaluated Genetic Algorithms. In *Genetic Algorithms and their Applications: Proceedings of the First International Conference on Genetic Algorithms*, pp. 93–100. Lawrence Erlbaum, 1985.

19. Surry, PD, and Radcliffe, NJ, The COMOGA Method: Constrained Optimisation by Multiobjective Genetic Algorithms. *Control and Cybernetics*, 1997; 26(3): 391-412.

20. Parmee, IC, and Purchase, G, The Development of a Directed Genetic Search Technique for Heavily Constrained Design Spaces, In IC, Parmee (ed.), *Adaptive Computing in Engineering Design and Control-'94*, pp. 97–102, Plymouth, UK, 1994. University of Plymouth.

21. Coello Coello, CA, Treating Constraints as Objectives for Single-Objective Evolutionary Optimization. *Engineering Optimization*, 2000; 32(3): 275–308.

22. Coello Coello, CA, and Aguirre, AH, Design of Combinational Logic Circuits through an Evolutionary Multiobjective Optimization Approach. *Artificial Intelligence for Engineering, Design, Analysis and Manufacture*, 2002; 16(1): 39–53.

23. Coello Coello, CA, Constraint-handling Using an Evolutionary Multiobjective Optimization Technique. *Civil Engineering and Environmental Systems*, 2000; 17: 319–346.

24. Fonseca, CM, and Fleming, PJ, Genetic Algorithms for Multiobjective Optimization: Formulation, Discussion and Generalization. In S Forrest (ed.) *Proceedings of the Fifth International Conference on Genetic Algorithms*, pp. 416–423, San Mateo, California, University of Illinois at Urbana-Champaign, Morgan Kaufmann Publishers, 1993.

25. Coello Coello, CA, and Mezura-Montes, E, Handling Constraints in Genetic Algorithms Using Dominance-Based Tournaments. In IC Parmee (ed.), *Proceedings of the Fifth International Conference on Adaptive Computing Design and Manufacture (ACDM 2002)*, vol. 5, pp. 273–284, University of Exeter, Devon, UK, Springer-Verlag, 2002.

26. Horn, J, Nafpliotis, N, and Goldberg, DE, A Niched Pareto Genetic Algorithm for Multiobjective Optimization. In *Proceedings of the First IEEE Conference on Evolutionary Computation, IEEE World Congress on Computational Intelligence*, vol. 1, pp. 82–87, Piscataway, New Jersey, June 1994. IEEE Service Center.

27. Deb, K, and Goldberg, DE, An Investigation of Niche and Species Formation in Genetic Function Optimization. In JD Schaffer (ed.), *Proceedings of the Third International Conference on Genetic Algorithms*, pp. 42–50, San Mateo, California, George Mason University, Morgan Kaufmann Publishers, 1989.

28. Mezura-Montes, E, Uso de la Técnica Multiobjetivo NPGA para el Manejo de Restricciones en Algoritmos Genéticos. Master's thesis, Universidad Veracruzana, Xalapa, México, 2001 (in Spanish).

29. Camponogara, E, and Talukdar, SN, A Genetic Algorithm for Constrained and Multiobjective Optimization. In JT Alander (ed.) *3rd Nordic Workshop*

*on Genetic Algorithms and Their Applications (3NWGA)*, pp. 49–62, Vaasa, Finland, University of Vaasa, 1997.

30. Chankong, V and Haimes, YY, Multiobjective Decision Making: Theory and Methodology. In AP, Sage (ed.), *Systems Science and Engineering*. North-Holland, 1983.

31. Jiménez, F and Verdegay, JL, Evolutionary Techniques for Constrained Optimization Problems. In *7th European Congress on Intelligent Techniques and Soft Computing (EUFIT'99)*, Aachen, Germany, 1999. Springer-Verlag.

32. Surry, PD, Radcliffe, NJ, and Boyd, ID, A Multi-Objective Approach to Constrained Optimisation of Gas Supply Networks : The COMOGA Method. In TC, Fogarty (ed.) *Evolutionary Computing. AISB Workshop. Selected Papers*, Lecture Notes in Computer Science, pp. 166–180. Springer-Verlag, Sheffield, U.K., 1995.

33. Ray, T, Kang, T, and Chye, SW, An Evolutionary Algorithm for Constrained Optimization. In D Whitley, D Goldberg, E Cantú-Paz, L Spector, I Parmee, and H Beyer (eds.), *Proceedings of the Genetic and Evolutionary Computation Conference (GECCO'2000)*, pp. 771–777, San Francisco, California, Morgan Kaufmann, 2000.

34. Hinterding, R, and Michalewicz, Z, Your Brains and My Beauty: Parent Matching for Constrained Optimisation. In *Proceedings of the 5th International Conference on Evolutionary Computation*, pp. 810–815, Anchorage, Alaska, 1998.

35. Koziel, S, and Michalewicz, Z, Evolutionary Algorithms, Homomorphous Mappings, and Constrained Parameter Optimization. *Evolutionary Computation*, 1999; 7(1): 19–44.

36. F, Jiménez, AF, Gómez-Skarmeta, and G, Sánchez, How Evolutionary Multi-objective Optimization Can Be Used for Goals and Priorities Based Optimization. In E Alba, F Fernández, JA Gómez, F Herrera, JI Hidalgo, J Lanchares, JJ Merelo, and JM Sánchez (eds.)*Primer Congreso Espaõl de Algoritmos Evolutivos y Bioinspirados (AEB'02)*, pp. 460–465, Mérida España, 2002. Universidad de la Extremadura, España.

37. Ray, T, Constraint Robust Optimal Design using a Multiobjective Evolutionary Algorithm. In *Proceedings of the Congress on Evolutionary Computation 2002 (CEC'2002)*, vol. 1, pp. 419–424, Piscataway, NJ, May 2002. IEEE Service Center.

38. Deb, K, and Agrawal, RW, Simulated Binary Crossover For Continuous Search Space. *Complex Systems*, 1995; 9: 115–148.

39. Kannan, BK, and Kramer, SN, An Augmented Lagrange Multiplier Based Method for Mixed Integer Discrete Continuous Optimization and Its Applications to Mechanical Design. *Journal of Mechanical Design. Transactions of the ASME*, 1994; 116:318–320.

40. Belegundu, AD, *A Study of Mathematical Programming Methods for Structural Optimization*. Department of Civil and Environmental Engineering, University of Iowa, Iowa, 1982.

41. Coello Coello, CA, A Comprehensive Survey of Evolutionary-Based Multiobjective Optimization Techniques. *Knowledge and Information Systems. An International Journal*, 1999; 1(3):269–308.

42. Richardson, JT, Palmer, MR, Liepins, G, and Hilliard, M, Some Guidelines for Genetic Algorithms with Penalty Functions. In JD Schaffer (ed.) *Proceedings*

of the Third International Conference on Genetic Algorithms (ICGA-89), pp. 191–197, San Mateo, California, June 1989. George Mason University, Morgan Kaufmann Publishers.

43. Runarsson, TP, and Yao, X, Stochastic Ranking for Constrained Evolutionary Optimization. IEEE Transactions on Evolutionary Computation, 2000; 4(3): 284–294.

44. Hamida, SB, and Schoenauer, M, An Adaptive Algorithm for Constrained Optimization Problems. In M Schoenauer, K Deb, G Rudolph, X Yao, E Lutton, JJ Merelo, and HP Schwefel (eds.), Proceedings of the Parallel Problem Solving from Nature VI Conference, pp. 529–538, Paris, France, Lecture Notes in Computer Science No. 1917, Springer, 2000.

# 11

# Multi-criteria Optimization of Finite State Automata: Maximizing Performance while Minimizing Description Length

Robert Goldberg and Natalie Hammerman

**Summary.** This chapter presents a new operator which, when added to a genetic algorithm (GA), improved the performance of the GA for locating optimal finite state automata. The new operator (termed MTF) reorganizes a finite state automaton (FSA) genome during the execution of the genetic algorithm. MTF systematically renames the states and moves them to the front of the genome. The operator was tested on the ant trail problem. Across different criteria (failure rate, processing time to locate a solution, number of generations needed to locate a solution), the MTF-enhanced GA realized speedups between 110% and 579% over the non-enhanced version. In addition, the successful FSAs found by the genetic algorithm augmented with MTF were 25% 46% smaller in size than those found by the original GA.

## 11.1 Introduction

The versatility of a finite state automaton (FSA) genome as the operand of a genetic algorithm (GA) is evident by the different types of applications it has been used for. Tomita [1] utilized it to locate language acceptors within a population. MacLennan [2] implemented an FSA genome to study the development of communication within an evolving population. Jefferson et al. [3] used the FSA genome to represent a trail following strategy; this was used as the starting point for the research presented in this chapter.

A genetic algorithm with an FSA genome was implemented to search the space of FSAs with 32 or fewer states for strategies to traverse an evaporating chemical trail within a given time frame. The work of Jefferson et al. [3] was recreated as the benchmark, and then augmented with the new reorganization operator. Experimentation was carried out with two disjoint seed sets for the random number generator, three different population sizes, and different loop limits for the maximum number of generations to be bred.

The rationale for the new reorganization operator is based on the following observation: because a single FSA can have many different representations by simply assigning the states different names or numbers, underlying schema that characterize families of finite state automata from their genomes are often not apparent. The consequence of this is that equivalent FSAs (differing only by state name) can force related schemata to compete against each other and hindering the growth of useful schemata from within the genetic algorithm. To compensate for this disadvantage a new operator MTF was designed. It systematically reorganizes FSA genomes during GA execution so that the following two conditions hold true for each member of the current parent pool:

- equivalent FSAs with the same number of states will have identical representations, and
- the significant data will reside in contiguous bits at the front of the genome.

Not only does this reorganization avoid competition between equivalent FSAs with different representations and the same number of states, but it also reduces schema length [4]. According to schema theory, shorter defining lengths are more beneficial to the growth of useful schemata [5], which in turn enhances convergence rates.

The next section describes the benchmark used for the experimentation. Then in Section 11.3 the new operator is presented. Sections 11.4 and 11.5 describe the results and analysis of the experimentation with/out the new operator, while the last section gives the conclusions and directions for further research.

## 11.2 The Benchmark

This chapter applies the genetic algorithm with a finite state automaton genome to the trail problem. It is based on the work of Jefferson et al. [3] and was recreated for the benchmark for the experimentation (of Sections 11.4 and 11.5). The next Section presents the trail problem in general and then, in Section 11.2.2, specific problem details are provided to understand how the GA with the FSA genome is applied.

### 11.2.1 The Problem to be Solved

This section describes the problem that was used to test the effectiveness of the reorganization algorithm. For the benchmark the work of Jefferson et al. [3] was recreated. The reader is referred to Figure 11.1 for an illustration of the trail now described. An ant is positioned facing the first step of the John Muir Trail. The trail represents an evaporating chemical trail. It is wrapped around a torroidal grid, which can be represented as a 32 × 32 square grid with top-bottom/left-right borders adjacency. The numbers in Figure 11.1 indicate the trail steps that have retained their chemical marking; the boxes with an × represent the trail steps that have lost their chemical marking as a

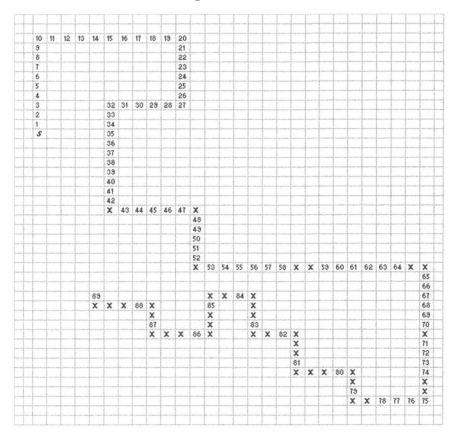

**Figure 11.1.** John Muir trail.

result of evaporation. There are 89 marked trail steps and 38 unmarked trail
steps which the ant must navigate in 200 time steps.

The ant is represented as a 32-state FSA. (See the next subsection for
genome description.) A time step represents an application of a transition
rule of the FSA. Based on the present state of the ant and whether the trail
step immediately in front of the ant is marked (FSA input = 1) or unmarked
(input = 0), the ant can turn 90° to the right (FSA output = 0) or left
(output = 1), move onto the trail step directly in front (output = 2), or do
nothing (output = 3). An output of 3 permits the ant to change state without
taking any additional action. Initially the ant is positioned in the box with an
$S$ facing the box marked 1 (Figure 11.1). The next subsection describes the
FSA implementation in a genome.

## 11.2.2 An FSA Genome

This section describes the genetic algorithm implemented for the benchmark. The GA is used to locate an ant (FSA) that can complete the John Muir Trail (Figure 11.1) within 200 time steps. A 32-state FSA is sufficient to encode a solution to the trail problem. The reader is now referred to Table 11.1 for the genome map. The start state can be any one of the 32 states. Thus, bits 0 through 4 of the genome (first data line of Table 11.1) contain the start state number. Then, each state (including the start state) needs 14 bits to describe the next state that the automaton will move to state (0-31) and the corresponding output (0-3) for each input (0 and 1). Hence, 2 inputs × (5 bits for next state + 2 bits for output) = 14 bits are required. Each line of the FSA table represents a given state with its next state and output for inputs 0 and 1. In general, for state $i \in \{ 0, 1, 2, \ldots, 31 \}$ with input $j \in \{ 0, 1 \}$, bits $5+14i+7j$ through $9+14i+7j$ of the genome indicate the next state, and bits $10+14i+7j$ and $11+14i+7j$ contain the corresponding output.

**Table 11.1.** State table of the 32-state/453-bit FSA genome.

| Present State | INPUT0 | | INPUT1 | |
|---|---|---|---|---|
| | Bits for next state | Bits for output | Bits for next state | Bits for output |
| **Start State** **(Bits 0-4)** | – | – | – | – |
| 0 | $5 - 9$ | $10 - 11$ | $12 - 16$ | $17 - 18$ |
| 1 | $19 - 23$ | $24 - 25$ | $26 - 30$ | $31 - 32$ |
| $\vdots$ | $\vdots$ | $\vdots$ | $\vdots$ | $\vdots$ |
| $i$ | $5+14i -$ $9+14i$ | $10+14i -$ $11+14i$ | $12+14i -$ $16+14i$ | $17+14i -$ $18+14i$ |
| $\vdots$ | $\vdots$ | $\vdots$ | $\vdots$ | $\vdots$ |
| 30 | $425 - 429$ | $430 - 431$ | $432 - 436$ | $437 - 438$ |
| 31 | $439 - 443$ | $444 - 445$ | $446 - 450$ | $451 - 452$ |

## 11.2.3 Genetic Algorithm

This section introduces the genetic algorithm that manipulates the genome pool (termed population) in its search to find a solution to the problem with best "fitness." Fitness is a metric on the quality of a particular genome (solution), and in the context of the trail problem is simply the number of marked steps of the trail traversed within the given time frame. The genetic algorithm shell that is used by many researchers is based on Goldberg [5]. The outline now presented also indicates step 3a that will be the insertion point for the new reorganization operator, MTF. The details of MTF will be presented in the next section.

The outline of the genetic algorithm is as follows. Step 3a incorporates the new operator.

1. Generate the initial population.
2. Find the fitness of each member of the present population.
3. Identify the parent pool as the top p percent of the population.
   [3a) Apply MTF to each member of the parent pool.]
4. Select mating pairs from the parent pool without regard to fitness.
5. Apply crossover and mutation to produce a single child from each mating pair.
6. The children bred in steps 3 through 6 become the present population.
7. Repeat from step 2 until a solution is found, or until the loop limit for the number of generations is reached.

Within the context of FSA genomes (Section 11.2.2), this algorithm (without Step 3a) will be considered the benchmark of Jefferson et al. [3]. Jefferson et al. initialized the GA with a population of 64K (65,536) randomly generated FSAs. The fitness of each FSA was the number of distinct marked steps the ant covered in 200 time steps. Based on this fitness, the top 5% of each generation was retained to parent the next generation. Once the parent pool was established, mating pairs were randomly selected from this pool without regard to fitness. Each mating pair produced a single offspring. Mutation and crossover were carried out at a rate of 1% per bit on the single offspring. To implement the per bit crossover rate, one parent was selected as the initial bit donor. Bits were then copied from the parent genome into the child genome. A random number was generated as each bit was copied. When the random number was below 0.9, the bits of the donating parent were used for the next bit of the child; otherwise, the other parent became the bit donor for the next bit. Step 3a is not used by the benchmark and refers to the operator introduced in the next section.

## 11.3 MTF Operator

In this section, MTF (move to front), the newly designed reorganization operator, is introduced (Section 11.3.1) and algorithmic details are provided (Section 11.3.2). MTF was designed to enhance schema growth based on the schema theory developed by Goldberg [5]; therefore an understanding of schema theory is critical to understanding why MTF is expected to improve the efficiency of a GA. The reader is referred to Hammerman and Goldberg [4] for further elaboration on this matter and a complete C code implementation of the algorithms presented in this section.

### 11.3.1 The Basis

The finite state automaton M1 of Figure 11.2 is a solution to the trail problem of Section 11.2.1, as well as any isomorphic automaton differing only in state names. However, although state 25, for example, could appear in any number of FSAs isomorphic to M1, it would have very different roles in each of the corresponding FSAs. There is no apparent useful shared schema when these two FSAs are represented in the genome of Table 11.1 (Section 11.2.2). Within a GA these equivalent FSAs would compete against each other to pass their genetic material onto the next generation instead of supporting each other in that task.

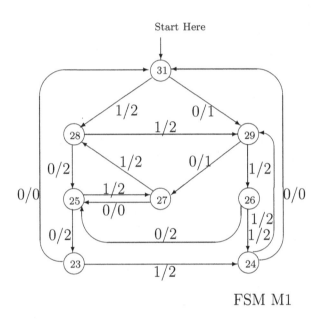

FSM M1

**Figure 11.2.** Equivalent FSA solutions to the trail problem.

In general, the genome data for automaton solutions is typically spread across the whole or almost all of the genome format. By renaming the states of FSA M1 in Figure 11.2 with numbers 0 through 7, as indicated by FSA M2 in Figure 11.3 (after applying the MTF operator), all the relevant data would be <u>m</u>oved <u>t</u>o the <u>f</u>ront of the genome, thus inducing useful schemata less susceptible to disruption due to crossover. Since the automata solutions to the ant trail problem presented here have 8 states, they need only 3 bits for determining the start state + 8 states × 2 input values per state × (3 bits for the next state designation + 2 bits for the output) = 83 bits of the genome, instead of the full 453 bits originally specified (Table 11.1). This represents an 82% reduction in genome length. It has been shown [4] that this situation holds true even with the selection process and per bit crossover implemented in this study. As a result of the systematic manner in which the states are renamed, equivalent automata now have identical representations.

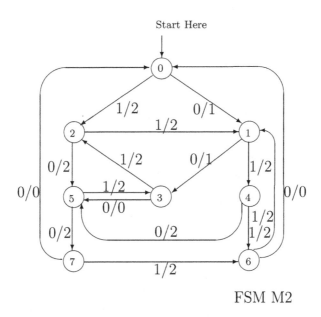

FSM M2

**Figure 11.3.** FSA of Figure 11.2 after MTF.

## 11.3.2 Algorithmic Details

The Java code in Figure 11.4 presents the details of the MTF algorithm. Within the figure, procedures **interchange_ next_ states_ and_outputs** and **change_ states_ in_ next_ state_ part_ of_table** implement the renaming of individual states and thus each have two states as arguments. Procedure **interchange_ next_ states_ and_outputs** exchanges the 14 bits of genome data for the two states in its arguments. Procedure **change_ states_ in_ next_ state_ part_ of_table** scans the next state parts of the FSA table for its two arguments; if either of the arguments appears, the state found is replaced with the other one in order to reflect the interchange of the two states. MTF performs a breadth-first search on the graph induced by the FSA table. It reassigns state numbers sequentially starting with state 0 for the start state (line 4 of Figure 11.4). As states are processed, they are entered into a FIFO (first-in, first-out) **QUEUE**. The reader may be interested in comparing FSA M1 in Figure 11.2 with FSA M2 of Figure 11.3 to understand how this operator works. Figure 11.4 presents Java code for the MTF operator and is now analyzed.

1. public void MTF (Automata *FSA*)
2. { // begin MTF

3.     // START_STATE conventionally set to zero.
4.     START_STATE = 0;
5.     NEXT_AVAILABLE_STATE = 1;
6.     **interchange_next_states_and_outputs**
7.         (START_STATE, *FSA*.START_STATE);
8.     **change_states_in_next_state_part_of_table**
9.         (START_STATE, *FSA*.START_STATE);
10.    *QUEUE*.**initialize**();
11.    *QUEUE*.**add**(START_STATE);

12.    // PROCESS THE *FSA*
13.    while ( !*QUEUE*.**empty**() )
14.    { // begin while loop

15.        CURRENT_STATE = *QUEUE*.**remove**();

16.        for (INPUT = 0; INPUT < *FSA*.NUM_OF_INPUTS; INPUT++)
17.        { // begin for loop

18.            NEXT_STATE =
19.                *FSA*.STATE_TABLE[CURRENT_STATE, INPUT];

20.            if (NEXT_STATE >= NEXT_AVAILABLE_STATE) // $\geq$
21.            { // begin if $\geq$

22.                if (NEXT_STATE > NEXT_AVAILABLE_STATE) then
23.                { // begin if >

24.                    **interchange_next_states_and_outputs**
25.                        (NEXT_STATE, NEXT_AVAILABLE_STATE);
26.                    **change_states_in_next_state_part_of_table**
27.                        (NEXT_STATE, NEXT_AVAILABLE_STATE);

28.                } // if (NEXT_STATE > NEXT_AVAILABLE_STATE)

29.                *QUEUE*.**add**(NEXT_AVAILABLE_STATE);
30.                NEXT_AVAILABLE_STATE++; // increment

31.            } // if (NEXT_STATE $\geq$ NEXT_AVAILABLE_STATE)

32.        } // for INPUT

33.    } // while ( !*QUEUE*.**empty**() )

34. } // MTF

**Figure 11.4.** Java code for the MTF algorithm.

States are only processed once. Processing a state means to reassign the state number with the next state number available. The data for the old and new state names are exchanged in the state table. Because new state numbers are assigned sequentially, it is easy to determine whether a state has already been reassigned: namely, if a state number in the FSA table is less than the next number available for state reassignment, then the state in the FSA table has previously been processed by the algorithm (tested by the inequality in line 20 of Figure 11.4.) When the state numbers are not the same, the old and new states are exchanged. This requires two steps. First, the 14 bits of data for the two states are exchanged by procedure **interchange_ next_ states_ and_outputs** (lines 6-7 for state 0 and lines 24-25 for the other states, Figure 11.4). Second, every occurrence of either state in the next state part of the table must be replaced with the other one by procedure **change_ states_ in_ next_ state_ part_ of_table** (lines 8-9 and 26-27 of Figure 11.4.) One last step is necessary whether or not the old and new state numbers are the same. The new state number must be added to the **QUEUE** (lines 11 and 29 of figure 11.4) so its next states can be processed in turn, and the **NEXT_AVAILABLE_STATE** is then incremented to the "next available state" (lines 5 and 30 of Figure 11.4).

MTF starts by renaming the start state as state 0 (line 4). State 0 is processed (lines 6-9) and placed on the **QUEUE** (lines 10-11). As long as the **QUEUE** is not empty (line 13), a state is removed from the **QUEUE** (line 15) and its next states are processed (lines 16-32) if they have not yet been processed (line 20). MTF terminates when all of the FSA states have been processed, that is, when the **QUEUE** is empty (line 13). The reader is referred to [4] for a C implementation of the entire algorithm, and for an example of a step-by-step walk-through of the algorithm as it is applied to a given FSA.

It is only necessary to reorganize the top 5% of the population, which forms the parent pool. MTF was designed to enhance schema retention and growth during the crossover operation; hence the 95% of the population, which is not used to form the next generation, is thus left alone.

The beginning of this section gave a motivation for the MTF operator based on an empirical example showing how equivalent automata can compete with each other instead of supporting the underlying similar schemata. The next section provides experiment results that support this supposition.

## 11.4 Experimentation and Results

In order to determine the effects of the MTF operator on the Jefferson et al. GA [3], two types of experiments were carried out. The first set of experiments (this section) was designed to track the evolutionary process and the second set of experiments (next section) explored the efficiency of B and MTF. The genome of Section 11.2.2 was used within the context of the genetic algorithm presented in Section 11.2.3 (benchmark) and augmented with the MTF operator (Section 11.3). For simplicity, the GA used for this study randomly generated 57 bytes (with values of 0 through 255) for each individual of generation 0; the three extra bits for each individual resulting from this method were discarded. (Jefferson et al. randomly generated individual bits for each genome.) In this section and next, the different types of experimentation/data collection are described and the results are presented. Data was collected for the benchmark (also referred to as algorithm B), and the benchmark augmented with the MTF reorganization algorithm (henceforth called algorithm MTF).

### 11.4.1 Tracking the Evolutionary Process

The first set of experiments was designed to track the evolutionary process. For these experiments, data were collected for each generation. Experiments were conducted using populations of 64K and 16K FSAs. Define *maxgen* as the maximum number of generations that the GA will be permitted to breed. For the 64K population *maxgen* was set to 70 generations; for the 16K, *maxgen* was 125 generations. In both sets of data, the GA was allowed to breed *maxgen* generations for evolutionary tracking, regardless of whether a solution was found prior to generation *maxgen*. (A *solution* is defined as an FSA which completely traverses the trail within the given time frame.) For each population size (64K and 16K) and each method (B and MTF), 30 runs were executed. For all experiments, run number $i$ used the same seed for the random number generator; and, thus for each population size, run $i$ started with the same initial population. The maximum fitness appearing in each generation of each run was recorded. Then for each population size/method/generation triplet, the maximum fitness was averaged over the 30 runs.

### 11.4.2 Results of the Experimentation

Figures 11.5 and 11.6 contain the data for the experiments using the 64K and 16K size populations respectively. In both cases, MTF attains a higher maximum fitness average per generation than the benchmark in the early generations. Although both methods are heading towards the maximum attainable value of 89, MTF moves the population fitnesses towards that value at a faster pace. Thus, the graphs in Figures 11.5 (64K, 70 generations) and 11.6 (16K, 125 generations) indicate that when MTF was incorporated into the GA, the evolutionary process was more efficient in moving towards more-fit individuals.

While these data are encouraging, the purpose of the GA is to locate a solution and the "efficiency" in locating a solution is the primary concern. Efficiency can be measured by the number of generations or by the amount of processor time an algorithm uses to locate a solution. In addition, the number of failed runs should be taken into account. These issues are discussed in the next section.

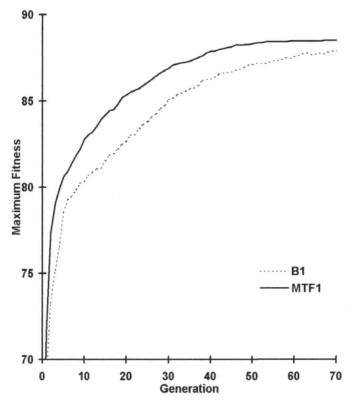

**Figure 11.5.** Comparison of B and MTF. Population size is 64K. The maximum fitness is the average over 30 runs of the maximum fitnesses for each generation.

## 11.5 Efficiency of MTF

In this section an additional set of experiments is discussed to determine the effect of MTF on the efficiency of the GA in locating a solution. During this experimentation it was observed that MTF exhibited solutions with fewer states, so this issue was also explored. The next three subsections describe the experimentation (Section 11.5.1), the criteria used to compare the results (Section 11.5.2), and the results obtained from these experiments (Section 11.5.3).

### 11.5.1 Further Experimentation

This subsection describes the experiments carried out to study the effect of MTF on convergence and automaton size. For this set of experiments, three population sizes were used: 64K, 32K, and 16K. For the experiments implementing a population size of 64K FSAs, data were collected for *maxgen* = 50, 60, and 70, where *maxgen* is the loop limit for the number of generations

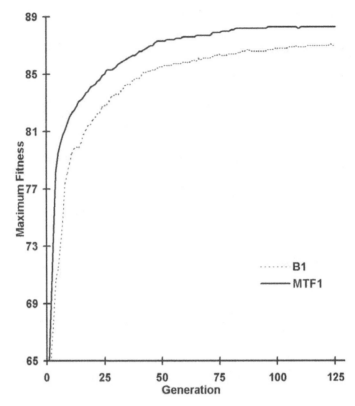

**Figure 11.6.** Comparison of B and MTF. Population size is 16K. The maximum fitness is the average over 30 runs of the maximum fitnesses for each generation.

bred. For the 32K population, data for *maxgen* = 75 and 100 were recorded, and for 16K, the values of *maxgen* were 100 and 125. The GA was halted when a solution was located (an FSA which covered all 89 marked steps within the given time frame) or if *maxgen* was reached.

For each method/population size pair, two disjoint sets of seeds were used. One set consisted of the 30 seeds that were used to track the evolutionary process. The other set consisted of 100 new seeds. The results for the 30 original seeds were considered separately because of the additional data available (Section 11.4.1) for this seed set. For all of the other experiments, run *i* for a seed set started with the same seed for the random number generator regardless of the context of the run. Hence, for a given population size and given seed set, run *i* started with the same initial population. For each method/population size/seed/*maxgen* quadruple, for those runs which find a solution before or by generation *maxgen*, the generation number in which the solution was found and the smallest number of states in the solutions located were saved along with the processor time for the run. The next subsection describes the different criteria used to evaluate the results of these experiments.

### 11.5.2 Criteria for Evaluation

This subsection describes the criteria used to compare the convergence performance of the two methods (B and MTF). To determine how MTF affects the efficiency of the GA, the evaluation of the data was based on different criteria. The speedup is calculated for given measures (number of generations, processor time, number of runs). Formally, speedup is defined as $V_B/V_{MTF}$ where $V_B$ is the value of the measure for the benchmark, and $V_{MTF}$ is the value of the measure for MTF [1]. A U-test (also called the Mann-Whitney or Wilcoxon test [7], is used to obtain a degree of confidence that MTF is more efficient than the benchmark for averages over the successful runs.

The criteria for evaluation are as follows:

Average: $G_{AV}$ is the average number of generations the GA bred in order to locate a solution, and $T_{AV}$:$S$ is the corresponding average processor time. These averages are taken over the $S$ successful runs for a given experiment for a seed set consisting of $n$ seeds. Speedups for $G_{AV}$ and $T_{AV}$: $S$ are calculated and a U-test is implemented.

Failed Runs: $F = n$-$S$ is the number of runs which did not find a solution by generation *maxgen*. With probability z, $K = \log(1\text{-}z)/\log(F/n)$ is the number of independent runs (on the average) that the GA is expected to execute to locate an FSA which can traverse the complete trail within the given time frame [8]. K is then used to calculate the speedup. For this study, z was set to 0.99.

Another issue is the percentage decrease in the average size of the successful FSAs for MTF with respect to the benchmark. In the next subsection these results are presented.

### 11.5.3 The Results

The computed results based on the data collection and criteria described in the previous two subsections are presented in this subsection and summarized in Tables 11.2 and 11.3. In all cases MTF surpasses the performance of the benchmark, with a high degree of confidence when the U-test is applicable. The number of failures, F, is used to find K (Section 11.5.2), the number of independent runs expected to be executed. z, the probability that a solution will be found in K runs, was set to 0.99. Across the experiments, the speedups of MTF over B, based on K, fall between 1.37 and 5.79 (Figure 7.9). For $G_{AV}$, the average generation in which a solution is found, the speedups vary from a low of 1.10 to a high of 1.53. Due to the allocation of system resources, reliable timing data is available only for the 30-seed/16K population experiments. The speedup based on $T_{AV}{:}S$ for $maxgen = 100$ is 1.26, and for $maxgen = 125$ this speedup is 1.27, where $maxgen$ is the loop limit for the last generation to be bred. In both cases the U-test degree of confidence that MTF is better than B is 0.999. This available timing data indicates that MTF is more efficient than the benchmark in locating a successful FSA, but the speedups are less than for the corresponding values for the number of generations due to the additional work that MTF does to reorganize the FSAs in the parent pool.

**Table 11.2.** Experiment results to determine efficiency. $maxgen$ is the loop limit for the last generation to be bred. The U-test indicates the degree of confidence that MTF is better than B. When this number is missing there are an insufficient number of data points to apply the U-test.

| # Seeds: Pop. Size: Max Gen. | $F_B$ | $F_{MTF}$ | $K_B$ | $K_{MTF}$ | Speedup based on K | $\frac{G_{AV}}{B}$ | $\frac{G_{AV}}{MTF}$ | Speedup based on $G_{AV}$ | U–test degree of confidence for $G_{AV}$ |
|---|---|---|---|---|---|---|---|---|---|
| 30:64K:50 | 24 | 12 | 20.64 | 5.03 | 4.11 | 46.67 | 41.06 | 1.14 | – |
| 30:64K:60 | 21 | 9 | 12.91 | 3.82 | 3.38 | 49.89 | 42.95 | 1.16 | 0.99 |
| 30:64K:70 | 16 | 8 | 7.33 | 3.48 | 2.1 | 55.36 | 44.05 | 1.26 | 0.999 |
| 30:32K:75 | 17 | 8 | 8.11 | 3.48 | 2.33 | 62.15 | 45.27 | 1.37 | 0.999 |
| 30:32K:100 | 13 | 8 | 5.51 | 3.48 | 1.58 | 69.41 | 45.27 | 1.53 | 0.999 |
| 30:16K:100 | 20 | 12 | 11.36 | 5.03 | 2.26 | 79 | 59.06 | 1.34 | 0.99 |
| 30:16K:125 | 17 | 10 | 8.11 | 4.19 | 1.93 | 86.62 | 64.2 | 1.35 | 0.99 |
| 100:64K:50 | 85 | 39 | 28.34 | 4.89 | 5.79 | 43 | 39.1 | 1.1 | 0.98 |
| 100:64K:60 | 60 | 36 | 9.02 | 4.51 | 2 | 50.8 | 39.77 | 1.28 | 0.999 |
| 100:64K:70 | 44 | 29 | 5.61 | 3.72 | 1.51 | 54.52 | 42.13 | 1.29 | 0.999 |
| 100:32K:75 | 66 | 37 | 11.08 | 4.63 | 2.39 | 57.68 | 48.14 | 1.2 | 0.999 |
| 100:32K:100 | 48 | 30 | 6.27 | 3.82 | 1.64 | 68.62 | 51.79 | 1.33 | 0.999 |
| 100:16K:100 | 62 | 49 | 9.63 | 6.46 | 1.49 | 67.82 | 59.1 | 1.15 | 0.98 |
| 100:16K:125 | 54 | 43 | 7.47 | 5.46 | 1.37 | 75.7 | 65.05 | 1.16 | 0.98 |

With respect to automaton size, MTF consistently located smaller solutions than the benchmark. The data indicate (Table 11.3) that the average number of states of the successful FSAs located by MTF uses just over a third of the number of states allowed, and hence just a little more than the front third of the genome. The next section summarizes the conclusions of the two different types of experiments.

## 11.6 Conclusions and Further Directions

Jefferson et al. [3] used an FSA genome as the operand of a genetic algorithm to find a strategy that would traverse the John Muir Trail (Figure 11.1) within a given number of time steps. Their GA did locate such an FSA, but that approach did not seem to readily enhance schema growth. To promote

**Table 11.3.** Experiment results with respect to automaton size. *maxgen* is the loop limit for the last generation to be bred. The U-test indicates the degree of confidence that MTF is better than B. When this number is missing there are an insufficient number of data points to apply the U-test.

| Seed set : Population Size : maxgen | Average machine size (# of states) for B | Average machine size (# of states) for MTF | Machine Size (# of states): percent decrease of MTF with respect to B | U-test degree of confidence for percent decrease |
|---|---|---|---|---|
| 30 : 64K : 50 | 17.17 | 12.78 | 25.57% | – |
| 30 : 64K : 60 | 17.89 | 13.05 | 27.05% | 0.99 |
| 30 : 64K : 70 | 18.71 | 12.95 | 30.79% | 0.999 |
| 30 : 32K : 75 | 21 | 11.32 | 46.10% | 0.999 |
| 30 : 32K : 100 | 19.94 | 11.32 | 43.23% | 0.999 |
| 30 : 16K : 100 | 22.2 | 12.89 | 41.94% | 0.999 |
| 30 : 16K : 125 | 21.15 | 12.65 | 40.19% | 0.999 |
| 100 : 64K : 50 | 20.27 | 12.56 | 38.04% | 0.999 |
| 100 : 64K : 60 | 18.98 | 12.61 | 33.56% | 0.999 |
| 100 : 64K : 70 | 18.27 | 12.7 | 30.49% | 0.999 |
| 100 : 32K : 75 | 19.24 | 13.46 | 30.04% | 0.999 |
| 100 : 32K : 100 | 18.79 | 13.51 | 28.10% | 0.999 |
| 100 : 16K : 100 | 18.53 | 12.73 | 31.30% | 0.999 |
| 100 : 16K : 125 | 19.41 | 12.51 | 35.55% | 0.999 |

such growth in the Jefferson et al. model, a new operator was designed and incorporated into this model.

MTF, the new operator, reorganizes an FSA genome. It sets the start state of a given finite state automaton to 0, and sequentially renames (reassigns) the next states of the FSA. This reorganization is applied to the parent pool while the GA is executing and results in the following: (1) equivalent FSAs with the same number of states having identical representations, and (2) relevant data compressed into a shorter bitstring thus yielding schemata with shorter defining lengths.

Two different types of experiments were undertaken. The first set of experiments tracked the evolutionary process by recording data for each generation and averaging the results over 30 runs. Experimentation was carried out for two different population sizes. The second set of experiments was designed to determine the efficiency of the MTF-enhanced GA. Efficiency is determined by the number of generations needed to locate a solution, the processor time needed to find a solution, and the success/failure rate. In addition, it was suspected that MTF would locate smaller solutions. For this second set of experiments, data were collected with respect to the termination of each run (success or failure in finding a solution, number of generations bred by the run, processor time of the run, and number of states in the smallest successful FSA.) This second set of experiments was carried out using two disjoint seed sets, and three different population sizes.

Based on the results of the experimentation (Sections 11.4 and 11.5), it was found that incorporating MTF into a GA had three positive effects:

- It sped up the evolutionary process (Section 11.4.1).
- It found solutions faster (Section 11.5.3).
- It located solutions with fewer states (Section 11.5.3).

While the specific results varied with different parameter values, incorporating MTF into the GA improves efficiency and induces smaller solutions across different population sizes and different values of *maxgen*. It would be interesting to track the progression of automaton genomes in terms of fitness and description length from generation to generation. This could possibly give extra insight into the positive effect MTF has on an FSA genome population.

## Acknowledgments

This chapter is dedicated to the memory of Jacob Shapiro, a colleague and mentor. This chapter is the third in a series representing the ongoing collaborative research on new operators for genetic algorithms. Partial support is acknowledged from PSC-CUNY research awards.

## References

1. Angeline, PJ, and Pollack, JB, Evolutionary Module Acquisition. In DB Fogel and W Atmar (eds.) Proceedings of the Second Annual Confer- ence on Evolutionary Programming, pp. 154-163, Palo Alto, California, 1993. Morgan Kaufmann Publishers.
2. Freund, JE, Mathematical Statistics with Applications, Seventh Edition. Englewood Cliffs, NJ, Prentice Hall, 2003.
3. Goldberg, DE. Genetic Algorithms in Search, Optimization and Machine Learning, Reading, MA, Addison-Wesley, 1989.
4. Hammerman, N and Goldberg, R, Algorithms to Improve the Convergence of a Genetic Algorithm with a Finite State Machine Genome, In LD Chambers (ed.) The Practical Handbook of Genetic Algorithms Vol III: Complex Coding Systems, pp. 119-238. CRC Press, Boca Raton, Florida, 1999.
5. Jefferson, D, Collins, R, Cooper, C, Dyer, M, Flowers, M, Korf, R, Taylor, C, and Wang, A. Evolution as a Theme in Artificial life: The Genesys/Tracker System, In CG Langton, C Taylor, JD Farmer, and S Rasmussen (eds.) Artificial Life II, pp. 549-578, Reading, MA, Addison-Wesley, 1992.
6. Koza, JR, Genetic Evolution and Co-evolution of Computer Programs. In CG Langton, C Taylor, JD Farmer, and S Rasmussen (eds.) Artificial Life II, pp. 603-629, Reading, MA, Addison-Wesley, 1992.
7. MacLennan, B, Synthetic Ethology: An Approach to the Study of Communication. In CG Langton, C Taylor, JD Farmer, and S Rasmussen (eds.) Artificial Life II, pp. 631-658, Reading, MA, Addison-Wesley, 1992.

8. Tomita, M, Dynamic Construction of Finite Automata from Examples Using Hill-climbing. In DB Fogel and W Atmar (eds.) Proceedings of the Fourth Annual Conference of the Cognitive Science Society, pp. 105-108, Ann Arbor, MI, The Cognitive Science Society, 1982.

# 12

# Multiobjective Optimization of Space Structures under Static and Seismic Loading Conditions

Nikos D. Lagaros, Manolis Papadrakakis, and Vagelis Plevris

**Summary.** This chapter presents a evolution strategies approach for multiobjective design optimization of structural problems such as space frames and multi-layered space trusses under static and seismic loading conditions. A rigorous approach and a simplified one with respect to the loading condition are implemented for finding optimal design of a structure under multiple objectives.

## 12.1 Introduction

In single-objective optimization problems the optimal solution is usually clearly defined, this does not hold in real-world problems having multiple and conflicting objectives. Instead of a single optimal solution, there is rather a set of alternative solutions, generally denoted as the set of Pareto-optimal solutions. These solutions are optimal in the wider sense that no other solution in the search space is superior to them when all objectives are considered. In the absence of preference information, none of the corresponding trade-offs can be said to be better than the others. On the other hand, the search space can be too large and too complex, which, the usual case of real-world problems, to be solved by the conventional deterministic optimizers. Thus, efficient optimization strategies are required that are able to deal with the multiple objectives and the complexity of the search space. Evolutionary Algorithms (EAs) have several characteristics that are desirable for this kind of problems and most frequently outperform the deterministic optimizers. The application of EA in multiobjective optimization problems has received considerable attention in the last five years due to the difficulty of conventional optimization techniques, such as the gradient-based optimizers, to be extended to multi-objective optimization problems. For dealing with the multi-objective optimization problems there are some typical methods, such as linear weighting method, distance function method and constraint method. In treating such a problem using gradient based optimizers, we have to combine them with the typical methods. On the other hand, the structure of the EA optimizers have been recognized to be more appropriate to multiobjective optimization problems since early in their development [1]. EA optimizers employ multiple individuals that can search for multiple solutions in parallel. Using some modifications on the operators used by the EA optimizers the search process can be driven to a family of solutions representing the set of Pareto-optimal solutions.

Structural sizing optimization at its early stages of development was mainly single-objective. The aim was to minimize the weight of the structure under certain restrictions imposed by design codes. Although some work has been published in the past dealing with multi-objective optimization [2-7] this was restricted to simple academic examples. Optimization of large-scale structures, such as sizing optimization of multi-storey 3D frames and trusses is a computationally intensive task. The optimization problem becomes more intensive when dynamic loading is involved [8]. The feasible design space in structural optimization problems under dynamic constraints is often disconnected or disjoint [9, 10] which causes difficulties for many conventional optimizers. Due to the uncertain nature of the seismic loading, structural designs are often based on design response spectra of the region and on some simplified assumptions of the structural behavior under earthquakes. In the case of a direct consideration of the seismic loading the optimization of structural systems requires the solution of the dynamic equations of motion which can be orders of magnitude more computationally intensive than the case of static loading.

In this work, both the rigorous approach and the simplified one with respect to the loading condition are implemented and their efficiency is compared in the framework of finding the optimum design of a structure under multiple objectives. In the context of the rigorous approach a number of artificial accelerograms are produced from the design response spectrum of the region for elastic structural response, which constitutes the multiple loading conditions under which the structures are optimally designed. The elastic design response spectrum can be seen as an envelope of response spectra, for a specific damping ratio, of different earthquakes most likely to occur in the region. This approach is compared with the approximate one based on simplifications adopted by the seismic codes. The Pareto sets obtained for a characteristic problem indicate the difference of the two Pareto sets obtained by the rigorous approach and the simplified one.

## 12.2 Single-objective Structural Optimization

In sizing optimization problems the aim is to minimize a single-objective function, usually the weight of the structure, under certain behavioral constraints on stress and displacements. The design variables are most frequently chosen to be dimensions of the cross-sectional areas of the members of the structure. Due to fabrication limitations the design variables are not continuous but discrete since cross-sections belong to a certain set. A discrete structural optimization problem can be formulated in the following form:

$$
\begin{aligned}
&\min && f(s)\\
&\text{subject to } && g_j(s) \le 0 \ j = 1,\ldots,k\\
&&& s_i \in R^d, \quad i = 1,\ldots,n
\end{aligned}
\tag{12.1}
$$

where $R^d$ is a given set of discrete values and the design variables $s_i$ ($i = 1,\ldots,n$) can take values only from this set.

In the optimal design of 3D frames and trusses the constraints are the member stresses and nodal displacements or inter-storey drifts. For rigid frames with I-shapes, the stress constraints, under allowable stress design requirements specified by Eurocode 3 [11] are expressed by the non-dimensional ratio $q$ of the following formulas

$$
q = \frac{f_a}{\sigma_a} + \frac{f_b^y}{\sigma_b^y} + \frac{f_b^z}{\sigma_b^z} \le 1.0 \quad \text{if } \frac{f_a}{\sigma_a} \le 0.15
\tag{12.2}
$$

and

$$
q = \frac{f_a}{0.60 \times \sigma_y} + \frac{f_b^y}{\sigma_b^y} + \frac{f_b^z}{\sigma_b^z} \le 1.0 \quad \text{if } \frac{f_a}{\sigma_a} > 0.15
\tag{12.3}
$$

where $f_a$ is the computed compressive axial stress, $f_b^y, f_b^z$ are the computed bending stresses for $y$ and $z$ axis, respectively. $\sigma_a$ is the allowable compressive axial stress, $\sigma_b^y, \sigma_b^z$ are the allowable bending stresses for $y$ and $z$ axis, respectively, and $\sigma_y$ is the yield stress of the steel. The allowable inter-storey drift is limited to 1.5% of the height of each storey.

Space truss structures usually have the topology of single or multi-layered flat or curved grids that can be easily constructed in practice. Most frequently the constraints are the member stresses, nodal displacements, or frequencies. The stress constraints can be written as $|\sigma| \le |\sigma_a|$, where $\sigma$ is the maximum axial stress in each element group for all loading cases, $\sigma_a = 0.60 \times \sigma_y$ is the allowable axial stress and $\sigma_y$ is the yield stress. Similarly, the displacement constraints can be written as $|d| \le d_a$, where $d_a$ is the limiting value of the displacement at a certain node, or the maximum nodal displacement.

Euler buckling occurs in truss structures when the magnitude of a member's compressive stress is greater than a critical stress that, for the first buckling mode of a pin-connected member, is equal to

$$
\sigma_b = \frac{P_b}{A} = -\frac{1}{A}\left(\frac{\pi^2 EI}{L^2}\right)
\tag{12.4}
$$

where $P_b$ is the computed compressive axial force, $I$ is the moment of inertia, $L$ is the member length. Thus, the compressive stress should be less (in absolute values) than the critical Euler buckling stress $|\sigma| \le |\sigma_b|$. The values of the constraint functions are normalized in order to improve the performance of the optimization procedure as: $\sigma/\sigma_a \le 1$ for tension member $\sigma_a = 0.60 \times \sigma_y$, $\sigma/\sigma_b \le 1$ for compression member $\sigma_b = E\left(\pi/(l/r)\right)^2$ and $d/d_a \le 1$.

The sizing optimization methodology with EA proceeds using the following steps: (1) At the outset of the optimization the geometry, the boundaries and the loads of the structure under investigation have to be defined. (2) The design variables, which may or may not be independent to each other, are also properly selected. Furthermore, the constraints are also defined in this stage in order to formulate the optimization problem as in (12.1). (3) A finite element analysis is then carried out and the displacements and stresses are evaluated. (4) The design variables are being optimized using the selection, crossover and mutation operators. If the convergence criteria for the optimization algorithm are satisfied, then the optimum solution has been found and the process is terminated, else the optimizer updates the design variable values and the whole process is repeated from Step (3).

## 12.3 Multiobjective Structural Optimization

In practical applications of structural optimization of 3D frames and trusses the weight rarely gives a representative measure of the performance of the structure. In fact, several conflicting and incommensurable criteria usually exist in real-life design problems that have to be dealt simultaneously. This situation forces the engineer to look for a good compromise design between the conflicting requirements. These kinds of problems are called optimization problems with many objectives. The consideration of multiobjective optimization in its present sense originated towards the end of the last century when Pareto presented the optimality concept in economic problems with several competing criteria [12]. The first applications in the field of structural optimization with multiple objectives appeared at the end of the seventies [2-7]. Since then, although many techniques have been developed in order to deal with multiobjective optimization problems and a number of structural optimization problems have been dealt with multiobjectives, the corresponding applications were confined to mathematical functions or Pareto-structural optimization problems under only static loading conditions [13-21].

### 12.3.1 Criteria and Conflict

Any engineer who looks for the optimum design of a structure is faced with the question of which criteria are suitable for measuring the economy, the performance, the strength and the serviceability of a structure. Any quantity that, when changed, has a direct influence on the economy and/or the performance, the strength and the serviceability of the structure, can be considered as a criterion. On the other hand, those quantities that must only satisfy some imposed requirements are not criteria but they can be treated as constraints. Most of the commonly used design quantities have a criterion nature rather than a constraint nature because in the engineer's mind these should take the minimum or maximum possible values. Most of the structural optimization problems are treated with a single objective, usually the weight of the structure, subjected to some strength constraints. These constraints are set as equality or inequality constraints using some upper and lower limits. Some times there is a difficulty in selecting these limits and these parameters are treated as criteria.

One important basic property in the multi-criterion formulation is the conflict that may or may not exist between the criteria. Only those quantities that are competing should be treated as independent criteria whereas the others can be combined into a single criterion to represent the whole group. The concept of the conflict has deserved only a little attention in the literature while on the contrary the solution procedures have been studied to a great extent. According to the latter presentation the local conflict between two criteria can be defined as follows: The functions $f_i$ and $f_j$ are called locally collinear with no conflict at point $s$ if there is $c > 0$ such that $\nabla f_i(s) = c\nabla f_j(s)$. Otherwise, the functions are called locally conflicting at $s$.

According to the previous definition any two criteria are locally conflicting at a point of the design space if their maximum improvement is achieved in different directions. The global conflict between two criteria can be defined as follows: The functions $f_i$ and $f_j$ are called globally conflicting in the feasible region $\Im$ of the design space when the two optimization problems $\min_{s\in\Im} f_i(s)$ and $\min_{s\in\Im} f_j(s)$ have different optimal solutions.

## 12.3.2 Formulation of a Multiple Objective Optimization Problem

In formulating an optimization problem the choice of the design variables, criteria and constraints certainly represents the most important decision made by the engineer. The designs, which will be considered here, are fixed at this very early stage. In general the mathematical formulation of a multiobjective problem includes a set of $n$ design variables, a set of $m$ objective and a set of $k$ constraint functions and can be defined as follows:

$$
\begin{aligned}
\min_{s\in\Im} \quad & [f_1(s),\dots,f_m(s)]^T \\
\text{subject to } & g_j(s) \le 0 && j = 1,\dots,k \\
& s_i \in R^d, && i = 1,\dots,n
\end{aligned}
\tag{12.5}
$$

where the vector $s = [s_1,\dots,s_n]^T$ represents a design variable vector and $\Im$ is the feasible set in design space $R^n$. It is defined as the set of design variables that satisfy the constraint functions $g(s)$ in the form:

$$
\Im = \{s \in R^n | g_j(s) \le 0\}.
\tag{12.6}
$$

Usually there exists no unique point which would give an optimum for all $m$ criteria simultaneously. Thus the common optimality concept used in scalar optimization must be replaced by a new one, the so-called Pareto optimum: A design vector $s^* \in \Im$ is Pareto optimal for the problem of Equation 12.5 if and only if there exists no other design vector $s \in \Im$ such that $f_i(s) \leq f_i(s^*)$ for $i = 1, \ldots, m$ with $f_j(s) < f_j(s^*)$ for at least one objective $j$.

According to the above definition the design vector $s^*$ is considered as a Pareto-optimal solution if there is no other feasible design vector that improves at least one objective without worsening any other objective. The solution of optimization problems with multiple objectives is the set of the Pareto-optimal solutions. The problem of Equation 12.5 can be regarded, as being solved after the set of Pareto-optimal solutions has been determined. In practical applications, however, it is necessary to classify this set because the engineer wants a unique final solution. Thus a compromise should be made among the Pareto-optimal solutions.

### 12.3.3 Solving the Multiobjective Optimization Problem

Typical methods for generating the Pareto-optimal set combine the objectives into a single, parameterized objective function by analogy to the decision making search step. However, the parameters of this function are not set by the decision making but systematically varied by the optimizer. Basically, this procedure is independent of the underlying optimization algorithm. Three previously used methods [ 4-7] are briefly discussed and are compared in this study in terms of computational time and efficiency with the proposed modified ES for treating multiobjective optimization problems.

### Linear Weighting Method

The first method, called the linear weighting method, combines all the objectives into a single scalar parameterized objective function by using weighting coefficients. If $w_i, i = 1, \ldots, m$ are the weighting coefficients, the problem of Equation 12.5 can be written as follows:

$$\min_{s \in \Im} \sum_{i=1}^{m} w_i f_i(s) \qquad (12.7)$$

with no loss of generality the following normalization of the weighting coefficients is employed:

$$\sum_{i=1}^{m} w_i = 1 . \qquad (12.8)$$

By varying these weights it is now possible to generate the set of Pareto-optimal solutions for Equation 12.5. The weighting coefficients correspond to the preference of the engineer for each criteria. Every combination of those weighting coefficients correspond to a single Pareto-optimal solution, thus, performing a set of optimization processes using different weighting coefficients it is possible to generate the full set of Pareto-optimal solutions.

In real-world problems there is not a common unit for the objectives leading to differences of some orders of magnitude between the values of the objectives. It is therefore suggested that the objectives should be normalized according to the following expression:

$$\tilde{f}_i(s) = \frac{f_i(s) - f_{i,\min}}{f_{i,\max} - f_{i,\min}} \tag{12.9}$$

where the normalized objectives $\tilde{f}_i(s) \in [0, 1], i = 1, \ldots, m$, use the same design space with the non-normalized ones, while $f_{i,\min}$ and $f_{i,\max}$ are the minimum and maximum values of the objective function $i$.

## Distance Function Method

The distance methods are based on the minimization of the distance between the set of the objective function values and some chosen reference points belonging to the criterion space. Whereas criterion space is defined as the set of the objective function values that correspond to design vectors of the feasible domain. The resulting scalar problem is:

$$\min_{s \in \Im} d_p(s) \tag{12.10}$$

where the distance function can be written as follows:

$$d_p(s) = \left\{ \sum_{i=1}^{m} w_i \left[ f_i(s) - z_i \right]^p \right\}^{1/p} \tag{12.11}$$

where $p$ is an integer number.

This technique has been widely used in structural optimization. The reference point $z^{id} \in R^m$ that is selected by the engineer is also called ideal or utopian point. A reference point that is frequently used is the following:

$$z^{id} = \left[ f_{i,\min}, \ldots, f_{m,\min} \right]^T \tag{12.12}$$

where $f_{i,\min}$ is the optimum solution of the single-objective optimization problem where the $i$th objective function is treated as the unique objective. The normalization function Equation 12.8 for the weighting factors $w_i$ is also used. In the case that $p = \infty$ Equation 12.10 is transformed to the minimax problem:

$$\min_{s \in \Im} \max_i \left[ w_i f_i(s) \right], i = 1, \ldots, m . \tag{12.13}$$

In the case of $p = 1$ the formulation of the distance method is equivalent to the linear method when the reference point used is the zero $\hat{z} = 0$, while the case of $p = 2$ the method is called the weighted quadratic method.

**Constraint Method**

According to this method the original multi-criterion problem is replaced by a scalar problem where one criterion $f_k$ is chosen as the objective function and all the other criteria are removed into the constraints. By introducing parameters $\varepsilon_i$ into these new constraints an additional feasible set is obtained:

$$\Im_k(\varepsilon_i) = \{s \in R^n | f_i(s) \leq \varepsilon_i, i = 1, \ldots, m \text{ with } i \neq k\} . \qquad (12.14)$$

If the resulting feasible set is denoted by $\bar{\Im}_k = \Im \cap \Im_k$ the parameterized scalar problem can be expressed as:

$$\min_{s \in \bar{\Im}_k} f_k(s) . \qquad (12.15)$$

The constraint method gives the opportunity to obtain the full domain of optimum solutions, in the horizontal or vertical direction using one criterion as the objective function and the other as the constraint.

**Modified Evolution Strategies for Multiobjective Optimization**

The three above-mentioned methods are the typical ones. The typical methods have been used in the past combined with mathematical programming optimization algorithms where one design point was examined at each optimization step as an optimum design candidate. In order to locate the set of pareto-optimal solutions a family of optimization runs have to be executed. On the other hand evolutionary algorithms instead of a single design point, they work simultaneously with a population of design points, which is a population of optimum design candidates, in the space of design variables. This characteristic has been proved very useful since it is easy to implement these methods in a parallel computing environment. Due to this characteristic, evolutionary algorithms have a great potential in finding multiple optima, in a single optimization run, which is very useful in Pareto optimization problems. Since the early 1990s many researchers have suggested the use of evolutionary algorithms in multiobjective optimization problems [22-26] an overview of all these methods can be found in Fonseca and Fleming [1] and Zitzler [27].

In our study the method of Evolution Strategies (ES) is used, and some changes have to been made in the random operators that are usually used in order to implement ES in multiobjective optimization problems and guide the convergence to a population that represent the set of Pareto-optimal solutions. The idea in those changes is (1) the selection of the parent population at each generation has to be changed in order to guide the search procedure towards the set of pareto optimum solutions, and (2) to prevent convergence to a single design point, and preserve diversity in the population in every generation step. The first demand can be fulfilled if the selection of the individual is chosen for reproduction potentially a different objective [22]. A random selection of the objective is implemented in this study. While in order to preserve diversity in the population and fulfill the second requirement, fitness sharing is implemented [28]. The idea behind sharing is to degrade those individuals that are represented in the higher percentage of the population. The modified objectives after sharing are the following:

$$f_i'(s) = \frac{f_i(s)}{\sum_h sh\big(d(s, h)\big)} \tag{12.16}$$

where the sharing function used in the current study is as follows:

$$sh\big(d(s, h)\big) = \begin{cases} 1 - \left(\frac{d(s,h)}{\sigma_{share}}\right)^a & if \ d(s, h) < \sigma_{share} \\ 0 & \text{otherwise} \end{cases} \tag{12.17}$$

The distance function used is in the objective space:

$$d(s, h) = \|f(s) - f(h)\| . \tag{12.18}$$

## 12.4 Structural Design under Seismic Loading

The equations of equilibrium for a finite element system in motion for the $i$th design vector, can be written in the usual form:

$$M(s_i)\ddot{u}_t + C(s_i)\dot{u}_t + K(s_i)u_t = R_t \tag{12.19}$$

where $M(s_i)$, $C(s_i)$ and $K(s_i)$ are the mass, damping and stiffness matrices for the $i$th design vector $s_i$; $R_t$ is the external load vector, while $u_t$, $\dot{u}_t$ and $\ddot{u}_t$ are the displacement, velocity, and acceleration vectors of the finite element assemblage, respectively. The solution methods of direct integration of equations of motion and of response spectrum modal analysis, which is based on the mode superposition approach, will be considered in the following paragraphs.

The Newmark integration scheme is adopted in the present study to perform the direct time integration of the equations of motion where the equilibrium Equation 12.19 is considered at time $t + \Delta t$

$$M(s_i)\ddot{u}_{t+\Delta t} + C(s_i)\dot{u}_{t+\Delta t} + K(s_i)u_{t+\Delta t} = R_{t+\Delta t} \tag{12.20}$$

and the variation of velocity and displacement are given by

$$\dot{u}_{t+\Delta t} = \dot{u}_t + [(1 - \delta)\ddot{u}_t + \delta\ddot{u}_{t+\Delta t}]\Delta t \tag{12.21}$$

$$u_{t+\Delta t} = u_t + \dot{u}_t\Delta t + [(\frac{1}{2} - \alpha)\ddot{u}_t + \alpha\ddot{u}_{t+\Delta t}]\Delta t^2 \tag{12.22}$$

where $\alpha$ and $\delta$ are parameters that can be determined to obtain integration accuracy and stability. Solving for $\ddot{u}_{t+\Delta t}$ in terms of $u_{t+\Delta t}$ from Equation

12.22 and then substituting for $\ddot{u}_{t+\Delta t}$ in (12.21) we obtain equations for $\ddot{u}_{t+\Delta t}$ and $\dot{u}_{t+\Delta t}$ each in terms of the unknown displacements $u_{t+\Delta t}$ only. These two relations for $\ddot{u}_{t+\Delta t}$ and $\dot{u}_{t+\Delta t}$ are substituted into Equation 12.20 to solve for $u_{t+\Delta t}$. As a result of this substitution the following well-known equilibrium equation is obtained at each $\Delta t$

$$K_{\text{eff}}(s_i)u_{t+\Delta t} = R_{t+\Delta t}^{\text{eff}} \, . \tag{12.23}$$

### 12.4.1 Creation of Artificial Accelerograms

The selection of the proper external loading $R_t$ for design purposes is not an easy task due to the uncertainties involved in the seismic loading. For this reason a rigorous treatment of the seismic loading is to assume that the structure is subjected to a set of artificial earthquakes that are more likely to occur in the region where the structure is located. These seismic excitations are produced as a series of artificial accelerograms compatible with the elastic design response spectrum of the region.

In this work the implementation published by Taylor [29] for the generation of statistically independent artificial acceleration time histories is adopted. This method is based on the fact that any periodic function can be expanded into a series of sinusoidal waves:

$$x(t) = \sum_k A_k \sin(\omega_k t + \varphi_k) \tag{12.24}$$

where $A_k$ is the amplitude, $\omega_k$ is the cyclic frequency and $\phi_k$ is the phase angle of the $k$th contributing sinusoid. By fixing an array of amplitudes and then generating different arrays of phase angles, different motions can be generated which are similar in general appearance but different in the 'details'. The computer uses a random number generator subroutine to produce strings of phase angles with a uniform distribution in the range between 0 and $2\pi$. The amplitudes $A_k$ are related to the spectral density function in the following way:

$$G(\omega_k)\Delta\omega = \frac{A_k^2}{2} \tag{12.25}$$

where $G(\omega_k)\Delta\omega$ may be interpreted as the contribution to the total power of the motion from the sinusoid with frequency $\omega_k$. The power of the motion produced by Equation 12.24 does not vary with time. To simulate the transient character of real earthquakes, the steady-state motion is multiplied by a deterministic envelope function $I(t)$:

$$Z(t) = I(t) \sum_k A_k sin(\omega_k t + \varphi_k) \, . \tag{12.26}$$

The resulting motion is stationary in frequency content with peak acceleration close to the target peak acceleration. In this study a trapezoidal intensity envelope function is adopted. The generated peak acceleration is artificially modified to match the target peak acceleration, which corresponds to the chosen elastic design response spectrum. An iterative procedure is implemented to smooth the calculated spectrum and improve the matching [29].

Five artificial uncorrelated accelerograms, produced by the previously discussed procedure and shown in Figure 12.1, have been used as the input seismic excitation for the numerical tests. The elastic design response spectrum considered in the current study is depicted in Figure 12.2 for damping ratio $\xi = 2.5\%$. The corresponding response spectrum of the first artificial accelerogram is also depicted in Figure 12.2.

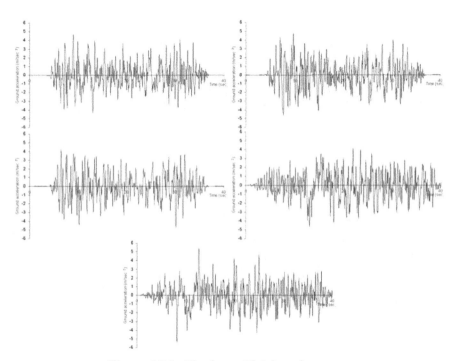

**Figure 12.1.** The five artificial accelerograms

## 12.4.2 Response Spectrum Modal Analysis

The response spectrum modal analysis is based on a simplification of the mode superposition approach with the aim to avoid time history analyses which are required by both the direct integration and mode superposition approaches. In the case of the response spectrum modal analysis, Equation 12.19 is modified according to the modal superposition approach, for the $i$th design vector, in the following form:

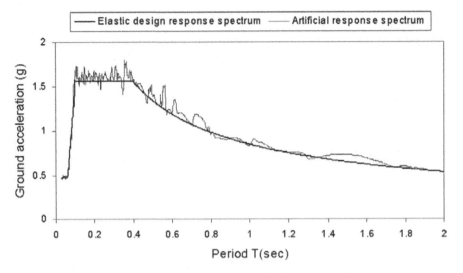

**Figure 12.2.** Elastic design response spectrum of the region and response spectrum of the first artificial accelerogram ($\xi = 2.5\%$).

$$\bar{M}(s_i)\ddot{u}_t + \bar{C}(s_i)\dot{u}_t + \bar{K}(s_i)u_t = \bar{R}_t \tag{12.27}$$

where

$$\bar{M}(s_i) = \Phi_i^T M_i \Phi_i \tag{12.28}$$

$$\bar{C}(s_i) = \Phi_i^T C_i \Phi_i \tag{12.29}$$

$$\bar{K}(s_i) = \Phi_i^T K_i \Phi_i \tag{12.30}$$

$$\bar{R}_t = \Phi_i^T R_t \tag{12.31}$$

are the generalized values of the corresponding matrices and the loading vector, while $\Phi_i$ is an eigenmode shape matrix to be defined later. For simplicity $M(s_i)$, $C(s_i)$, $K(s_i)$ are denoted by $M_i$, $C_i$, $K_i$, respectively. These matrices correspond to the design, which is defined by the $i$th vector of the design parameters, also called the design vector. According to the modal superposition approach the system of $N$ simultaneous differential equations, is transformed to a set of $N$ independent normal-coordinate equations.

In the response spectrum modal analysis a number of different formulas have been proposed to obtain reasonable estimates of the maximum response based on the spectral values without performing time history analyses for a considerable number of transformed dynamic equations. The simplest and most popular of these is the square root of the sum of the squares (SRSS) of the modal responses. According to this estimate the maximum total displacement is approximated by

$$u_{\max} = \sqrt{u_{1,\max}^2 + \cdots + u_{N,\max}^2} \tag{12.32}$$

where $u_{j,\max}$ corresponds to the maximum displacement calculated from the $j$th transformed dynamic equations over the complete time period. The use of Equation 12.32 permits this type of "dynamic" analysis by knowing only the maximum modal coordinates $u_{j,\max}$.

The following steps summarize the response spectrum modal analysis adopted in this study and by a number of seismic codes around the world:

1. Calculate a number $m' < N$ of eigenfrequencies and the corresponding eigenmode shape matrices, which are classified in the following order $(\omega_i^1, \ldots, \omega_i^{m'})$, $\Phi_i = [\phi_i^1, \ldots, \phi_i^{m'}]$, respectively, where $\omega_i^j$, $\phi_i^j$ are the $j$th eigenfrequency-eigenmode corresponding to the $i$th design vector. $m'$ is a user specified number, based on experience or on previous test analyses, which has to satisfy the requirement of Step 6.
2. Calculate the generalized masses, according to the following equation:

$$\bar{m}_i^j = {\phi_i^j}^T M_i \phi_i^j \ . \tag{12.33}$$

3. Calculate the coefficients $L_i^j$, according to the following equation:

$$L_i^j = {\phi_i^j}^T M_i r \tag{12.34}$$

   where $r$ is the influence vector, which represents the displacements of the masses resulting from static application of a unit, ground displacement.
4. Calculate the modal participation factor $\Gamma_i^j$, according to the following equation:

$$\Gamma_i^j = \frac{L_i^j}{\bar{m}_i^j} \ . \tag{12.35}$$

5. Calculate the effective modal mass for each design vector and for each eigenmode, by the following equation:

$$m_{\text{eff},i}^j = \frac{L_i^{j^2}}{\bar{m}_i^j} \ . \tag{12.36}$$

6. Calculate a number $m < m'$ of the important eigenmodes. According to Eurocode the minimum number of the eigenmodes that has to be taken into consideration is defined by the following assumption: The sum of the effective eigenmasses must not be less than 90% of the total vibrating mass $m_{tot}$ of the system, so the first $m$ eigenmodes that satisfy the equation

$$\sum_{j=1}^{m} m_{\text{eff},i}^j \geq 0.90 m_{\text{tot}} \tag{12.37}$$

   are taken into consideration.
7. Calculate the values of the spectral acceleration $R_d(T_j)$ that correspond to each eigenperiod $T_j$ of the important modes.

8. Calculate the modal displacements according to equation

$$(SD)_j = \frac{R_d(T_j)}{\omega_j^2} = \frac{R_d(T_j) \times T_j^2}{4\pi^2} \,. \tag{12.38}$$

9. Calculate the modal displacements:

$$u_{j,\max} = \Gamma_i^j \times \phi_i^j \times (SD)_j \,. \tag{12.39}$$

10. The total maximum displacement is calculated by superimposing the maximum modal displacements according to Equation 12.32.

## 12.5 Solution of the Optimization Problem

The optimization problem is solved with evolution strategies. Evolution strategies were proposed for parameter optimization problems in the 1970s by Rechenberg [30] and Schwefel [31]. Similar to genetic algorithms, ES imitate biological evolution in nature and have three characteristics that make them different from other conventional optimization algorithms: (1) in place of the usual deterministic operators, they use randomized operators: mutation, selection as well as recombination; (2) instead of a single design point, they work simultaneously with a population of design points in the space of variables; (3) they can handle continuous, discrete, and mixed optimization problems. The second characteristic allows for a natural implementation of ES on parallel computing environments. The ES were initially applied for continuous optimization problems, but recently they have also been implemented in discrete and mixed optimization problems.

### 12.5.1 ES for Discrete Optimization Problems

The multi-membered ES adopted in the current study, based on the discrete formulation, use three operators: recombination, mutation, and selection operators that can be included in the algorithm as follows:

**Step 1 (recombination and mutation)**

The population of $\mu$ parents at $g$th generation produces $\lambda$ offsprings. The genotype of any descendant differs only slightly from that of its parents. For every offspring vector a temporary parent vector $\tilde{s} = [\tilde{s}_1, \ldots, \tilde{s}_n]^T$ is first built by means of recombination. For discrete problems the following recombination cases can be used:

$$\tilde{s}_i = \begin{cases} s_{\alpha,i} \ or \ s_{b,i} \ \text{randomly} \\ s_{m,i} \ or \ s_{b,i} \ \text{randomly} \\ s_{bj,i} \\ s_{\alpha,i} \ or \ s_{bj,i} \ \text{randomly} \\ s_{m,i} \ or \ s_{bj,i} \ \text{randomly} \end{cases} \tag{12.40}$$

where $\tilde{s}_i$ is the $i$th component of the temporary parent vector $\tilde{s}$, $s_{a,i}$ and $s_{b,i}$ are the $i$th components of the vectors $s_a$ and $s_b$ which are two parent vectors randomly chosen from the population. The vector $s_m$ is not randomly chosen but is the best of the $\mu$ parent vectors in the current generation. In case C of (12.40), $\tilde{s}_i = s_{bj,i}$ means that the $i$th component of $\tilde{s}$ is chosen randomly from the $i$th components of all $\mu$ parent vectors. From the temporary parent $\tilde{s}$ an offspring can be created following the mutation operator.

Let as consider the temporary parent $s_p^{(g)}$ of the generation $g$ that produces an offspring $s_o^{(g)}$ through the mutation operator as follows:

$$s_o^{(g)} = s_p^{(g)} + z^{(g)} \tag{12.41}$$

where $z^{(g)} = [z_1^{(g)}, \ldots, z_n^{(g)}]^T$ is a random vector. The mutation operator in the continuous version of ES produces a normally distributed random change vector $z^{(g)}$. Each component of this vector has a small standard deviation value $\sigma_i$ and zero mean value. As a result of this there is a possibility that all components of a parent vector may be changed, but usually the changes are small. In the discrete version of ES the random vector $z^{(g)}$ is properly generated in order to force the offspring vector to move to another set of discrete values. The fact that the difference between any two adjacent values can be relatively large is against the requirement that the variance $\sigma_i^2$ should be small. For this reason it is suggested that not all the components of a parent vector, but only a few of them (e.g. $k$), should be randomly changed in every generation. This means that $n-k$ components of the randomly changed vector $z^{(g)}$ will have a zero value. In other words, the terms of vector $z^{(g)}$ are derived from

$$z_i^{(g)} = \begin{cases} (\kappa+1)\delta s_i & \text{for } k \text{ randomly chosen components} \\ 0 & \text{for } n-k \text{ other components} \end{cases} \tag{12.42}$$

where $\delta s_i$ is the difference between two adjacent values in the discrete set and $\kappa$ is a random integer number, which follows the Poisson distribution

$$p(\kappa) = \frac{(\gamma)^\kappa}{\gamma!} e^{-\gamma} \tag{12.43}$$

where $\gamma$ is the standard deviation as well as the mean value of the random number $\kappa$. This shows how the random change $z_i^{(g)}$ is controlled by the parameter $\gamma$. The choice of $k$ depends on the size of the problem and it is usually taken as $1/5$ of the total number of design variables. The $k$ components are selected using uniform random distribution in every generation according to Equation 12.42.

## Step 2 (selection)

There are two different types of the multi-membered ES:

- $(\mu + \lambda)$-ES: The best $\mu$ individuals are selected from a temporary population of $(\mu+\lambda)$ individuals to form the parents of the next generation.
- $(\mu, \lambda)$-ES: The $\mu$ individuals produce $\lambda$ offsprings $(\mu \leq \lambda)$ and the selection process defines a new population of $\mu$ individuals from the set of $\lambda$ offsprings only.

In order to implement ES in Pareto optimization problems the selection operator is based on randomly chosen objectives. For discrete optimization the procedure terminates when the following termination criteria is satisfied: when the ratio $\mu_b/\mu$ has reached a given value $\varepsilon_d$ (=0.5 to 0.8) where $\mu_b$ is the number of the parent vectors in the current generation with the best objective function value.

### 12.5.2 ES in Multiobjective Structural Optimization Problems

The application of EAs in multiobjective optimization problems has received a lot of attention in the last five years [21-28]due to the difficulty of conventional optimization techniques, such as gradient based methods, to be extended to multiobjective optimization problems. EAs, however, have been recognized to be more appropriate to multiobjective optimization problems since early in their development [1]. Multiple individuals can search for multiple solutions in parallel, taking advantage of any similarities available in the family of possible solutions to the problem.

In the first implementation where the typical methods are used, the optimization procedure, in order to generate a set of Pareto-optimal solutions, initiates with a set of parent design vectors needed by the ES optimizer and a set of weighting coefficients for the combination of all objectives into a single scalar parameterized objective function. These weighting coefficients are not set by the engineer but are being systematically varied by the optimizer after a Pareto-optimal solution has been achieved. There is an outer loop which systematically varies the parameters of the parameterized objective function, and is called the decision making loop. The inner loop is the classical ES process, starting with a set of parent vectors. If any of these parent vectors gives an infeasible design then this parent vector is modified until it becomes feasible. Subsequently, the offsprings are generated and checked if they are in the feasible region. The number of parents and offsprings involved affects the computational efficiency of the multi-membered ES discussed in this work. It has been observed that values of $\mu$ and $\lambda$ equal to the number of the design variables produce better results.

The ES algorithm when combined with the typical methods for multiobjective structural optimization applications under seismic loading can be stated as follows:

*Outer loop - Decision making loop*
Set the parameters $w_i$ of the parameterized objective function
*Inner loop - ES loop*

1. Selection step: selection of $s_i$, $(i = 1, 2 \ldots, \mu)$ parent vectors of the design variables
2. Analysis step: solve $M(s_i)\ddot{u} + C(s_i)\dot{u} + K(s_i)u = R_t$, $(i = 1, \ldots, \mu)$
3. Evaluation of parameterized objective function
4. Constraints check: all parent vectors become feasible
5. Offspring generation: generate $s_j$, $(j = 1, \ldots, \lambda)$ offspring vectors of the design variables
6. Analysis step: solve $M(s_j)\ddot{u} + C(s_j)\dot{u} + K(s_j)u = R_t$, $(j = 1, \ldots, \lambda)$
7. Evaluation of the parameterized objective function
8. Constraints check: if satisfied continue, else change $s_j$ and go to step 5
9. Selection step: selection of the next generation parents according to $(\mu + \lambda)$ or $(\mu, \lambda)$ selection schemes
10. Convergence check: If satisfied stop, else go to step 5

*End of Inner loop*
*End of Outer loop*

In the second implementation the special characteristic of the EA optimizers are used. The ESMO algorithm for multiobjective structural optimization applications under seismic loading can be stated as follows:

1. Selection step: selection of $s_i$, $(i = 1, 2 \ldots, \mu)$ parent vectors of the design variables
2. Analysis step: solve $M(s_i)\ddot{u} + C(s_i)\dot{u} + K(s_i)u = R_t$, $(i = 1, \ldots, \mu)$
3. Evaluation of parameterized objective function
4. Constraints check: all parent vectors become feasible
5. Offspring generation: generate $s_j$, $(j = 1, \ldots, \lambda)$ offspring vectors of the design variables
6. Analysis step: solve $M(s_j)\ddot{u} + C(s_j)\dot{u} + K(s_j)u = R_t$, $(j = 1, \ldots, \lambda)$
7. Evaluation of the parameterized objective function
8. Constraints check: if satisfied continue, else change $s_j$ and go to step 5
9. Selection step: random selection of the potential objective for each individual and selection of the next generation parents according to $(\mu + \lambda)$ or $(\mu, \lambda)$ selection scheme
10. Fitness sharing
11. Convergence check: If satisfied stop, else go to step 5

## 12.6 Numerical Results

Three benchmark test examples, one six-storey space frame and one multi-layered space truss, are investigated. The following abbreviations are used in this section: *DTI* refers to the Newmark Direct time Integration Method; *RSMA* refers to the Response Spectrum Modal Analysis; *LWM* refers to the Linear Weighting Method; *DFM* refers to the Distance Function Method; CM refers to the Constraint Method and *ESMO* refers to the proposed Evolution Strategies for treating Multiobjective Optimization problems.

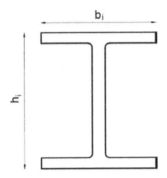

**Figure 12.3.** I-shape cross section.

### 12.6.1 Six-storey Space Frame

The modulus of elasticity is 200 GPa and the yield stress is $\sigma_y = 250$ MPa. The cross section of each member is assumed to be an I-shape and for each member two design variables are considered, as shown in Figure 12.3. The objective functions considered for the problems are the weight of the structure, the maximum displacement and the first eigen period. The first two objective functions have to be minimized while the third one has to be maximized. The constraints are imposed on the inter-storey drifts and on the maximum non-dimensional ratio $q$ of Equations 12.2 and 12.3 for each element group under a combination of axial force and bending moments. The values of allowable axial and bending stresses are $F_a = 150$ MPa and $F_b = 165$ MPa, respectively, whereas the maximum allowable inter-storey drift is limited to 4.5 cm which corresponds to 1.5% of the height of each storey. The test example was run on a Silicon Graphics Power Challenge computer.

The space frame consists of 63 elements with 180 degrees of freedom as shown in Figure 12.4. The beams have length $L_1 = 7.32$m and the columns $L_2 = 3.66$m. The structure is loaded with a 19.16 kPa gravity load on all floor levels and a static lateral load of 109 kN applied at each node in the front elevation along the $z$ direction. The element members are divided into 5 groups, each one having two design variables resulting in ten total design variables.

The Pareto-optimal set of solutions was first computed with the LWM. The performance of this method for the case of seeking the simultaneous minimization of weight and maximum displacement is depicted in Figures 12.5 and 12.6 for both static and seismic loading conditions. In Figures 12.5 and 12.6 the performance of the DFM and ESMO methods are also presented.

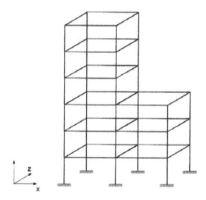

**Figure 12.4.** Six-storey space frame.

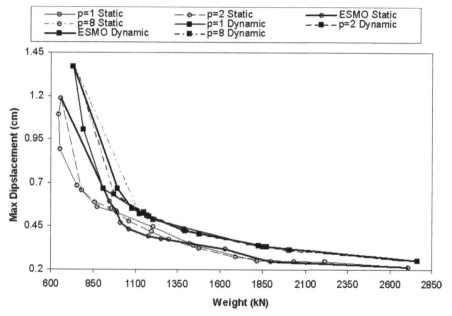

**Figure 12.5.** Six-storey frame: Linear (p = 1), Distance method and ESMO (both static and seismic loading conditions) using LVM.

For the case of the DFM the zero (0) point was considered as the utopian point, while three different schemes of the DFM were also examined, p = 1: equivalent to the LWM, p = 2: called quadratic LWM and $p = 8$: equivalent to the $p = \infty$. The case when the weight and the first eigenperiod are considered as the objectives of the problem is depicted in Figure 12.9.

The CM is implemented with the following variations: (1) The weight as the only criterion and the maximum displacement or the first eigenperiod as constraint; and (2) the maximum displacement or the first eigenperiod

292    Lagaros et al.

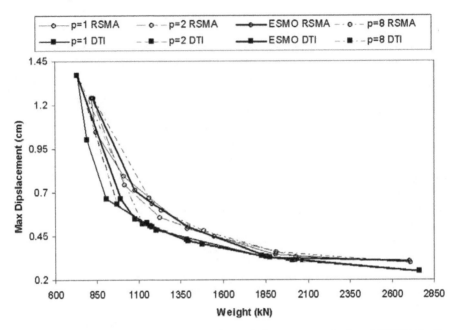

**Figure 12.6.** Six-storey frame: Linear (p = 1), Distance method and ESMO (both static and seismic loading conditions)using LVM.

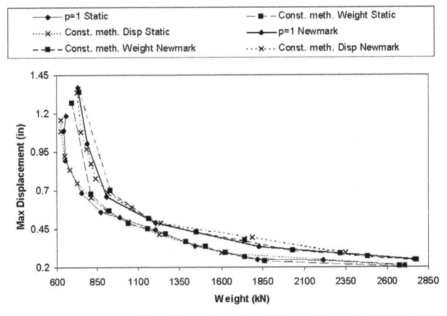

**Figure 12.7.** Six-storey frame: Linear (p = 1) and Constraint method (both static and seismic loading conditions) using CM.

as the only criterion and the weight as constraint. In Figures 12.7 and 12.8 we can see the performance of the CM, for the simultaneous minimization of weight and maximum displacement. These sets of Pareto optimal solutions are produced for the following cases: (1) different upper limits for the maximum displacement, and (2) different upper limits of the weight of the structure. In Figure 12.10 we can see the performance of the CM, for the simultaneous minimization of weight and the first eigenperiod and for the cases: (1) with different upper limits for the first eigenperiod, and (2) for different upper limits of the weight of the structure.

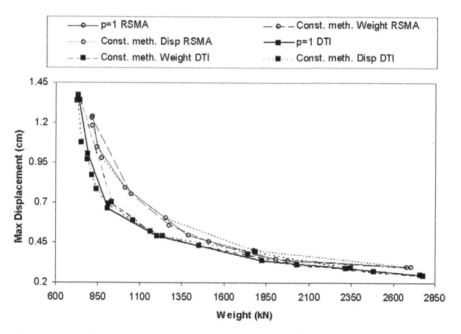

**Figure 12.8.** Six-storey frame: Linear (p = 1) and Constraint method (both static and seismic loading conditions)using CM.

It can also be seen from Figures 12.6 and 12.8 that the Pareto optimal solutions achieved by the direct time integration approach under the multiple loading conditions of the five artificial accelerograms given in Figures 12.6 and 12.8 is less than the corresponding design given by the response spectrum modal analysis. In figures 12.5, 12.6 and in 12.9, 12.10 we can see that there is little difference in the performance of the typical methods and the ESMO method, while as can be seen from Table 12.1 there is a difference in the computing time.

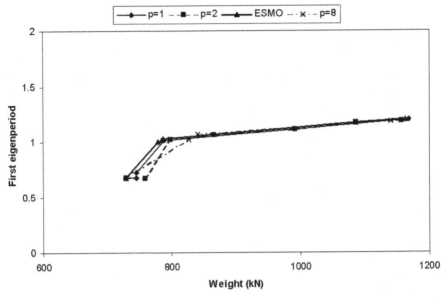

**Figure 12.9.** Six-storey frame: Linear (p = 1), Distance method and ESMO method.

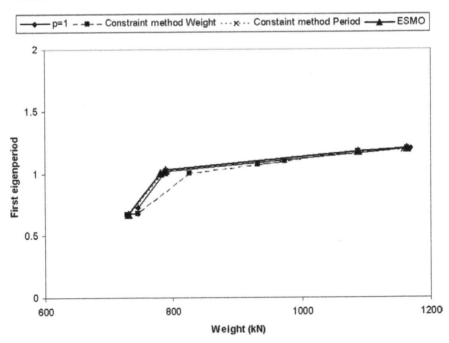

**Figure 12.10.** Six-storey frame: Linear (p = 1), Constraint method and ESMO method

**Table 12.1.** Example 1 - Time required by classical and EA methods for dealing with multiobjectives for dynamic loading conditions.

| Method | Time (sec) | Generations | FE analyses |
|---|---|---|---|
| p = 1 DTI | 254,112 | 372 | 2,609 |
| ESMO DTI | 35,788 | 28 | 367 |
| p = 1 RSMA | 109,803 | 411 | 2,901 |
| ESMO RSMA | 15,171 | 31 | 401 |

### 12.6.2 Multi-layered Space Truss

The optimum design with multiple objectives of a long span aircraft hangar is investigated. The objective functions considered for the problems are the weight of the structure and the maximum deflection, both of which are to be minimized. The members of the space truss were grouped as follows: Group 1: Longitudinal members of the top and bottom flanges. Group 2: Cross girders of the top and bottom flanges. Group 3: Bracing diagonals connecting top and bottom flanges to top and bottom chords of the space frame. Group 4: Top and bottom chords of the space frame. Group 5: Diagonal bracing members connecting top and bottom chords of space frame to middle chords. Group 6: Middle chords of the space frame. The hangar comprises 3,614 nodes (10,638 d.o.f.) and 12,974 members. Members of group 1 to 3 are to be selected from the structural sections listed in Table 12.2 and members of groups 4 to 6 from the tube sizes given in Table 12.3. Taking advantage of the symmetry of the structure, the formulation of the problem was made only for one half of the hangar which results in a model with 5,269 d.o.f. (see Figure 12.11). A constraint of 750 mm on the maximum deflection was imposed in addition to the stress constraints.

The performance of the LWM for the case of the simultaneous minimization of weight and maximum displacement is depicted in Figure 12.12. In Figure 12.12 the DFM with $p = 1$, 2 and 8 and ESMO methods are also presented. For this test example two cases are considered: (1) The weight as the only criterion and the maximum displacement as constraint; and (2) The maximum displacement as the only criterion and the weight as constraint. Figure 12.13 depicts the performance of the CM, for the simultaneous minimization of weight and maximum displacement. These sets of Pareto-optimal solutions, are produced for different upper limits for the maximum displacement and for different upper limits of the weight of the structure. In Figures 12.12 and 12.13 we can see that there is little difference in the performance of the typical methods and the ESMO method, while as can be seen from Table 12.4 there is significant difference in the computing time.

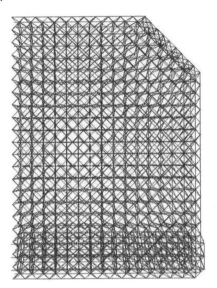

**Figure 12.11.** Multi-layered space truss.

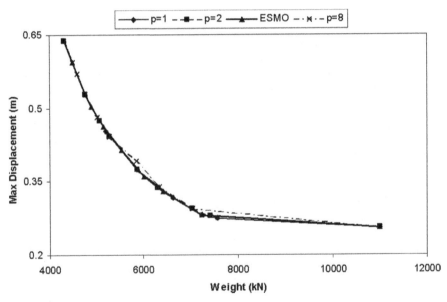

**Figure 12.12.** Multi-layered space truss: Linear, Distance and ESMO method.

**Table 12.2.** Properties of the structural members (Database 1).

| Section number | Type | Area $(mm^2)$ |
|:---:|:---:|:---:|
| 1 | ISMC 100 | 1170 |
| 2 | 2 x ISMC 75 | 1740 |
| 3 | 2 x ISMC 100 | 2340 |
| 4 | 2 x ISMC 125 | 3238 |
| 5 | 2 x ISMC 150 | 4176 |
| 6 | 2 x ISMC 175 | 4878 |
| 7 | 2 x ISMC 200 | 5642 |
| 8 | 2 x ISMC 225 | 6802 |
| 9 | 2 x ISMC 250 | 7734 |
| 10 | 2 x ISMC 300 | 9128 |
| 11 | 2 x ISMC 350 | 10732 |
| 12 | 2 x ISMC 400 | 12585 |
| 13 | 2 x ISMC 400 with 2 x 8mm thick MS Plates | 14986 |
| 14 | 2 x ISMC 400 with 2 x 12mm thick MS Plates | 16186 |
| 15 | 2 x ISMC 400 with 2 x 16mm thick MS Plates | 17386 |
| 16 | 2 x ISMC 400 with 2 x 25mm thick MS Plates | 20086 |
| 17 | 4 x ISMC 400 | 25172 |
| 18 | 4 x ISMC 400 with 2 x 8mm thick MS Plates | 30772 |
| 19 | 4 x ISMC 400 with 2 x 16mm thick MS Plates | 36372 |
| 20 | 4 x ISMC 400 with 2 x 20mm thick MS Plates | 39172 |
| 21 | 4 x ISMC 400 with 2 x 25mm thick MS Plates | 42672 |
| 22 | 4 x ISMC 400 with 2 x 32mm thick MS Plates | 47572 |
| 23 | 4 x ISMC 400 with 4 x 20mm thick MS Plates | 51172 |
| 24 | 4 x ISMC 400 with 4 x 25mm thick MS Plates | 57672 |
| 25 | 4 x ISMC 400 with 4 x 32mm thick MS Plates | 66772 |
| 26 | 4 x ISMC 400 with 4 x 40mm thick MS Plates | 77172 |
| 27 | 4 x ISMC 400 with 4 x 50mm thick MS Plates | 90172 |

**Table 12.3.** Properties of the structural members (Database 2).

| Section number | Outer diameter | Thickness | Area $(mm^2)$ |
|:---:|:---:|:---:|:---:|
| 1 | 60.30 | 3.25 | 582.73 |
| 2 | 76.10 | 4.50 | 1012.63 |
| 3 | 88.90 | 4.85 | 1281.16 |
| 4 | 114.30 | 5.40 | 1848.19 |
| 5 | 139.70 | 5.40 | 2279.26 |
| 6 | 152.40 | 5.40 | 2494.80 |
| 7 | 165.10 | 5.40 | 2710.34 |
| 8 | 193.70 | 5.90 | 3482.35 |
| 9 | 219.10 | 5.90 | 3953.34 |
| 10 | 273.00 | 5.90 | 4952.80 |

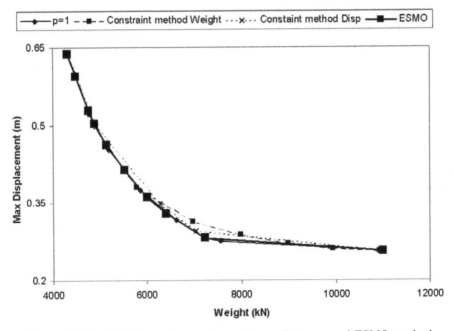

**Figure 12.13.** Multi-layered space truss: Linear, Distance and ESMO method.

**Table 12.4.** Example 2 – Time required by classical and EA methods for dealing with multi-objectives

| Method | Time (sec) | Generations | FE analyses |
|--------|-----------|-------------|-------------|
| p = 1  | 7.917     | 195         | 1.163       |
| ESMO   | 2.119     | 28          | 312         |

## 12.7 Conclusions

Evolution strategies can be considered as an efficient tool for multiobjective design optimization of structural problems such as space frames and multi-layered space trusses under static and seismic loading conditions. The LWM and CM methods compared to the ESMO method appear to be robust and reliable for treating multiobjective structural optimization problems giving almost identical results. A generalization of the LWM for $p > 1$ called the CM is also examined in this study. The results obtained by the DFM were somewhat different than those taken by the other two methods, while for large values of $p$ it produces either too close or disperse points in the Pareto sets.

In terms of computational efficiency it appears that all three typical methods considered require similar computational effort, with approximately the same number of generation steps. On the other hand the ESMO method requires one order of magnitude less computing time than the typical methods.

The presented results indicate that it is possible to achieve an optimal design under seismic loading. Both design methodologies based on a number of artificially generated earthquakes and the response spectrum modal analysis adopted by the seismic codes have been implemented and compared. The more rigorous dynamic approach based on time history analyses gives more economic designs than the approximate response spectrum modal analysis, at the expense of requiring more computational effort.

# References

1. Fonseca, CM, and Fleming, PJ, An Overview of Evolutionary Algorithms in Multiobjective Optimization, Evolutionary Computations, 1995; 3: 1-16.
2. Stadler, W, Natural Structural Shapes of Shallow Arches, Journal of Applied Mechanics, 1977; 44: 291-298.
3. Leitmann, G, Some Problems of Scalar and Vector-valued Optimization in Linear Viscoelasticity, Journal of Optimization Theory and Applications, 1977; 23: 93-99.
4. Stadler, W, Natural Structural Shapes (The Static Case), Quarterly Journal of Mechanics and Applied Mathematics, 1978; 31: 169-217.
5. Gerasimov, EN, and Repko, VN, Multi-criteria Optimization, Soviet Applied Mechanics, 1978; 14: 1179-1184.
6. Koski, J, Truss Optimization with Vector Criterion, Publication No. 6, Tampere University of Technology, 1979.
7. Cohon, JL, Multi-objective Programming and Planning, New York, Academic Press, 1978.
8. Papadrakakis, M, Lagaros, ND, and Plevris, V, Optimum Design of Space Frames Under Seismic Loading, International Journal of Structural Stability and Dynamics, 2001; 1: 105-124.
9. Cassis, JH, Optimum Design of Structures Subjected to Dynamic Loads, PhD Thesis, University of California, Los Angeles, 1974.
10. Johnson, EH, Disjoint Design Spaces in Optimization of Harmonically Excited Structures, AIAA Journal, 1976; 14: 259-261.
11. Eurocode 3, Design of Steel Structures, Part1.1: General Rules for Buildings, CEN, ENV 1993-1-1/1992.
12. Pareto, V, Cours d'economique Politique, vol. 1&2, Lausanne, Rouge, 1897.
13. Adali, S, Pareto Optimal Design of Beams Subjected to Support Motion, Computers and Structures, 1983; 16: 297-303.
14. Baier, H, Structural Optimization in Industrial Environment, In H Eschenauer and N Olhoff (eds.) Optimization Methods in Structural Design, Proceedings of the Euromech-Colloquium 164, University of Siegen, Bibliographisches Institut A6, Zurich, pp. 140-145, 1983.
15. Diaz, A, Sensitivity Information in Multiobjective Optimization, Engineering Optimization, 1987; 12:281-297.
16. Hajela, P, and Shih, CJ, Multi-objective Optimum Design in Mixed Integer and Discrete Design Variable Problems, AIAA Journal, 1990; 28: 670-675.
17. Rozvany, GIN Structural Design via Optimality Criteria, Dordecht, Kluwer, 1989.

18. Goicoechea, A, Hansen DR, and Duckstein L, Multi-objective Decision Analysis with Engineering and Business Applications, New York, Wiley, 1982.

19. Koski, J, Bicriterion Optimum Design Method for Elastic Trusses, Acta Polytechnica Scandinavica, Mechanical engineering series No 86, Dissertation, Helsinki, 1984.

20. Sandgren, E, Multicriteria Design Optimization by Goal Programming, In H Adeli (ed.) Advances in Design Optimization, Chapman & Hall, pp. 225-265, 1994.

21. Kamal, CS, and Adeli, H, Fuzzy Discrete Multicriteria Cost Optimization of Steel Structures, Journal of Structural Engineering, 2000; 126: 1339-1347.

22. Schaffer, JD. Multiple Objective Optimization with Vector Evaluated Genetic Algorithms, PhD thesis, Vanderbilt University, 1984.

23. Fonseca, CM, and Fleming, PJ, Genetic Algorithms for Multiobjective Optimization: Formulation, Discussion and Generalization, In S Forrest S (ed.) Proceedings of the $5^{th}$ International Conference on Genetic Algorithms, San Mateo, California, Morgan Kaufmann, pp. 416-423, 1993.

24. Horn, J, Nafpliotis, N, and Goldberg, DE, A Niched Pareto Genetic Algorithm for Multiobjective Optimization, In Proceedings of the $1^{st}$ IEEE Conference on Evolutionary Computation, IEEE World Congress on Evolutionary Computation, Volume 1, Piscataway, NJ, pp. 82-87, 1994.

25. Deb, K, and Goldberg, DE, An Investigation of Niche and Species Formation in Genetic Function Optimization, In JD Schaffer (ed.) Proceedings of the $3^{rd}$ International Conference on Genetic Algorithms, San Mateo, California, Morgan Kaufmann, pp. 42-50, 1989.

26. Hajela, P, and Lin, CY, Genetic Search Strategies in Multicriterion Optimal Design, Structural Optimization, 1992; 4: 99-107.

27. Zitzler, E, Evolutionary Algorithms for Multiobjective Optimization: Methods and Applications, PhD thesis, Swiss Federal Institute of Technology Zurich, Computer Engineering and Networks Laboratory, 1999.

28. Goldberg, DE, and Richardson, J, Genetic Algorithms with Sharing for Multimodal Function Optimization, In JJ Grefenstette (ed) Genetic Algorithms and Their Applications, Proceedings of the $2^{nd}$ International Conference on Genetic Algorithms, Hillsdale, NJ, Lawrence Erlbaum, pp. 41-49, 1987.

29. Taylor, CA, EQSIM, A Program for Generating Spectrum Compatible Earthquake Ground Acceleration Time Histories, Reference Manual, Bristol Earthquake Engineering Data Acquisition and Processing System, December, 1989.

30. Rechenberg, I, Evolution Strategy: Optimization of Technical Systems According to the Principles of Biological Evolution, Stuttgart, Frommann-Holzboog, 1973.

31. Schwefel, HP, Numerical Optimization for Computer Models, Chi Chester, UK, Wiley & Sons, 1981.

# Index